> *An octogenarian, planting saplings,*
> *Amazed three teenage boys, smart alecks, local striplings.*
> *"To build at your age would be dumb, but planting trees,"*
> *They said, "that's crazy!"... He'd lost it, plain to see.[1]*
>
> "The Old Man and the Three Young Ones"
> by Jean de La Fontaine

---

1. *The Complete Fables of La Fontaine,* trans. Craig Hill (New York: Arcade Publishing, 2008), 291.

Justice Lifts the Nations

by Paul Robert

Justice Lifts the Nations

Paul Robert's *Justice Lifts the Nations* "is on the stairway in the old Supreme Court Building in Lausanne where the judges had to pass each time before going to try a case. Robert wanted to remind them that the place which the Reformation gave to the Bible provided a basis not only for morals but for law. Robert pictured many types of legal cases in the foreground and the judges in their black robes standing behind the judges' bench. The problem is neatly posed: How shall the judges judge? On what basis shall they proceed so that their judgment will not be arbitrary? Above them Robert painted Justice standing unblindfolded, with her sword pointed not vertically upward but downward toward a book, and on the book is written 'The Law of God.' This painting expressed the sociological base, the legal base, in northern Europe after the Reformation. Paul Robert understood what the Reformation was all about in the area of law. It is the Bible which gives a base to law."[1]

— Francis A. Schaeffer

---

1. Schaeffer, Francis, *How Should We Then Live?* (Wheaton, IL: Crossway, 2005), 106.

Table of Contents

Publisher's Note . . . . *xxi*
Translator's Preface . . . . *xxiii*
Pierre Courthial: A Brief Biography . . . . *xxvii*
Foreword . . . . *xxxv*
Introduction . . . . *xlix*

Part 1: The Ancient Order of the World

1 **God and His Covenant** 3
   Before the Fall: The Prelapsarian Covenant 4
      The Transcendent-Immanent God   4
      Two Possibilities: Theonomy or Autonomy   5
      Two Ends: Life or Death   6
      Historical and Symbolic Perspectives   7
      Two Sacramental Trees   7
   After the Fall: The Postlapsarian Covenant . . . 8

2 **The Mountains of God** 11
   The Mountain of Eden 12
      The Cultural Mandate at Creation   13
      Original Sin   14

Judgment and Grace	15
THE MOUNTAIN OF ARARAT	16
Sons of Men and Sons of God	16
Noah's Sacrifice	17
The Rainbow	19
THE MOUNTAIN OF MORIAH	20
The Nations	21
God — The One and the Many	21
Abraham (around 2000 B.C.)	22
The Three Promises	24
Circumcision	24
THE MOUNTAIN OF SINAÏ	26
The Two Moments at Sinaï	27
First Moment	27
The Passover	27
Approximately 1400 B.C.	28
The Holy People	29
Second Moment — The Decalogue	29
The Blood of the Covenant	30
Judgment and Grace	31
The Tabernacle	31
THE MOUNTAIN OF ZION	34
Judges	34
Samuel	35
Saul	35
David	36
The Covenant Confirmed	36

3 THE LORD, HIS LAW, AND HIS PEOPLE 39

GOSPEL AND LAW FOR ADAM AND EVE 40
NOAH 41
ABRAHAM 41
THE TORAH 42
AN ORGANIC WHOLE 43
THE MORAL AND CEREMONIAL LAWS OF THE TORAH . .44
THE UNITY OF THE TWO FAMILIES OF LAWS 45
AN OBEDIENCE ROOTED IN LOVE 45

GOSPEL AND LAW 46
THE ECCLESIAL TRADITION AND THE WORD OF GOD . .47
THE REMNANT. 49
THE MINISTRY OF THE PROPHETS 49
THE COUNCIL OF GOD .50
JUDGMENTS 53
THE SAGES. 54
THE SONG OF SONGS 54
DANIEL. 56
THE RETURN OF THE JEWS AND
    THE REBIRTH OF ISRAEL. 58

PART 2: THE TURNING OF THE AGES

4   THE EARTHLY LIFE OF CHRIST: A.D. 1–30. 63
    PRELIMINARY REMARKS 63
    THE MYSTERY OF THE INCARNATION 64
        The Incarnation of God the Son   64
        The Nicene Creed   65
        The Council of Chalcedon   65
        The Abasement of the Only-Begotten Son   66
    THE OPENINGS OF THE FOUR GOSPELS 67
        John the Baptist   68
        The Faithful Remnant Gathered Round the Child   69
        Two Significant Names   70
        Wise Men and Shepherds   71
    THE OBEDIENCE OF JESUS 71
        Jesus Grows   72
        The Obedience of Jesus   73
    THE PROLOGUE OF JOHN 76
        First Point: Creation   76
        Second Point: Tabernacle   77
        Third Point: *Heséd* and *Eméth*   77
    THE BAPTISM AND ANOINTING OF CHRIST 78
        The Old Priests . . .   80
        . . . and the New Priest   80
        His Baptism-Anointing   81

According to the Order of Melchizedek	82
The Baptism of Christ as Head of His Body	84

THE PROPHETIC TEACHING OF JESUS 86

The Two Perspectives of Christ's Prophecy	86
The "Poor" of Israel	89
The Pharisees	89
The Sadducees	90
Six Antitheses	91
The King and His Kingdom	93

THE END OF THE AGE.................95

The Context	96
"This Generation"	97
The Seven Warning Signs	98
The Sign of the Son of Man in Heaven	98
The High Priestly Prayer	99
First Part	*99*
Second Part	*99*
Third Part	*100*

5 THE APOSTOLIC PERIOD: A.D. 30–70 101

FROM EASTER TO PENTECOST 101

From Humiliation to Glorification	101
The Resurrection	101
The Fifty Days	102
The Forty Days	102
The Ascension	103
The Ten Days	103
Pentecost	104

THE EARLY DAYS OF THE APOSTOLIC CHURCH 105

"The Last Times"	106
"The Last Days"	107
"The Last Hour"	107

THE MISSION OF THE APOSTOLIC CHURCH 109

Israel + the Nations = the Church	109
The Missionary Mandate	110
Make Disciples of the Nations	112

THE APOSTLES 114

Part 3: The New Order of the World

6 The Genuinely *Catholic* Ecclesial Tradition 151

Preliminary Remarks 151
   The Ecclesial Time   151
   Removing the Veil from the Hebraic Bible   153
   A Warning to All Unfaithful Churches   154
   God's Sovereignty and Man's Responsibility   155
   The Covenant of Grace and Law   156
   Viewing the Catholic Ecclesial Tradition
      in Light of the Covenant   158
What to Make of Traditions? 158
   Introduction   158
   The Ecclesial Tradition   161
   "Tota Scriptura" and the "Catholic" Tradition   162
   The Progress of the Ecclesial Tradition   164
   The Two Great Epochs in the Progress of Ecclesial
      Tradition   166
The Epoch of the Early Ecumenical Councils . . . 167
   The Early Heresies and
      the First Four Ecumenical Councils   167
      The Heresy of Arius (256–336)   169
      The Heresy of Apollinarius (Died 390)   169
      The Heresy of Nestorius (380–451)   170
      The Heresy of Eutychius (378–453)   170
   The Fifth and Sixth Ecumenical Councils   170
   Returning to Chalcedon   171
East and West after Chalcedon 172
   The Orthodox Churches of the East after Chalcedon   172
   The Catholic Church of the West after Chalcedon   174
The Epoch of the Reformation 178
   Introduction   178
   The Necessity of the Reformation   180
   The Abiding Significance of
      the Pre-Reformation Ecclesial Tradition   182
The Soteriological Dogma 186

Peter	*115*
Paul	*116*
John	*117*
Jews against Jews	*119*

THE SEVEN SIGNS................................. 120
    The Seven Warning Signs Fulfilled   *120*
    Sign #1 — "False Christs" (Luke 21:8)   *120*
    Sign #2 – "Wars and Rumors of Wars"   *121*
    Sign #3 — "Famines and Earthquakes"   *121*
        Josephus' The Jewish Wars   *122*
    Sign #4 — The Martyrdom of Those
        Who Endure to the End   *124*
        Hupomonè   *124*
        The Beginning of the Roman Persecution
            of Christians under Nero   *126*
    Sign #5 — The Apostasy of a Great Number   *128*
    Sign #6 — The Gospel Preached to All the Nations   *130*
    Sign # 7 — The Abomination of Desolation   *131*

THE COMING OF THE LORD.......................... 134
    The Sign of the Son of Man in Heaven   *134*
    Cosmic Images in Biblical Prophecy   *134*
    Dies Irae, Dies Illa   *136*
    Nunc   *137*
    Et in Hora Mortis Nostrae Sursum Corda!   *138*
    Amen! Come Lord Jesus!   *138*
    "This Generation"   *139*
    Lamentations for the End   *139*
    The Carcass and the Eagles   *141*

THE SCRIPTURAL CANON............................ 142
    The Closing of the Biblical Canon   *142*
        The Canonical List   *142*
        The Dogmatic Canon   *144*
    The Tradition of the Apostles   *145*

Justification by Faith before the Reformation	*186*
Justification by Faith Expounded by the Reformers	*189*
An Alien Righteousness	*192*
Sanctification Accompanies Justification	*193*
Faith and Works	*195*
The Spiritual Battle	*197*

THE SCRIPTURAL DOGMA *199*

Opening Remarks	*199*
First Remark —	
Scripture's Own Testimony Concerning Itself	*199*
Second Remark —	
The Apostolic Faith in the Inspiration of Scripture	*200*
Recognizing the Doctrine of Scripture as the Dogma of Scripture	*202*
The Essential Points of the Dogma of Scripture	*206*
Which Texts Are Ultimately Authoritative	*206*
The Written Word Must Be Heard in the Church	*209*
The Scriptural Dogma Clarifies that the Church Is the Servant of the Faith	*212*

7 THE CHURCH SICK WITH HUMANISM. **216**

THE AGE OF FAITH *216*

The "Age of Faith" Mispresented as the "Middle" or "Dark" Ages	*216*

THE HUMANIST CONTAGION. *220*
HUMANISM AND SCHOLASTICISM *223*
HUMANISM AND THE RENAISSANCE *227*

Introduction	*227*
Erasmus and the Spirit of Renaissance Humanism	*228*
Luther's Response to Erasmus concerning "Free Will"	*229*

HUMANISM AND THE ENLIGHTENMENT *235*

Introduction	*235*
The Influence of Immanuel Kant	*235*

THE HISTORICAL-CRITICAL METHOD *237*

The History and Presuppositions of the Historical-Critical Method	*237*
The Contribution of Louis Gaussen's *Theopneustia*	*241*

CRITIQUING BIBLICAL CRITICISM 244
THE WORKS OF REFORMED SCHOLARSHIP. 246

8 HUMANISM DEFEATED BY THE LAW OF GOD . . 251

THE COVENANT: GOSPEL AND LAW 251
   Introduction   251
THE RISE OF THE CONTEMPORARY
   THEONOMIC MOVEMENT 256
   The Knowledge of Good and Evil   259
   Common Grace   260
   The Theonomic Challenge to Humanistic Autonomy   262
THE MORAL LAW OF GOD EXTENDED 267
   Israel and the Nations   267
   From the Ancient Church to the New Israel   271
      The Upholding of the Moral Law in its Entirety   271
      The Case Laws   274
      The Judicial and Political Laws   276
   Penology and Penal Law   280
      "An eye for an eye…"   282
THE MORAL LAW OF GOD DEEPENED 284
   The Law of God Deepened in the TaNaKh   284
   The Law of God Deepened in Jesus' Teaching   289
      Hierarchical Order within the Law   289
      The Law Aims at the Heart   291
      The Identification of Love with Law   291
   The Law of God Deepened in
      the Conscience and Life of the Faithful   292
   The Law of God Deepened in the Church and the World   295

Appendix: My Meeting with Pierre Courthial. 308
History Index 313
Scripture Index 321
General Index 341

Publisher's Note

THE PUBLICATION OF THIS BOOK CAME INTO BEING MORE BY A unique meeting of Providence than by the usual contact between author and publisher.

In July 2004, I traveled to Switzerland to work on a book regarding the sixteenth-century Swiss Reformation. At the end of the trip, I arrived in Lausanne to meet writer and theologian Jean-Marc Berthoud at his Christian bookshop (La Proue). It was there that Jean-Marc introduced me to the life and works of Pierre Courthial, and encouraged me to translate Courthial's two most important books: *A New Day of Small Beginnings* and *The Bible in the Bible*.

Soon afterward, the rights to the books were secured from Reverend Courthial and his original French edition publisher, Éditions L'Age d'Homme, Lausanne. At Jean-Marc's suggestion, Matthew Miller was engaged to translate both books into English.

We are indebted to Reverend Matthew Miller for his time and careful labors to produce a translation that is theologically accurate and true to the author's intent.

We are also indebted to Dr. Douglas Kelly, a friend of Courthial, for his insightful and inspiring foreword.

Of course, our special acknowledgment is to Jean-Marc Berthoud. This important work never would have been published in French without Jean-Marc's continued encouragement to his dear friend

Pierre Courthial to write his theological masterpiece.

We are grateful to Éditions L'Age d'Homme, Dr. Louise Bentley, and Tim Bloedow for their excellent proofing of the text, and to others who helped with the production of the book: R. A. Sheats, E. Ray Moore, Bethany Sheats, Tiffany Griffin, Erica Sheats, Karrah Oliver, Emily Shackleton, Molly Orr, Luis Lovelace, Jr., Kyle Shepherd, Shelby Shepherd, Madison Cormick, and Lauren LaFleur. We also greatly appreciate Reedy Creek Presbyterian Church, Paul Dorr, Dr. Michael and Nancy Miller, Dr. Drew and Laura Miller, Todd W. Miller, and Kevin Wolfswinkel for their generous financial contribution toward the printing of the book.

Finally, concerning our small Christian publishing house, I cannot imagine, considering our long list of future translations, a more important work we could bring to print than *A New Day of Small Beginnings*.

I trust the book will have a wide circulation and will be in print for many years. I am convinced it will have a tremendous influence on a coming generation of Christian leaders who will be inspired by Courthial's thoroughly Biblical vision to give a courageous, faithful, and comprehensive witness to the lordship of Christ over all peoples and nations.

Thomas Ertl, President
Zurich Publishing Foundation

Translator's Preface

TRANSLATING PIERRE COURTHIAL'S MASTERFUL TREATMENT of the Covenant of Grace has been one of the greatest privileges of my life. I first learned of *Le jour des petits recommencements* (*A New Day of Small Beginnings*) in a theology course at Reformed Theological Seminary in Charlotte, NC, where I jotted down the title after hearing the work extolled by the professor, Dr. Douglas Kelly. Two years later, while studying theological French at Harvard Divinity School, I ordered the book and began to work through its pages. The following year, through God's remarkable providence and through a connection made by Swiss author and theologian Jean-Marc Berthoud, I came under contract to translate this and another book by Courthial (*De Bible en Bible*, forthcoming) for Zurich Publishing.

As a translator, my aim, in simplest terms, was to produce a translation that feels as little as possible like a translation, and to do so without losing Courthial's unique style in the process. As those familiar with Courthial's writing warned me before I began, this would prove to be no simple undertaking. Concerning the author's distinctive style, Pierre Marcel (1910–1992) has aptly described it as "a liturgical language." Marcel observed:

> Pierre Courthial is a granite block of total conviction founded on prayer. At every instance his writing pulses with intellectual or

emotional "vibrations" bordering on wonder, at that subtle point where perception and quivering, singing emotion meet. There you will find nothing wizened, nothing stiffened, nothing shriveled, such as we all too often discover amongst our "evangelical" authors.

As for his style, I know of no other like it. His is a liturgical language crafted in multiple voices... The phrases are carefully coordinated with architectural skill... And these perceptive little parentheses, with their exclamation points, jar us back to order as well as reason! In some parts of Courthial's writings, the reader finds himself immersed in the fullness of polyphony.[1]

Impressive in the French, several of Courthial's tightly woven and often multi-layered sentences approach a half-page in length. Carefully constructed, these sentences proved difficult to divide into shorter sentences.

Nonetheless, for the sake of readability (by our English standards), I have frequently broken the longer sentences into two, three, and, sometimes, four sentences. For the sake of fluidity (by our English standards), I have often lifted a thought or phrase out from between the author's characteristic parentheses or dashes, giving it instead a sentence of its own and expressly stating, when needed, its relation to the idea it qualifies. But wherever possible, to the best of my ability, I have tried to convey Courthial's "architectural skill" (Marcel) by maintaining the layers, the seeming interruptions, the unexpected exclamations, and other devices so deliberately used by the author to help us see what he sees, and even to feel what he feels, with his exact and often elegant expression. Whether I have been successful at this is for others to determine, and certainly any errors or shortcomings in the translation are entirely my own.

Additionally, several editing decisions played into this translation. These decisions were originally made in actual conversation and correspondence with Courthial before his death in 2009, and after 2009 with the ongoing assistance and help of his good and trusted friend, Jean-Marc Berthoud. Pierre Courthial gave us a degree of latitude in dealing with the peculiarities of his style. In the rarest of instances, these edits consist of a phrase that was removed because it was thought

---

1. From Marcel's introduction to Pierre Courthial, *Fondements pour l'avenir* (Aix-en-Provence, France: Kerygma, 1981), v.

unnecessary (Courthial graciously agreed.) Occasionally a phrase or sentence was added to aid clarity. The bulk of the edits consisted in the addition of transitional sentences to indicate and summarize a section now completed, and briefly introduce the section that now lies ahead. In one place — the second paragraph of chapter one — a paragraph was composed to aid the introduction of the work (it is also marked by a footnote indicating as much). If our aim with these edits has been achieved, then the reader will simply feel more assured of his place and progress in the work as he paces himself through it.

In Scriptural quotations, I have preferred the New King James Version (NKJV). This decision was made with regard to Courthial's own position on the Greek manuscripts: he was an advocate for the Textus Receptus and a strong critic of the "Critical Text." Moreover, in most places the NKJV, based on the same manuscripts, matches Courthial's presentation of Scripture quotations in French (which were sometimes his own translation). Where necessary, another English version is used — usually the English Standard Version (ESV), New International Version (NIV), or New American Standard (NAS) — either in place of, or occasionally in combination with, the NKJV.

Two final matters regarding the translation should be of great interest to the reader. The first concerns Courthial's choice of words to describe the project of the sixteenth- and seventeenth-century reformers. In French, a significant distinction used to exist between the verbs *réformer* and *reformer* (or, concerning persons, *les réformateurs* and *les reformateurs*). With the accent, *réformer* means "to revolutionize, to advance according to a novel pattern," etc. Without the accent, *reformer* means "to recover, to go back to the original pattern." To make the point that the Protestant Reformation self-consciously pursued the latter (a recovery) and not the former (a revolution), Courthial deliberately retrieved and employed the older word, without the accent, in his writings about *le Reformation* and the goals of *les reformateurs*. While this distinction cannot be properly translated into English, an awareness that this distinction exists in the French text will help the reader more fully appreciate Courthial's understanding of the historical flow of dogma and, in particular, of the position and posture of the Reformation in that flow.

The second concerns Courthial's use of the term "theonomy." Douglas Kelly has ably clarified in the "Foreword" how the "theonomic dogma" Courthial advocates aligns with, and differs from, the theonomic position advanced by leading American theonomists (see page xlv below). I would only add that in his subsequent and final book (*De Bible en Bible*, 2001; English translation forthcoming), Courthial notably privileges a new term — "theocosmonomy" — to define his vision. There he gleans from the work of Herman Dooyeweerd the term, "cosmonomy" (*cosmos*, "world," + *nomos*, "law"), and uniquely adds *theos* ("God") as a prefix. He unfolds this "theocosmonomic vision" over the last third of that work, drawing more heavily from Dooyeweerd than any other theologian. Accordingly, I believe that the genuinely unique nature of Courthial's "theonomic dogma" in *A New Day of Small Beginnings* becomes even more apparent in his development of the idea, including the employment of a new term (theocosmonomy), in *De Bible en Bible*.

I wish to express special thanks to Rev. Colin Ambrose, Dr. Louise Bentley, Jean-Marc Berthoud, R. A. Sheats, and Timothy Bloedow for their careful reading of later drafts of the translation and invaluable suggestions. I also benefited in several places from an earlier effort at translating this work by Mrs. Ellen Myers. Kyle Shepherd also identified several places where corrections were needed in his excellent and careful work of formatting the text. I am immeasurably grateful to the publisher, Thomas Ertl, for his vision, his patience, and his constant encouragement, without which this *magnum opus* of one of the great Reformed minds of the twentieth century would still remain unavailable to the English-speaking world. And lastly, I wish to give thanks to my wife, Lindsay, whose unwavering support and numerous sacrifices made it possible for me to finish this work during hours and days that belonged to her, and which she chose to give.

My prayer is that this translation will help numerous Christians in the ongoing work of the Great Commission, with its comprehensive charge from our risen and ascended Lord of "teaching them to observe *all that I have commanded you*" (Matthew 28:19), the full meaning of which Courthial beautifully unpacks in this book, and returns to in its closing lines.

Rev. Matthew S. Miller
Erskine Theological Seminary
Greenville, South Carolina

Pierre Courthial: A Brief Biography

Birth and Education

Pierre Courthial was born in St. Cyr-au-Mont-d'Or, France, in August 1914. His father, a businessman, was Protestant, and his mother was Catholic. It was at the age of sixteen, while studying in Lyon, that he came across the writings of Calvin and the Reformer's colleague, Pierre Viret, writings which would form the backbone of his theology over the next seventy-five-plus years. After a year of studying business, he opted to switch his concentration to theology, and was admitted to the Faculté de Théologie de Paris, where he sat under the teaching of the great French Reformed theologian of the twentieth century, August Lecerf. Courthial also befriended a more senior student in the program who shared and helped develop the younger Courthial's Reformed convictions. That student was Pierre Marcel.

After completing his university coursework in theology, he joined his parents in Shanghai, where his father was on business (as an eleven-year-old boy, he and his family had also lived in Saigon before returning to France). In Shanghai, Courthial found someone to tutor him in Dutch, since he was eager to read the writings of the great nineteenth- and twentieth-century Dutch theologians. In June of 1937, he returned to Paris from Shanghai largely (and memorably) via the trans-Siberian railway, stopping in Moscow along the way. Back in Paris, he began work on his thesis under Henri Monnier. In the meantime, Lecerf had secured a scholarship for Courthial to begin doctoral work at the Free University of Amsterdam. He was very much looking forward to this next step when it was unexpectedly interrupted.

Ministry

The Protestant Church in Lyon (L'Eglise libre des Terreaux) was expecting the arrival of their new minister, Roland de Pury, but it happened that de Pury would not be able to quit his former congregation for another year. At Roland de Pury's request, Pierre Courthial forewent his year in Amsterdam in order to pastor the congregation in Lyon until de Pury could arrive. As the Lord would have it, Courthial would be a pastor and churchman the rest of his life (except for the brief time that he served in the French army during World War II, during which he was part of the Dunkirk Evacuation in which he crossed the English Channel to Ramsgate at 1:00 AM on June 3) His time in Lyon was also significant since it was there, while leading a study on the Heidelberg Catechism, that he met Hélène, who became his wife, and with whom he would have five children.

Immersed in pastoral ministry, Courthial held fast to crucial advice given him by Lecerf — namely, that a pastor should devote two hours each day to personal study independent of his immediate duties. Accordingly, Courthial pursued a decades-long reading plan that took him carefully along the route of historical theology, beginning with the church fathers, in the 1940s. He also remained current on present controversies throughout those years. Finally, though his Reformed convictions were deep and unshakable, he displayed a keen openness toward ecumenical dialogue, which he believed was necessary for the health and future of the Church (one should remember here that his mother was Roman Catholic). Courthial persistently distinguished between a weak and flimsy ecumenism, for which he had no tolerance, and a strong, robust, vivacious ecumenism, which he pursued. Courthial saw this latter kind of ecumenism as centered on the four grand dogmas of the Church: the dogmas of the Trinity, the Incarnation, salvation by grace, and the authority of Scripture.

Along these lines, when, in 1941, Courthial was named pastor of a Reformed parish in La-Voulte-sur-Rhône, he befriended Paul Evdokimov, an Orthodox theologian living in a neighboring village. The two met regularly to read through the Church Fathers, and it was through Evdokimov that Courthial became acquainted with the best of modern orthodox theologians: Serge Bulgakov, Vladimir Lossky, and Vladimir Soloviev among them.

His growing ecumenical dialogue raised eyebrows back in Paris, and at the end of 1944, he was called to Paris to give an account of his theological positions. He was required to stay in Paris for several months for the purpose of putting in writing his theological views and his posture toward ecumenism. At the end of this time, any concerns that his ecumenical engagements were coming at the expense of his Reformed convictions were allayed — he was cleared of suspicion and allowed to return to his parish that May.

In February of 1951, Courthial received a letter from Pierre Maury, the very pastor who had called him to Paris to give an account of his theology. This time, however, it was a letter calling Courthial to Paris not to give an account of his theology, but rather to join Maury on the ministry staff at the eminent L'Eglise Réformée de l'Annonciation, where Marc Boegner was the senior minister. Courthial accepted the offer, and would soon thereafter (after Boegner's retirement in 1953) succeed Maury (who died in 1956) as the senior minister. Thus began the longest stage of his pastoral career. He would serve L'Eglise Réformée de l'Annonciation for twenty-three years.

Even as he assumed the responsibilities of this large and vibrant church, he remained engaged with theological study and engagement, continuing to devote the two hours per day to study, as Lecerf had advised. Significant time was given to sermon preparation and Bible studies, and he was diligent in visiting the elderly, the sick, and all who called upon him. He used the Heidelberg Catechism to train each member of the church.

Broader Ministry

Outside of his immediate pastoral responsibilities, he became co-editor of *La Revue réformée* at the request of Pierre Marcel, also contributing several articles, including notable critiques of Karl Barth. He also served on several educational and missions boards, and collaborated with Henri Blocher to found the Center of Evangelical Theological Studies in 1967, which met monthly.

In 1970, Courthial and Blocher established an ecumenical evangelical theological review to counter the growing doctrinal laxity and limp ecumenism pervading theological literature. *Ichthus* (as it was called) aimed to promote rigorous theological reflection intended for Lutherans, Reformed, Baptists, and Independents. The circulation grew to four thousand issues. The high point was when the managing board organized an Evangelical meeting in Nîmes which, on the 7th and 8th of June, 1980, drew more than 17,000 people. Differing factors led to the review's decline in subsequent years, but it continued until its last issue in 1986.

Continuing his personal studies, from the 1970s on, Courthial devoted his attention substantially to the works of Dutch Reformed theologians (Abraham Kuyper, Herman Bavinck, Herman Dooyeweerd, Klaas Schilder, and lastly, Herman Ridderbos, with whom Courthial sought and obtained a meeting Holland in 1975); then, more and more, to those of the Americans (in particular, Cornelius Van Til, Vern Poythress, John Frame, R. J. Rushdoony, Greg Bahnsen, Gary North, David Chilton, and James B. Jordan). Faced with the strident and all-pervasive anti-Christianity coming to the fore in Europe, which he called "an ecumenism of Arius," he found in these unabashed Reformed thinkers, and particularly in the self-named Christian Reconstructionists, a full-orbed application of God's Word to all of life, as he had already encountered in the works of Augustine and Calvin. He was convinced that only a careful but unflinching application of the whole of God's Word (he preferred the phrase "tota scriptura" to "sola scriptura") to all of life could counter the sweeping force of atheistic humanism. He called this line of theology "the ecumenism of Athanasius" — that is, the ecumenism of those who live and work, as Athanasius did, *contra mundum* ("against the world").

In the fall of 1973, Courthial was invited to help found a faculty of Protestant theology in Aix-en-Provence. Eugene Boyer, Pierre Filhol, Paul Wells, and Peter Jones all visited him and asked him to join them in this undertaking. In many respects the seminary's success would depend upon the stamp of legitimacy that only an established churchman such as Courthial could give. For Courthial, this was not a clear-cut decision, for he would be leaving the mainline Protestant denomination in France to give support to a much smaller, younger denomination. After much reflection, he accepted their invitation, moving to Aix-en-Provence, where he served as the seminary's first dean and taught apologetics and practical theology until his retirement in 1984. William Edgar (now professor at Westminster, Philadelphia) and Pierre Berthoud (who succeeded him as Dean) also joined the budding faculty, and Courthial esteemed their friendship to the end of his life.

During this time, he also continued his ecumenical engagement, establishing a fellowship in Aix-en-Provence among his seminary students and the brethren of the *Communauté des moines apostoliques*. Their meetings were open to laymen as well, and their discussions centered on a rigorous interpretation of Scripture. There were differences between them, to be sure, but he considered the engagement to be a fruitful one.

These years were also dotted with trips to South Africa, the United States, and Canada. In September of 1979, he traveled to Philadelphia at the invitation of Westminster Theological Seminary. The seminary, founded in 1929, was celebrating its Jubilee year, and as a climax of that celebration, Courthial was among four distinguished recipients chosen to receive Westminster's first honorary doctorates. Accompanying this honor, Dr. Courthial was invited to give a lecture at the seminary ("John 3:12: Implications for Hermeneutics") and contribute a chapter to the *feschrift* for Professor Paul Wooley, which was edited by W. Stanford Reid and entitled *John Calvin: His Influence in the Western World* (Courthial wrote the fourth chapter, "The Golden Age of Calvinism in France, 1533–1633").

Major Writing Projects

It was, surprisingly, only some years after his retirement in 1984 that Dr. Courthial applied himself to his two major writing projects, which would culminate in *Le jour des petits recommencements* ("A New Day of Small Beginnings"), 1996, and *De Bible en Bible* ("The Bible in the Bible"), 2001. Courthial undertook the first of these with the encouragement of his good friend in Switzerland, Jean-Marc Berthoud, who saw that the fields of Courthial's extensive, lifelong studies were ripe for the harvest. Berthoud would call him almost weekly over the two-year writing period to urge him on in the work. Accordingly, Courthial, having dedicated the book to his dear wife Hélène, also publicly acknowledged this debt to his long-time friend.

Reviewing the finished work, theologian Paul Wells would deem the book you now hold in your hands as one of the most important theological works of the second half of the twentieth century.

Courthial completed *A New Day of Small Beginnings* at the age of eighty-two. Over the course of the next ten years, until his death in 2009, Courthial maintained correspondence with friends and theologians from his home in Paris. Though the state of the church in France, and of his home country at large, continued to crumble, Courthial continued to maintain great hope for the future. Though he didn't believe he would live to see it, he was confident that the next generation might see a restoration of Christianity, even in the West, of a magnitude comparable to the sixteenth-century Reformation.

Influence

Having completed the works he had been created in Christ Jesus to do, Pierre Courthial passed into the presence of the Lord in Paris on April 23, 2009.

He left behind his wife of sixty-seven years, five children, and an unknown host of people affected by his ministry and inspired by his writings.

Undoubtedly, his influence was limited in his time by a context that could hardly have been less friendly to his biblical critique and proposals for reform. In the words of his former colleague, Paul Wells, delivered at Courthial's memorial service:

> In a France so rapidly and thoroughly secularized after 1968, it was impossible that the gifts and capacities of a man with Pierre Courthial's convictions would be appreciated and utilized. If he had lived in the nineteenth century, we'd be talking about Courthial alongside Spurgeon; if he'd lived in the eighteenth century, alongside Whitefield; if in the sixteenth century, alongside Calvin, Luther, and Bucer; and if in the fourth century, we'd speak of Courthial alongside Athanasius.
>
> But in the twentieth century, Christianity in Europe experienced no revival, but only continual decline. Who wanted to take seriously a pastor-theologian who longed for the Church "to be reformed according to the Word of God"?

And yet, despite proclaiming the Word of God year-in-year-out, decade-in-decade-out, in a setting that could hardly be less receptive to it, Courthial maintained an upbeat posture towards the future. Wells remarks that although Courthial saw with great clarity the extent and depth of the problems in the church:

> He nonetheless showed an indefatigable optimism. His eyes were constantly searching, like a sentinel from his tower, for signs of light in the night.... His hope stood against the wind and the waves, for he loved his Church which he never ceased to regard, despite her infidelities, as the Bride of Christ.

This hopeful outlook, unwavering in the face of one of the most spiritually-crushing centuries in Western Christianity (the twentieth century, in France no less!), permeates nearly all of Courthial's published works, and remained a remarkable character trait of the author to the end of his days (for more on that, see the Appendix: "My Meeting with Pierre Courthial").

Rev. Matthew S. Miller
Erskine Theological Seminary
Greenville, South Carolina

Foreword

ERASMUS, THE EMINENT RENAISSANCE SCHOLAR AND ALL-European man, once wrote that France was the envy of the other kingdoms of Europe at that time. With its ancient royal dynasty and King Francis I, who called himself "the most Christian King of France," the Roman Church styled France as "the eldest daughter of the Church." The premier university of Europe was in Paris: the Sorbonne, which had boasted the leading theological faculty of the Catholic world for a good three centuries by the time of the outbreak of the Protestant Reformation in the 1520s. This very conservative bastion of traditional Roman Catholicism was not amused when the Reformation began in neighboring Germany and began spilling over into the French kingdom. The theologians of the Sorbonne had behind them the police power of the strong French state, which they readily used to stop the Protestant Reform movement among their people.

It cannot be our purpose here to follow the complex history of the Reformation in France, with the religious wars that ensued, showing both the remarkable spread of Reformation concepts and worship (perhaps as many as one-fourth of the population was in one way or another touched by the Reformation), as well as large-scale suppression of the French Protestants. I cannot say whether Robert L. Dabney of nineteenth-century Virginia was right about post-Reformation French history (in his essay on "The Uses and Results of

Church History"), but having lived in France in my student days, and always having immensely admired its language and culture, I have often wondered about what he said. Dabney suggests that the terrible mistreatment of the French Huguenots by the royal government in the seventeenth century was visited in a sort of divine retribution by the atheistic revolution in 1789, which violently toppled the very throne that had killed or driven out the Calvinists after 1685.

I cannot say, and will not attempt to judge such a matter, but it was interesting to note a not dissimilar suggestion from a rather different perspective; a widely read book by a former official of the government of Gen. Charles de Gaulle, Alain Peyrefitte, *Le Mal Francais* (published in 1976). Peyrefitte (without entering into questions of divine providence) states that a possible reason why the "Anglo-Saxons" arrived on the moon first was because the French government had driven out the very talented, creative Huguenots in the seventeenth century, who then went and offered their talents to Switzerland, Holland, Britain, and the United States after the Revocation of the Edict of Nantes in 1685 (which had up to that time given religious toleration to the Calvinist Protestants).

What must be noted by anyone familiar with the history of the French culture is its brilliance, beauty, and creativity in multifarious realms over countless centuries. The part it played in the "Revival of Letters" (such as the groundbreaking classical linguistic and Patristic publications of G. Bude), its superb poetry (such as that of the members of "the Pleiades"), its architecture, music, and its sixteenth-century advancements in nearly every realm, leave one in awe.

Out of this brilliant and creative context came that giant of the sixteenth-century Reformation, John Calvin: a man of immense culture, linguistic erudition, self-sacrificing diligence, and a natural teacher (although personally a shy man). John Calvin seems to have been converted to the Reformation cause about 1532, at age twenty-three. A logo frequently printed in his post-conversion works shows a burning heart, and under it these words: "Prompte et sincere in opere Domini" ("prompt and sincere in the work of the Lord"). This is an accurate representation of his Christian life till its earthly end some thirty-two years later: a fervent piety, joined to profound integrity, intellectual brilliance, and tireless, selfless labor in the good cause. Not long after his conversion to Christ, he found refuge from persecution by the

French government (strongly loyal to the papacy at that period) in the city of Geneva. There he literally poured out his life expounding the Word of God: preaching several sermons a week, writing various tracts and treatises and Biblical commentaries, and especially that summary of how most faithfully to interpret the Bible, *Institutes of the Christian Religion*, not to mention his voluminous number of letters, his work as Christian statesman, missionary leader, educator and social reformer, and active pastor and counselor. He died in 1564, worn out at age fifty-five.

But his mighty influence waxed ever stronger in many a nation over centuries to come. There can be no doubt that "Anglo-Saxon" liberties to a significant degree owe much of their development to the powerful stream of Calvin's Biblical teaching (generally known as "Calvinism"). The beneficent influence of "Calvinism" as a whole upon culture was perhaps best set forth by the Dutch theologian and statesman, Abraham Kuyper, in his 1898 "Stone Lectures" at Princeton, New Jersey, under the simple title, *Lectures on Calvinism*.

Calvin cannot fairly be summarized under any particular doctrine, as best I can tell (a procedure that was so popular among nineteenth-century German historians of doctrine). Reading his sermons and other writings leaves one with the main impression that above all else he wishes to be faithful to all parts of Holy Scripture; to set forth all of it in orderly fashion so that the transforming truth of God's inspired revelation can shine into the minds and hearts of ordinary men and women as well as into the most educated and privileged. He sought to bring all of human life and every aspect of culture under the holy light of the written Word of God in every part of it. He believed that (as the twentieth-century Scottish expositor, William Still, used to say) "the whole Christ is in the whole Word" and thus, to find His fullness, one must range through the whole Word to be impacted by every angle and attribute of His divine and human character and grace in the larger bearing of all the truths of God in all sixty-six books of the Bible. That is precisely why Calvin preached so many thousands of sermons and wrote commentaries on most of the Bible. That is how his influence pushed northern Europe heavenwards.

Of course, he taught that the written Word must always be accompanied by the power of the Holy Spirit to make it effective. Indeed, he is the one who originated the practice of the Wednesday night prayer meeting at the Cathedral of St. Pierre in Geneva early on in his ministry there (as one will see from vol. I of *The Registers of the Consistory of Geneva*, published only in 1996). He knew that the Spirit is given in answer to prayer (Luke 11:13), and thus, that "the sword of the Spirit, which is the Word of God" and "the weapon of all prayer" (cf. Ephesians 6:12ff.) would transform broken, self-centered human lives and push, the culture — and nations themselves in due time — towards the living God.

Although I would resist the encapsulation of Calvin under any one theological topic (for he is too thoroughly Biblical and too "catholic," in the best sense of that good word, for such a limitation), it does appear from years of reading his material that they have a way of bringing one into the very presence of God. I know of one talented Calvin translator who was actually converted while translating some of his important writings! I know of many more whose eyes and hearts have been opened to see all aspects of the created order (and of their place in it) as God's marvelous creation, well worth the best creative efforts of their short earthly lives, whether in theology, science, agriculture, politics, literature, or whatever. From this perspective, certainly it is not an exaggeration to say that Calvin's life and the body of writings he left to the next 500 years have been peculiarly "theocentric." Those who "follow in his train" have a way thereafter of viewing all of life in terms of what David wrote in Psalm 16:8: "I have set the LORD always before me: because he is at my right hand, I shall not be moved."

For all of these reasons, particularly because the sovereign God in Christ is ever gracious and all-powerful to bless, transform, and deliver those who "seek his face" (cf. Psalm 27) in the written Word and in the Holy Spirit (who originally inspired it and now illumines it to seeking hearts), I suspect that the influence of John Calvin can only grow stronger in the next 500 years than it has in the last 500 years since his home-going. It is because our faces are turned towards God's victorious work in the future expansion of Christianity that we most appreciate the epoch-making work of Pierre Courthial of France during the now-concluded twentieth-century. He has proven one of the truest heirs, most fruitful and perceptive interpreters, and evangelistic conveyors of the entire legacy of John Calvin for the last hundred years in Calvin's native land (and indeed, for the entire half millennium since Calvin's birth). Thereby, Courthial points the entire Christian Church towards a bright future.

Pierre Courthial was born into a cultured and religious home in St. Cyr-au-Mont-d'Or in 1914. His father was French Reformed and his mother Roman Catholic, but young Pierre was brought up as a Protestant. He was a communicant member of the "Eglise Reformee de France," the church of his forefathers; a church that looked largely to John Calvin as its major human progenitor (the main influence behind its central confession, that of "La Rochelle" of 1571, composed not long after his death). Dr. Courthial states that from age thirteen, he began gleaning in the field of the Holy Scriptures, and from age sixteen, he began studying the Doctors of the Church (such as Augustine and Anselm), as well as becoming familiar with John Calvin's *Institutes of the Christian Religion* and the *Christian Instruction* of Pierre Viret (Swiss Reformer of Lausanne, and colleague of Calvin).

Having felt a clear call to the ministry, Pierre Courthial studied from 1932 to 1936 at the Protestant Faculty of Theology in Paris. That prestigious faculty had long since felt the all-pervasive influence of the liberal theology that accompanied the "Higher Criticism" coming out of nineteenth-century Germany and, lying behind that, the secularism and unbelief of the European Enlightenment, especially of the eighteenth century. Much like my own experience some forty years ago (in the late 1960s in Virginia), Courthial in the Paris Faculty of the 1930s had to deal intellectually with straight liberalism — though conveyed through technically "Reformed," Protestant professors, when he learned a great deal about the modern, naturalistic world view. His wholesale rejection of that view is not because he did not know what it is.

But there were other, altogether more God-honoring, influences in his theological education in the Paris of the 1930s. As a student, he gladly came under the sway of the justly famous Calvinist scholar, author, and professor, Auguste Lecerf. Although Calvinism had largely been rejected long before by so many in the Reformed Church of France, in the interests of appearing "enlightened" (in terms of eighteenth-century Enlightenment philosophy and nineteenth-century Higher Criticism of the Scriptures), Lecerf through his teaching and writing kept displaying a bright flame of God-centered truth, filled with vibrant hope for the future. Courthial "rejoiced in that light" that reflected the beauty of the Gospel of Christ and the overarching purpose of the Triune God.

During those seminal years of study, and afterwards in the parish ministry, Courthial read the great French Calvinist, Pierre Du Moulin, as well as Abraham Kuyper, H. Dooyeweerd, and K. Schilder of the Netherlands; William Cunningham and John Murray of Scotland; Charles Hodge and Cornelius Van Til of the U.S., and many others. In his parish ministry in Paris he was in a reading group for years that dipped deeply into both Roman Catholic and Eastern Orthodox fathers and writers. He had the privilege of being a colleague of the distinguished Calvinist pastor and author, Pierre Marcel in Paris. These two stalwarts carried on a strongly Biblical and Calvinist witness in the Reformed Church of France, minority though they were. Thus, while always a Reformation-type Calvinist, Courthial has been at the same time a true "catholic": a proponent of the main-line, age-old Catholic tradition, grounded in the Scriptures and affirmed and safe-guarded in the historic Creeds and Confessions of the first five centuries of the undivided Church. He sees himself as a true follower of John Calvin in this "catholic" regard (much as he feels it necessary to critique thoroughly some of the aberrations of the Medieval and Counter-Reformation Roman Church). But his critique, though open, unabashed, and straight-forward, is charitable and never vicious (as regards both Roman Catholics and Protestant Liberals). It seems to me that his criticism always has in it a certain tender pleading and a quiet hope for better things to come.

I am particularly pleased that Courthial (who helped re-start the Conservative-Evangelical and Reformed Seminary at Aix-en-Provence in France in the 1970s, and served for many years as its dean, thus lending it considerable credibility among Reformed Protestants in France) has written *Le Jour Des Petits Recommencements*, and that it has been ably and beautifully translated into English (as *A New Day of Small Beginnings*) by my former student-assistant and good friend, the Rev. Matthew Miller of Erskine Theological Seminary in Greenville, South Carolina, and generously backed by Christian businessman, Thomas Ertl of Florida. Monsieur Jean-Marc Berthoud, a Reformed lay scholar of Lausanne, has helpfully looked over every word of this translation. For several years, I used parts of this translation as a required text in my "Covenant Theology" class at Reformed Theological Seminary in Charlotte, NC. It was much appreciated by the large class of students.

This book, *A New Day of Small Beginnings*, should help make available the God-centered witness flowing in a living stream from John Calvin's theology, in a vital, intelligible, and far-reaching manner to future generations of many branches of the Christian Church. He makes sense of the grand, overarching story of redemption both in Holy Scripture and in the two thousand years of Church history since the Apostolic Age, and, above all else, he *applies* the broad range of divine truth to the whole of human life and duty. This volume robustly follows the witness of John Calvin: it presents the whole Christ in the whole Word, in the context of the one Covenant of Grace, and all of this in the bosom of the historic Christian Church. Its firm grasp of historical Biblical truth is why it is so alive with confident hope for the present and future.

Courthial traces all the covenants of Holy Scripture under the one overarching Covenant of Grace: from Adam and Noah, through Abraham, David, and Moses, down to the New Covenant, which is based on "better promises" (Hebrews 8:6), carried out in "a greater and more perfect tabernacle" (Hebrews 9:11); that is to say, the human nature of the God-man, who fulfilled in perfection all of the Old Testament types, and carried through in letter and spirit all aspects of the divine law, so that after His "once-for-all" sacrifice was acclaimed by the Father, the Holy Spirit was sent down in fullness to inhabit the Church, so that it immediately, from the inside out, "knows the Lord" (cf. Jeremiah 31:34; Hebrews 8:11), and makes others to know Him to their eternal salvation (cf. Matthew 28:18–20).

In Part I, he discusses the grace and requisite (and yet graciously provided) obligation of the various covenants in historic-redemptive order. While grace is the theme in every one of them (especially the central covenant promise: "I will be their God, and they shall be my people"), he constantly includes the personal response of faith and obedience, required of and given to all of the elect people of God across the long ages. Throughout, he shows that God deals with us as persons, created in His image, and not as mere machines of whom no response is required. On the contrary, we have been created and redeemed to function in terms of His holy character. Grace does not cut out that response, but makes possible a substantial fulfillment of it by means of the written Word and the present power of the Holy Spirit in the communion of the saints.

Part II summarizes perceptively the great moments of the history of redemption from sin and rebellion to grace and glory by means of focusing upon "the mountains of God": Eden (where we "sinned in Adam"), Ararat (where the Ark of Noah landed, and the human race made a new beginning), Moriah (where Isaac was to be sacrificed before a substitute was provided), Sinai (where the holy law was revealed through Moses, and atoning sacrifice and representative priesthood were established), and Zion (or Calvary, where Christ paid the supreme sacrifice, upon which the veil of the Temple was rent in twain, giving all the people of God immediate access to the Lord Himself). Thus, the whole of Scripture is drawn together in light of the eternal plan of God to redeem a people for Himself, and to renew the entire cosmos.

Part III opens "the new order of the world," running from the apostolic age to the return of Christ in glory. Here you will find one of the most luminous discussions of the proper place of dogma in the Church and in the life of every true believer. Here his wide and deep reading in Eastern Orthodox, Western Catholic, and Reformation sources (both ancient and modern) is brought to bear. Like Calvin and other Reformers (and later Puritans such as John Owen), he cordially accepts and incorporates the ecumenical councils and creeds of the first five centuries (from Nicea to Chalcedon), but definitely rejects (as unfaithful to the clear teaching of Holy Scripture) the seventh ecumenical council: the Second Council of Nicea (with its approval of the cult of images). He makes these assessments in accord with chapter 2 of the "Posterior Helvetic Confession" of 1566, taken over into the French Confession of La Rochelle (1571). It speaks of the Protestant Reformational relationship to the doctrines of the ancient Church Fathers and the Medieval theologians as follows: "We modestly refrain from agreement with them whenever we find that they propose something far removed from the Scriptures, or contrary to them."

He rejoices in the clear discovery and powerful exposition of justification by grace through faith in the sixteenth-century Reformation (a discovery that led to widespread revival in northern Europe and opened the way for a new missionary expansion of the Apostolic Faith throughout the world). He believes that a certain intuitive grasp of salvation by grace had always been somewhere in the heart of the

Church, but its coherent explication by the Reformers (distinguishing plainly justification from regeneration and sanctification) opened the way for a renewed preaching of the Gospel, accompanied by the joy of assurance of salvation and a life set free from fear to be "zealous of good works" so as to reach out as never before to lost men and women of all nations. In this regard, he lays all due emphasis on the necessity of the doctrine of "imputation" (a doctrine now criticized by many in "the New Perspective on Paul").

In the latter part of this third section, Courthial takes us through the declining faith of the Middle Ages and into the secularistic humanism of the eighteenth and nineteenth centuries, which is what we have faced for the last hundred years, and into which context we must preach and live out the changeless Gospel. A central issue here is the setting of the human mind above God and His Word, a mind that is supposedly not fallen and a Word that is not a thoroughly true revelation of God. Courthial demonstrates the philosophical, antitheistic program of so much of the liberal "historical criticism" of the Scriptures, as having been a prime way the followers of the humanistic Enlightenment emasculated the final authority of Holy Scripture within the churches of the West, in order to facilitate its functional replacement by the statist word of liberated mankind (or rather, the elite who claim to represent them). One of the values of this book is that its author does far more than offer criticism of heresy and rank unbelief: he lucidly provides a coherent response of faith concerning the authority, canonicity, and sound interpretation of the Bible. On this subject of the true history of the text of Scripture and of how it should be faithfully interpreted, Courthial makes as much sense as anything I have ever read. That is characteristic of his book: he is at points negative in order to set forth a gloriously positive alternative. Probably, that is why the book (unlike some conservative writing) is so free from bitterness, rancour, and hopelessness. It lifts one up rather than depressing him.

With this clash of authorities in mind, we can see that since the French Revolution of 1789, the general approach of the rich Western nations has been to turn their backs on their own sin, to reject God's holy law and the assistance of His Holy Spirit to walk in its light, in favor of multifarious statute legislation, concocted by humanistic legislatures in regimes that are taking more and more control over every aspect of the lives of their citizens. The remedy for all is in Christ. The French Revolution of 1789 and the Marxist Revolution of 1917 were supposed to lead the nations of the world into a sort of statist paradise by virtue of total planning by the omnicompetent state. The Marxist dream (or nightmare) was largely cast off after the fall of the Berlin wall in 1989 and the unraveling of the Soviet Union in 1991. But as the great Christian philosopher of atheism, A. Del Noce, pointed out near the end of the twentieth century, although Marxism has failed, secularistic atheism is still the reigning philosophy of our opulent Western society. He suggested that neither the "religious aspects" of Marxism, nor historic Christianity were acceptable to maintain our wealthy self-centeredness: only atheism is desired as the basis of life and law by our multinational elites. Anything else — any higher authority — might restrain them from their projects. One sees here the reappearance of the tempter to our first parents: "Ye shall be as gods, knowing good and evil."

It is one of the great virtues of *A New Day of Small Beginnings* that it faces with eyes wide open the atheism and statism characterizing the societies in which we live. He takes no joy in merely denouncing it; he points a better way forward in company with the ancient and ever-living Christian tradition. In place of man pretending to be as god, he would have us bow to and live our lives in the presence of the only true and living God: the Holy Trinity, our Creator, Redeemer and Lord; a sovereign Lord who has revealed the whole range of His will through law, prophets, and apostles: and supremely, in the Incarnation and Gospel of His only-begotten Son. In his lucid ranging through the many constituent parts of the Holy Scriptures, Courthial reminds us of the divinely-given interconnection in all of these parts between the Gospel of free salvation and the all-encompassing disciplines of life lived in the paths of God's holy law and in the power of the Holy Spirit. He is the unseen One who writes that law in our hearts and brings forth the fruit of the character of the God who gave it, as we abide in vital union with the risen Christ whom He supernaturally makes present to us. The author has traced in an intriguing manner this interconnection between Gospel and law through the various Biblical covenants in the earlier section of his book; his concluding section shows how it is manifested in Christian life today in a fallen and rebellious world and how it is *the* solution to the corroding "acids of modernity" that are eating away the face and very heart of our secularized culture.

He proposes that the contemporary Church may be on the verge of a fuller development of its theological tradition. He calls it the development of a "theonomic dogma." There is no doubt that this word ("theonomy") bitterly divided many good Reformed Christians in the U.S. during the 1970s and 80s, especially in response to the writings of R. J. Rushdoony. As a general rule, the vast majority of Reformed American Christians rejected theonomy as being a harsh imposition of Old Testament civil law onto modern states, which would signal the return of all sorts of capital crimes in a kind of politically imposed modern theocracy. But if I have read Courthial aright, that does not appear to be what he is really advocating.

He states what he thinks this theonomic dogma would be: "God alone, the Father, the Son, and the Holy Spirit, is the LORD and Savior and there is none other besides Him" (page 256). Courthial believes that the Swiss Reformer Pierre Viret, more than Calvin, set this forward (in his *Instruction Chretienne en la doctrine de la Loi et de l'Evangile* of 1564). Courthial summarizes it: "God alone, in His Scripture, has sovereignly defined and decreed, once for all, the foundations of ethics and law" (271). Referring to Calvin's *Commentary on Deuteronomy* (CR 52,49,131), he quotes: "God is not submitted to laws, because He Himself *is* the law for Himself and for all others" (263). Hence Courthial writes that Holy Scripture is "the moral law revealed by God to Israel, the covenantal people," and that it "is normative for all men and all nations" (270).

He clearly admits important discontinuity between Israel and the nations (270, 284), and in that spirit appears to accept what Chapter XIX, par. 4 of the *Westminster Confession of Faith* says about the application of Old Testament civil laws to modern states: "To them also [i.e. Israel], as a body politic, he gave sundry judicial laws, which expired together with the state of that people, not obliging any other, now, further than the general equity thereof may require." I assume that this is what he means when he states (after affirming the threefold division of the law in the Reformed Confessions between moral, ceremonial, and civil), concerning socio-political and ceremonial laws: "though no longer having a direct and literal application," these laws "do nevertheless maintain an indirect and *typical* authority" (272). And in this regard he makes helpful reference to the first eight chapters of *The Shadow of Christ in the Law of Moses* by Vern S.

Poythress (1991). So, it appears, Courthial is seeking to work out "the general equity of the law." He makes it very clear that he is not seeking a state run by the church, but rather a state and church that acknowledge in their own different ways the source of all law and right in the holy character of God (220, 278). Yet in his section on the penal law, he does seem to me to go much further than Calvin and most of the Reformers have gone (280–284).

But apart from significant details such as this one (where many Calvinists will likely disagree with some aspects of his thesis), I believe that most will be able to agree with his main point, which should be both clear and convincing for all who hold to the authority of God speaking in Holy Scripture. It is this: the Word of God written, with its saving Gospel, Holy Spirit power in the Church, and with the guidance of its moral law and the general equity of all of its other types of law, is the light in which we are universally to walk — both in Church and in state, at home and abroad. Humanistic law, if and when it is contrary to the divinely revealed principles of the Word, is to be resisted and, where possible, replaced. That is what Courthial sees as the continuing issue between humanist revolution and Christian Reformation:

> Revolutions of human origin, *coups de force* aroused by "power religion," openly violate God's laws, scoff at liberties, and end by installing dictators who are determined to achieve their goals at all costs, even if that means the bloody sacrifices of many human lives. The system they establish is a veritable form of slavery. Their hatred of men in God's image reveals their hatred for God Himself. Reformations of divine origin, on the other hand, peacefully and patiently pursue the extension of the Kingdom of God on earth and a deeper understanding of His Law, which they diligently keep and practice. In the end, such Reformations progressively liberate many men from slavery, work toward a renewal of culture, invest great efforts into all kinds of educational and relief efforts which serve not only to address short-term needs but also improve conditions in the long-term. There will then be a *Christianization* of society, a new *Christendom*, rising from the large number of those who are *converted* and *come back* to the Faith as a result of the faithful communication of the Word-Gospel-Law of God under the sovereign working of the Holy Spirit. (300–301)

Here we see the two different streams that flow from the gigantic, creative influence of France: the atheistic "mother" revolution and the humanistic socialism that still flows from it, versus the theocentric godliness of such Reformers as John Calvin and Theodore Beza, and their spiritual heir, Pierre Courthial. Both of these streams still water the nations of our world and have much to do with the fruit they bear. One leads to humanistic bondage and the other to Christian freedom and renewal. If we follow the right stream, the one so beautifully channeled with such ready accessibility to our contemporary culture by Courthial, our future can be as bright as the promises of God, and many of us may yet live to give (in the words of one of Jonathan Edwards' titles of his reports on the New England revival) *A Narrative of Surprising Conversions* and, after that, a renewed and updated *History of the Work of Redemption*. Courthial would be surprised should it not be so, for he knew that in due season "we shall reap if we faint not" (Galatians 6:9) as, by Gospel faith, we go forth in loving obedience, invisibly united to the Lord of the harvest, the revealer of all truth, the Savior of our souls, the renewer of our cultures, and the sovereign dispenser of the Holy Spirit, who has long been in the business of "making all things new" (2 Corinthians 5:17).

If reading Courthial's book affects you the way it did me, it will cause you "to lift up your eyes unto the hills, from whence cometh your help: from the Lord which made heaven and earth" (Psalm 121:1, 2). You will be in good company as you follow the author along the hills of God, from Eden to Zion, until you find yourself gazing by faith upon "that city which hath foundations, whose builder and maker is God" (Hebrews 11:10). Those who look most to their citizenship in *that* city have a way of making the greatest beneficial differences in the cities and cultures here below.

The Lord called this grand old saint to his heavenly home on April 22, 2009, after a long and fruitful Christian life. Psalm 92:14 beautifully describes his life: "They shall still bring forth fruit in old age; they shall aye be flourishing," as do these words in Hebrews 11:4 (said of Abel): ". . . he being dead yet speaketh."

Douglas F. Kelly
Reformed Theological Seminary
Charlotte, North Carolina
January, 2018

Introduction

FROM MY ADOLESCENCE ON, I HAVE SPENT MY DAYS GLEANING.
It began at the age of thirteen (1928), when I began to glean *the vast field of the Scriptures*, reading and rereading these Words, though, alas, I too often fell short of them in my everyday life. For me these Scriptures have been always the Word(s) of God.

From the age of sixteen (1931), I have also gleaned *the fields of the ecclesial Tradition*, those of the Fathers (beginning with St. Augustine's *Confessions*), of the Doctors of the Age of Faith (beginning with Anselm's *Proslogion*), and of the Reformers (beginning with John Calvin's *Institutes* and Pierre Viret's *Christian Instruction*).

Since my university days in the Faculty of Protestant Theology in Paris (1932–1936), I have not stopped gleaning in particular from *the fields of the confessing Reformed*, whether those fields be French (from Pierre du Moulin to Auguste Lecerf), Dutch (from Abraham Kuyper to Herman Dooyeweerd and Klaas Schilder), Scottish (from William Cunningham to John Murray), South African (from Hendrik Stoker to Jan Taljaard), or American (from Charles Hodge to Cornelius Van Til). It has been with an ever-increasing appreciation and joy that I have found in each of these a living orthodoxy, unshakably committed to remaining faithful to *the Bible* of Israel (so regrettably called the "Old Testament") and to *the Apostolic Tradition* (so regrettably called the "New Testament"). Moreover, this gleaning of *the confessing*

Reformed has never prevented me (if anything it has encouraged me) from gleaning farther afield: in those fields of the Eastern Orthodox or Roman Catholics, both of clergy and laymen.

Thus my biblical model (both historical and symbolic) could well be Saint Ruth the Moabite. In the second chapter of that biblical book which bears her name we find, no less than a dozen times (and nowhere else in Scripture), the verb "to glean" (in Hebrew, *laqat*). As Ruth said, so can I say, from my own place in the field, that by the authorization and unmerited grace of the Landowner, "I have gone out into the field and gleaned and gathered among the sheaves after the reapers" (Ruth 2:3).

After these prolonged gleanings, which have enabled me to gather together many things (which may appear to some as just odds and ends), I sought to bring these together in a synthesis, a *covenantal* synthesis, of which this book is the fruit.

*

I am not presenting to the reader an easy book. I am well aware of that. My aim was to put into the reader's hands a book that would encourage his reflection on certain essential themes of Holy Scripture, on a number of decisive moments in the history of the Church, and on the major and indisputable affirmations from the early creeds and councils as well as the Reformed confessions of faith of the sixteenth and seventeenth centuries. To that end, numerous quotations are found in these pages, some of them quite lengthy. These quotations must not be skipped over or even skimmed through, but must be examined and studied closely, for they have altogether more weight and importance than the words that link and surround them, and the reader who gives his careful attention to them will be rewarded for his effort. I do not believe the reader will find the effort required to be beyond his reach; rather, he will find that a proper perseverance will suffice to carry him to the goal.

When it's all said and done, we must each be convinced and overcome by the written Word of God, centered from its first to its last words on the incarnate Word, our Savior, the Lord Jesus Christ.

I write here words, imbued with a mysterious light, which speak of that very Word of God which is indeed the Scripture:

I SOUGHT A MASTERPIECE BOTH ABSOLUTE AND UNIQUE. I DREAMT OF A BOOK THAT BY ITS VERY BEAUTY COULD RESTORE THE WORLD.... BUT THIS UNIQUE BOOK, THIS ABSOLUTE BOOK, COULD IT BOTH BE JUDGMENT AND KINGDOM, ALL AT ONCE?[1]

There are several persons I would like to thank, among many others:

— Aline Dielman, librarian of the Reformed Theological Faculty of Aix-en-Provence,[2] who always helped me find, or took it upon herself to find for me, many books, both mentioned and unmentioned, in this book;

— Marie de Védrines, who provided constant encouragement and brought both a friendly vigilance and critical spirit (I greatly profited from both) to the task of reading, rereading, typing, and preparing the manuscript for the publisher;

— Professor Paul Wells, pastors Roger Barilier and Arthur-Louis Hofer, as well as Henri-Jean Faber, each of whom read my manuscript and provided corrections;

— and Jean-Marc Berthoud, who, in a fraternal spirit, successfully persuaded me to undertake these labors, and who generously accepted to include the pages which follow in the publication he edits, *Messages*.

Lastly, the title of my book is taken from Zechariah 4:10 — "For whoever has despised the day of small things (or 'small beginnings') shall rejoice..."

Pierre Courthial
Aix-en-Provence
September 1994–March 1996

---

1. Andréi Makine, *Le testament français* (Mercure de France, Paris, 1995), 293.
2. Now named *Faculté Jean Calvin*.

PART ONE

The Ancient Order of the World

From the Origins to Our Era

1

God and His Covenant

2

The Mountains of God

3

The Lord, His Law, and His People

1

GOD AND HIS COVENANT

IN HOLY SCRIPTURE, WE LEARN THAT GOD'S GRACE IS REVEALED and given in the context of the relationship that He has sovereignly established with those whom He calls to be His people, a relationship known as the Covenant of Grace.[1] Scripture furthermore reveals the history of God's relationship with His people in terms of the historical development of the Covenant of Grace, tracing for us the growing reach and depth of the covenant as it carries on, according to God's plan, through various stages and administrations. Against the backdrop of these diverse stages and administrations — again, all according to God's plan — we come to see clearly the underlying unity and continuity of the covenant from its foothold in the Garden of Eden to its fulfillment in the New Jerusalem.

And just as Holy Scripture reveals to us the Covenant of Grace, so, in turn, does the Covenant of Grace throw light back upon how we understand the nature of Holy Scripture. The inseparable relationship between the two is rooted ultimately in the relation of each to God Himself, for each has God for its sovereign Author. And in choosing then to reveal His covenant (and its foundations) in His Holy Scripture, God established that each should be understood only in relation to the other. Thus we find Scripture referring to itself, quite fittingly, as "the Book of the Covenant" (Exodus 24:7), or as the covenant treaty.

---

1. The Hebrew word for "grace" is *hen*, which means "benevolence" or "favor."

The aim of this work is to unfold the Covenant of Grace through its successive manifestations (or, as we shall come to see they are called, successive "covenants") as revealed in Scripture, with the ultimate and urgent goal of understanding more fully what the Scriptures, in light of the covenant, reveal concerning how the Church in the twentieth century has fallen into such confusion and sickness, and how the Church may face the century to come with confident hope. Beginning in the Garden of Eden and ending with the Great Commission (and connecting the two), we will look at the covenant revealed to Adam, Noah, Abraham, Moses, and David, and then fulfilled in Christ, preached by the apostles and evidenced in the Fall of Jerusalem in A.D. 70. We will see the perennial relationship between God and His true people, between the Gospel and the Law, between the Scripture and the true tradition of the Church, and between faith and obedience. We will then survey the history of the Church's struggle against challenges and heresies, both ancient and modern (and "postmodern"), in the light of which we can better understand our present predicament and the path forward.[2]

In these opening pages, we must carefully lay the groundwork by considering the basic aspects of the Covenant of Grace (both in its prelapsarian and postlapsarian stages), before going on to give a more detailed exposition of the covenant in each of its successive manifestations (or, again, successive "covenants").

We begin with the covenant before the fall.

Before the Fall: The Prelapsarian Covenant[3]

Everything begins with the opening chapters of Genesis, the unavoidable starting point of the Bible, and with the first man, Adam. Here we find the beginning of the covenant and its history.

The Transcendent-Immanent God

The covenant is the unmerited gift from the transcendent God to the human creature, His image-bearer. God is God. From Him comes

---

2. *Translator's Note*: This paragraph was composed and inserted by the translator, in consultation with M. Jean-Marc Berthoud (see "Translator's Preface").

3. *Lapsus* is Latin for "fall"; prelapsarian means "before the fall" of Adam; postlapsarian means after this fall.

"every good and perfect gift" (James 1:17). From the beginning, it is He who creates, He who speaks, He who blesses, He who warns and commands. Moreover, God is transcendent, which is to say that He is qualitatively and infinitely distinct from His creatures.

And yet His transcendence — His being before all time and unbound by space — does not mean that He is distant from His creatures. Just the opposite! It is precisely because He is transcendent that He is able to be present to *all* His creatures, and present in such a way that he remains wholly unconfused with them (otherwise He would be mixed *with them* — à la *pantheism* — and not present *to them*). Thus we may say of God that His transcendence actually occasions His immanence.

The only reason that the Covenant of Grace between God and His people exists at all is the wisdom and kindness of the personal, one-and-many, transcendent-and-immanent God who established it by His sovereign will at the very beginning of human history. And the same goes for those who would ask why the covenant has continued through history, or who would seek to know its ultimate meaning. Such inquiries must lead us to acknowledge with gratitude the wisdom and kindness of God, for there is no further reason.

Two Possibilities: Theonomy or Autonomy

The human creatures, who receive the covenant as God's gift, are called to find the whole orientation of their lives in relation to the covenant, and thus to God Himself. In fact, the covenant establishes their very freedom and responsibility (*liberté-responsabilité*) as human creatures — a *liberté-responsabilité* bestowed on them by God's grace and subject entirely to His authority. Adam and Eve are called to live as faithful partners to the covenant in time and in history, and called to do so both as individuals and as a couple, in their roles both distinct and shared.

We must be careful not to mistake *liberté-responsabilité* for autonomy. Autonomy — being a law unto oneself — belongs to God alone. As the transcendent Creator, He is before all and over all, and subject to none. The *liberté-responsabilité* given to human beings, the creatures in His image, is therefore theonomic in nature (from *theos* = God and *nomos* = law); that is, set under the sovereignty of God and

His Word. This theonomic situation in no way diminishes, distorts, devalues, or destroys human *liberté-responsabilité*; rather, it is the only thing that makes freedom and responsibility possible, authentic, and meaningful. Apart from this situation, this theonomic relation, human *liberté-responsabilité* would simply not exist (freedom to what end? responsibility to whom?).

We see the establishment of a theonomic *liberté-responsabilité* from the very outset of God's relationship with His human creatures: "And God blessed them. And God said to them, 'Be fruitful and multiply and fill the earth and subdue it and have dominion…'" (Genesis 1:28). No sooner does God bestow His blessing upon man (Gospel!) than He gives His commandments (Law!), showing that the two (Gospel and Law) are inseparable. God commands the human creature to fill the earth and subdue it; to exercise dominion over the sub-human world (animals, vegetation, minerals) and to name the creatures; to tend and to keep the garden and to eat from all but one of the trees (1:28–29; 2:15, 20). It was forbidden to eat from "the tree of the knowledge of good and evil" (2:9).

In this blessing, calling, and warning, God grounded the *liberté-responsabilité* of our first parents — and in them that of the whole human race to come — in the context of a theonomic ethic. Whether they use their freedom to carry out the call of the Covenant of Grace, or use it in the rebellious pursuit of autonomy (which is ultimately destructive of their freedom), they are, from the very beginning, inescapably responsible to their gracious and sovereign Creator.

Two Ends: Life or Death

In addition to the blessing and commands (or Gospel and Law) found in Genesis 1:28–29, the covenant includes positive and/or negative sanctions. The text of Genesis next leads us to consider these.

As long as the human partner of the covenant remains faithful and responds with gratitude to God's grace, he enjoys open access to "the tree of life" standing in the middle of the garden. However, should he become inexplicably unfaithful, should he cease to acknowledge and serve God as God — if, pretending to autonomy like a madman, desiring to be "like God," to be a law unto himself, he should take of the forbidden tree — he will suffer death. He will be driven out from the garden. From that time onward "the way to the tree of life" will be closed off to him, guarded by the Cherubim with flaming sword (Genesis 3:24).

Man experiences death in two stages. First comes spiritual death, which he experiences immediately, for he is no longer in communion with God; then, later, comes physical death. If he is born again, his resurrection will likewise be in two stages. First comes spiritual resurrection, also experienced immediately, because his fellowship with God is restored; then, at the end of time, the resurrection of his body.

Historical and Symbolic Perspectives

Only within the context of the whole Bible can the full meaning of the opening pages of Genesis be grasped. This means that the reader should employ both the Bible's own historical perspective (we shall revisit this when we consider the several stages and developments of the covenant) and the symbolic perspective (found especially in the prophetic or poetic books in the Old Testament and in Revelation in the New Testament) by which the Bible often requires us to "visualize" what we are reading. The need for both perspectives becomes apparent as we turn our attention to the two trees in the Garden of Eden.

Two Sacramental Trees

The two trees in the garden were vital to the revelation of God's covenant to our first parents and remain vital for our understanding of that same covenant, which is why they are given such prominence in the biblical account. Historically speaking they were ordinary trees in every way; symbolically speaking they had a sacramental function as signs and seals of the covenant.

The tree of the knowledge of good and evil stands in the garden as the symbol and banner of God's Lordship in this covenant with the human creature, His image. By refraining from eating of this tree, the human creature demonstrates his submission to God. On the other hand, should he disobey God by eating from this tree, it would constitute an act of high treason; and not only that, it would be to choose — and to love — death (Proverbs 8:36). The very sight of this tree would remind Adam and Eve of their place under God's Law.

The tree of life stands in the garden as the symbol and banner of salvation, of the fullness of life found only in God. The sight of the tree of life, as well as the nourishment Adam and Eve took of it, would remind them that their Creator is the Author and Sustainer of their lives.

The glory of God as the Savior of the covenant and of the creation — as the one holding the power of life and of death — was visually represented to our first parents by these two sacramental trees. If the human creature reaches for the first tree and eats of it — by some act of incomprehensible revolt! — he will be deprived of the second tree and will experience death.

When, as is proper, the historical and symbolic characters of the text are brought together, it becomes clear that Adam finds himself in the garden with his future before him, beholding a dazzling array of possibilities that are not only beautiful to imagine, but would be good to bring to fruition — good both for him, as a creature in God's image fulfilling his divine calling, and also for the creation set under his dominion. This future hangs on but one condition: that he remain faithful to the One who gives him life while revealing to him how he should honor the Covenant of Grace.

Adam lives only by the grace, benevolence, and favor of the Lord, His Creator and Savior. He has no justification in and of himself. He neither has merited — nor can merit — anything at all. He can and must live only by faith, hope, and love. His motivation to be faithful comes only from his gratitude for the grace which has been given him and in which he lives. It is as if God had said to him: "I will be your God and you will be my faithful servant!" and Adam had answered: "Amen! ('so be it') my Lord and my God!"

After the Fall: The Postlapsarian Covenant

All throughout history, God has upheld and will continue to uphold His Covenant of Grace, and that by His Word (His Gospel-Law). Just as it was God who established this covenant, so it will be God who will renew it, God who will confirm it, and God who will fulfill it.

The man and woman are expelled from the garden after the revolt, the disobedience, the fall of Adam (which we shall consider next in greater detail), when he heard the harsh words of condemnation — "Cursed is the ground for your sake; in toil you shall eat of it all the days of your life . . . by the sweat of your face you shall eat bread till you return to the ground, for out of it you were taken" (Genesis 3:17–19). Their expulsion is an act of justice. But before they are driven away, and even before the words of condemnation fall on them, the man and woman first hear sure and certain words of hope — words revealing the Lord's patience toward them and His loving concern for them, and words laden already with the pain that the Lord takes upon himself in anticipation of the coming of Jesus Christ: "I will put enmity between you and the woman, between (the) seed (of the serpent) and (the) seed (of the woman); he shall bruise his head (of the serpent) and you shall bruise His heel (of the woman)" (Genesis 3:15; Revelation 12). The enmity that is foretold supposes a conflict between two lines: the one following in the ways of Satan, the deceiver; the other line upheld as partners of the covenant by the grace of God that looks toward the forgiveness of sins, the doing away with the penalty (spiritual and physical death) for their sins, and the victory over their adversary, in the crucifixion and resurrection of Christ.

Although the covenant is immediately resumed with Adam and Eve and continued with Seth and his descendants (called "the sons of God" in Genesis 6:2–4), the word "covenant" itself (*berîth* in Hebrew) does not make its first appearance in the Bible until the account of Noah. In Genesis 6:17–18, God says to Noah: "I Myself am bringing floodwaters on the earth . . . but I will confirm My covenant with you."

English translations too often render it: "I will *establish* My covenant." While the Hebrew verb *qûm* (in the *hiphil* form) can mean "to establish," it can equally well mean "to ratify, to confirm." Now whenever it concerns the covenant — as in Genesis 6, 9 and 17 and Exodus 6 — we must prefer the translation "to confirm" rather than "to establish." Why? Quite simply, the general context preceding these instances plainly shows, as we have seen, that the Covenant of Grace already existed with Adam (and even with Adam before the fall!). Furthermore, the more immediate context of Genesis 6 makes clear that Noah was already in the covenant before this episode in which God confirms it with him, his family, and his descendants. Several verses before Genesis 6:18, it is said: "Noah obtained favor in the eyes of the Lord. . . . Noah was a righteous man, having integrity in his generations. Noah walked with God" (6:8–9). Now it is impossible that anyone can obtain God's favor, be righteous, and have integrity, or walk with God, unless he is *in* the Covenant of Grace — this covenant which God calls *My covenant*. Thus we infer from this testimony concerning Noah that he was already a member of the Covenant of Grace which, just prior to and in view of the coming Flood, God confirms with him.

Holy Scripture reveals the establishment of the Covenant of Grace with Adam at creation. From that point on it reveals to us the basic history of this covenant running from generation to generation as it is successively resumed, renewed, confirmed, modified, and deepened over time. We find that each stage of its history is marked by promises, commandments, warnings, and sacraments.

We must not fail to note that the New Testament twice refers to these stages of the covenant as successive "covenants" in the plural (Romans 9:4; Ephesians 2:12). The New Testament also (in the Epistle to the Hebrews) distinguishes between the "old covenant" and the "new covenant." These are not separate and unrelated covenants — as if God has fundamentally changed the way he relates to his human creatures — but distinct epochs in the history of the one Covenant of Grace, wherein the "old covenant" epoch of the Covenant of Grace is comprised of the several historical stages which precede and anticipate the coming of Christ, while the "new covenant" epoch of the Covenant of Grace refers to the fulfillment in Christ of all that has come before. That is why among these various "covenants" we find both unity and progressive development, testifying to the fact that the plan of the personal, one-and-many, transcendent God has been the same from the very beginning.

2

The Mountains of God

It may come as a surprise to many readers that the historical stages of the covenant are clearly marked out for us in Scripture according to the particular mountain on which each stage was inaugurated. Accordingly, it seems apropos that Psalm 121, the second of the "psalms of ascent," opens with these often-misunderstood words: "I will lift up my eyes to the mountains; From where shall my help come?" (NASB). In the following pages, under the titles of "the mountain of...," we will consider one by one the stages and arrangements of the history of the covenant as it unfolds with Adam, Noah, Abraham, Moses, and David (the culmination of the covenant in Jesus Christ will be our focus in Part II). We will lift our eyes to the main mountains of Scripture, "the mountains of God," to find our help. From mountain to mountain, we will lift up our hearts, beginning with the garden where it all began and culminating with the heavenly City above. God "will make me walk on my high hills" (Habakkuk 3:19). Did not Isaiah prophesy: "Now it shall come to pass in the latter days, that the mountain of the Lord's house shall be established on top of the mountains, and shall be exalted above the hills; and all nations shall flow to it" (Isaiah 2:2)?

The Mountain of Eden

> 1. *As for that part of the Garden, my beloved,*
>   *which is situated so gloriously*
>   *at the summit of that height*
>   *where dwells the Glory,*
>   *not even its symbol*
>   *can be depicted in man's thought...*
>
> 2. *Perhaps that blessed tree,*
>   *the Tree of Life,*
>   *is, by its rays,*
>   *the sun of Paradise...*
>   *In the breezes the other trees*
>   *bow down as if in worship*
>   *before that sovereign*
>   *and leader of the trees.*[1]

The story of Adam and of the covenant begins on a mountain, east of Eden, in a garden (Genesis 2:8; a garden no doubt set on a plateau on the mountainside). The river that "went out of Eden to water the garden" branched into four arms which descended down the mountain. God would say later to the King of Tyre, a distant descendant of Adam mysteriously identified with him: "You were the seal of perfection, full of wisdom and beauty. You were in Eden, the garden of God.... I established you; you were on the holy mountain of God" (Ezekiel 28:12–14).

The Genesis account of what transpired on this first mountain introduces us to the fundamental ground motive of Holy Scripture: Creation-Fall-Redemption.[2] This ground motive courses through the whole Bible until it reaches its climactic exposition in Revelation ("the Apocalypse"), received and written down by St. John (cf. Isaiah 51:3, Ezekiel 36:33–36).

---

1. *Translator's Note*: Courthial quotes from *St. Ephraim the Syrian* (306–373), *Hymnes sur le Paradis*, III, "Sources chrétiennes" no. 137. The English rendering is here taken from *Hymns of Paradise*, trans. Sebastian Brock (St. Vladimir's Seminary Press, 1990), 90–91.

2. *Translator's Note*: Courthial appears to be borrowing the phrase "ground motive" (*motif-de-base*) from the Dutch Reformed philosopher Herman Dooyeweerd (whom he much admired and read extensively), to refer to the basic organizing principle of a thought-system.

The Cultural Mandate at Creation

To enter into God's covenant, into the communion of love, as well as to be able to carry it forward into the future, it was necessary that the man in God's image be created perfect. Accordingly, we are told that the man in God's image was created "good," and even "very good" (Genesis 1:31). Once created, the man in God's image is charged with a major mission, the cultural mandate. Earthly life would be the stage of his activity, for from the earth he was formed and over it he was to exercise dominion.[3] God's covenant with man is forward-looking from the beginning.

The trees in the garden present to man, naturally and symbolically, the vast array of life's possibilities which lie before him — all of the occupations, arts, and sciences for developing a culture. His life's work will be to glorify the Lord by being — and seeking always to become more and more — His image and likeness.

To this end, the man-image of God is given three callings — to be a king, a priest, and a prophet.

As king, he is called to exercise dominion over the creation, exploring and studying it, naming the creatures with ever-greater precision and transforming the sub-human (that is, "put-under-man") world with his advancing capabilities. But success in this calling depends upon his asking for and receiving that wisdom which begins with, and finds its living principle in, the fear of the Lord; that is, that worshipful respect which can only express itself in full and unreserved submission to His Word (Job 28:28; Psalm 111:10; Proverbs 1:7; 9:10).

As priest, he is called to keep and serve the house of God where he has been placed (originally, that is the garden, cf. Meredith Kline's *Kingdom Prologue*). It is the role of a priest to discern and maintain the distinctions, the boundaries, which the Lord has established (cf. Ezekiel 44:23). Already in the opening chapter of Genesis several such divinely-established "separations" have been revealed: light-darkness, waters above and waters below, land-sea, good-evil, male-female.[4]

---

3. "Cultural" mandate according to both senses of the word: the culture of man's physical environment ("agriculture") as well as the human culture that would be developed.

4. The importance of maintaining these first separations of the creation is emphasized in later parts of Scripture. For example, Isaiah 5:20 ("Woe to those who call evil good and good evil, who put darkness for light and light for darkness"); and Deuteronomy 22:5 ("A woman shall not wear a man's garment, nor shall a man put on a woman's cloak, for whoever does these things is an abomination to the Lord your God").

Moreover, as priest, he is called to render thanksgiving for all things, offering everything — most especially his very self — back to God. This is his "logical" worship; that is, worship according to the Logos, the Word of God (Romans 12:1).

As prophet, man is called to remain in fellowship with the Council of the one-and-many God who, by His revelation, makes known to him, in part, His secret — "Surely the Lord GOD does nothing, unless he reveals His secret to His servants the prophets" (Amos 3:7; cf. Jeremiah 23:18). To maintain this privileged relationship, he must be always fighting off the slightest temptation or urge to be autonomous. When Adam was cut off from Eden after the fall, he was also cut off from the Council of God which God, by grace, had once shared with him. It is only by the prophets — first with Abraham, then above all with Moses — that God will share anew His Council with the men of the covenant.

We cannot fail to notice that the commandments of the Edenic covenant are addressed not only to individual *persons* — to Adam and Eve — but *communities* as well. Most broadly, *the whole human race* in Adam, and with him as its head and representative, is included in the commandments to "man." More specifically, with Adam and Eve, God establishes *marriage* and *the family* (Genesis 1:26–28; 2:18–24). The covenant applies equally to communities and individuals, from which ensue responsibilities both individual and corporate in nature. This dual aspect of the covenant confronts us time and again throughout Scripture in the course of which it becomes clearer and more far-reaching.

Original Sin

Adam transgressed the covenant (Hosea 6:7). His eating from the sacramental tree of good and evil revealed disregard for God's specific prohibition, as well as, more generally, his rejection of theonomy, of the authority of the Law of God (and thereby of the Gospel!). This mad act of revolt was driven by his craving for autonomy, to be a law unto himself, to be "like God" in an evil sense, for which the human race, with Adam and in Adam, has paid the consequences to this day ("the wages of sin is death"; Romans 6:23).

Indeed, the man in God's image was called to be "like God," and to become ever more "like God," but to become so in his place as a creature and out of gratitude for theonomy. Adam's longing to be "like God," however, sprang from his insane desire to substitute his own law (his autonomy) for the Law of the Lord (theonomy). Whereas he ought to have heeded the covenantal communication by which a man in communion with God hears and follows what the personal, one-and-many God tells him — from mouth to ear, from heart to heart — Adam, at the instigation of "the adversary," made his own autonomous and absurd voice, the voice of a man-making-himself-god, to take the place of what God had clearly said... in order to go against it. His pride swelled to the point that God's rightful claim over him — to be able to tell him, as his Creator, what kind of man he should or shouldn't be, what kinds of things he should or shouldn't do — became unbearable to him.

If Adam's sin, the *original* sin that the human race and each human creature would thereafter bear within themselves, could somehow be explained (as owing to an imperfection in the divine work of creation, or to something lacking in man's created condition), it could then be excused (which is exactly what Adam and Eve tried to do with their blaspheming; Genesis 3:11–13). But the *original sin* (that is, Adam's sin and ours with and in Adam) is truly without excuse, *precisely because it is truly inexplicable.* Thus Adam and Eve, and every human creature, have nothing to say but *mea culpa, mea maxima culpa*, absent even the slightest attempt to supply a reason for what they have done.

Judgment and Grace

And yet, right after the fall, on the mountain, still in the Garden of Eden, the Covenant of Grace resumes. Aware of their "nakedness" now that they have willfully stripped themselves of grace, and afraid of the God of the covenant who is looking for them, Adam and Eve attempt to hide from Him in the garden and cover their nakedness with "fig leaves" sewn together (Genesis 3:7–10). But the "Lord God" (His name as Lord of the covenant) calls to them to announce both His righteous judgment (Law!) and the grace that He will renew to them (Gospel! — the grace that *He renews to them* is also the grace that *renews them*). Now under His judgment, the human creatures are going to be chased from the garden and from Eden into the rest of the earth, entering a new situation in history, one full of dangers, pains, and tensions between themselves and their environment. They know already and have still more to learn, in great dread, about what was meant by the warning: "You will die" (Genesis 2:17 and 3:16–19).[5]

The LORD God's grace, received with faith and repentance, allows Adam to name his wife. He names her Eve, meaning "Living" (she is the mother of all the living). This grace is signified and sealed by the fact that God makes tunics of skin with which to cover them. These tunics of skin are sacramental precursors of redemption, that redemption which is to be prefigured by the blood of the sacrifices offered repeatedly and temporarily under the old covenant epoch of the Covenant of Grace, then fulfilled at last by the blood of the once-for-all and perfect sacrifice of Christ Jesus, "God made man" for us and for our salvation, in the new covenant epoch of that same Covenant of Grace. It was true even in the garden that "without the shedding of blood there is no forgiveness" (Hebrews 9:22; cf. Hebrews 10:5–10); and salvation is still likened to being "clothed" in God's gracious covering even after Christ has come: "For as many as were baptized into Christ have put on (lit. 'dressed themselves with') Christ Jesus" (Galatians 3:27).[6]

THE MOUNTAIN OF ARARAT

Who then has seen such flowers
as those which one gathers
in the holy Books,
on the Mountains?[7]

Sons of Men and Sons of God

As the story of the covenant moves beyond Adam and Eve, the nature of the covenant becomes clarified in light of two of their sons,

---

5. The *kerûbîm* now guard the way to the tree of life with a flaming sword (Genesis 3:24; the *kerûbîm* are not angels in the ordinary sense, but spirits, spiritual creatures who, in their prayer and unceasing worship, accompany the presence and the majesty of the Lord: they are nothing like the cherubs (or cupids) in our sentimental modern art! Cf. Exodus 25:22; 37:7–9; 1 Samuel 4:4; Ezekiel 9:3; 10:3–22; Hebrews 9:5; Revelation 4:6–9).

6. See also Job 29:14; Isaiah 61:10; Matthew 6:30; 2 Corinthians 5:4; Revelation 19:13.

7. St. Ephraim the Syrian, "Hymnes sur la Résurrection," II, *Célébrons la Pâque*, "Les Pères dans la Foi," Migne, 1995, 158.

Cain and Seth, and their respective descendants. Cain's descendants were "the sons of men," Adamite rebels of the covenant. But in Seth's descendants God raised up "the sons of God," Adamites faithful to the covenant. This division of the human race into two peoples lasted until "the sons of God" began marrying "the daughters of men," which led to a worldwide rebellion of the human race against the Lord and His covenant. The "wickedness of man" became so great ("every intent of the thoughts of his heart was only evil all the time") that the Lord was "grieved in his heart" and decided to blot out men and animals from the face of the earth (Genesis 6:5–7 and 11–12). This was the Flood. Noah, a man faithful to the Covenant of Grace, along with his family and numerous pairs of animals, were the only ones spared (Genesis 6:13–8:19). The Covenant of Grace was renewed and confirmed with Noah and his line on the mountain of Ararat (Genesis 8:20–9:27).

Out of faithfulness to the covenant, Abel, son of Adam, had offered the sacrifice "of the firstborn of his flock and of their fat" which "the LORD looked upon favorably" (Genesis 4:4). Likewise, out of the same faithfulness, when he went out of the ark on the mountain of Ararat (a new *mountain of God*, located perhaps just above the site of the old mountain of Eden), Noah built an altar to the Lord, offering a sacrifice of "clean animals" that the Lord accepted.

Noah's Sacrifice

After this sacrifice was offered and accepted, the story of Genesis continues with the monologue that takes place when the one-and-many God says "in His heart:"

> I will never again curse the ground for man's sake, although the imagination of man's heart is evil from his youth; nor will I again destroy every living thing as I have done. While the earth remains, seedtime and harvest, cold and heat, winter and summer, and day and night shall not cease (Genesis 8:21–22).

Then God renews the covenantal blessing on Noah and his sons, the same blessing pronounced previously on our first parents: "Be fruitful and multiply, fill the earth" (Genesis 9:1; cf. Genesis 1:26). He restates here more precisely what he had affirmed in Genesis 1: "Subdue the earth; have dominion over the creatures" (animals and vegetation). He gives His covenantal precepts concerning the use of vegetables and animals for food. And whereas God had earlier set a mark on Cain, the murderer, to protect him (Genesis 4:15), He now makes clear that anyone who murders a human creature, image-of-God, will be justly punished by death (Genesis 9:2–7). The Lord also declares that the Covenant of Grace concerns "perpetual generations," or "generations to come" (Genesis 9:12).

He concludes by reminding man that because those faithful to the covenant occupy a place over nature (mineral, vegetable, animal), the renewed Covenant of Grace will encompass the whole cosmos. This was already implied by the words God said in His heart when Noah offered sacrifices after exiting the ark. He expressly states that the Covenant of Grace extends to animals as well, and even to the whole realm of nature — "I will remember my covenant which is between Me and you and every living creature of all flesh" (Genesis 9:11–17; cf. Romans 8:18ff.). From that time on, for as long as the earth remains, the God who is faithful to the Covenant of Grace and its members will preserve and protect the order of nature — and this to the benefit of all humanity.

The survivors of the Flood — eight persons in all, including Noah — form a kind of "faithful remnant" of the Covenant of Grace. At that moment in history, on the mountain of Ararat, these eight are the embryo of the future people of the new Adam to come (cf. 1 Peter 3:20–21). According to the promise of the Lord, this embryo of the covenantal people will be fruitful, multiply, and fill the earth; it will subdue the earth and exercise dominion over the creatures.

One significant development is that, after the diluvian judgment, God authorizes and ordains the legitimate defense of the members of the Covenant of Grace against the malice of their adversaries. The mark of protection that He had set on Cain (Genesis 4:15; 9:5–7) is withdrawn: the death penalty must be pronounced on every murderer.

In this way the renewal of the Covenant of Grace on the mountain of Ararat marks a new stage, an advance in relation to what happened during Adam and Eve's time on the mountain of Eden and in subsequent history up to the Flood.

Now that the fall has happened and original sin has corrupted the human race, now that "the imagination of man's heart is evil from his youth" (something felt most keenly by the members of the Covenant of Grace!), the renewed covenant, with its promises, commands, warnings, and signs, must be grasped, more than before, in terms of forgiveness, in terms of redemption. This redemption, though prefigured by the blood of temporary and imperfect sacrifices like those offered by Seth and Noah, will be accomplished by the blood of the one-and-only and perfect new Adam to come, God made man. Accordingly, the texts of Genesis must now be read through the lens of the new Adam.

The Rainbow

The renewal of the covenant on the mountain of Ararat is accompanied by the sacramental sign of the rainbow.

From the time of the Flood — which brought about deep and indescribable upheavals in the life of the world, and for as long as the earth remains — there has been and will be the rainbow. Though given as a visual sign and symbol for the faithful of the Covenant of Grace (which none can fail to receive! Genesis 9:17), it is presented to us in Genesis 9:9–17 more as a memorial for God Himself: "I will remember My covenant which is between Me and you and every living creature of all flesh: the waters shall never again become a flood to destroy all flesh. The rainbow shall be in the cloud, and I will look on it to remember the everlasting covenant between Me and every living creature of all flesh that is on the earth." Emphasis is given to the phrase "My covenant" (*berîthî*) by its threefold use, and the phrase "sign of the covenant" and the word "rainbow" each appear three times as well. It seems fitting, then, to look at three other Bible verses speaking of the rainbow.

First, when Ezekiel has his vision of the glory of God, he will say: "Like the appearance of a rainbow in a cloud on a rainy day, so was the appearance of the brightness all around it. This was the appearance of the likeness of the glory of the Lord" (Ezekiel 1:28).

Second, when the apostle John has his vision of God while on the isle of Patmos, he will see "a rainbow around the throne, in appearance like an emerald" (Revelation 4:3).

And, third, when this same John has the vision of Jesus Christ in his glory, he will describe it as "an angel coming down from heaven, clothed with a cloud. And a rainbow was on his head, his face was like the sun, and his feet like pillars of fire" (Revelation 10:1).

And so it is that, when God, surrounded by the cloud of His glory, looks upon His world and His people, He sees them always through the rainbow, the luminous memorial of His Covenant of Grace.

Following the Noahic covenant, the seventy *nations* (*goyîm*) are established — the number "seventy" being both historical and symbolic. It is historically meaningful in that it refers to the seventy descendants of Noah: the sons and grandsons of Japheth (14), those of Ham (30), and those of Shem (26). These seventy were the ancestors of the clans from which originated the first *nations*, each distinguished by their own country and language. The number "seventy" is symbolically meaningful in that it refers to the *totality* (10 x 7) of nations, all the nations that will exist on earth in the course of history from the Flood to the end of the world (Genesis 9:7–17; 10:32). Every nation (as well as every family and *fatherland*; cf. Ephesians 2:14) takes its name, that is, derives its reality, from God the Father, who, in His eternal plan, conceived its establishment, in its time, in history — "He has made from one blood every nation of men to dwell on all the face of the earth, and has determined their pre-appointed times and the boundaries of their dwellings…" (Acts 17:24–28; cf. also Deuteronomy 32:7–8; Psalm 22:28; 86:8–10; Matthew 28:18–20). The divine plan for the nations was indicated beforehand in the Edenic covenant, in which obedience to the prophetic commandments — "be fruitful and multiply and fill the earth" — were intended to propel the human race outward and across the whole earth, subduing and exercising dominion over it as they multiplied. God is so zealous for the diversity of the nations that he will not allow totalitarian one-worldism to stand, whether it be the tower of Babel (Genesis 11) or the proud empires which have risen and fallen one after another.

The Mountain of Moriah

It is His Word which is
that treasure of treasures,
When He opens it
all His creatures are enriched.[8]

---

8. St. Ephraim the Syrian, "Hymnes sur les Azymes," XX, *Célébrons la Pâque*, "Les Pères dans la Foi," 97.

Before the Flood, the only major differentiation known to the human race, the Adamic race, was that which existed between the Cainites from the Sethites. The Cainites, first in the image of Cain, then in the image of Lamech (the seventh generation from Adam through Cain), lived and breathed murder and envy (Genesis 4:23–24). The Sethites, in the image of Enoch (the seventh generation from Adam through Seth) sought to "walk with God" and respect the sign of protection that the Lord had set on Cain and his descendants. The Cainites took advantage of that protection, exploiting the Sethites' inability to defend themselves in order to gain ascendancy over them. Finally these "sons of God," no longer prizing their identity as the faithful line, "saw" that the daughters of the Cainites, the "daughters of men," were "beautiful" (just as Eve had "seen" that the forbidden tree was "pleasant to the eyes"; Genesis 3:6). They took wives from among them, and thus began down the road that would lead to their ruin. God would now come to "regret" having made man on the earth. The judgment of God arrived (Genesis 6:1–7).

The Nations

As we have said above, the human race after the Flood is going to be divided into nations, each having to some degree, and gaining over time, its own geographic area, government and language.

We should take note of two things in the passage. First, among the list of nations there appears one named Eber, an ancestor of Abraham and descendant of Shem, from whom will come the Hebrews. Second, the Greek translation of the Jewish Bible — carried out between 250 and 130 B.C. — is called the version of the Seventy, or, more briefly, "the Septuagint" (LXX), because it was intended to be read by those besides the Jews, that is, by the people of the nations.

God — The One and the Many

Obstinately longing for autonomy and full of pride, men rejected the plan of the one-and-many God and sought to build for themselves "a city and a tower whose top is in the heavens" with which to "make a name for ourselves" (Genesis 11:4).

We should note here that the true God presents Himself as both one and many ("Come, let Us go down and confuse their language";

Genesis 11:7), as He does throughout the whole Bible. In the Old Testament, the most frequent name for God (it appears more than 2,500 times) is *Elohîm*, a word which is, at the same time, both singular and plural: *El* meaning God, the one God; and the suffix *îm* indicating plurality. Furthermore, the Spirit of God (e.g. Genesis 1:2; 2 Chronicles 24:20; Job 33:4; Isaiah 11:2; 34:16; Ezekiel 11:5; 37:9ff) and the Angel of the LORD (Genesis 16:7; 22:11, 15; 24:7, 40; 31:11; 32:24ff. [cf. Hosea 12:4]; Genesis 48:16) are clearly two persons in the one God, distinct from the third, the Father, there being three persons in all. Finally, as it concerns the Old Testament witness, there are certain passages in Genesis that we have already cited in which God says "Us" instead of "I" (Genesis 1:26 and 11:7). In the New Testament, the one-and-many God is plainly revealed as the Father, the Son, and the Holy Spirit.

But at Babel, the Lord confuses the conceited plans of men and their pretension to autonomy and "scatters them abroad throughout the earth" (Genesis 10 and 11:1–9). This historical judgment of God brings an end to the empire-building enterprise at Babel. Such will be the fate of every empire, every "pseudo-mountain," every tower and pyramid intended to be a man-made version of the "mountains of God" (cf. Daniel 2:31–45).

*

The book of Genesis is made up of a series of tablets. The longest of these concern Abraham, Isaac, Jacob, and Joseph. With the tablet of Abraham, the focus narrows from the story of the nations to the patriarchal stage of the Hebrew clan, a clan that is going to develop apart from the other Semites (= descendants of Shem) and form its own family-church, descending from four successive patriarchs: Abraham, Isaac, Jacob, and Joseph. The Hebrew clan is not a state, nor is it yet a people or nation. At this stage it is but the embryo of the people of Israel.

Abraham (around 2000 B.C.)

The figure of Abraham — first named *Ab-ram* (high father), becoming *Ab-raham* (father of a multitude) — is that of an earthly father (*ab* means "father") walking in close communion with the Heavenly

Father, so much so that he would become His living parable on the mountain of Moriah (Genesis 22).

This tablet of Genesis tells us of eight meetings between God and Abraham, "the friend of God" (cf. 2 Chronicles 20:7; James 2:23). In each of these meetings, God speaks (or shows Himself and speaks) to Abraham and Abraham believes and obeys (Genesis 12:1–4; 12:7–8; 13:14–18; 15; 17; 18; 21:12–14 and 22:1–9).

The first of these meetings took place in Ur of the Chaldeans, the native land of Abraham's parents. The other seven took place in Palestine, in the land of Canaan: first at Shechem, in the middle of the country, then and most often to the south at Hebron, and finally on the mountain of Moriah, the site of the future Jerusalem, perhaps at the very hill where the foundation of the Temple would be laid (2 Chronicles 3:1).

Wherever these meetings took place, which was often where he was residing or had pitched his tents, Abraham built altars (a miniature model of the holy mountains to "lift our hearts and hands to God in heaven"; Lamentations 3:41). On these altars he offered, with adoration and prayer, sacrifices of birds and beasts great and small to extol the Lord, His covenant, His promises, commandments, and warnings. The climactic sacrifice in the life of Abraham came when, in obedience to God's extraordinary and mysterious command, he offered in his heart and by his own hands (and he would have gone through with it), his only and beloved son, Isaac. He laid Isaac on the altar "concluding that God was able to raise him up, even from the dead" (Hebrews 11:19). This is why the mountain of Moriah represents the most moving encounter — a living parable — between the Lord, the heavenly Father, and Abraham, the earthly father *par excellence* (Genesis 22). We are confronted here with a dramatic symbol (Hebrews 11:19).

In the course of the sixth meeting (Genesis 18), Abraham had the unique and distinguished honor of receiving three mysterious visitors who manifested the Holy Trinity (as the text indicates, though in a veiled manner). As the "father of all those who believe" (Romans 4:11–12, 16; Galatians 3:7), Abraham had the faith, love, and hope to address the three as one ("My *Lord*"; Genesis 18:2–3) and the one as three ("rest *yourselves* under the tree"; Genesis 18:4–5).

The Three Promises

As the Covenant of Grace is confirmed to Abraham on several occasions (Genesis 12–22), three inseparable promises are made to him:

- a people will descend from him and will be the holy people, the people of God;
- a land will be given to this people and will be the holy land;
- this people and their land will be the instruments of a *universal blessing*.

Historically, the promise of a people is fulfilled during the time of Moses; the people come into full possession of the land during the time of David; and the people and their land will manifest the universal blessing only with the coming of Jesus Christ, God-made-man for the salvation of the world.

As far as Abraham was concerned, the great people descending from him were for a long while but a promise. Then, with Isaac, they existed solely in his only son. Concerning the promised land, Abraham, at his death, possessed only a field there, before Mamre, near Hezron. He had purchased this field himself from Ephron, the Hittite, to be a place truly his own to bury his wife, Sarah. And it was there, in the cave of Machpelah, located on this property, that Abraham's two sons (Isaac, son of Sarah, and Ishmael, son of Hagar the servant) buried his body next to Sarah's (Genesis 23 and 25:7–11).

A man faithful to the God of the Covenant of Grace, Abraham "believed in the LORD, and He accounted it to him for righteousness" (Genesis 15:6; quoted in Romans 4:3, Galatians 3:6, and James 2:23). "For he waited for the city which has foundations, whose builder and maker is God.... Therefore from one man, and him as good as dead, were born (descendants) as many as the stars in the sky in multitude — innumerable as the sand which is by the seashore" (Genesis 15:5; Hebrews 11:10, 12).

Circumcision

During His fifth meeting with Abraham, God instituted the sacrament of circumcision (Genesis 17:9–14, 23–27). This sacrament sealed the triple promise made by God to the father of all believers. With this mark, the promise was henceforth, we can say, inscribed on the body of every male member of the Covenant of Grace. This practice would continue for as long as the *berîth olam*, the perpetual covenant, lasted (in Hebrew, *olam* is related to a time, an age, an era, lasting until the time of its fulfillment). In fact, circumcision, as a sacrament of the covenant, would have to be maintained up to the fulfillment of the last of the three promises: the universal blessing in Jesus Christ.

According to verses 23 and 27 of Genesis 17, all the males in the Abrahamic clan, young and old alike, were circumcised. According to verses 12 and 13, every male child, whether born a descendant of Abraham or adopted into the patriarch's clan, was to be circumcised when he was eight days old.

Circumcision signified and sealed the covenantal adoption by God of the one circumcised and his standing as a member of the Covenant of Grace, a privileged place to be honored both by other members of the covenant and by himself. For the one circumcised, the sacramental mark of circumcision exacted a spiritual demand on him: namely, that he recognize the special claim that God had over him. Moreover, it placed him under the promises of the covenant, but not without also placing him in the realm of the Lord's righteous threats and warnings. Therefore, the Lord commanded Abraham and his descendants to "keep My covenant" (Genesis 17:9) and to "keep the way of the Lord by doing what is right" (18:19, NIV).

God had appeared to Abraham at that time with a new name, *El Chaddaï*, the all-powerful God. God had full power to keep His promises and execute His judgments.

At this same meeting, God declared to the father of believers that through Ishmael, his son by the servant, would come a great nation, but the people of the covenant would come through the son promised to him by Sarah — "I will bless [Sarah] and also give you a son by her... and she shall be a mother of nations; kings of peoples shall be from her" (Genesis 17:15–22).

It must be noted that, in Hebrew, one does not "agree to" a covenant, but one "cuts" a covenant (*kârath berîth*). In Genesis 15:9–12 and 17ff., the Lord orders Abraham to bring a heifer, a goat, and a ram and to *cut* them in two. Then, at dusk, the Lord *cuts* the covenant with Abraham by renewing the promises to him after a smoking furnace and burning torch passed between the animals *cut* in two. In circumcision, the cutting, the removal of the foreskin, served to mark on the body of the one circumcised his calling to be faithful to the covenant *cut* by God. The rest of the Torah (Exodus, Leviticus, Numbers, and Deuteronomy) will make clear that if the circumcised one should become unfaithful and deny the covenant, they will be justly *cut off* from the covenant. The Hebrew verb *kârath* can be translated equally well by "to cut" or "to remove," "to cut off" (for example, Genesis 17:14 — "that person shall be cut off from his people").

Circumcision demonstrates visually and sacramentally that natural, physical descent from Abraham is not sufficient to become one of the true spiritual descendants of Abraham, the father of all who believe. The natural, physical descendants of Abraham were no less affected by original sin and its consequences than the rest of the human race since Adam's fall. The salvation of the people of the covenant will be a justifying and sanctifying work that God must see to Himself — to be received by grace, through faith. The blood of circumcision, like that of the bloody sacrifices of animals, pointed typologically (*typos* is Greek for "figure, image, example"; cf. Romans 5:14; Hebrews 8:5) to the sacrifice of the only-begotten Son of the Father. Abraham, "while still uncircumcised," Paul says, "received the sign of circumcision, a seal of the righteousness of the faith" (Romans 4:11). Deuteronomy explicitly states the spiritual implication of circumcision: "Therefore circumcise the foreskin of your heart and be stiff-necked no longer.... And the LORD God will circumcise your heart, and the heart of your descendants, to love the LORD your God with all your heart and with all your soul, that you may live" (10:16; 30:6).

The Mountain of Sinaï

> *Moses, who instructs all men*
> *with his celestial writings,*
> *He, the master of the Hebrews,*
> *has instructed us in his teaching —*
> *the Law, which constitutes*
> *a very treasure house of revelations...*[9]

---

9. St. Ephraim the Syrian, *Hymnes sur Paradis*, I, "Sources chrétiennes," no. 137, 35. Translator's Note: The English rendering comes from *Hymns of Paradise* (1990), 77.

The covenant, with the triple promise, the triple oath of God to Abraham (Genesis 26:3; 22:15–18), was confirmed once to Isaac (Genesis 26:2–5), then twice to Jacob (Genesis 28:12–22 and 35:6–15). It is because of His covenant, as renewed with Abraham, Isaac, and Jacob, that God heard the groaning of the descendants of Jacob-Israel (Genesis 35:9–10) when they were slaves in Egypt (Exodus 2:24–25).

The Two Moments at Sinaï

Two of the great moments in the history of the covenant occurred at Sinaï. The first was God's meeting with Moses at the burning bush (Exodus 3 and 4). The second was the confirmation of the covenant with the people of Israel (Exodus 9 to 40 and the last three books of the Torah).

First Moment

In the course of the first episode on the mountain of God, at Horeb (another name for Sinaï), "the Angel of the Lord," God Himself, appears to Moses "in a flame of fire in the midst of a bush," but the bush is not consumed. He reveals His Name for all eternity to Moses: the unpronounceable YHWH (I Am), which the Jews, followed by many Christians, have replaced with *Adonaï* ("the Lord"). He announces that the time has come for the fulfillment of the first of the three promises made to Abraham: the people of the covenant, who have been formed in Egypt, are going to be brought out of the house of bondage. In order to make it unmistakably clear that this constitutes a major step in the history of the covenant, God refers to Himself three times as "the God of Abraham, Isaac, and Jacob" (Exodus 3:6, 16; and 4:5).

In Exodus 5–11, we read of the great conflict between God and Pharaoh, between the living God and the gods of Egypt. When Moses voices God's demand, "Let my people go that they may serve Me!" Pharaoh, wanting to keep his slaves, obstinately responds, "No!"

Then God unleashes the first of nine plagues on Egypt.

The Passover

On the eve of the tenth and last plague on Egypt, the death of every first-born among the Egyptians, God institutes the Passover, the second of the great sacraments for the people of Israel (the first being the continued practice of circumcision).

The practice of keeping the Passover effectively made priests of every head of household in Israel. This practice would give rise to the institution of the Tabernacle (which we shall address shortly) and the sacrificial system of Israel.

Approximately 1400 B.C.

In Exodus 12:1–25 we read about the institution of the Passover. God instructs Moses and Aaron how to observe the Passover, the memorial of God's "passing" over Egypt resulting in judgment for Egypt and salvation for the people of Israel.

According to the Lord's command, Israel's calendar year will begin in the spring, in the month of the Passover (*Nisan*, March-April). "On the tenth of this month every man shall take for himself a lamb, according to the house of his father, a lamb for a household," says the Lord, continuing:

> And they shall take some of the blood and put it on the two doorposts and on the lintel of the houses where they eat it. Then they shall eat the flesh on that night.... Now the blood shall be a sign for you on the houses where you are. And when I see the blood, I will pass over you; and the plague shall not be on you to destroy you when I strike the land of Egypt. So this day shall be to you a memorial.... And you shall observe this thing as an ordinance for you and your sons forever. It will come to pass when you come to the land which the Lord will give you, just as He promised, that you shall keep this service. And it shall be, when your children say to you, "What do you mean by this service?" that you shall say, "It is the Passover sacrifice of the Lord!" (Exodus 12:7–8, 13–14, 24–27)

On that night, the Lord struck Egypt with the last of the ten plagues. This plague finally broke Pharoah's hardened heart, and Israel was freed to render to the Lord the worship they owed Him. We should notice that the people of God pass from a Master-Tyrant who forcibly enslaved them, to a Master-Lord who calls them to be free servants. True liberty is not found in a pretended, anarchic autonomy, but in a grateful obedience due to the Creator-Savior whose laws are holy, just, and good, intended for the well-being of men and their growth in conformity to His image.

The Holy People

A significant development occurs with the Exodus from Egypt to Sinaï. From that point on, it is no longer with individuals and their descendants alone that the Covenant of Grace continues (as with Adam and Noah), nor with clans alone forming family-churches (as during the time of the patriarchs). The Covenant of Grace will continue with a people that has been liberated and saved from the bondage in Egypt, where they were forged not without sufferings. With this the first promise made to Abraham is now fulfilled: there is a *people of Israel*. From Genesis 50:20 through the rest of the Torah, God will say "My people" just as he had already said "My covenant" — "I have surely seen the oppression of My people in Egypt" (Exodus 3:7); "I will take you as My people" (Exodus 6:7). Moses will later say to Israel: "The Lord has taken you and brought you out of the iron furnace, out of Egypt, to be His people, an inheritance" (Deuteronomy 4:20); "For you are a holy people to the Lord your God, and the Lord has chosen you to be a people for Himself, a special treasure above all the peoples who are on the face of the earth" (Deuteronomy 14:2). From then on, an affirmation, a promise, a commandment, is going to run like a leitmotif throughout all of Scripture: *I will be your God and you will be My people* (Exodus 29:45; Leviticus 26:12; Jeremiah 24:7; 31:33; 32:38; Ezekiel 11:20; 37:23, 27; Zechariah 8:8; 2 Corinthians 6:16; Hebrews 8:10; Revelation 21:7).

Second Moment — The Decalogue

In the course of the second episode on the mountain of God at Sinaï, God solemnly and publicly renews the Covenant of Grace. By the mediation of Moses, he warns His people Israel: "Now, therefore, if you will obey My voice and keep My covenant, then you shall be a special treasure to Me above all people; for all the earth is Mine. And you shall be to Me a kingdom of priests and a holy nation" (Exodus 19:5–6). God then gives the Decalogue, the Ten Words, the ten basic principles of conduct, to His people. The Decalogue is immediately followed by laws of application for various cases: moral laws relating to both individual and social situations, as well as sacrificial and ceremonial laws. An expansion of these laws of application will be found not only in the rest of the Torah, but throughout all of Holy Scripture as well (we will come back to this in the second and third parts of the book).

After a preamble recalling who it is that addresses them (the Lord of the people of the covenant) and a prologue recalling what He has just done (He has saved His people from bondage), the Decalogue then reveals His Ten Words, a series of commandments accompanied by affirmations, promises, blessings, and warnings.

When Moses had told the people "all the words of the Lord and all the judgments," the whole people responded with one voice: "All the words which the Lord has said we will do" (Exodus 24:3).

The Blood of the Covenant

The gravity of the occasion, of this renewal of the Covenant of Grace, was then marked and sealed by a sacrifice. Moses built an altar, set up twelve memorial stones for the twelve tribes of Israel, and sacrificed a bull as a peace offering to the Lord. He sprinkled half the blood on the altar and saved the other half in basins. Finally, after having read the Book of the Covenant to the people, the book which he had written and of which the people again said: "All that the Lord has said we will do, and be obedient," Moses took the blood which he had saved and sprinkled it on the people, and said: "This is the blood of the covenant which the Lord has made [lit. "cut"] with you according to all these words" (Exodus 24:1–8).

All this took place at the foot of the mountain of Sinaï, the mountain on which God had come down and Moses had gone up (Exodus 19:20). This momentous event had been accompanied by signs. The thick cloud of the glory of God came on the mountain, the mountain had shaken violently, and the people had seen a burning fire on the mountaintop. There had been thunder and lightning. The blast of the trumpet had sounded several times and became louder and louder (Exodus 19:16–19).

Judgment and Grace

And yet it took no time for Israel to commit her first apostasy with the worship of a pretended image of God, the golden calf which approximated the representations of Egyptian gods. In his anger, Moses broke the two tablets of stone on each of which were written the Ten Words (one tablet of the covenant for the Lord, one tablet of the covenant for Israel: the signed pact). He then had the faithful Levites execute three thousand apostates. Had not God just said: "You shall not make for yourself a carved image and bow down to it" (Exodus 20:4), and "He who sacrifices to any god, except to the LORD only, he shall be utterly destroyed" (Exodus 22:20)? And so three thousand were "cut off" from the people of the covenant, from this covenant that had just been twice ratified.

After having spoken to Moses "face to face, as a man speaks to his friend" (Exodus 33:11), and Moses having interceded for the people, God renewed the Covenant of Grace yet again, saying that He was "merciful and gracious, longsuffering and abounding in goodness and faithfulness." The tablets of the covenant were replaced by new ones cut by Moses. For forty days and forty nights, Moses stayed on Sinaï with the Lord. Moses wrote the Ten Words on the new tablets (34:27). We are told that "the skin of his face shone while he talked with the LORD" (34:29).

The Tabernacle

It was then that the Lord commanded the construction of the Tabernacle, but not before first reiterating through Moses the command to consecrate and observe the *Sabbath* (which, long-neglected, had not been observed since perhaps the time when Noah and his sons entered into the Ark; cf. Genesis 2:3; 7:10–13; Exodus 31:12–17; 35:1–3).

Now that there is a "people," a "nation," there is going to be a distinction between (let us say!) Church and state.

The government of the state was first assumed by Moses, who, though remaining all the while a *Prophet*, was also a *Judge* of the people, making "known the statutes of God and His laws" (Exodus 18:13, 16). However, following the advice of his father-in-law, Jethro, Moses quickly ceded government of the state to the "elders," to "men of truth," who were placed over the people as rulers of tens, of hundreds, and of thousands (Exodus 18:17–26). Such is the biblical principle of subsidiarity, whereby everything is governed at the lowest possible level, the level nearest the people, and matters are sent up the hierarchical order only when they cannot be settled at the lower level. Under the universal authority of God and His Word, governments should be arranged from the bottom up, beginning at the most basic level where each individual governs himself according to God's Law-Word (real decentralization). The satanic, totalitarian hierarchy is always the inverse, arranged from the top down (centralization). This same biblical principle of subsidiarity, applied to the state by Moses, is applied to the Church by the Lord Jesus Christ (Matthew 18:15–18).

The institution of the Tabernacle introduces a new development in Israel's worship practice. In the time of the patriarchs the worship of family-churches had been practiced in many sanctuaries throughout the land. This had then taken the form of "holy assemblies" (future synagogues?) led by Levites on sabbath days with the reading and application of the Word of God accompanied by prayer (Deuteronomy 14:27, 29), and with the annual paschal meals led by the heads of families in their homes. Now the worship of Israel was to include the institution of the Tabernacle as the center of worship for the newly constituted people, the Tabernacle being led by the priests drawn only from the family of Aaron, the descendant of Levi, the son of Jacob, with the help of the Levites.

1. *The Tabernacle and its surrounding courtyard* represent a scaled-down version of the House of the God of creation which includes both heaven and earth: "Heaven is My throne, and the earth is My footstool" (Isaiah 66:1). The Tabernacle, or Tent of Meeting (of the meeting between God and His people), is made of high-quality materials (beautiful fabrics and skins for the wall coverings, acacia wood for the boards, etc.) overlaid with various articles made of gold, silver, and bronze.
    - *The Holy of Holies* symbolizes the heaven of heavens: in its center is the Ark of the Covenant, the visible throne of the invisible God who sits on the *Kerûbîm* (= the cherubim); only the high priest may enter once a year into God's very presence.
    - *The Holy Place* symbolizes the heavens of the earth: in it are the golden lampstand providing light, the table all set with its

dishes, cups, and pitchers for food, and the altar of incense, where "sweet incense" was burned to accompany prayer (Exodus 26:23–40; 30:1–10). Only the priests could enter here.
- *The courtyard* around the Tabernacle, enclosed by curtains of fine linen hanging from pillars of bronze, symbolizes the earth. In the part of the courtyard extending from the entrance to the Holy Place and the Holy of Holies stood the laver for washings (30:17–21) and the altar for sacrifices (27:1–8) where the priests, sons of Aaron, would daily offer two one-year-old lambs, one in the morning, one in the evening; this was the perpetual sacrifice.

2. *The Tabernacle and its courtyard* represent a scaled-down version of the mountain of God joining earth and the heavens. In this sense, the mountain of God is always with the holy people wherever they are and wherever they go. It is from the summit of the mountain, the Holy of Holies, that God speaks, giving His instructions, His Torah — "You have seen that I have talked with you from heaven" (Exodus 20:22). Holy Scripture, which begins at the same time as the people of God, is placed beside the Ark of the Covenant in the Holy of Holies (Deuteronomy 31:26).

3. *The Tabernacle and its courtyard* represent a scaled-down version of the people of God who are to remain in communion with their Lord and Savior. They are the city in which God lives, the body to which He gives life. When the citizens of the city, the members of the body, become "unclean," the Tabernacle and the courtyard become "unclean." This requires that all receive forgiveness and cleansing, from the High Priest (Leviticus 16:1–14) down to the least Israelite (Leviticus 4–5).

*

Out of the warmth of His affection for Israel (Deuteronomy 7:8; 23:5), out of His desire to meet with Israel, out of the close intimacy that He wants to have with Israel, God goes so far as to pitch His tent among the tents of Israel; that their lives might be centered on Him, He chooses to live right in their midst. "I will be with you," the Lord had promised. The Tent of Meeting, the Tabernacle, is the movable memorial to the promise that He will go with His people every step of the way from Sinaï to Jerusalem. "And let them build Me a sanctuary, that I may dwell among them," the Lord had declared before indicating in detail the way He would require the Tabernacle to be built (Exodus 25:8), adding shortly thereafter: "And there I shall meet with the children of Israel, and the tabernacle shall be sanctified by My glory" (29:43).

The Mountain of Zion

The Church
gathers in the Scriptures
the sweetness of the Holy Spirit[10]

Judges

From Moses to David, from Sinaï to Jerusalem and to the mountain of Zion, long is the history of the Covenant of Grace and of the people of the covenant. About four centuries pass from Moses to David, with Joshua, the Judges, and Saul in between (from roughly 1400 to 1000 B.C.). It was a time marked by periods of renewal and progress, but all too often by periods of backsliding as well, as Israel and her leaders went back and forth between faithfulness and unfaithfulness to the promises (Gospel!) and commands (Law!) of the Word of God, of the Torah of Moses. We read of this long history in the books of the *Nebîîm richonîm*, "the former prophets:" Joshua, Judges, 1 and 2 Samuel, and 1 and 2 Kings.

The time of *Joshua*, whom God called to succeed Moses after his death on Mount Nebo (Deuteronomy 34; Joshua 1), was largely a time of blessing. Under Joshua's authority, the land promised to Abraham was partially conquered and distributed among the tribes of Israel.

The time of the *Judges*, following Joshua, was largely a time of cursing. Israel, unfaithful, refused to hear the voice of God. Time and again the situation degenerated to the point that His people cried out to Him, and each time God, in his mercy, sent a judge, a truly charismatic leader who saved Israel and was able to turn things for the

---

10. St. Ephraim the Syrian, "Hymnes sur la Résurrection," IV, *Célébrons la Pâque*, 169.

better, at least locally. However, no sooner were they delivered than Israel would again turn from God as King, each doing whatever was right in his own eyes (Judges 21:25). The result was anarchy and idolatry.

Thus between the fulfillment of the first promise made to Abraham — that his descendants would become a people, which was fulfilled with Moses — and the fulfillment of the second promise made to Abraham — that a land would be given to this people, which will be truly and fully fulfilled only with David — a very long time lapsed.

Samuel

Like Joshua at the beginning of this long history, Samuel, at the end, would emerge as the dominating figure. Obedient to the Lord who called him, and speaking in His name, Samuel was the first to respond to Israel's insolent demand for "a king like all the nations" — a demand betraying a rejection of God as king (1 Samuel 8).

Saul

The Lord then commanded Samuel to test the people by giving them what they wanted. And so, heeding what the Lord told him, Samuel anointed Saul as king. Samuel hoped to give the people a king who would not be "a king like all the nations," but one who would rule according to the principles anticipated by the Torah of Moses:

> When you come into the land . . . you shall surely set a king over you whom the Lord your God chooses. . . . But he shall not multiply horses for himself. . . . Neither shall he multiply wives for himself . . . nor shall he greatly multiply silver and gold for himself. . . .
>
> Also it shall be, when he sits on the throne of his kingdom, that he shall write for himself a copy of this law in a book. . . . And it shall be with him, and he shall read it all the days of his life, that he may learn to fear the Lord his God and be careful to observe all the words of this law and these statutes, that his heart may not be lifted above his brethren, that he may not turn aside from the commandment to the right or to the left, and that he may prolong his days in his kingdom, he and his children in the midst of Israel (Deuteronomy 17:14–20).

Sadly, the faithfulness that marked the beginning of Saul's reign, together with his victories over the Philistines, did not last, as he turned more and more from God and His commands. In the end, God rejected him as king when Saul refused to carry out His command to utterly destroy the Amalekites (after defeating them in battle, Saul chose instead to spare Agag, their king, and kept the best of their possessions rather than offer them as sacrifices to God).

Again, it was Samuel who secretly anointed David as king of Israel, doing so in obedience to the Lord who had rejected Saul (1 Samuel 15 and 16). David, the Lord's anointed, effectively and publicly became king after Saul's death (1 Samuel 31 and 2 Samuel 1).

David

The account of David's reign is recorded for us in 2 Samuel and 1 Kings 1–2 (along with parallel sections recorded in 1 Chronicles 11–29; that is, in the "early prophets").

Being both a judge and a prophet, Samuel had been God's Word-bearer to both the people of Israel ("the LORD was your king"; 1 Samuel 12:12) and to King Saul ("you have not kept what the LORD your God commanded you. . . . Because you have rejected the word of the LORD, He also has rejected you from being king"; 1 Samuel 13:14; 15:23). And so it was Samuel, this judge and prophet, who initiated David into his service as the vassal-king to the true King, and anointed him with oil to consecrate him as such (1 Samuel 16).

David reigned over Judah for his first seven and a half years as king, residing principally at Hebron. He then moved to Jerusalem, which he had taken from the Jebusites. Jerusalem became "his city," and there he reigned for the next thirty-three years over all Israel and all Judah (2 Samuel 5:1–10).

The Covenant Confirmed

David had the Ark of the Covenant, "the ark of God whose name is called by the Name, the LORD of hosts, who dwells between the *Kerûbîm*," brought up to Jerusalem, the city of David, on the mountain of Zion (how much like the mountain of Moriah! — Oh father Abraham!). As the Ark made its way up, David, in a kind of joyous confession amidst the shouts of the people and the sound of the trumpet (and disregarding the reproach of his wife, Michal, Saul's daughter), "danced before the LORD with all his might." The Ark of the Covenant was set "in its place in the middle of the tabernacle that David had erected for it" (2 Samuel 6). (Note that the Ark, which the Philistines had stolen in one of their victories soon after the calling of Samuel, was not brought back to the Tabernacle when it was sent back by the Philistines and recovered by Israel (1 Samuel 3–6). The Tabernacle "pilgrimed" one route, the Ark another, which must be seen as a time of death for the Tabernacle. The Tabernacle would once again come to life only when integrated within the Temple built by Solomon, David's son.)

The Ark, the visible throne of the invisible God, was now set in its place on the mountain of Zion. It was thus there that king David, vassal of the Lord, received the word of the confirmation and renewal of the Covenant of Grace.

David had offered burnt offerings and peace offerings. He had blessed the people in the name of the Lord. He had distributed to everyone a cake of bread, a portion of meat, and a cake of raisins (2 Samuel 6). Shortly afterward, he said to Nathan the prophet, "See now, I dwell in a house of cedar, but the ark of God dwells inside tent curtains." Later that night, Nathan was commanded by God to answer David, saying:

> I have not dwelt in a house since the time that I brought the children of Israel up from Egypt, even to this day, but have moved about in a tent and in a tabernacle.... I took you from the sheepfold, from following the sheep, to be a ruler over My people, over Israel.... I will appoint a place for My people Israel, and will plant them, that they may dwell in a place of their own and move no more.... [Your son] shall build a house for My name, and I will establish the throne of his kingdom forever. I will be his Father, and he shall be My son.... And your house and your kingdom shall be established forever before you. Your throne shall be established forever. (2 Samuel 7:1–16)

David prayed:

> You have... spoken of your servant's house for a great while to come. Is this the manner of man, O Lord GOD?... Therefore You are great,

O Lord God. For there is none like You, nor is there any God besides You.... Now, O Lord God, the word which You have spoken concerning Your servant and his house, establish it forever and do as You have said.... And let the house of Your servant David be established before You.... Now therefore, let it please You to bless the house of Your servant, that it may continue before You forever; for You, O Lord God, have spoken it, and with Your blessing let the house of Your servant be blessed forever. (2 Samuel 7:18–29)

With this renewal, this confirmation of the Covenant of Grace, God thus declared that the holy people had been granted a place — they had indeed received the promised land, the fulfillment of the second promise made to Abraham. On this same occasion God renewed the third promise. In a future time, beyond Solomon and the Temple that he would build, there would arise the Son of David, the Son of God, one who would be King, Temple, and eternal Blessing. David hailed that distant day with hope, a hope expressed in his prayer full of confidence and assurance.

3

The Lord, His Law, and His People

HOLY SCRIPTURE ASCRIBES SIMILAR ATTRIBUTES TO THE LAW and to the one-and-many God, the Law-Giver.

The Lord is Spirit (John 4:24); the Law likewise is spiritual (Romans 7:14). The Lord is Holy — He is qualitatively distinct from His creation (Psalm 22:3; Isaiah 6:3; Revelation 4:8); He is the Righteous One, the Just One (Psalm 7:10; Acts 3:14); He is Good (Psalm 145:9; Matthew 19:17). His Law, as a reflection of who He is, is likewise "holy, just, and good" (Romans 7:12; cf. Psalm 119).

The Law simultaneously witnesses both to the immanence of the transcendent God — that is, His intimacy with and involvement in the life of His creatures — and to His moral character.

To fear the Lord is to live before Him with intimate, worshipful respect; it is to have that fear that is the beginning of wisdom (Job 28:28; Psalm 111:10; Proverbs 1:7; 9:10). Whoever has such fear of the Lord can only "tremble" with adoration for Him before His commandments (Ezra 10:3). The conclusion of Ecclesiastes is: "Fear God and keep His commandments" (Ecclesiastes 12:13).

Gospel and Law for Adam and Eve

From the creation of Adam and Eve, from the beginning of the Covenant of Grace, the Gospel precedes and undergirds every commandment. But this does not mean that the Gospel and the Law are separate; rather, no sooner do we read of the Gospel, God's blessing (Genesis 1:28), than we find the Law given to accompany it — inseparably. *At no point in history, not even when our first parents were created, have human beings had to establish their righteousness by obeying the Law. Righteousness has always been received in the Gospel of grace, the Gospel of steadfast love, the Gospel of blessing.* This righteousness was conveyed to Adam and Eve before any commandment was issued, so that it was not in their own works, but in God their Creator, and in the Gospel of His freely-given blessing, that they were to place and keep their faith, and in which they would have always found their justification.

Adam and Eve, after the fall, were able to regain their justification in the same way they had originally received it — only by the Gospel. But from the fall onwards, this Gospel would include, as its first and foremost blessing, the blessing of forgiveness — a forgiveness merited in a way as yet unknown to the first human creatures: forgiveness by the blood of the divine sacrifice of "the Lamb slain before the foundation of the world" (Revelation 13:8). It was the same Gospel that had always called them to faith, but which after the fall called them to repentance as well. God's commands (His Law) would remain the same for Adam, Eve, and their descendants: marriage and procreation (Genesis 1:28; 2:23–24); weekly rest in the image of God's rest after the six days of creation (Genesis 2:2–3); and the cultural mandate (Genesis 1:28–30; 2:15–16, 19–20). What distinguished life after the fall from life before was the fact of original sin. With the introduction of sin, human beings now faced a hard and bitter spiritual fight (Genesis 3:15) up to the agony of death (Genesis 2:17; 3:19), and had to struggle against difficulties in every area of life for the woman, the man, and the two as a couple as they sought to exercise the cultural mandate over their environment (animal, vegetation, and mineral), an environment now altered by the curse (Genesis 3:14–19). Man, the image of God, had been set over the sub-human creatures, over the whole of creation (Genesis 1:26) as king, priest, and prophet. Therefore, the effects of his fall were not limited to his own corruption: even the sub-human creation "was subjected to futility," reduced to a state of "bondage," from which it has been groaning and waiting ever since for the revelation of the sons of God (Romans 8:18–22).

Noah

With the renewal of the Covenant of Grace with Noah and his family after the Flood, one could say that everything began afresh. Consider the ark itself — did it not symbolize creation in miniature form? For example, the three decks of the ark (Genesis 6:16) correspond to the three tiers of creation as they appear to our senses and as they are spoken of in Genesis 1: above, the heavens; below, the earth; and below the earth, the sea. And the dove hovering over the sea — does it not call to mind the Holy Spirit hovering over the waters at the beginning of creation (Genesis 1:2; 8:8–12)?

When God renews the covenant with Noah, His commandments concerning the cultural mandate are the same as those given to Adam (Genesis 9:1 and 1:28). There are only two differences. The first concerns food (the animals are given to Noah and his descendants for food; Genesis 9:3; cf. 1:29). The second, previously mentioned, concerns the right to legitimate defense given to the members of the Covenant of Grace, a right providing even for capital punishment (Genesis 9:6).

Abraham

When the covenant is renewed with Abraham (with the three promises of the people, the land, and the universal blessing, together with the institution of the sacrament of circumcision; Genesis 12:2–3; 17:1–14), we do not find a new set of specific commandments for "Abraham's descendants" (we learn who is counted among Abraham's descendants in John 8:31–40, Romans 9:7 and Galatians 3:29). But God does have two things to say to Abraham pertaining to him and his descendants, commands which, though not new, can and must be received (and which we have already cited):

I am Almighty God; walk before Me and be blameless (Genesis 17:1);

For I have known [Abraham], in order that he may command his children and his household after him, that they keep the way of the LORD, to do righteousness and justice, that the LORD may bring to Abraham what He has spoken to him. (Genesis 18:17–19)

Moreover, there are implicit commands that oblige everyone in subsequent generations to follow the examples of faith and obedience left by the father of all who believe (cf. Hebrews 11:8–12; James 2:20–23).

The Torah

When the Apostle John writes his Gospel, it will say: "The Law was given through Moses" (John 1:17). This had already been announced by the Torah itself: "Moses commanded a law for us" (Deuteronomy 33:4).

The Law (the Torah, our Pentateuch) is the first and fundamental writing of all of Holy Scripture. The first five books of the Bible, beginning with Genesis, transmit God's commands to His people, commands dealing not only with personal morals, but social morals as well. These commands deal with every aspect of human existence, including our relation to every aspect of creation. God is one and many, and so His Law is a whole, truly one, in its variety of aspects.

As a living and morally perfect person, *the one God* tells us in His Law what it is to be a moral person in His image. As the Trinity of God the Father, of the Angel of the Lord, and of the Spirit, a living and morally perfect society, *the plural God* tells us in His Law what it is to be a moral society in His image. In both creation and redemption, the image of God is found in each human person and is reflected in each true human society, beginning with the husband-wife relationship.

The Law is to be constantly read, meditated on, scrutinized, and taught even in its most minute details (Jesus will refer to the smallest letters and least strokes of the pen in his Sermon on the Mount; Matthew 5:18). But these most minute details can only be understood under the light — one and diverse — of the whole Torah.

The one-and-many God, the living God, has given to His people, through Moses, His commandments for every imaginable area of earthly life. If there were a single area of existence that was not under the divine Law, we would have to excuse and make allowance for polytheism, since there would be some area of life under a law — or laws — other than the one Law of God. None but God, the Creator and Savior, has the power and sovereign right, the authority, to command men in His image how to live in His universe.

An Organic Whole

The Law was not given to us as a body of dead and/or incomprehensible articles, but as an amazingly organic whole with one commandment at its center, a commandment ruling all the others and constituting their *raison d'être*: "Hear, O Israel: The Lord our God, the Lord is one! You shall love the Lord your God with all your heart, with all your soul, and with all your strength" (Deuteronomy 6:4–5).[1] Man being made in God's image, a second command follows immediately and inseparably from this central commandment, and should be taken as its echo: "You shall love your neighbor as yourself: I am the Lord" (Leviticus 19:18). Around this central commandment gather other commandments which develop and clarify its meaning: namely, the Ten Words (Exodus 20:2–17; Deuteronomy 5:7–21). Next, as though forming a third great circle around the first two, with the commandments of the short Book of the Covenant (Exodus 21–23), come the great many commandments of the Torah, many of which are case-by-case applications (casuistic, in the proper, legal sense of the word) of the central commandment, of the Ten Words, or of other

---

1. *Translator's Note:* John Murray draws attention to "the close-knit organic unity of the whole of Scripture," maintaining that "[w]e must understand that the whole Bible stands together and that the fibres of organic connection run through the whole Bible connecting one part with every other part and every one truth with every other truth" ("The Study of the Bible," *Collected Writings of John Murray*, vol. 1 [Banner of Truth Trust, 1976], 5). Likewise, in his comments on "the righteous requirement of the law" in Romans 8:4, C. E. B. Cranfield makes the following remark regarding the unity of the Law: "The use of the singular is significant. It brings out the fact that the law's requirements are essentially a unity, the plurality of commandments being not a confused and confusing conglomeration but a recognizable and intelligible whole, the fatherly will of God for His children" (*A Critical and Exegetical Commentary on the Epistle to the Romans*, vol. 1 [T&T Clark, ed. 2004], 384).

divine commandments. In fact, the many commandments of the Torah are the revealed explanations-applications of one or more of the Ten Words, as the Ten Words themselves are an explanation-application of the central commandment of the Law.

In the last part of this work we will come to see how the Church should endeavor to faithfully receive, hear, and interpret the organic whole of the Mosaic Law, doing so in and through Jesus Christ and by the Holy Spirit.

The Moral and Ceremonial Laws of the Torah

The Torah includes two great families of laws: ceremonial and moral. To the family of ceremonial laws belong the sacrificial laws together with the laws of separation concerning "the clean and the unclean"; to the family of moral laws belong laws dealing with both individuals and societies.

The family of ceremonial laws include firstly the *sacrificial laws*, which govern everything relating to the sacrifices, the priests, the Tabernacle, the sacraments of Circumcision and the Passover, expiation of sin and guilt by blood, etc. The ceremonial laws also include the *laws of separation*, which govern everything relating to the principle of things clean and unclean with the resulting consequences for animals, human beings, places, food, clothing, individual and societal boundaries (in particular the boundaries between Israel and the nations), contact with impure things and necessary purifications, etc.

The family of moral laws concerns everything that pertains to the *individual* as well as *social life*: marriage, family, education, work, state, law, etc.

In other words, the Torah reveals the commandments of theocracy, an expression that does not mean either clericalism (rule by a religious class of persons) or ecclesiasticism (rule by the institution of the Church), but refers to the sovereign and universal authority of God as the One to whom each and every individual (including clerics) and independent institution (including the Church) is directly accountable.

The *ceremonial laws* (sacrificial laws and laws of separation) are found mainly in those sections dealing with the laws concerning the altar (Exodus 20:22–26), the Tabernacle and its service (Exodus 25–31 and 35–40), and in Leviticus (1–25), Numbers (1:47–6:21; 8:1–19; 15:1–31; 18 and 19; 28:1–30:17; 35:1–36:13), and Deuteronomy.

The *moral laws* (dealing with both persons and societies) are found mainly in the small Book of the Covenant (Exodus 21–23), in the book of Numbers (27:1–11), and at the end of Deuteronomy (23:15–30:20). These laws establish the boundaries that human persons and societies have no right to cross, the transgression of which will result in destruction, misery and death:

> Behold, I set before you today a blessing and a curse: the blessing, if you obey the commandments of the Lord your God . . . and the curse, if you do not obey the commandments of the Lord your God, but turn aside from the way which I command you today (Deuteronomy 11:26–28).

The Unity of the Two Families of Laws

Though the two families of laws are distinct, we cannot fail to see that they are interrelated. The ceremonial laws are, as a matter of necessity, morally significant, since they demand obedience to the thrice-holy God; and the moral laws have an inescapable significance for the ceremonial laws (worship practices) since they set forth the manner of life that demonstrates the fear (worshipful respect) due to the Lord. In fact, all of the commands of the Law are so interrelated and interdependent that they form a living organism, one that serves to support the people of God in their call to remain faithful to the covenant. Upon the commandments of the Law hang the life or death of Israel. The laws concerning sacrifices and things "clean and unclean" have to do simultaneously with sin and forgiveness — each of these being moral categories. The moral laws dealing with persons and societies have to do with the sacrifices and divine worship that the members and people of the covenant owe to their Lord.

An Obedience Rooted in Love

Let us observe furthermore that the human partners of the covenant do not owe a merely external obedience to the Law, but an obedience from the heart, an obedience from love, as the human creatures find their joy and well-being in the Lord of the covenant:

> And now, Israel, what does the Lord your God require of you, but to fear the Lord your God with all your heart and with all your soul, and to keep the commandments of the Lord and His statutes which I command you today for your good? Indeed heaven and the highest heavens belong to the Lord your God, also the earth with all that is in it.... Therefore circumcise the foreskin of your heart, and be stiff-necked no longer. For the Lord your God is God of gods and Lord of lords, the great God, mighty and awesome, who shows no partiality.... He administers justice for the fatherless and the widow, and loves the stranger, giving him food and clothing. Therefore love the stranger, for you were strangers in the land of Egypt. You shall fear the Lord your God; you shall serve Him, and to Him you shall hold fast.... He is your praise, and He is your God. (Deuteronomy 10:12–21)

Gospel and Law

The Torah, the Book of the Covenant, the very Word of God, teaches that there is a close relationship between the Gospel and the Law, like that between faith and obedience. In every passage bearing directly on the covenant (for example, in the accounts of the institution of the covenant with Adam — before, then after, the fall — or in those which confirm and renew the covenant, in particular with Noah, Abraham, and Moses) the Gospel always precedes the Law, but is nonetheless immediately accompanied by the Law, just as faith leads immediately to obedience. Put another way, requirements are not external to the Gospel, but every requirement is *enfolded within* the Gospel; and thus true faith is never without works.

Of course, any notion of human *merits* is totally excluded (in this sense, one cannot speak of a Covenant of Works). But the Law, *being itself of grace* (cf. Psalm 119:29), is included within the Covenant of Grace — it cannot be that God's people, the members of the covenant, should have faith without works.

When the Lord of the covenant comes to His people, He comes *by* grace, and He comes *with* promises and commandments. These promises (Gospel!) and commandments (Law!) of the Covenant of Grace expect, call for, and require the believer to respond with obedience born of faith, with the consequence that, in the short or long term, blessings or cursings follow according to the faithfulness or unfaithfulness of the members of the covenant.

The bloody sacrifices and sacraments of the covenant prescribed by God in the Torah find both their ultimate and provisional meaning in their future (though not fully known or disclosed at that time) orientation toward the one and only sacrifice of the "Lamb slain from the foundation of the world" (Revelation 13:8). Taken as a whole, these sacrifices serve to show that the way of true repentance and forgiveness remains open to all those who, having been in the covenant, have departed from it, and would seek to return and be reestablished in it. This right and dignity is theirs by the unmerited grace of the covenant.

Consider this passage from Leviticus — the Word of God:

> But if they confess their iniquity and the iniquity of their fathers, with their unfaithfulness in which they were unfaithful to Me, and that they also have walked contrary to Me... if their uncircumcised hearts are humbled, and they accept their guilt — then I will remember My covenant with Jacob, and My covenant with Isaac and My covenant with Abraham I will remember; I will remember the land.... But for their sake I will remember the covenant of their ancestors, whom I brought out of the land of Egypt in the sight of the nations, that I might be their God: I am the Lord. (Leviticus 26:40–45)

The Ecclesial Tradition and the Word of God

When considering the history of the covenant, we must be careful to distinguish between what God reveals and commands (His Gospel; His Law) and what actually happens in the lives of the human partners of the covenant — what they actually believe, think, say, and do. The Word of God itself gives ample testimony to this inconsistency on the part of God's people!

God is always faithful to His covenant, and His Word is always true. The same cannot be said of the people who are the members of the covenant, for their faithfulness to Him varies. During certain times, during certain epochs (though too seldom), their faithfulness triumphs; they make headway; they stay on course. But it all too often happens that, during other times and epochs, their unfaithfulness prevails; they backslide; they go off course, sometimes going so far as to break the covenant. From this arises an important difference between the Word of God and the ecclesial tradition. The Word of God is certain and true, and as, over time and under the guidance of the breath of God, it is written down as Scripture, it communicates His ineffable truth to the people of God in a language understood by men. The ecclesial tradition,[2] on the other hand, is never beyond need of reexamining and critiquing itself under the light and normative judgment of the Word of God, of Holy Scripture.

From the moment on the mountain of Sinaï when the people of the covenant and the Book of the Covenant began to coexist according to the sovereign plan of the Lord (so that the two develop together stage by stage), the people of God have been called, leaders and members alike, to grow *normatively* (that is, "under the norm/standard"). They do this by keeping the covenant, by heeding the voice of God (Exodus 19:5), by probing ever more deeply the Ten Words (Exodus 20), and by putting into practice "all that the LORD has said" — in short, by obeying (Exodus 24:7).

The rest of the history told in the Bible shows us how often and how badly the leaders and kings of Israel, as well as the priests and members of the people called "of God," backslid; into what apostasies they sometimes fell; and how they cut themselves off from the Gospel-Law. This history also reveals the constant exception: the abiding *remnant* that, sometimes considerable in number, other times less so, stays faithful to the covenant — and this always by grace.

The general moral lives of the people and members of the covenant (their actual behavior, in thought, word, and deed) were constantly confronted by God's stated expectations and rarely in conformity with them. Likewise, the ecclesial tradition, individual and social, pursued a course in disregard for the Torah, for the commandments of God, thus placing itself under the historical judgments that are contained in the warnings announced by the Word of God.

---

2. That is, the tradition of the people of God — in Hebrew, *qahal*, translated much later in the Greek Bible by *ekklesia*.

The Remnant

The prophets Isaiah, Jeremiah, Ezekiel, Joel, Micah, and Zephaniah speak of the faithful remnant (or faithful survivors). Because of God's merciful grace (Ezra 9:8; Jeremiah 23:3; 50:20), His jealous zeal (2 Kings 19:31; Isaiah 37:32), His desire to protect (Isaiah 1:9; Ezekiel 14:22; Micah 2:12), His redemption (Isaiah 11:11; Jeremiah 31:7), His kingly glory (Isaiah 28:5; 66:19ff.), and His plan for worldwide evangelization (Isaiah 66:19ff.), there has always been a faithful remnant, those who have not fallen away from the covenant and through whom the people of His covenant on earth have been preserved (without gaps or breaks). In history, they have always been "like dew from the Lord" (Micah 5:7).

The Ministry of the Prophets

In the constant back-and-forth between God and the human partners of the covenant, in which God does the speaking and they the responding, positively or negatively, faithfully or unfaithfully, the biblical prophets play an important role and exercise a decisive ministry.

Their mission is three-fold. To begin with, they are to set the people of the covenant — its leaders, priests, and members — squarely before the Torah of God, the Gospel-Law, so that they neither forget it nor fail to apply it to their lives. Additionally, and at the same time, they are to confirm the people's faithfulness or condemn their unfaithfulness. Finally, they are to announce the blessings or cursings that are going to come upon them.

Although the origin and etymology of the Hebrew word for prophet (*navi*, singular, *nevi'im*, plural) is unknown, or at least uncertain, the Greek word used to translate it (*prophétes*, the prefix *pro* added to the verb *phémi*, meaning "to speak") is explicit and indicates a one- and three-fold meaning.

The *pro*-phet is one who speaks:

1. *for* God;
2. *to* the people or to a certain member of the people, such as the king;
3. *before* a thing comes to pass in order to declare it.

Holy Scripture, which is often its own best dictionary, defines *the true prophet*, the one who does not make himself a prophet but who becomes a prophet by the call of God, in the following way:

1. He is the word-bearer of God (in Exodus 4:15, God says to Moses: "I will be with your mouth"; in Exodus 7:1–2, He says to him: "You shall speak all that I command you"; cf. Jeremiah 1:6–7).
2. He addresses the one and/or those to whom, or against whom, God sends him, regardless of status and, if it is required of him, at the price of his own interests, his reputation, or even his life (for example: Elijah prophesying against King Ahab (1 Kings 18); or Jeremiah prophesying against the inhabitants of Jerusalem; Jeremiah 5ff.).
3. He declares beforehand what benediction or judgment is to come (for example: Ezekiel 34; Daniel 2).

The biblical meaning of the word *prophet* is yet more expansive since the prophet of God is a "seer" (2 Samuel 24:11; Isaiah 30:10), a "man of God" (Deuteronomy 33:1; 1 Samuel 2:27; 9:6; 1 Kings 13:1; 2 Kings 4:9; etc.), a "servant of the Lord" (2 Kings 17:13; 21:10; Jeremiah 7:25), a "watchman" (Jeremiah 1:11–12; Ezekiel 3:17), or a "messenger" (Nahum 2:13; 2 Chronicles 36:16).

It was by the power of the sovereign Spirit of the Lord falling upon them that the prophets, the *nevi'im*, spoke and/or wrote (Ezekiel 11:5; Micah 3:8; Zechariah 4:6; Exodus 17:14; Joshua 24:26; Exodus 24:4; Jeremiah 30:1; Habakkuk 2:2).

But we must go deeper, beyond the generally accepted definitions...

The Council of God

The prophet is a member of the Council of God.

We must first understand the Council of God as that which is within God Himself — the one God in three persons of the Father, the Angel of the Lord, and the Spirit of God (Genesis 1:26; 3:22; 6:3; 11:7). God may add the angels, the heavenly army, to this Council (Job 1:6–12, 2:1–6). But the wider Council of God includes also the prophets.

In contrast to the prophets who are associated with the Council of

God, the false prophets "speak a vision of their own heart" and have not "stood in the council of the LORD and perceived and heard His word" (Jeremiah 23:16–18).

"The LORD God does nothing," declares the prophet Amos, "unless He reveals His Council (*sôd*) to His servants the prophets" (Amos 3:7, NASB). The Hebrew word *sôd* is better translated as "meeting, deliberation, council," rather than "secret."

Abraham is the first man to be called *prophet* in the Bible (Genesis 20:7). He is so named only after his meeting by the oak trees of Mamre with the three persons who are yet one and had come to him to declare the coming birth of his only son (Genesis 18:1–16). Just as the Lord had not "hidden" this extraordinary birth to Abraham, so, in Genesis 19, He decides not to hide any longer from Abraham His plan to bring terrible judgment on Sodom and Gomorrah (Genesis 18:17 and 19:1–19).

Moses, the great Prophet of the old covenant (Deuteronomy 34:10), the greatest before John the Baptist (Matthew 11:9–14), went up the mountain of Sinaï on several occasions to take part in the Council of God. He also took part in the Council of God when he went to the Tabernacle, the tent of meeting (Exodus 33:3–11). God says to him: "He is faithful in all My house. With him I speak mouth to mouth (that is, he faithfully repeats My words; what My mouth says, his mouth says), clearly, and not in riddles, and he beholds the form of the LORD" (Numbers 12:7–8, ESV). Being a member of the Council of God, it sometimes happens that Moses changes the Lord's mind (Exodus 32:7–14, 30–35; Numbers 14:13–20).

Micaiah reports that he had been in the Council of the Lord with the angels (1 Kings 22:19–23), as does *Isaiah* (Isaiah 6:1–7). *Amos*, in the Council, moves God to relent from what He had earlier determined to do (Amos 7:1–3).

When the Spirit of God brings a man of the covenant into His Council, He does so by taking hold of him in a specific historical situation and communicating to him through visions, thoughts, words, sometimes in response to a reflection, prayer, or experience that He has caused the man to have (cf. Daniel 9). During this specific time and through these various means, the Spirit of God communicates to the man the speeches, phrases, and even the very words that He would have him take to the people (the prophet then communicates his message either orally, through signs, or in writing, or by any combination of the three). For a long, or a very brief, time, the prophet is engaged body and soul in this *communication*, first an inner communication from God to him, and then through him to those to whom God sends him, a communication from the breath of God Himself. By the Spirit of the Lord, his senses, mind, heart, and faith are enabled to grasp exactly what the Lord would have him say to His people. Astounding what the simple sight of an almond tree branch or a boiling kettle can then unleash (Jeremiah 1:11–14)!

Ezekiel shows us both literally and symbolically the meaning of this prophetic communication:

> Now when I looked, there was a hand stretched out to me; and behold, a scroll of a book was in it. Then he spread it before me; and there was writing on the inside and on the outside, and written on it were lamentations and mourning and woe.
>
> Moreover He said to me, "Son of man, eat what you find; eat this scroll, and go, speak to the house of Israel." So I opened my mouth, and He caused me to eat that scroll. And He said to me, "Son of man, feed your belly, and fill your stomach with this scroll that I give you." So I ate, and it was in my mouth like honey in sweetness. (Ezekiel 2:9–3:3)

*

Abraham, Moses, and all the prophets after him from Samuel to John the Baptist, could describe, with increasing clarity, the image of the Lord God whom they had met, seen, and heard in His Council — such Majesty! Such Holiness! Such Glory! (cf. Exodus 3, Isaiah 6, and Ezekiel 1). Even their description itself served both to reinforce the moral character of the one-and-many God, transcendent-and-immanent, faithful to His covenant both in His grace and in His judgments, as well as to recall the law of the covenant, reflecting the character of its Author. The eyes of faith must be opened (Isaiah 35:5, 42:7) for the members of the covenant to receive this image of God drawn by the prophets, but their reception of this image must in no way lead them to attempt to make some kind of material representation of it, nor, less still, to make any image of God according to their own imaginations, desires, or thoughts. The second law of the Decalogue governs here.

The foundation of the prophetic preaching and the main weapon in this preaching was the Torah. It was the Torah to which they referred and it was the Torah which they quoted — not mechanically repeating its words in a parrot-like, incantational manner, but laboring to transmit it in a living and relevant way, rigorously faithful to its meaning. The Torah was so much in their hearts, in their memories, and on their lips, that it was woven throughout their message and writings.

From Samuel to Malachi, the prophets, with the Torah, were always with the people of the covenant — with their leaders, priests, and members — counseling and strengthening them with a word from God in the times of their faithfulness, in obedience to the Torah, condemning and calling them to repentance when they were unfaithful and disobedient.

JUDGMENTS

As early as the days of Moses, the people of God's covenant had been denounced as "a stiff-necked people" (Exodus 32:9; Deuteronomy 9:6, 13). They would begin to experience God's great judgments after the death of Solomon, the builder of the Temple, as a schism tore Israel into two kingdoms: the kingdom of Israel in the north and the kingdom of Judah in the south.

The preaching of the eighth-century (B.C.) prophets such as Amos, Hosea, and above all, Isaiah, could not prevent that next judgment which came with the capture of Samaria and the final destruction of the northern kingdom, the kingdom of Israel.

To the south, the kingdom of Judah, centered spiritually on the Temple in Jerusalem, would continue another century and a half. There would be some faithful kings of the Davidic dynasty who reigned with the Scripture in hand, such as Hezekiah and chiefly Josiah, the Reformer. But the fiery sermons of Jeremiah, like those of Habakkuk, Nahum, and Zephaniah, with their warnings of a terrible judgment, went unheeded, and so these judgments came upon Judah. Nebuchadnezzar came upon them, capturing Jerusalem and destroying the Temple, then taking a great number of the city's inhabitants into exile (including Daniel and Ezekiel). With this judgment came the end of the kingdom of Judah. From that time on, neither Judah nor the larger Israel would have a member of David's messianic family sitting on its throne. What is more, with the loss of the Temple a whole part of the Torah could no longer be put into practice! It was as if the presence of God had left the people of God.

THE SAGES

The development of the prophetic preaching was accompanied by the development of a growing body of wisdom teachings. While this wisdom tradition, like the prophetic preaching, went back to the time of Moses, it would only be with David, and more particularly with Solomon, that a body of *wisdom literature*, borne by the Spirit of God, would be established in Israel. This wisdom literature would come to include the book of Job, a number of Psalms (37; 49; 112; 122; among others), the book of Proverbs, and Ecclesiastes.

The sages wrote in a manner different from the prophets. They composed literary works that took up and developed the *inspired symbols* of the Torah with the goal of applying its commands to their new covenantal situations (King Solomon himself, when acted upon by the Spirit of God, was one such sage). This is not to say that they set aside or fundamentally altered any parts of the Torah. Rather, like the prophets, they were all the more strictly faithful to the meaning of the content of the Torah, which cannot change and must not be changed, as they were led to renew its *form* under changing circumstances. For example, we learn from the book of Job that the "righteous man" must often suffer though he has done nothing to bring such suffering on himself. We also learn in both Job and Ecclesiastes that we cannot determine a person's or group's standing before God simply by looking at the visible blessings or cursings they are experiencing.

With these developments from one stage to the next of the covenantal Revelation, Holy Scripture, as it grows, closes in more and more on the "meaning" of the Torah, further clarifying and elucidating it.

THE SONG OF SONGS

The Jewish Bible is ordered according to three major divisions — the Law (the *Torah*), the Prophets (the *Nevi'im*), and the Writings (the

Ketuvim).³ Within this last division are included five shorter books known as the *Hamesh Megillot*, or "the five scrolls:" the Song of Songs, Ruth, Lamentations, Ecclesiastes, and Esther.⁴ The most beautiful of these five — the Song of Songs, meaning "the Song (or poem) *par excellence*" — merits particular attention on account of its deep reflection on the nature of the covenant. Indeed, the Song of Songs could be called "the heart of the Bible."

This little book has two levels of meaning. It celebrates not only the faithful love enjoyed within the covenant of marriage, but also the love, in the Covenant of Grace, between the Lord and His Bride, between the Lord and His Church, between the Lord and His people.

These few pages (only 117 verses) have been read, re-read, repeated, and pored over throughout the centuries. At the beginning of the second century, Rabbi Aqiba said: "The world had neither value nor meaning before the Song of Songs was given to Israel." The medieval Doctors such as Saint Bernard in the twelfth century, the great Puritans such as John Owen and John Gill of the seventeenth and eighteenth centuries, meditated and commented on this book, celebrating this mystical union of love pulsing at the center of the Covenant of Grace.

> Hear O Israel: The Lord our God, the Lord is one! You shall love the Lord your God with all your heart, with all your soul, and with all your strength. (Deuteronomy 6:4–5)

The mystery of the covenant is a mystery of love. The history of the covenant is a history of love.

---

3. The Law (the *Torah*) includes Genesis to Deuteronomy, the Prophets (the *Nevi'im*) includes Joshua to Malachi, and the Writings (the *Ketuvim*) includes the Psalms through 2 Chronicles. Thus, the Jewish Bible, according to the traditional Hebrew canon, is known as the *TaNaKh* (*Torah + Nevi'im + Ketuvim*), for short. For a fuller discussion of the merits of the Hebrew canon for the Christian's understanding of the Old Testament, see Pierre Courthial, *De bible en bible* (2003).

4. *Translator's Note*: Ecclesiastes is the only book among "the five scrolls" that is also considered a piece of wisdom literature. As a genre, it belongs to the class of "wisdom literature," while as a book within the canon of the Jewish Bible, it belongs among "the five scrolls."

Daniel

Some remarks need to be made here concerning the Book of Daniel, which draws on both the prophetic and wisdom books, and which is counted in the Jewish Bible not among the *Nevi'im*, the Prophets, but among the *Ketuvim*, the Writings.

In Book X of his *Jewish Antiquities*, Flavius Josephus states expressly that Daniel was a "prophet of good things" and that "he also wrote and left behind him what made manifest the accuracy and undeniable veracity of his predictions."[5]

After being deported to Babylon, Daniel became a fearless witness of God before Nebuchadnezzar, the great Babylonian king who, having persecuted Daniel and his companions (Daniel 1–3), came eventually to "praise and extol and honor the King of heaven, all of whose works are truth, and His ways justice. And those who walk in pride He is able to put down" (Daniel 4:34–37). The prophet, a Jew, subsequently became a considerable statesman, first serving the successive Babylonian rulers, then those from Medo-Persia and even Cyrus (Daniel 6:1–2, 28; 10:1).

In addition, Daniel received an extraordinary gift of historical foresight. This vision (given directly or by the intermediary of the angel Gabriel) of the long-view of history allowed him to:

- foresee and declare the succession of four great empires (Babylonian, Medo-Persian, Greek, and Roman) that would collapse at the coming of the Kingdom of God in Christ (Daniel 2:31–45);
- foresee and declare the Ascension of the Son of Man who would go up to God on the clouds of heaven to be enthroned as the eternal King over all the nations (Daniel 7:13–14);
- foresee and declare, in a short and amazingly dense passage (Daniel 9:24–27), the seventy weeks of years decreed by the Lord that would span almost five centuries, "from the going forth of the command to restore and build Jerusalem" until the coming of Messiah the Prince who will be "cut off." (Let us note, in passing, that the Jewish Bible has two passages in which "days" are taken to mean "years:" Numbers 14:34 and Ezekiel 4:6.)

---

5. *The Works of Josephus*, trans. William Whitson (Hendrickson Publishers, 2006), 285.

Let us look at this matter more closely. Daniel declares that the seventy weeks will be comprised of three successive stages:

1. Seven sevens (7 × 7 = 49 years), from the edict of Cyrus until the reconstruction of the Temple is completed.
2. Sixty-two sevens (62 × 7 = 434 years), from the reconstruction of the Temple until the coming of Messiah the Prince.
3. One seven (7 years), in the middle of which the Christ will be "cut off" and the Covenant of Grace will be confirmed for many (remember that in Hebrew one "cuts a covenant"; cf. Genesis 15:10ff.).

This chronology is more than just a timeline (49 + 434 + 7 = 490 years); it is also symbolic chronology, loaded with sabbatical and messianic implications. Essentially, the seven sevens of years (7 × 7 = 49) is the length of time leading to the fiftieth year, the year of Jubilee. The seventy sevens (7 × 7 × 10 = 490), which would span ten Jubilees, constitutes a chrono-symbolic indication of the coming of Christ for the salvation of the world, since Christ will bring, with Him and in Him, the ultimate and long-awaited Jubilee: "to preach good tidings to the poor, to heal the brokenhearted, to proclaim liberty to the captives, and the opening of the prison to those who are bound; to proclaim the acceptable year of the Lord," as had been announced by the prophet Isaiah (Isaiah 61:1–3) and as Jesus would fulfill according to His word (Luke 4:16–21). Nearly a millennium and a half before Jesus Christ, God had said to Moses: "And you shall count seven sabbaths of years for yourself, seven times seven years; and the time of the seven sabbaths of years shall be to you forty-nine years. Then you shall cause the trumpet of the Jubilee to sound on the tenth day of the seventh month; on the Day of Atonement you shall make the trumpet to sound throughout all your land. And you shall consecrate the fiftieth year, and proclaim liberty throughout all the land to all its inhabitants. It shall be a Jubilee for you" (Leviticus 25:8–10).[6]

According to our dense prophecy (Daniel 9:24–27) and the Lord's sovereign decree, six things will be fulfilled (in three pairs) during the time of Christ:

---

6. The word *jubilee* derives from the Hebrew word *yôbél* meaning either "jubilee" or "ram," because the trumpet used to sound the Jubilee was a ram's horn.

Pair I   1. The end, the accomplishment of the last transgression against the Holy of Holies,
        2. the sealing up of this sin.

Pair II 3. The expiation of the transgression and of sin,
        4. the work of the One who brings in everlasting righteousness.

Pair III 5. The sealing up of vision and prophecy,
        6. the anointing of the Holy of Holies.

All of that is encapsulated in verse 24 alone.

During the last seven of seven years (which comes after the first sixty-nine sevens [7 + 62]), in the middle of this seven, the Christ will be "cut off" and the Covenant of Grace will be fully confirmed for many. The second half of this seven (three and a half years after the crucifixion of our Lord) will begin with the turning of the covenant from Israel to the nations with the calling of the Apostle to the nations, St. Paul (Acts 7:55–8:1; 9:15).

Let us conclude these remarks on the Book of Daniel by noticing the *addenda* of sorts at the end of verse 26 and in verse 27, which speak of the destruction of the city, the end to sacrifice and offering, etc. These verses declare the tragic events of the year A.D. 70 (the destruction of Jerusalem and the Temple) that will come shortly as a result of the confirmation of the renewed covenant.

The Return of the Jews and the Rebirth of Israel

When the edict of Cyrus put an end to the seventy years of exile (2 Chronicles 36:22ff.; Ezra 1:1–4), the Jews (the new name by which the Israelites and the inhabitants of Judah are now known; cf. Jeremiah 34:9; Ezra 4:12) who came back from Babylon, together with those who had remained in the homeland, undertook to rebuild the Holy City and the Temple, which also symbolized the restoration of Israel.

The prophets had foretold this return and restoration. Isaiah had declared long before that Cyrus would accomplish the will of God, the Redeemer of His people, and that Jerusalem and the sanctuary would be rebuilt (Isaiah 44:24–28). Jeremiah had predicted that the exile would last seventy years (Jeremiah 25:11–12). And in these events was realized, at least in part, what Ezekiel had said:

> Therefore thus says the LORD God: "Now I will bring back the captives of Jacob, and have mercy on the whole house of Israel; and I will be jealous for My holy name . . . when I have brought them back from the peoples and gathered them out of their enemies' lands, I am hallowed in them in the sight of many nations, then they shall know that I am the LORD their God, who sent them into captivity among the nations, but also brought them back to their land. . . . And I will not hide My face from them anymore; for I shall have poured out My Spirit on the house of Israel," says the Lord GOD. (Ezekiel 39:25–29)

Although the exile was indeed a terrible judgment of the Lord visited on His holy people, it was not, by the Lord's grace, without fruit.

Firstly, the great dispersion of the northern kingdom, the great *Diaspora* of Israel, resulted in the establishment of a strong Jewish colony along the Euphrates where many chose to settle. It also prompted a large number of Jews to emigrate, by land and by sea, to the nations (*goyîm*) where, by their witness, they would make many proselytes.

Secondly, the loss of the Temple led to the multiplication of synagogues not only in Babylon and in other foreign lands but even in Judah. Jews would gather in these synagogues, sometimes daily, for prayer and for the study of Scripture. Although the priests and most of the Levites remained centered on the Temple and its service after it was rebuilt, a few Levites and an increasing number of laymen would lead these synagogues and become scholarly scribes, maintaining the text and its teaching. These scribes, sometimes called "doctors of the law," would take the place of the prophets and sages. We are told that Ezra, the priest and scribe (Nehemiah 8:9), "had prepared his heart to seek the Law of the LORD, and to do it, and to teach *His* statutes and ordinances in Israel" (Ezra 7:6, 10).

Finally, the time of exile (without the Temple!) and the time of waiting (without losing hope!) during the exile brought about a kind of spiritual maturation among a great many Jews. Not only did it stir up their desire to be more faithful, but it also made them more open to witnessing to the nations about the Lord and His Word.

PART TWO

The Turning of the Ages

The Seventy Years: A.D. 1–70

4
The Earthly Life of Christ: A.D. 1–30

5
The Apostolic Period: A.D. 30–70

4

The Earthly Life of Christ: A.D. 1–30

Preliminary Remarks

The seventy years beginning our era (A.D. 1–70) witnessed historic events of capital and decisive importance, which together constituted the turning of the ages.

This period also saw the revelation of the fourth and final part of Holy Scripture.

The Old Testament or Jewish Bible (consisting of three parts called the *Torah*, the *Nevi'im*, and the *Ketuvim* — that is, the Law, the Prophets, and the Writings) presents the origin and development of the old administration of the Covenant of Grace from Adam to the time of Israel's restoration after the Babylonian exile.

The New Testament (constituting the fourth and final part of Holy Scripture, which may be called *the Tradition of the Apostles*, consisting of twenty-seven writings from the apostolic circle) presents the origin and development of the new administration of the Covenant of Grace in effect since the coming of the second Adam, Jesus Christ, and for all time thereafter.

In this way we can think of the whole of the Bible, now completed, as *the Treaty of the Covenant of Grace*.

These seventy years (A.D. 1–70) comprise two periods. The first thirty years are those of the earthly life of Christ, from His birth to His ascension. The last forty years are those of the apostolic times, from the Ascension of Christ to the destruction of the Temple in Jerusalem.

These two periods are so inseparable, so deeply united, that we can know the first only in light of the writings of the second. Moreover, it is only against the backdrop of the whole seventy years that inaugurate our era (and not just the first thirty) that we can truly appreciate the revelation of Christ as the central event in history.

The Mystery of the Incarnation

Contrary to the views of Judaism in its present form (a Judaism that has strayed from its own Bible!), contrary to the views of Islam today and contrary to the many ancient and modern heresies, the God who reigns over history is not a "solitary God." Rather, He is the one-and-many God, the living God who has revealed Himself as Trinity, as the God who is not love because He loves us, but who loves us because He is eternally love in Himself, because He is the undivided unity of the three divine Persons, the one who can say "I," "you," or "we" in the love that is His life. That is the God who reigns over history.

The Incarnation of God the Son

The Incarnation of the only-begotten Son of God is the crowning achievement of the creative will of the One who has "made known to us the mystery of His will, according to His good pleasure which He purposed in Himself, that in the dispensation of the fullness of the times He might gather together in one all things in Christ, both which are in heaven and which are on earth — in Him" (Ephesians 1:9–10).

In His only-begotten Son, God has "rent the heavens" and "come down," the "mountains shaking at His presence" (Isaiah 64:1), the mountains from Eden to Zion, passing through Ararat, Moriah, and Sinaï (Haggai 2:6; Hebrews 12:26).

The Nicene Creed

For us men and for our salvation, [the Son of God] became incarnate from the Virgin Mary, and was made man. (*Nicene Creed*, A.D. 325)

Jesus Himself said, "God sent His Son into the world that the world through Him might be saved" (John 3:17).

The Lord personally and actually entered into time and history, which is why the years A.D. 1–30 occupy a central place at the heart of — and indeed over — all time and all histories. The thought of it boggles the mind, but such is the creativeness of the love of God!

The Council of Chalcedon

Meditating on Holy Scripture and being fully faithful to it, the Fathers of the Council of Chalcedon confessed in 451,

> one and the same Son, our Lord Jesus Christ, at once complete in Godhead and complete in manhood, truly God and truly man... of one substance with the Father as regards his Godhead, and at the same time of one substance with us as regards his manhood; like us in all respects, apart from sin;
>
> as regards his Godhead, begotten of the Father before the ages, but yet as regards his manhood begotten, for us men and for our salvation, of Mary the Virgin, the God-bearer;
>
> one and the same Christ, Son, Lord, Only-begotten, recognized in two natures, without confusion, without change, without division, without separation;
>
> the distinction of natures being in no way annulled by the union, but rather the characteristics of each nature being preserved and coming together to form one person and subsistence,
>
> not as parted or separated into two persons, but one and the same Son and Only-begotten God the Word, Lord Jesus Christ.

In this beautiful confession, we have nothing other than the development of the baptismal formula: "in the name of the Father and of the Son and of the Holy Spirit" (Matthew 28:19). The Name is "one"; the Father, the Son, and the Holy Spirit are "three." As it says in the liturgy of John Chrysostom (344–407): "Grant that with one mouth and one heart we may praise thine all-honorable and majestic name: of the Father, and of the Son, and of the Holy Spirit."[1]

Not as an intermediary, but as the Mediator, being true God and true man, God-the-Son-made-man alone had the power to bring men back to God.

By His incarnation, God the Son took hold of time and history from within, from their origin to their end. The historic stages of the Covenant of Grace, with their promises, commands, warnings, and sacraments, presupposed all along this incarnation, this time, from the years 1 to 30, that would prove decisive and unique for all history.

The Lord through whom all things were made is indeed the Redeemer. And His Word (Gospel-Law) is sealed for all time by the blood of the sacrifice of the only-begotten Son who came, through the Spirit, from the Father. Therefore the Apostle Paul did not hesitate to speak of the blood of God (Acts 20:28).

The heavens were rent open; God descended in His Son to fight with and wrest victory from the enemy — the Devil, sin, and death.

The Abasement of the Only-Begotten Son

In His abasement, as determined by the Trinitarian Council, God the Son voluntarily stripped Himself, all without ceasing to be God, in order to assume fully His humanity.

> ...He made Himself nothing, taking the form of a bondservant, and coming in the likeness of men. And being found in appearance as a man, He humbled Himself and became obedient to the point of death, even the death of the cross. (Philippians 2:7–8)

In covenantal language, the One who is autonomous, a Law unto Himself, and the Giver of the Law to all creatures, willed, in His Son, to place himself under the Law, to live under the Law, to become... theonomic.

That is what took place with the sacrificial humiliation — covenantal and freely chosen, out of love "for us and our salvation." Without ceasing to be God, or more precisely because He is the living God

---

1. Jaroslav Pelikan and Valerie Hotchkiss, eds. *Creeds and Confessions of the Faith,* vol. I (New Haven, CT: Yale University Press, 2003), 288–289.

and is Love, the only-begotten Son took on the condition of a servant, a condition similar to our own, undergoing the most difficult temptation, the most difficult trial ("temptation" and "trial" are both meant by the Greek word *peirasmos*), even unto the hellish trial of separation from God in our stead — "My God, My God, why have You forsaken Me?" (Matthew 27:46; cf. Psalm 22). Whether in the desert immediately after his baptism (Matthew 4:1–11) or during Peter's satanic suggestion that He not go to the cross (Matthew 16:21–23), or finally at Gethsemane shortly before his arrest, Jesus underwent unimaginable temptations and trials, in the course of which, "tempted as we are, yet without sin . . . though He was a Son, yet He learned obedience by the things which He suffered" (Hebrews 4:15; 5:8).[2]

Jesus fully assumed all that is human and, in that humanity, faced temptations and trials in their full force. Whereas the first Adam on the mountain of Eden succumbed and fell, Jesus persevered and triumphed — He "offered up prayers and supplications, with vehement cries and tears to Him who was able to save Him from death, and was heard because of His godly fear" (Hebrews 5:7).

The Openings of the Four Gospels

In the Gospels we find the earthly life of our Lord presented in four specific "series of historic images." These four versions are four angles from which to view the one and same Gospel; and each "angle," as well as the comprehensive picture emerging from them as a whole, was and continues to be borne along by the Holy Spirit.

The Gospels of Matthew and Luke do not begin with the vital mystery of the Incarnation (of which we have just spoken). Rather, each gives a genealogy of Jesus — Matthew right from the start of his introduction (Matthew 1:1–17), Luke a little after his introduction (Luke 3:23–38). These genealogies — Matthew's in particular — include some figures one might not expect to find there, but their inclusion speaks significantly to our human condition: notorious sinners such as Tamar, Rahab, David, the wife of Uriah, and Solomon; and foreigners who

---

2. Let us note that each *peirasmos* is at once a *temptation* in the plan conceived by Satan, and a trial in the sovereign plan willed by God. Whereas the temptation invites evil, the trial calls faith to victory over that evil (1 John 5:4).

are also significant on another level, such as Ruth the Moabitess (and, again, Tamar and Rahab, both Canaanites; cf. Genesis 38 and Ruth 2). These genealogies serve to emphasize the humanity of Jesus, in every degree like ours, only without sin.

The Gospels of Mark and John, on the other hand, begin immediately with the mystery of the Incarnation. Mark's opening line is, "The beginning of the gospel of Jesus Christ, the Son of God." John's whole prologue highlights the same (John 1:1–18).

John the Baptist

If the introductions of Matthew and Luke, the opening line of Mark, and the prologue of John were removed, the four Gospels would all begin with John the Baptist (Matthew 3:1; Mark 1:2; Luke 3:1; John 1:19).

John the Baptist occupies a singular place in the history of the Covenant of Grace. The last Prophet, and the greatest, of the old covenant, in some ways like Samuel, or even more like Elijah, he was sent from God as a special messenger to herald and introduce the Christ "that all through him might believe" (Matthew 11:7–15; John 1:6–7).

Together with John, and through John's hands and mouth, all the saints and prophets of the old covenant point to Jesus and say: "Behold, the Lamb of God, who takes away the sin of the world!" (John 1:29). Did not Isaiah say: "The chastisement for our peace was upon Him, and by His stripes we are healed.... As a lamb led to the slaughter... He bore the sin of many" (Isaiah 53:5–12)?

The time of the old covenant had reached its fulfillment! The Kingdom of God would make its entrance into history in the person of the King Himself! And John hailed the One who, though coming after him, was indeed before him since He was "the Son of God" (John 1:30, 34).

The mission of John the Baptist, the precursor, had reached its culmination: to prepare, to make smooth, the way of the Lord. And so John calls Israel to repent, warning the nation that if they do not repent, Jesus will baptize Israel with the fire of judgment. Indeed, His winnowing fan is in His hand to clean out His threshing floor. A *remnant*, the wheat, will be gathered into the barn, but the chaff He will burn with unquenchable fire. Saying "we have Abraham for our father!" will count for nothing if there is not repentance. Already the axe is laid to the root of the trees (Matthew 3:1–12; Mark 1:4; Luke 3:1–9, 16–17).

With John the Baptist we reach the turning of the ages, the decisive turning of the history of the covenant and of the world. We come to that time which the New Testament calls "the last times," or "the last days," or even more succinctly, "the last hour." This turning of the ages marks the end of *a* world, of an ancient era, of the old "aeon." Adamic time, measured from the creation of the world, will give way to the time of the second Adam, the Christian era, an era that will last until the end of *the* world — that is, until the Christ's return in glory, until the resurrection of the dead, until the final Judgment, until the transfiguration of the universe, the *apokatastasis*, that is, "the times of *restoration* of all things" of which Peter speaks (Acts 3:21).

The Faithful Remnant Gathered Round the Child

Several significant events in the life of Jesus and His parents are reported to us in only two of the four Gospels: Matthew and Luke. These events include:

- the conception and miraculous birth of John, who would become the Baptizer (Luke 1:5–25 and 57–80);
- the visit paid by one expectant mother, Mary, to another, her cousin Elizabeth (Luke 1:39–56);
- the divine conception of Jesus and his virgin birth (Matthew 1:18–25; Luke 1:26–38 and 2:1–6);
- the visits of the shepherds and the wise men to the child in Bethlehem (Luke 2:8–20; Matthew 2);
- the circumcision of Jesus on the eighth day according to the commandment of the Torah and His presentation to the Temple in Jerusalem on the fortieth day (Luke 2:21–40);
- the pilgrimage of Jesus and His parents when He was twelve years old to the same Temple from Nazareth (Luke 2:41–52);
- and the dramatic preaching of John the Baptist in the desert (Matthew 3:1–12; Luke 3:1–20).

These opening episodes introduce us to various members of the remnant, those faithful to the covenant. We meet:

- the high priest Zechariah and his wife Elizabeth;
- the parents of John the Baptist;
- the virgin-mother Mary and her husband Joseph, the parents of Jesus;
- the prophet Simon who takes the baby Jesus up in his arms;
- and the prophetess Anna, far-advanced in years.

To these men and women — depicted as literary icons (especially so by Luke, who had undoubtedly learned of all these events from Mary's own lips, she who "kept all these things and pondered them in her heart"; Luke 2:19) — to these members of the *remnant* of Israel we owe several psalms, namely the Song of Mary (*Magnificat*), that of Zechariah (*Benedictus Domine Deus*), and that of Simon (*Nunc Dimittis*).

The introductions of Matthew and Luke make the Hebraic and Jewish roots of Jesus impossible to miss ("salvation is of the Jews," Jesus himself would say; John 4:22). These roots — the roots of the faithful remnant that heeded John the Baptist's message — would grow and bear their first fruits in the lives of the apostles, the disciples, the whole Church in Jerusalem (the first church, the mother church), and the first martyrs after Jesus, beginning with Stephen. All of these were Jews. Their lives give evidence to the continuity of the Covenant of Grace as the old aeon, the old era, gives way to the new.

Two Significant Names

When speaking of the virgin birth (with such delicacy, such respect, full of the fear and wisdom that God gives!), Matthew brings up two names whose explicit (and marvelous!) meaning can only be understood in the Jewish language. We learn that God commanded Joseph to name the child *Yehoshuah* (*Iêsous* in Greek, *Jesus* in English), which means "God saves" ("that which God does through Jesus," or "that which Jesus, being God, does Himself": He saves!). The other name then, the one indicated beforehand by the prophet Isaiah (Isaiah 7:14), is *Emanu-El*, meaning God (*El*) with us (*Emanu*). The child is named *Emanu-El* because He is truly God and truly man, together and inseparably, with our humanity, except without sin.

Wise Men and Shepherds

The wise men, the sages, the scholars from the East (from Mesopotamia perhaps or from Persia?) were not Jews, but they believed in the Lord and King of the Jews (there were a few such non-Jewish believers before them and many more after!). They had followed the route marked out for them by the bright star of the glory of God and had come to Bethlehem (Hebrew for "house of bread") to worship the child with joy. They had been preceded in this by the shepherds of Israel, who had been visited by the angels and told where to go, and who had heard the first *Gloria* in honor of Jesus.

As for King Herod, he responded to this news by massacring "all the male children who were in Bethlehem and its surrounding districts from two years old and under" (Matthew 2:16). Jesus escaped, however, Joseph taking Him and His mother to Egypt after being warned by an angel. Had not Simon declared to Mary: "Behold, this Child is destined for the fall and rising of many in Israel, and for a sign which will be spoken against" (Luke 2:34)? While some celebrated Christmas with the angels, others celebrated in their own way with the demons.

THE OBEDIENCE OF JESUS

We have only one story from Jesus' childhood. We know that when He was twelve years old His parents made their pilgrimage to the Temple in Jerusalem to celebrate Passover, accompanied for the first time by their son (the age of twelve marked the end of childhood — the *bar-mitsva* of the Jews). Other than that, we have no biographical details in the New Testament, not even in the Gospels, about Jesus' first thirty years.

Let us note in passing that our Savior was most probably born in September of the year 3 B.C. The shepherds made their visit when Jesus was still a newborn (Luke 2:12), while the wise men made theirs when he was a little older than one year, while he was living with his parents in a house in Bethlehem (cf. Matthew 2:11, 16). When Jesus and His parents came back from their time as refugees in Egypt to their pleasant town of Nazareth, in Galilee, Jesus was more than two years old (cf. Matthew 2:19–23).

Jesus Grows

In Nazareth, where Joseph was a carpenter (Matthew 13:55), Jesus grew "in wisdom and stature, and in favor with God and men" (Luke 2:40, 50–52). We know that He had brothers: James, Joseph, Simon, and Jude (John 2:12; Mark 6:3).

Although we are not given the slightest description of His appearance, we can highlight some of the important points of His development and maturation from when He was two until He was thirty-three (A.D. 1–30).

How was Jesus educated within his family? We know that He was under the authority of His parents as commanded by the Torah (Luke 2:51). Joseph, who undoubtedly died during Jesus' adolescence (since we hear nothing about him in the Gospels after that time), was "a just man," which is to say a man of faith and prayer, obeying the commands of God. Betrothed to Mary, he certainly faced a real trial during the mystery of the conception and virgin birth of his "son," a trial he overcame (Matthew 1:18–24). Mary always sought to be "the maidservant of the Lord" (Luke 1:38). Mother of God according to His humanity, favored and blessed among women (Luke 1:42, 48), she was a faithful member *par excellence* of the remnant of Israel, a remnant that also included her relatives, Zechariah and Elizabeth, "both righteous before God, walking in all the commandments and ordinances of the Lord, blameless" (Luke 1:6), their son John (the Baptizer), and Mary's husband Joseph. Here was a whole community of saints who lived in the "fear" of God and under His mercy (Luke 1:50), a spiritually "hungry" people whom God filled with His good things (Luke 1:53).

Mary, though descended from the royal Davidic line (like Joseph), was of modest circumstances (Luke 1:27, 69; 2:4). She surely suffered much: from the great strain put on her relationship with Joseph when it was first announced that she would be pregnant, to the indignity of giving birth to her son in a stable, to the fearful flight to Egypt under Herod's dire threats. But God, both in heaven and in her arms on earth, strengthened her in all these things. She knew a sword would pierce her own soul; but as Elizabeth had told her, "Blessed is she who believed!" (Luke 1:45).

The faithfulness of Mary and Joseph led them to raise Jesus with a respect mixed with adoration (it was indeed the case!), in a life of daily prayer, in a devout attention to the commands of the Torah (especially as it relates to the education of children) that constantly occupied their minds and graced their lips. And so Jesus, first as a tiny babe, then as a young child, then as an adolescent, raised with the Scriptures, surrounded by the love and example of his family, grew in wisdom, obedience, and grace.

Quite early on Jesus was "full of wisdom," of that wisdom rooted in the fear of God (Psalm 111:10) and in observing His commandments, the Torah (Deuteronomy 4:6). As the Second Adam, the Adam of the new covenant, of the fully renewed covenant, He sought in everything to depend on that grace by which He lived His human existence.

We are now ready to look more closely at the obedience of Jesus — the obedience that was required of Him to learn, the obedience that He desired to learn, Him whom "even the winds and the sea obey" (Matthew 8:27).

The Obedience of Jesus

Jesus fulfilled the Law in two ways by His obedience. He fulfilled it by obeying all that the Law calls for, that is, its precepts and commandments. But He also fulfilled it by submitting to the righteous punishments that the Law declares and requires.

Jesus, the new and second Adam, the head of a new and saved humanity, having assumed the condition of a servant by setting aside His glory, desired to obey the Law of God perfectly, in contrast to the first Adam who rebelled against God's Law and so became the head of a humanity made subject to original sin. Whereas the sin of the first Adam resulted in the death and perdition of us all, the obedience of the second Adam is going to result in the new birth and salvation of all the elect, all who are going to believe in Him and take the first steps of obedience.

Jesus is going to "learn obedience," though not in the sense of moving from disobedience to obedience, for He is the one without sin from conception. He is going to "learn obedience" in that He is going to grow more and more, and better and better, in obedience. The first Adam, created obedient, became inexplicably disobedient. The second Adam, conceived obedient, *is going to increase in obedience*, an obedience that will cost Him more than one could possibly imagine, for it will lead him to the point of separation from God, of accepting to be cursed of God — in our place, for our sin, so that righteousness might come from the righteous punishment of the sins of the human race, committed by all men with and in Adam, the first Adam.

As Jesus grows in obedience, he will do so, even from the very beginning, with the hellish and cursed death of the cross constantly in view (Deuteronomy 21:23; Galatians 3:13). From the beginning Jesus has to envisage, and willingly move toward, the unbearable: namely, that He, the only true Righteous One without sin, will suffer death on the cross. The temptation and trial (*peïrasmos*) which Jesus will undergo throughout His life, and especially at the end, is to accept, or not to accept, to experience the hell of separation from God, the curse of God the Holy One on sin and on sinners — in our place, in the place of those for whom he desires to be the only and perfect Savior. A Holy One, cut off from Him who is holiness itself: that is what Jesus chose to be; that is what Jesus chose *to experience in his death* — to accept, out of love for His own, precisely that which He finds intolerable, unacceptable.

From the Incarnation to the cross, Jesus reveals God's love and righteousness. His whole life, and especially the end of it, is one of full and complete obedience to the Law, the Law that is expressed not only in commandments, in precepts, but also in the condemnation of separation from God for the sins of sinners such as we all are, we of Adam's fallen race.

In our fallen state, we eagerly desire the love of God, but we deny His justice. If we must, we accept that God has indeed given His Law, but a Law that we would strip of its warnings, threats, and condemnations. Jesus, on the other hand, took on himself the full burden, embraced His whole vocation in His love for us: as much the commandments of the Law as the condemnations of the same. For us and our salvation "it was necessary" (ah! this little word *deï* which punctuates the Greek text of the New Testament!), "it was fitting," "it was needed," not only for Jesus to obey the Law fully, but also for Him to take upon Himself and for Himself, in our place, the chastisement of all the sins of sinners from Adam's first sin to the sins of the last repenting and believing men who will walk the earth.

In this way the cursed death of the cross is the final act of an obedience that began with the Incarnation. The Christ, God the Son become man, truly man, had to learn more and more, and better and better, what was the fullness of His obedience.

The physical pain of the crucifixion paled in comparison to the unimaginable moral pain experienced by the One who, holy and innocent, willingly bore God's curse, the hellish separation from God. Yet it was what Christ had chosen once and for all:

When He came into the world, He said:

> "Sacrifice and offering You did not desire,
> But a body You have prepared for me.
> In burnt offerings and sacrifices for sin
> You had no pleasure.
> Then I said, 'Behold, I have come —
> In the volume of the book it is written of Me —
> To do Your will, O God.'"

(Hebrews 10:5–7; cf. Psalm 40:7–9)

The human obedience of Jesus, which began when He was a tender child, will culminate with the supreme offering, the supreme prayer of Gethsemane on the morning of His death:

> O My Father, if it is possible, let this cup pass from Me; nevertheless, not as I will, but as You will!

and then:

> O My Father, if this cup cannot pass away from Me unless I drink it, Your will be done!

and finally, that afternoon, His cry of dereliction:

> *Eli, Eli, lama sabachtani?*" that is, "My God, My God, why have You forsaken Me?" (Matthew 26:39, 42; 27:46)

The Prologue of John

In the prologue of his Gospel, John moves quickly to highlight the close relationship between the Torah of Moses and the person of Jesus Christ.

First Point: Creation

With liturgical style, the Johannine prologue celebrates the same Word who, being God, brought the created universe into being, and who, being made flesh, brought the new creation — or the renewal of the creation that is salvation in and through this new creation (cf. 2 Corinthians 5:17 and Revelation 21:5).

> In the beginning was the Word, and the Word was with God, and the Word was God.... All things were made through Him.... In Him was life, and the life was the light of men. And the light shines in the darkness, and the darkness did not overcome it.... That was the true light which, coming into the world, gives light to every man. He was in the world, and the world was made through Him, and the world did not know Him. He came to His own, and His own did not receive Him. But as many as received Him, to them He gave the right to become children of God, to those who believe in His name: who were born, not of blood, nor of the will of the flesh, nor of the will of man, but of God.
>
> And the Word became flesh and dwelt among us, and we beheld His glory, the glory as of the only begotten of the Father.... And of His fullness we have all received, and grace for grace.... No one has seen God at any time. The only begotten Son, who is in the bosom of the Father, He has declared Him. (John 1:1–18)

Like Genesis, the Johannine prologue opens with the words: "In the beginning...God." And, also like Genesis, it deals immediately with the creation, the creation of light overcoming the darkness, of life and of human beings.

Second Point: Tabernacle

John 1 literally says: "The Word became flesh and 'pitched His tent' ('tabernacled') among us."

The Greek verb used here by John, *skénoô*, has the same root as the noun *skénôma*, which in the Greek of both the Septuagint and the New Testament refers to the Tabernacle, the Temple of God (Acts 7:46), or the human body (2 Peter 1:13–14). In being made flesh, the only-begotten Son of God took to Himself a human body, He assumed the life of men among men; but He was also that Temple of God concerning which He will say to the Pharisees: "Destroy this temple, and in three days I will raise it up" (John 2:19–22). This same verb *skénoô* appears twice in the book of Revelation. The first time, speaking of the martyrs, it says: "They are before the throne of God, and serve Him day and night in His temple. And He who sits on the throne will dwell among them" (Revelation 7:15). The second time, the Bridegroom of the Church — Jesus Christ — is referred to in this way: "Behold, the tabernacle of God is with men, and He will pitch His tent among them, and they shall be His people. God Himself will be with them and will be their God" (Revelation 21:3).

With the incarnation of the Son of God, three promises are realized. The first, from the Torah: "I will set My tabernacle among you, and My soul shall not abhor you. I will walk among you and be your God, and you shall be My people" (Leviticus 26:11–12). The second, from the Prophets: "I will set My sanctuary in their midst forevermore. My tabernacle also shall be with them; indeed I will be their God, and they shall be My people" (Ezekiel 37:26–27). And the third, from the Writings: "In the secret place of His tabernacle He shall hide me; he shall set me high upon a rock" (Psalm 27:5).

Third Point: Heséd and Eméth

John 1:17 declares: "The Law (the Torah) was given through Moses; grace and truth came through Jesus Christ."[3]

This sentence links Moses and Jesus Christ together, inextricably so. The first part of this verse, as we have already mentioned, echoes what

---

3. Many versions read: "*but* grace and truth came through Jesus Christ." The adversative, "but," is not included in the Greek text, and tends to support the Marcionite notion that Law and Gospel are opposed to one another.

the Torah itself says: "Moses commanded a law for us" (Deuteronomy 33:4). As we shall come to see, Jesus Himself says at the beginning of His ministry: "Do not think that I came to destroy the Torah.... I did not come to destroy but to fulfill... till heaven and earth pass away, one jot or one tittle will by no means pass away from the Torah" (Matthew 5:17–18).

Nor are "grace and truth" new ideas added to the old commandments of the Torah, for we find them in the Torah (for example, Exodus 34:6). "Grace" and "truth" (in Hebrew, *héséd* and *éméth*) characterize the Covenant of Grace. *Héséd*, which is also translated as "lovingkindness," signifies God's faithfulness, in the positive sense, to the promises of the covenant (His "wrath," or His "vengeance," being His faithfulness, in the negative sense, to the warnings and threats of His covenant; cf. Numbers 11:33; Deuteronomy 11:17; Matthew 3:7; Luke 21:22–23). *Éméth*, translated as "truth," signifies God's loyalty, sincerity, uprightness, and surety concerning everything that He says, whether addressed to His people, the members of the Covenant of Grace, or to those outside of His covenant to whom He has nonetheless addressed His Word. *Éméth* comes from the same root as *Amen*, the word that God uses to ratify what He says — "*Amen, Amen,* I say to you" — or that we use to ratify what God or another (perhaps an angel) says to us (Revelation 7:11–12). When the people say *Amen* after one has led them in prayer, for example, they are saying: "I agree! I join myself to this prayer!" To say *Amen* is an engagement; it is a serious word not to be pronounced casually. To say *Amen* is to say "yes." According to Revelation 3:14, Jesus Christ is "the *Amen*, the Faithful and True Witness, the Beginning of the creation of God." *Amen!*

The Baptism and Anointing of Christ

The written Gospels all attest to the one true Gospel. Likewise, the introductions of Matthew and Luke and the prologue of John are prefaces to this one true Gospel, all of them remarkable, invaluable, and indispensable. The first sentence of the Gospel of Mark (which serves as its heading) makes it very clear that the Gospel of Jesus Christ the Son of God — that is, the ministry of Jesus Christ — begins with His baptism and anointing (or "baptism-anointing"), an event reported in all four Gospels.

We have already looked at the mystery of the conception and virgin birth of Jesus, known as the *fiat* (that which would be done to me; Luke 1:38) of the Blessed Mary, called to be the *theotokos*, the mother of God. From beginning to end, this *fiat* was prepared, directed, enveloped, and seen through to the end in a special way by the sovereign grace of the Trinitarian God. Among the many attestations to this work of God are the Annunciation of the Angel Gabriel: "the Lord is with you" (Luke 1:28), the witness of Elizabeth, the mother of John the Baptist: "Blessed are you among women" (Luke 1:42), and Mary's own *Magnificat*: "My soul magnifies the Lord, and My spirit has rejoiced in God my Savior.... For He who is mighty has done great things for me" (Luke 1:47–49). Likewise, as we now consider the mystery of the baptism-anointing of Jesus, we come to the *fiat* (the "permit it to be so"; Matthew 3:13–17) of John the Baptist, called to be "a prophet who is more than a prophet" (Matthew 11:9; Luke 7:27–28).

The *fiat* of John, the Precursor (Luke 1:17, 76), was prepared, directed, enveloped, and seen through to the end in a wholly particular manner by the sovereign grace of the Trinitarian God. We acknowledge the work of God in the authority of the incarnate *Son* convincing John, who first opposed Him; in the descent and pre-pentecostal coming of the *Spirit* upon Jesus in the form of a dove; and in the voice of the *Father*, saying, "This is My beloved Son, in whom I am well pleased." Far more is taking place here than mere baptism, for it is the baptism by John, together with the opening of the heavens and the actions and pronouncements of the distinct persons of the Holy Trinity that come together to constitute inseparably the baptism-anointing of our Lord and Savior Jesus Christ.

Although the baptism-anointing of Jesus is rich with meaning, we must understand it firstly as that event which set apart Jesus as Christ (from the Greek *Christos*), as Messiah (from the Hebrew *Mashîah*), as the Anointed One (from the Latin *Unctus*) to be first and foremost Priest, but also Prophet and King.

It is also the baptism-anointing of Jesus Christ as Head of His Body, of His own people.

These two perspectives, these two meanings of Jesus' baptism-anointing come together, they join together closely, because this event signals the entrance of the one-and-only Mediator into His triple office, into His ministry for the glory of God and the salvation of all His people.

This does nothing to downplay the fact that Jesus, from His incarnation, is already filled with the Holy Spirit by whom He grows in wisdom and grace in His humanity. But Jesus' baptism-anointing was His ordination, His consecration into the public and manifested ministry of Mediator, into which He now enters. He is already the Mediator, but secretly. Over the course of perhaps two years, three at most, He is going to give witness and demonstration to the fact that He is the Mediator, up to the end of His life as a man and the end of His ministry, up to the cross where He is going to seal the Gospel by his blood, by the sacrifice costing Him the hellish and horrible torment of His separation from God.

The Old Priests…

In the old covenant, the priests — Aaron and his son — were anointed, invested, sanctified, that is, "set apart," to serve the Lord in the faithful offering of sacrifices (Exodus 28:41; 29:7; 40:12–15), to minister as holy priests to the Lord (Exodus 30:30). This anointing was done with "oil" (Leviticus 8:12; 21:12), a perfume carefully prepared from olive oil and blended with the finest spices (Exodus 30:22–25). The ceremony also included sprinkling with water, as we shall see shortly.

One was "consecrated" when this anointing was "poured on the head" by sprinkling.

Among the many specific commands given by the Torah concerning the High Priest and the Day of Atonement, it is stated that "the priest who is anointed … shall make atonement" (Leviticus 16:32).

In the old covenant, not only were priests anointed, but kings as well (1 Samuel 10:1; 16:3, 12, 13; 2 Samuel 2:4; 3:39; 1 Kings 1:34–45; 2 Kings 9:3–6; 11:12; 23:30). Sometimes the anointing was also received by prophets (for example 1 Kings 19:16). The anointing — priestly, kingly, prophetic — was the sacramental sign and seal of a pouring out of the Holy Spirit (1 Samuel 10:1, 6; 16:13; Isaiah 61:1).

The anointing of Christ is announced several times in the Old Testament (for example: 1 Samuel 2:10, 35; Psalm 2:2, 6; 45:8; Daniel 9:24–26).

…and the New Priest

Soon after His baptism-anointing, Jesus went into the synagogue in Nazareth on the Sabbath day. After reading Isaiah 61:1–2 ("The Spirit of the Lord is upon Me"), he declared to the congregation: "Today this Scripture is fulfilled in your hearing" (Luke 4:14–21).

When speaking with the Samaritan woman at Jacob's well, Jesus claims indeed to be the Christ, the Messiah, the Anointed One (John 4:25–26). Later, Jesus accepts Peter's confession: "You are the Christ (the Messiah, the Anointed One) of God" (Luke 9:20). And again, before the high priest on the day of His passion and crucifixion, Jesus will declare that He is the Christ (Mark 14:61–62; cf. also Acts 2:36 and Romans 1:4).

It is known how John refused to baptize Jesus at first, asking the same of him: "I need to be baptized by You, and are You coming to me?" But Jesus insists and commands: "Permit it to be so for now, for thus it is fitting for us to fulfill all righteousness" (Matthew 3:14–15). Those Jews faithful to the Torah knew that righteousness was observing everything that God commanded (Deuteronomy 6:25). Jesus, born under the Torah (Galatians 4:4), had always sought to fulfill all righteousness prescribed by the Torah. This is how the faithful remnant of Israel understood righteousness. This is what Jesus had learned from his parents.

His Baptism-Anointing

During His baptism, our perfect and only Priest was desirous that "all righteousness be fulfilled" and that everything "that the Torah taught be observed."

Three things were required for a priest to be ordained. He needed to wait until the age of thirty (Numbers 4:3, 47), He needed to be called (Exodus 28:1; cf. Hebrews 5:4), and He needed to be sprinkled with water by a priest (Leviticus 8:6; Exodus 29:4; 30:17–21; cf. for Levites: Numbers 8:6–7).

The baptism of Jesus, the sacramental act of His ordination, was conformed to the arrangements of the Torah. It is specifically said that He was baptized at the beginning of His ministry when he was thirty years old (Luke 3:23); He was duly called by God (Hebrews 5:4–10); and He was "sprinkled with water" by John, who was a lawful priest, being the son of the priest Zechariah (Luke 1:5, 13).

The priests of the old covenant were also anointed with oil. Better than oil, Jesus was anointed with the Holy Spirit, who descended and came upon Him as He came up from the waters (Matthew 3:16).

In claiming that Jesus' baptism-anointing was in fact His ordination, the obvious parallels between the event and the Old Testament prescriptions are not our only evidence. An episode reported in Matthew 21 and Mark 11 confirms that this was indeed his ordination. These two Gospels tell us that after He had made His entrance into Jerusalem to undergo His passion, Jesus chased the merchants from the temple, saying: "It is written, *'My house shall be called a house of prayer,'* but you have made it a *'den of thieves.'*" The Jewish authorities then intervene while Jesus is teaching in the Temple and approach Him to ask: "By what authority are You doing these things? Who gave You this authority?"

Jesus answers them, saying, "I also will ask you one thing, which if you answer Me, I likewise will tell you by what authority I do these things: The baptism of John — where was it from? From heaven or from men?"

Jesus establishes a link between His baptism-anointing and His authority to chase thieves from the Temple and teach there, and in so doing, shows that the right and responsibility of the office of Priest are His.

The offhand objection is raised: "But Jesus could not have been a priest since He was not from the family of Aaron! Jesus is not even from the tribe of Levi whose members were attached to the family Aaron for the temple ministry!" (Numbers 3:9–12). The New Testament itself provides the answer.

According to the Order of Melchizedek

Jesus was not a priest according to the order of Aaron for the simple reason that His priesthood, as both offerer and offering, was not, like that of the old covenant, for Jews only, but, according to the new covenant, for all nations of the world. He was made "priest according to the order of Melchizedek."

Psalm 110 announced:

The Lord (YHWH) said to my Lord (*Adonai*)...
The Lord shall send the rod of Your strength out of Zion...
The Lord has sworn
and will not relent,
"You are a priest forever
According to the order of Melchizedek."

The Epistle to the Hebrews, citing both Psalm 2 and Psalm 110 (5:5–6), tells us that Jesus, the only-begotten Son and the Christ, was proclaimed "High Priest according to the order of Melchizedek" (Hebrews 5:10; 6:20; 7:17).

The whole of the seventh chapter of the Epistle to the Hebrews celebrates the mysterious and qualitative superiority of Melchizedek (the King of Righteousness) over Moses himself, and the superiority of this priestly work according to the order of Melchizedek over the Aaronic priestly work in Israel. The high priests of the Israelite priesthood, of the priesthood of the old covenant — that is, of the old disposition of the Covenant of Grace — being men subject to weakness, needed to offer sacrifices continually. But Christ, the only-begotten Son, the High Priest according to the order of Melchizedek, has offered Himself once for all, "tak[ing] away the sins of the world," as John the Baptist said (John 1:29), by His perfect sacrifice.

Genesis 14 recounts the story of the meeting between Abraham and Melchizedek. This story radically and prophetically reveals to us that there is a priesthood, concealed in the Old Testament, revealed in the New, that is deeper and higher, broader and more universal, than the Aaronic and Levitical priesthood. The true archetypical priesthood of the Old Testament is that of Melchizedek, even though its historical realization, in the unique Sovereign High Priest, comes after the Levitical priesthood. Christ came after Abraham, after Moses, after Aaron, after the Prophets of the Old Testament, which include John the Baptist. And yet He was before them, being "the Lamb slain from the foundation of the world" (Revelation 13:8).

By giving a "tenth of all" to Melchizedek, Abraham confessed — such mystery of faith! — that the one who had given him "bread and wine" and "blessed" him was priest of the Most High God (Genesis 14:18–19). This king of Salem, this king of peace, was also "without father, without mother, without genealogy, having neither beginning of days nor end of life, but made like the Son of God, [who] remains continually" (Hebrews 7:3–4). Christ Jesus is indirectly referred to as King of Righteousness in the New Testament (e.g., Matthew 6:33; Revelation 15:3–4). Likewise, with royal authority, He gives His peace (John 14:27; 16:33; Acts 10:36; Romans 5:1; Ephesians 2:14).

In this we see Christ Jesus humbly obeying the Torah by receiving, as an ordinary priest, His water baptism by a human priest when He is thirty years old. In so doing He also fulfills the promises of the Jewish Bible, which, both in its description of the old priesthood ordained by God through Moses with a view toward Him who was to come, as well as in its depiction of the singular figure of Him who was to come in the image of Melchizedek, announced, prepared, and *typified* the Anointed One, the Messiah, the Christ to come, the extraordinary Priest, the one true Priest, whose priesthood would be "forever" (Hebrews 5:6), "perfect" (Hebrews 7:11), and "unchangeable" (Hebrews 7:24).

> For such a High Priest was fitting for us (*deî!*), who is holy, innocent, undefiled, separate from sinners, and has become higher than the heavens. (Hebrews 7:26)

The baptism-anointing of Jesus may be understood in two ways. It was firstly that of Christ as Priest, King, and Prophet; but as we are going to see, it was also that of Jesus Christ as Head of His body, as the Head of His people.

The Baptism of Christ as Head of His Body

Those coming to John for baptism heard his call to repent — the Kingdom of God is at hand! Jesus, of course, did not need to repent, for He was sinless. Yet He was not going to be a King without subjects, a Prophet without disciples, a Priest without those benefiting from His sacrifice. He was not going to be a Head without a body.

In his long prophecy running from chapters 40 to 55, Isaiah announced the coming of a *Shepherd* for his flock, his sheep and lambs (40:10–11); the coming of the *Redeemer* for His people (41:14); the coming of the *Chosen One* of God for all the nations (42:1, 4, 6); the coming of the *Lord* for the people of His covenant (49:8ff.); the coming of the *Liberator* for those whom He will crown with joy (51:11–12); the coming of the *Servant* for those whose punishment He will bear (53:4ff.).

The words from this prophecy are taken up by God when He says at Jesus' baptism-anointing: "Behold . . . My Chosen One in whom My soul delights" (42:1). And when John the Baptist says that Jesus "takes away the sin of the world," he is referring to Isaiah's prophecy about the Lamb (53:7), which prophecy he authenticates, for with his own eyes he "sees" it fulfilled, realized, in Jesus.

With His baptism-anointing by John, Jesus, as Head, begins that path that will lead to His passion for His people, His body. His baptism in the Jordan announces that baptism of sweat and blood that He will undergo in His redemptive death. It signals that Jesus, the Anointed Priest, is also the Anointed Sacrifice laden with the sins, the judgment, the condemnation, and the punishment of His people, of those sinners elect in Him, for the taking away of their sins and the securing of their salvation.

The goal of the baptism-anointing of Jesus, the Head, is the salvation of the body.

There, at His baptism-anointing, Jesus accepts to have the sins of His people fall on Him like the waters of the Jordan; He accepts to have the wrath, the righteous wrath of God, fall on Him to the point of becoming a "curse" (Galatians 3:13; cf. Deuteronomy 21:23). The water poured *on* Him signifies the wrath of God falling *on* the Head instead of the Body. The phrase: "the wrath of God on/upon/over" appears frequently in the Old Testament (cf. for example, 2 Chronicles 32:25) and in the New (cf. John 3:36; Romans 1:18; Ephesians 5:6).

Jesus is the Head of the Church; He is mystically one with her. He represents all of His people before the face of His Father, assuming, taking upon Himself, all the sins of the members of His body. With the water of His baptism-anointing, Jesus accepts in advance the punishment of the curse of the cross.

This was also done that all righteousness might be fulfilled — the sins of many being "taken away" because the Innocent One has "taken responsibility" for them, receiving the punishment for them, paying for them, out of love for His people and in their stead.

Baptizing Jesus according to His command, John the Baptist consecrated Him *Priest*. But by the free and sovereign will of the Trinity, this baptism signified that Jesus was also the vicarious *sacrifice* for His people that all righteousness might be fulfilled.

Luke makes a point of the fact that Jesus *prayed* during His baptism (3:21). This prayer can and must be understood together with Jesus' prayer on the Mount of Olives on the eve of His death.

As a true human being, struggling in prayer as He went down into the Jordan to be baptized, Jesus needed the full measure of the Holy Spirit. "And the Holy Spirit descended in bodily form like a dove upon Him, and a voice came from heaven which said, 'You are My beloved Son; in You I am well pleased'" (Luke 3:22).

The Lord and Savior's baptism takes place in the setting of an Epiphany, a Theophany, in which the Trinitarian God manifests Himself. The heavens were opened (Matthew 3:16; Mark 1:9; Luke 3:21; John 1:32). The sacrament! The mystery!

The Prophetic Teaching of Jesus

The Two Perspectives of Christ's Prophecy

Jesus exercises His prophetic ministry soon after His baptism-anointing. The-Word-of-God-made-man becomes the Prophet.

When considering the prophecy of Jesus (the whole of what He says: speeches, teachings, parables, sermons, aphorisms, etc.), one finds two perspectives — these two perspectives are sometimes distinct and at other times mixed together.

According to the first perspective, Jesus *consoles* (supports, holds up, encourages, strengthens) the Remnant of Israel and those who join it.

According to the second perspective, Jesus *issues a call* to the whole people of Israel, to all Israel. With greater and greater urgency, He makes it known that now is the time to hear and follow the Word of God: the Word written by the Spirit of God in the Torah, the Prophets, and the Writings; and Christ, the Word incarnate, come to His own as the Bible of Israel had foretold.

We discern two stages in His prophetic ministry in regard to this call. During the first stage, which continues from His baptism-anointing until His transfiguration and His journeying up to Jerusalem to die, Jesus mobilizes His disciples (the Twelve: Matthew 10; then the Seventy: Luke 10) to call the people of God to return, by turning back, to the life and death questions posed by the words of the covenant. These questions include:

1. Who is the Lord?
2. What has He done up to this point?
3. What are His commandments?
4. What blessings or cursings ought to be expected from Him as a consequence of faithfulness or unfaithfulness?

5. What future is there, what lies ahead, for the people of the covenant?

Those sent by Jesus — the Twelve, then the Seventy — have only a short time to fulfill their mission to "the lost sheep of the house of Israel." Thus they must not load themselves down with moneybags or possessions. If they are received, they are to stay only as long as necessary. If they are not received, they are to shake the dust from their feet and move on (Matthew 10:5–15; Mark 6:7–13; Luke 9:1–6 and 10:1–20). Let us note in passing that this missionary priority to Israel would not end with the departure of their Master, but would be continued after the coming of the Holy Spirit on the Day of Pentecost. It would be continued even at the price of martyrdom, even if they were hated by all for the sake of Jesus' Name. The Son of Man will come to judge Israel even before they have finished their mission (Matthew 10:16–23).

During the second stage, following His transfiguration and journey up to Jerusalem to die, things accelerate. Jesus is going to declare openly the judgment of God on His people. He says that they are like the tree without fruit that he curses and that "dried up from the roots" (Mark 11:11–26), or like vinedressers to whom the owner leased his vineyard and who then beat up the servants whom the owner sent "when the season came" — once, twice, three times — and who eventually kill his beloved son when the owner sends him (Mark 12:1–12).

These episodes and parables depict the Lord God, the Lord (Suzerain) and Founder of the covenant, bringing and pursuing a just legal action against His unfaithful vassal who has broken the covenantal pact. It's as if the Lord God came to issue an ultimatum to these rebels before executing His vengeance (Deuteronomy 32:35; Hebrews 10:30–31; Matthew 23:32–36).

It has often been said that the God of the Old Testament is terrible and wrathful, while the God of the New Testament is loving and lenient. This opposing of the God of the Old Testament against the God of the New Testament is a gross and incomprehensible error, a misinterpretation of the texts, for God is love and God is holy in the one testament as well as in the other. In fact, if the New Testament more fully reveals God's love, it more fully reveals His holiness as well.

We see the love and holiness of God clearly portrayed together in the Gospel of John, which is the most "predestinarian" of the Gospels (for example 3:5–8, 27; 6:37–39, 44, 65; 17:24), yet also has the most to say about the messianic judgment. It is common to quote — and misapply the meaning of — Jesus' statement: "For God did not send His Son into the world to condemn the world, but that the world through Him might be saved" (John 3:17), without quoting what immediately follows:

> He who believes in Him is not condemned; but he who does not believe is condemned already, because he has not believed in the name of the only begotten Son of God. And this is the condemnation, that the light has come into the world, and men loved darkness rather than light, because their deeds were evil. For everyone practicing evil hates the light and does not come to the light, lest his deeds should be exposed. But he who does the truth comes to the light, that his deeds may be clearly seen, that they have been done in God (John 3:18–21).[4]

And it is the fourth Gospel that reports this statement of Jesus: "He who does not believe the Son shall not see life, but the wrath of God abides on him" (John 3:36; cf. also John 5:21–30; 8:16; 9:39; 12:31).

Jesus, at the end of his ministry, comes to say that this generation — this "wicked," "adulterous," "sinful," "perverse" generation — will see the destruction of Jerusalem and the Temple, the coming upon them of the judgment of the Son of Man, the end of the world, the end of the era of the old covenant.

Jesus, the Israelite, weeps when he considers what is soon to happen: "O Jerusalem, Jerusalem, the one who kills the prophets and stones those who are sent to her! How often I wanted to gather your children together, as a hen gathers her chicks under her wings, but you were not willing!" (Matthew 23:37).

There were many who wept, many who were moved by the call of Christ, who thus became His disciples, hailed Him as the Messiah, and joined the faithful Remnant of Israel. But, as a whole, the generation followed false shepherds and stubbornly rejected Him. Many were called, but few were chosen (Matthew 22:14).

*

---

4. *Translator's Note:* The kind of selective quoting of John 3:17 against which Courthial warns is alive and well. For a recent example, see Rob Bell's *Love Wins: A Book About Heaven, Hell, and the Fate of Every Person Who Ever Lived* (New York, NY: HarperOne, 2011), 160.

In the Sermon on the Mount, in Galilee, at the beginning of His public ministry (Matthew 5, 6, and 7), Jesus exercises His prophetic office as He addresses His disciples who have come to His feet and the crowd of Jews who gathered round to listen.

The "Poor" of Israel

He declares the humble, the poor in spirit (those who form the faithful Remnant of Israel) to be "happy," "blessed," even — and most especially — when they suffer insults, slander, and persecutions for the name of the Lord. They are the salt of the land of Israel. Let not the salt lose its flavor, nor the light be put under a basket! With their simple obedience to the Torah, they glorify their Father in heaven before men.

The Pharisees

Next, Jesus warns his hearers about the teaching of the scribes, the teachers of the law, and the Pharisees.

The Pharisees — coming from the Hebrew word *Perushîm*, meaning the "set apart ones" — had been influential since the reign of John Hyrcanus (134–104 B.C.) and were divided into various schools (for example, the school of Hillel the Elder against the school of Shamaï). They claimed to follow the "traditions" supposedly going back to Moses, but these traditions often contradicted the Mosaic Law. Consequently, by way of these traditions, the Pharisees changed and twisted the meaning of the Torah so that it was not the true Torah, but a deformed Torah, that they promoted.

Beginning with the Sermon on the Mount, Jesus repeatedly and vigorously calls His hearers to reject these traditions of human invention and to return to the Word of God — that is, to the Word of God alone, and to the Word of God entire. In this vein, we find toward the end of His prophetic ministry His condemnation of the "scribes and Pharisees, hypocrites" in the form of *seven plus one* cursings, which corresponds to the *seven plus one* blessings He pronounced upon the "poor" and the "meek" of Israel, those who "hunger and thirst after righteousness." (I say *seven plus one*, and not *eight*, because in each case the eighth differs from the first seven in that it does not concern particular types of obedience or disobedience, but states universal outcomes experienced by those who will find themselves persecuted on the one hand, and those who become persecutors on the other [Matthew 5:10; 23:33–36].)

The Pharisees, their scribes, their teachers of the Law, and their elders (or *Rabbis*) were guilty of twisting the Torah on several counts.

First, by putting all of the focus on the external performance of certain rituals, they put things of secondary importance before things of primary importance (and this contrary to the clear teachings of Scripture). They have left undone the "weightier matters of the law: justice and mercy and faith" (cf. Micah 6:8; Zechariah 7:9–10), which things they "ought to have done, without leaving the others undone" (Matthew 23:23).

Secondly, they externalized the meaning of the Law instead of seeking to grasp the fullness and depth of its inner meaning (cf. Proverbs 6:16–18, 25). They were certainly right to recognize that the Law condemns evil actions, but they erred in downplaying or failing to recognize that it also condemns the sources of those evil actions which spring from the *heart*, from deep within the self — "Keep your heart with all diligence, for out of it spring the issues of life" (Proverbs 4:23; this biblical teaching is also found in Exodus 20:3, 17; Deuteronomy 5:20 and 8:2; Ezekiel 11:19–20; 36:25–27; etc.).

Finally, what made them hypocritical, self-sufficient, and proud was that they justified themselves before God, not seeing themselves as sinners (Matthew 9:10–13; Luke 16:15; 18:9–14). They failed to see that the Law was not given as a means for men to justify themselves, and that salvation comes only by grace. The Law does not give the ability to fulfill the Law; that ability comes to men only by grace.

The Sadducees

Alongside the Pharisees, the Gospels tell of the *Sadducees* (perhaps descendants of Zadok, the High Priest), many of whom were priests themselves. The Sadducees were well-regarded by the Hasmonean kings and leadership (of the family of Herod) until A.D. 65. Many of the members of the Sanhedrin were Sadducees. But after the destruction of the Temple in A.D. 70, their influence disappeared, while the influence of the Pharisees prevailed. For the Sadducees, only the Torah proper (our Pentateuch) had full authority. The Sadducees did not believe in the resurrection, the existence of spiritual creatures (angels or demons), or in judgment beyond the grave. They were devoted to the promotion of human autonomy.

*

We should not suppose that there is the slightest opposition between the Torah of Moses and the teachings of our Lord in the Sermon on the Mount. In fact, Jesus explicitly warns against any such opposition, saying: "I did not come to destroy, but to fulfill. For assuredly, I say to you, till heaven and earth pass away, one jot or one tittle will by no means pass from the law till all is fulfilled. Whoever therefore breaks one of the least of these commandments, and teaches men so, shall be called least in the kingdom of heaven; but whoever does and teaches them, he shall be called great in the kingdom of heaven" (Matthew 5:17–19).

In fact, in Matthew 5:17–48, Jesus opposes what is said by the elders (the teachers of the Law, the scribes and *rabbis*) with what is actually written in the Torah. *With authority* (Matthew 7:29), Jesus goes back to and emphasizes the normative authority of the Torah, of the Jewish Bible. Each of His statements beginning with "but I say to you..." couples His own Words (coming from the Word incarnate) with those of Holy Scripture, the Word inscripturated (carried by His own Spirit). Just as He had done during His temptation in the desert by the Devil, so He does here: He responds forcefully to the misuse of isolated (and thus misinterpreted) texts of Scripture with the true and full meaning of the words of Scripture, and in this way He confronts and corrects the *Halakhah* (the systematic compendium of teaching) of the Pharisaic scribes, of the *rabbis*, exposing their erroneous interpretation.

Six Antitheses

In light of the above, we see how Jesus sets forth six antitheses (Matthew 5:21–48), showing how the teachings of the *rabbis* are contrary to what the Torah, the Bible, truly says. Jesus appeals to Scripture as a whole, from its roots to its fruits, whereas the *rabbis* pick only parts, branches cut away from the whole and thus withering.

Although each "You have heard that it was said..." contains a verse of Scripture, we must recognize that the Pharisees and *rabbis* are using this verse to downplay, "superficialize," twist or misrepresent the meaning of what is written. The principle of *Sola Scriptura* (Scripture alone) is true only insofar as it lines up with *Tota Scriptura* (the whole of Scripture): the two must go together.

1. "You shall not murder," according to the *rabbis*, applied only to the act, and not to the unrighteous anger that gives rise to the act (Zechariah 7:10; 8:17). Jesus goes further still, showing that the sixth commandment also includes a positive aspect: being reconciled with the neighbor, love for neighbor (Matthew 5:23–26; cf. Leviticus 19:16–18).
2. Likewise, according to the *rabbis*, "You shall not commit adultery" did not apply to lust (cf. Exodus 20:17 and Job 31:1).
3. "Whoever divorces his wife, let him give her a certificate of divorce" (Deuteronomy 24:1), according to the *rabbis*, would allow a man to divorce his wife simply because he wanted to (cf. Malachi 2:14–16). The school of the *rabbi* Hillel, a contemporary of Jesus, allowed a man to divorce his wife for any cause: if he found her too loud, a poor cook, less attractive than before, etc.
4. To the *rabbis*, "You shall not swear falsely, but shall perform your oaths to the Lord" (Matthew 5:33, referencing Leviticus 19:12) meant that one could swear and make oaths in everyday life, with mental reservations, according to which one would swear "by this" or "by that" or "on the head of," etc. There is a legitimate place for oaths (the Lord Himself made them), such as in the public courtroom; but in everyday life our yes must be yes and our no, no; anything more than this is of the Evil One.
5. "An eye for an eye and a tooth for a tooth." The purpose of *lex talionis*, a principle affirmed in the Bible, is to ensure that the punishment fits the crime. But it was taken by the *rabbis* to justify personal revenge in private matters — situations in which Scripture, on the other hand, exhorts us to show mercy (Proverbs 19:22; 22:9; Isaiah 1:17; Zechariah 7:9).
6. The *rabbis* took the commandment of the Torah, "You shall love your neighbor," and perniciously added "and hate your enemy." The Bible, however, commands: "If your enemy is hungry, give him bread to eat; and if he is thirsty, give him water to drink" (Proverbs 25:21).

Jesus further expands upon the true meaning of the Bible, the Bible that was His own, saying, "But I say to you, love your enemies, bless those who curse you, do good to those who hate you, and pray for those who spitefully use you and persecute you.... You shall be perfect, just as your Father in heaven is perfect" (Matthew 5:44–48).

The King and His Kingdom

Having been consecrated Priest and Prophet by His baptism, Jesus Christ is also consecrated King — King of the Kingdom of God, of the Kingdom of Heaven.

At the beginning of His ministry Jesus "went about all Galilee ... preaching the gospel of the kingdom" (Matthew 4:23). He stressed the necessity of grace and of the Holy Spirit, as we find Him saying to Nicodemus who came to him by night: "Unless one is born from above, he cannot see the kingdom of God ... unless one is born of water and the Spirit, he cannot enter the kingdom of heaven" (John 3:3, 5).

All throughout His ministry Jesus declares that the Kingdom is near (Matthew 4:17; Mark 1:15; 12:34) since it has arrived, and, in His person, is in their midst (Luke 17:21).

His invitation is to "seek first the kingdom of God and its righteousness" (Matthew 6:33) and to ask for the Holy Spirit without whom no one can enter the kingdom and live out its righteousness (Luke 11:9–13). Moreover, the Kingdom and righteousness (righteousness is the fulfillment of the law) go together (Romans 8:4; 14:17). The righteousness of the disciples exceeds that of the scribes and Pharisees, for theirs, unlike that of the scribes and Pharisees, is the righteousness that God gives by grace to sinners who humble themselves and repent, and who know that they are far from perfect, but who press on toward the goal for the prize of the upward call of God in Christ Jesus, making every effort to live according to God's commandments in every area of life (cf. Philippians 3:8–14).

The Kingdom of God is the fifth kingdom announced by Daniel. Having explained to Nebuchadnezzar his vision of the statue and spoken of the *stone* that would shatter the statue and become a great mountain filling the whole earth (Daniel 2:31–35), the prophet and statesman concluded: "the God of heaven will set up a kingdom which shall never be destroyed ... and it shall stand forever" (Daniel 2:44). In

Revelation, the voices in heaven loudly proclaim: "The kingdoms of this world have become the kingdoms of our Lord and of His Christ, and He shall reign forever and ever" (Revelation 11:15).

We find Jesus' teaching on the Kingdom in the parables.

In one of these parables (a single sentence!), Jesus, at the end of his ministry, declares: "Most assuredly, I say to you, unless a grain of wheat falls into the ground and dies, it remains alone; but if it dies, it produces much grain" (John 12:24). The King, mysteriously bearing the Kingdom in Himself, must die in order to bear much fruit.

Another time, Jesus puts forth this parable: "The kingdom of heaven is like a mustard seed, which a man took and sowed in his field, which indeed is the least of all seeds; but when it is grown it is greater than the herbs and becomes a tree, so that the birds of the air come and nest in its branches" (Matthew 13:31–32). The Kingdom will grow *extensively* throughout the centuries up to the day when, in the end, "the earth shall be full of the knowledge of the LORD as the waters cover the sea" (Isaiah 11:9). The Torah announced the same (Leviticus 26:3–13; Deuteronomy 28:1–14).

Once more, Jesus says: "The kingdom of heaven is like leaven, which a woman took and hid in three measures of meal till it was all leavened" (Matthew 13:33). Here we learn that the Kingdom will also grow *intensively* — over time the Kingdom will penetrate and leaven the various aspects of reality until, eventually, no portion of human life is left untouched.

The King, the bearer of the Kingdom, will die alone, a single grain fallen to the ground, so that He might then, no longer alone, become an immense tree.

It is through His death, resurrection, and ascension that Christ, the King victorious over the Devil, sin, and death, will sit enthroned "far above all principality and power and might and dominion, and every name that is named, not only in this age but also in that which is to come" (Ephesians 1:20–21).

This reign of Christ, inaugurated in A.D. 30 and manifested in an extraordinary way from A.D. 30 to 70, is not *of* this world (John 18:36) since it exerts itself *from* heaven where Christ sits at the right hand of the Father. Nonetheless, the development of the Kingdom is progressive, as it extends and deepens in a somewhat embryonic manner in the early stages and then continues to exert itself more and more prominently, *"on earth* as it is in heaven," in every area of life, until it comes to the point of full flourishing announced in Isaiah 2:2–4 and Micah 4:1–4.

In heaven, from where He reigns more and more on earth, Jesus "became the author of eternal salvation to all who obey Him" (Hebrews 5:9). The progress of the Kingdom, of the Covenant of Grace, is not, however, strictly automatic. It moves forward and falls back according to the faithfulness or unfaithfulness, the perseverance or falling away, the obedience or disobedience, of the subjects of the Kingdom, of the members of the Covenant of Grace, to the Word-Law of God. Since the days of Jesus' earthly ministry, the proclamation of the coming Kingdom goes together with the call to obedience to the Law (Matthew 7:12–27).

In the *Te Deum*, the Church has sung throughout the centuries to the King of the Kingdom, the Guarantor of the Covenant of Grace: *"By Your victory over death you have opened the gates of the Kingdom to all who believe."*

The End of the Age

We come now to the Olivet discourse, which Jesus addressed to His disciples on the Mount of Olives at the end of His earthly ministry (Matthew 24; Mark 13; Luke 21).

Just beforehand, as the disciples are leaving the Temple, they are extolling its beauty. The year is A.D. 30. Though built after the return of the exiles four centuries earlier, this second Temple shines impressively under the sun, the result of a total restoration project begun a few decades earlier by Herod the Great (Herod, an Idumean king, sought by this move to win the Jews' favor). The finishing touches were still being added.

"Teacher," one of the disciples says, "See what manner of stones and what buildings are here!" To their amazement, Jesus responds: "Do you see all these things? Assuredly, I say to you, not one stone shall be left here upon another, that shall not be thrown down." The disciples decide to question Him on this.

Later, at the Mount of Olives where Jesus had taken His seat, they come to Him privately, saying, "Tell us, when will these things be? And what will be the sign of Your coming, and of the end of the aeon[5] [the era, the age, in which we are]?" It is to this question that Jesus responds.

The Context

Throughout His ministry, Jesus had already announced in various ways the end of the present era (which would thus become the ancient era): "And I say to you that many will come from the east and the west, and sit down with Abraham, Isaac, and Jacob in the kingdom of heaven. But the sons of the kingdom will be cast out into outer darkness. There will be weeping and gnashing of teeth" (Matthew 8:11–12). Another time He tells the parable of the wedding feast:

> The kingdom of heaven is like a certain king who arranged a marriage for his son, and sent out his servants to call those who were invited to the wedding; and they were not willing to come. Again, he sent out other servants, ... But [those invited] made light of it and went their ways ... and the rest seized his servants, treated them spitefully, and killed them. But when the king heard about it, he was furious. And he sent out his armies, destroyed those murderers, and burned up their city. Then he said to his servants, 'The wedding is ready, but those who were invited were not worthy. Therefore go into the highways, and as many as you find, invite to the wedding' ... and the wedding hall was filled with guests. (Matthew 22:2–10)

To the cities in Israel who refused His call, Jesus said:

> Woe to you, Chorazin! Woe to you, Bethsaida! For if the mighty works which were done in you had been done in Tyre and Sidon, they would have repented long ago in sackcloth and ashes. But I say to you, it will be more tolerable for Tyre and Sidon in the day of judgment than for you. And you, Capernaum, who are exalted to heaven, will be brought down to Hades; for if the mighty works which were done in you had been done in Sodom, it would have remained until this day. But I say to you that it shall be more tolerable for the land of Sodom in the day of judgment than for you. (Matthew 11:21–24)

---

5. The Greek word *aïon* is here used.

He also told the frightful parable of the vinedressers to whom a landowner had leased his vineyard. The landowner,

> when vintage-time drew near, sent his servants to the vinedressers,... and the vinedressers took his servants, beat one, killed one, and stoned another.... Then last of all he sent his son to them, saying, 'They will respect my son.' But when the vinedressers saw the son,... they took him and cast him out of the vineyard and killed him. Therefore, when the owner of the vineyard comes, what will he do to those vinedressers?... He will destroy those wicked men miserably, and lease his vineyard to other vinedressers who will render to him the fruits in their seasons. (Matthew 21:34–41)

Jesus then turned to the chief priests, Pharisees, and others hearing Him, and added:

> Therefore I say to you, the kingdom of God will be taken from you and given to a nation bearing the fruits of it. (Matthew 21:43)

Jesus then, after rebuking the leaders of Israel (Matthew 23:1–12), pronounced the *seven plus one* cursings upon them (Matthew 23:13–36). We are told that after this encounter Jesus wept over Jerusalem (Matthew 23:37–39). Finally, as He made His way up to the Place of the Skull, bearing His cross, He will say to the women lamenting over Him: "Daughters of Jerusalem, do not weep for Me, but weep for yourselves and for your children. For indeed the days are coming in which they will say, 'Blessed are the barren, wombs that never bore, and breasts which never nursed!' Then they will begin to say to the mountains, 'Fall on us!' and to the hills, 'Cover us!'" (Luke 23:28–30).

"This Generation"

Now that we have a sense of the context, we can better understand the Olivet discourse in which Jesus predicts the "days of vengeance" (Luke 21:22) which are coming upon the Temple, Jerusalem, and Israel, and are coming soon, since these events will happen during the lifetime of "this generation," before "this generation" passes away (Matthew 24:34; Mark 13:30; Luke 21:32). The Greek word *genea* is used thirty-three times in the Gospels and over forty times in the New Testament. In every instance it clearly and specifically means a *generation*, a *"group of contemporaries."* The sign of "the Son of Man in heaven," like the seven other signs that will precede and warn of it, must therefore come to pass before the present generation of Israel passes away, a generation that Jesus characterized as "wicked," "adulterous," and "sinful." This generation, consequently, was also the generation of the apostolic circle.

The Seven Warning Signs

In His discourse Jesus tells His hearers to be looking for seven warning signs — seven signs demanding the greatest attention, proceeding one to the next with growing precision, from the most general to the most specific.

They are:

1. False Christs who "will deceive many" (Matthew 24:4–5; Mark 13:6; Luke 21:8).
2. Wars and rumors of wars (Matthew 24:6–7; Mark 13:7; Luke 21:9–10).
3. Earthquakes and famines in various places (Matthew 24:7; Mark 13:8; Luke 21:11).
4. The martyrdom of those who faithfully endure to the end (Matthew 24:9, 13; Mark 13:9, 11 and 13; Luke 21:12–19).
5. The apostasy of many (Matthew 24:10–12; Mark 13:12; Luke 21:16).
6. The Gospel proclaimed to all nations in the *oïkoumené* (the inhabited world) (Matthew 24:14; Mark 13:10).
7. The abomination of desolation and the great tribulation (Matthew 24:15–28; Mark 13:14–23; Luke 21:20–26).

The Sign of the Son of Man in Heaven

After the seven warning signs, "the sign of the Son of Man will appear in heaven" (Matthew 24:29–35; Mark 13:24–31; Luke 21:25–33). This will be the Coming of the "Messiah and Judge" of His people; the destruction of the Temple, and the end of the old covenant era.

We will consider these historical prophecies in greater detail when we speak about their fulfillment at the end of the forty years from A.D. 30 to 70.

The High Priestly Prayer

John does not record Jesus' discourse on the Mount of Olives in his Gospel (though around A.D. 68, John, borne along by the Holy Spirit, wrote the Book of Revelation after receiving a series of visions on the isle of Patmos, a book intended to encourage Christians as the coming of Christ, the Judge of Israel, and the great tribulation draw near). But in John's Gospel, we find Jesus' prayer for the apostles and subsequent generations of disciples that are specific to the time in which they live and will live. We speak, of course, of the High Priestly Prayer of our Lord as recorded in John 17.

This prayer, addressed by the Son to the Father just prior to His passion, is composed of three parts, each concerning one of three successive epochs in our Christian era.

First Part

The hour having come in which the Son must glorify the Father, the Son asks the Father to glorify Him as He goes through the events which lie ahead: His imminent death on the cross, His resurrection, and His ascension. These impending events, together with the sufferings and victory encompassed in them, will culminate with Christ receiving from His Father "authority over all flesh" (cf. Matthew 28:18) and, in particular, authority to give eternal life to those whom the Father has given the Son (John 17:1–3). "I have glorified You on the earth. I have finished the work which You have given Me to do. And now, O Father, glorify Me together with Yourself, with the glory which I had with You before the world was" (verses 4 and 5).

The first part of the High Priestly Prayer deals with the years A.D. 1 to 30: *the time of Christ's earthly life.*

Second Part

The Father gave the members of the apostolic circle to the Son. These believed in the name of the Father and the Son and received and kept the Word (and the words!) given by the Father to the Son. Now the Son asks the Father to glorify the Son in them. The Son is leaving this world to go to the Father. Jesus asks the Father to keep the members of the apostolic circle in the name of the Father and the Son: "That they may be one as we are one!" Jesus kept the twelve and "none of them is lost except the son of perdition, that the Scripture might be fulfilled" (cf. John 13:18, quoting Psalm 41:9). He gave them the Word of the Father. They are still *in* the world; the world hates them because they are not *of* the world (verses 6 to 14). "I do not pray that You should take them out of the world, but that You should keep them from the evil one.... Sanctify them by Your truth. Your word is truth. As You sent Me into the world, I also have sent them into the world. And for their sakes I sanctify Myself, that they also may be sanctified by the truth" (verses 15 to 19).

This second part of the High Priestly Prayer concerns the years A.D. 30 to 70: *the period of the Apostolic Church.*

Third Part

Having now prayed for His glorification and the sanctification of the apostolic circle in the truth, the Son now prays for all who will believe thereafter, throughout the centuries until the resurrection of the dead, the Last Judgment, Christ's return in glory, and the universal transfiguration. "I do not pray for these alone (the apostles), but also for those who will believe in Me through their word; that they all may be one, as You, Father, are in Me, and I in You; that they also may be one in Us, that the world may believe that You sent Me, ... Father, I desire that they also whom You gave Me may be with Me where I am, that they may behold My glory which You have given Me; for you loved Me before the foundation of the world. O righteous Father! The world has not known You, but I have known You; and these have known that You sent Me. And I have declared to them Your name, and will declare it, that the love with which You loved Me may be in them, and I in them" (verses 20 to 26).

This third part of the High Priestly Prayer concerns the whole span of our era after A.D. 70: *the post-apostolic period of the Church.*

5

THE APOSTOLIC PERIOD:
A.D. 30–70

FROM EASTER TO PENTECOST

From Humiliation to Glorification

For a time, Christ, by His incarnation, refrained from manifesting and availing himself of the glory that was His in His divinity. In order to accomplish everything necessary for the salvation of His people, He assumed humanity and set himself under the Law. This humbling of Himself and submission to the Law was the decision of Trinitarian love. Theologians call this His *status humiliationis* — or, in the words of Paul, His "emptying" or "divesting" (Philippians 2:7) of Himself. However, with the Resurrection, our Lord enters into His *status exaltationis*, His glorification.

The Resurrection

For a time, Christ's body and soul were separated. But, by His resurrection, death is vanquished; believers, now united to Him, may rise to new life, finding in His resurrection a guarantee of their own bodily resurrection (Romans 8:11; 1 Corinthians 15:17, 54; Colossians 3:1–5; 1 Peter 1:3, 21).

The Fifty Days

From Easter to the Ascension were forty days, and from the Ascension to Pentecost — when the Holy Spirit came, the heavenly Jerusalem descended, and the reign of God on earth began — were another ten days. In all, between Easter and Pentecost, there were fifty days. It was a very specific time and a very mysterious time.

The Forty Days

Christ crossed from death to life in an act that was more than just a resuscitation or revival, more than simply again taking hold of life. He had, by His resurrection, taken hold of a transfigured, glorified, and immortal life. And yet what makes the forty days from Easter to the Ascension so mysterious is that, resurrected though He was, He had not departed from this world.

The individual identity of Christ's humanity remained, but in a condition, a status, of glorification. The tomb was empty but for the linen clothes and the face cloth lying where the body had been (John 20:3–8).

Over the course of forty mysterious days, the resurrected Christ appears many times as though still on earth. He is no longer bound by physical laws. He is there and yet He is not there. These were an extraordinary, incredible forty days during which Jesus could be seen, heard, and touched at one moment and completely beyond human perception the next. He is still in this world and yet already elsewhere. Christ, already raised to the Father, has not yet ascended to Him.

In this way and during this time, He is able to strengthen His people's faith in God and put His resurrection beyond doubt. He shows them His wounds and they touch His hands and feet. He eats with them (Luke 24:13–49), talks with them (John 21), gives them commands, and gathers them on a mountain in Galilee (Matthew 28:1–10; 16ff.). He explains the Scriptures to them and, after journeying with them, gives them the bread of communion.

He shows Himself, resurrected, to Mary Magdalene at the tomb. He shows Himself to the disciples, both in Jerusalem, where they were meeting behind closed doors, and some time later on the shores of the Sea of Tiberias as they fished (John 20:11 to 21:23). And though we are not told where, we know that He showed himself to more than five hundred brethren in all (1 Corinthians 15:6).

The Ascension

After having appeared over the course of forty days to the disciples, speaking to them concerning the things of the Kingdom of God — how slow they were to realize that it was not to be confused with the kingdom of Israel! — Jesus ascended to *heaven* (Acts 1:3–11):

> So shall My Word be that goes forth from My mouth;
> It shall not return to Me empty,
> But it shall accomplish what I please,
> And it shall prosper in the thing for which I sent it. (Isaiah 55:11)

This heaven is symbolized by the sky over our heads. In ascending visibly before the eyes of the disciples until a cloud received Him out of sight, Jesus showed them that He was leaving this world to enter into the "unapproachable light which no man has seen or can see," hidden from view "until our Lord Jesus Christ's appearing (*epiphane*), which He will manifest in His own time, He who is the blessed and only Potentate, the King of kings and Lord of lords" (1 Timothy 6:14–16).

The Ten Days

The mystery does not end there. Ten days followed during which Jesus, ascended to heaven and enthroned at the right hand of His Father, prays the Father to send His people another Paraclete, that is, the Holy Spirit (John 14:16). The Greek word *paraklètos* means one who is called alongside, an advocate, support, consoler, counselor, guide, and companion. The Paraclete, "the Spirit of truth," will lead the apostolic circle in all truth, speaking to them all things that He receives from the Son, in heaven, and telling them of things to come. He will glorify the Son on earth, taking what is His and declaring it to them. Jesus Christ, having still much to say to His apostles, will speak to them by the Paraclete whom He will send. Since Christ will be glorified, having received all power from the Father, it will be to their advantage that He go away — "for if I do not go away, the Paraclete will not come to you; but if I depart, I will send Him to you" (John 16:7–15).

During these same ten days here below, the apostles, heeding the command of their Master, return to Jerusalem, to the upper room where Jesus instituted the Lord's Supper, where, together "with the women and Mary the mother of Jesus, and with His brothers," they await the promised Holy Spirit (Acts 1:12–14).

Pentecost

What is sometimes called the "Pentecost of Christ" happened at the beginning of our Lord's public ministry, when the Holy Spirit descended upon Him in the form of a dove at His baptism. The day of Pentecost, fifty days after Easter, saw the Holy Spirit descend upon the Church and the world. Under the old administration of the Covenant of Grace, under various forms from Adam to John the Baptist, there were only *gifts and actions* of the Holy Spirit. With the Church's Pentecost, under the new administration of the Covenant of Grace, these gifts and actions remain (and more abundantly so, as the New Testament, beginning with Acts, attests). But even further, with this new era of the Covenant of Grace *the Holy Spirit Himself is personally present*, just as Jesus promised that another Paraclete would come, descend, and remain eternally in the world with Christ's disciples (John 14:16). This Paraclete will even be *in them* (John 14:17) and pray with and in them "with groanings which cannot be uttered" (Romans 8:26). Indeed, this personal presence of the descended Holy Spirit is different from that of the incarnate Son during His life, in that the Spirit is not visible, although He is at times visibly manifested in His gifts and actions. But His presence is now so intimate, so personal, that He makes His dwelling in the hearts of the faithful. With Him in their hearts, they may prove the unity of love between the Father and the Son and, making humble beginnings in obedience to His Law-Word, prove the unity of love that also exists between the-Father-and-the-Son and them (John 14:20–21). "You will see Me. Because I live, you will live also" (John 14:19b).

Truly speaking, Christ is intimately with and within His people by the Spirit. In fact, we may even speak of the Holy Spirit as Christ's "other self" since the Son and the Spirit of the Father, though distinct, are, together with the Father, *one*. Since it was necessary that Jesus first ascend to the Father before He could send the Spirit, we see that it was not in spite of the Ascension, but precisely because of it, that Jesus could say to His disciples: "*I am with you*, even to the end of the age" (of the new age, of the new beginning). He is with them; He will be with them, in the Holy Spirit, His other self. This presence and working of the Holy Spirit, the Spirit of Christ, is the principle of faith and sanctification by grace in the lives of the faithful.

The Early Days of the Apostolic Church

The Apostolic Church will experience rapid growth beginning at Pentecost in A.D. 30. By *Apostolic Church*, we mean, quite simply, the Church in the apostles' time — from A.D. 30 to 70. This is the Church raised upon the first *stones* of the "dwelling place of God in the Spirit," the Church "built on the foundation of the apostles and the prophets, Jesus Christ Himself being the chief cornerstone" (Ephesians 2:20–22).

Together with the apostles, this foundation is composed of the *prophets* — undoubtedly those who had received "the communication of the Holy Spirit" in a miraculous way. In the Apostolic Church, the apostles, in conformity with the spiritual authority they received from the Lord (John 14:26; 15:16, 26; 16:12–14; 17:6–19), were capable of both verifying and authenticating *prophecy* by incorporating it, when they deemed necessary, into their teaching. They could also include this prophecy when they put their teaching in writing, whether this was done by the apostles themselves or by their faithful companions. This is what we have in the Gospels, Acts, Epistles, and Revelation.

God Himself bore witness to the testimony and teaching of the apostolic circle "with signs and wonders, with various miracles and gifts of the Holy Spirit" (Hebrews 2:4; cf. Acts 2:43).

*

In its early existence, the vast majority of the Church was Jewish. The very first church — the mother church in Jerusalem — was even exclusively Jewish. On the day of Pentecost, all 3,000 baptized were Jewish, whether those who lived in Jerusalem or the land of Israel, or those who came "from every nation under heaven." The apostles, "filled with the Holy Spirit," spoke "as the Holy Spirit gave them utterance," and, miraculously, everyone present heard the apostles' message "in their own language" (Acts 2:4–11).

On that day the prophecy of Joel began to be fulfilled, as Peter made known:

And it shall come to pass in the last days, says God,
That I will pour out of My Spirit on all flesh;
Your sons and your daughters shall prophesy,
Your young men shall see visions,
Your old men shall dream dreams.
And on My menservants and on My maidservants
I will pour out My Spirit in those days;
And they shall prophesy.
And I will show wonders in heaven above
And signs in the earth beneath:
Blood and fire and vapor of smoke.
The sun shall be turned into darkness,
And the moon into blood,
Before the coming of the great and awesome day of the Lord.
And it shall come to pass
That whoever calls on the name of the Lord
Shall be saved. (Acts 2:17–21; cf. Joel 2:28–32)

Undoubtedly Peter understood Joel's "the last days" to refer not to a future time, but to his present time. Although there are a few rare occasions in the New Testament where "the last day" refers to the day of resurrection and final judgment (John 6:39; 11:24), far more often "the last day[s]," "the latter times," "last time," or even "the last hour" refer to the apostolic times from A.D. 30 to 70. Let us take a moment to consider the following texts:

"The Last Times"

"Now the Spirit expressly says that in the latter times some will depart from the faith (*future tense*), giving heed to deceiving spirits...." Since the prophecy was finding its fulfillment at the time of Paul's writing, Paul then switches to the present tense: "They are forbidding them to marry" (1 Timothy 4:1–3).

Remember the words which were spoken before by the apostles of our Lord Jesus Christ: how they told you that there *would be* mockers in the last time;... *and now these cause* divisions, being sensual persons not having the Holy Spirit. (Jude 17–19)

"The Last Days"

Citing the prophet Joel, the author of Acts writes: "And it shall come to pass in the last days, says God, that I will pour out My Spirit on all flesh. Your sons and your daughters *shall prophesy*...." But the preceding verse alludes to the events which were happening at that time on the day of Pentecost, specifying that "*this is what* was spoken by the prophet Joel" (Acts 2:16–17).

"But know this, that in the last days perilous times *will come*: men *will be* lovers of themselves, lovers of money...." Paul adds that "of this sort *are* those who creep into houses..." (2 Timothy 3:1–9).

> God... has *in these last days* spoken to us by His Son. (Hebrews 1:2)

In a remark made to the rich, James says: "You have heaped up treasure *in the last days*" (James 5:3).

"The Last Hour"

> Little children, *it is the last hour*... even now many antichrists have come, by which we know that *it is* the last hour. (1 John 2:18)

A careful look at these texts shows that the references were to times, events, and persons that were present during the generation of the apostles (we will speak of "the Day of the Lord" shortly).

The prophet Joel's references to "blood and fire and vapor of smoke," with the sun changed into darkness and the moon into blood, with "wonders in heaven above and signs in the earth beneath," speak together of a great day of judgment on Israel, a judgment from which only those who called on the name of the Lord would escape. As we shall see, the apostolic generation — the last times — culminates with a great judgment on Jerusalem in A.D. 70 that fulfils Joel's prophecy.

The miraculous gift of speaking in foreign languages was inaugurated on the day of Pentecost and continued during the apostolic times, that is, the last times. This gift, according to Paul, was the fulfillment of Isaiah's prophecy against the Israel that would reject Christ, "the cornerstone." Isaiah looks to a time "when the overflowing scourge passes through, then you will be trampled down by it" (28:18). It is a time when, "with men of other tongues and other lips" the Lord "will speak to this people" (1 Corinthians 14:21; citing Isaiah 28:11). "Yet they would not hear. But the word of the LORD was to them, 'Precept upon precept...line upon line...here a little, there a little,' that they might go and fall backward, and be broken and snared and caught. Therefore hear the word of the LORD, you scornful men, who rule this people who are in Jerusalem" (Isaiah 28:12–14; cf. Matthew 21:42–44 and 1 Peter 2:6–8).

The Jews remain a priority for the Apostolic Church, even as Paul's ministry begins to win many converts from the nations (the "uncircumcised"). After all, the Jews (the "circumcised") were "the sons of the covenant." Moreover, the extent of the Jewish Diaspora — both geographically and numerically — was considerable. In the Roman Empire far more than a million Jewish souls were spread along the banks of the Mediterranean.

The preaching and teaching of the Apostolic Church were based on the Jewish Bible as understood in light of the Gospel of Jesus and the apostles, the Gospel concerning the person and work of the Messiah Jesus, Son of God and Son of Man. And so the "sons of the covenant" were, as a matter of priority, called to conversion (Acts 3:12–26).

The first Christians in Jerusalem were baptized Jews who, while breaking the bread of life in their homes, continued also, "day by day," to frequent the Temple together (Acts 2:42–46). Among them were also many priests who carried out their service at the Temple (Acts 6:7). The Christians of Jewish origin believed that so long as the Temple was still standing and its service still active, the ceremonial law retained its authority. With this in mind, we can understand why Paul, even after the Jerusalem Council of A.D. 49 declared circumcision was not required of Gentile Christians, decided to circumcise his disciple Timothy himself — Timothy was "the son of a certain Jewish woman who believed, but his father was Greek" (Acts 16:1ff.). In his second letter to the Thessalonians, written around A.D. 50, Paul does not hesitate to speak of the Temple in Jerusalem as "the Temple of God" (2 Thessalonians 2:4). Shortly before his arrest in Jerusalem in A.D. 57, Paul, who continued to observe the feast days of the Temple, took a Nazirite vow (Acts 18:18; 21:15–26). The Nazirites (from the Hebrew verb *nazar*, meaning "to set apart," "to consecrate") were Jews who dedicated themselves to God; the Nazirites looked to Numbers 6 as their charter of sorts.

And so, with the ancient era not yet ended, and the new era already underway, there was, for a time, an overlap between the two.

The Mission of the Apostolic Church

Israel + the Nations = the Church

The old administration of the covenant had prepared for, and was comprised of, the special people, Israel, placed in the midst of the nations. Life outside of Israel, and even life within Israel when it strayed from the God of the covenant and His Word, was more or less shrouded in darkness: "They do not know, nor do they understand; they walk about in darkness; all the foundations of the earth are unstable.... Arise, O God, judge the earth; for You shall inherit the nations" (Psalm 82:5, 8).

The covenant most certainly had the nations in view. One of Israel's purposes was to grow in faithfulness to God so that she would model for every nation what such corporate faithfulness looked like (Deuteronomy 4:5–8). Moreover, Israel was called to attract and gather many from the nations into her expanding life and borders (Exodus 34:22–24), and thus she was commanded to be open to the nations she approached or those which came to her. To this end, and contrary to what was accepted everywhere else in the world, there was not to be one law for Israelites and another for foreigners in her midst, but one and the same law for both (Exodus 12:49).

It is significant in this respect that the Feast of Tabernacles (that is, tents, or shelters), which was also the Feast of Ingathering (Exodus 23:16), heralded the nations' conversion to the true faith. Long neglected until it was taken up again by the returnees from the Babylonian exile, this feast found its true sense in the preaching of the later prophets. Haggai announced: "I will shake all nations, and they shall come to the Desire of All Nations, and I will fill this temple with glory" (Haggai 2:7). Likewise Zechariah prophesied: "And it shall come to pass that everyone who is left of all the nations which came against Jerusalem shall go up from year to year to worship the King, the LORD of hosts, and to keep the Feast of Tabernacles" (Zechariah 14:16).

In its detailed description of how the Feast of Tabernacles (or Ingathering) was to be celebrated (Numbers 29:12–38), the Torah commands that seventy bulls be sacrificed, which serves both as a memorial to the seventy nations coming from Noah and as a promise of the ingathering of the seventy nations into the Kingdom of God.

The first foreshadowings of this ingathering of the nations can be found in the influence of the patriarch Joseph, God's light to Egypt, the influence of the prophet Jonah, through whom the Ninevites acknowledged God, and the influence of the statesman and prophet Daniel, whose witness led Nebuchadnezzar and Darius to glorify God. When the Queen of Sheba came to Jerusalem to visit King Solomon, did she not bless the LORD (1 Kings 10:1–13)?

But now the history of the Covenant of Grace will enter into the "time of the nations" (Luke 21:24). Now God is going to open "the door of faith to the nations" (Acts 14:27). Now "all the nations shall come and worship before You because His justice has been revealed" (Revelation 15:4), coming to the city of God, where "the nations of those who are saved shall walk in its light, and the kings of the earth bring their glory and honor into it" (Revelation 21:24; Isaiah 60:3). "In bygone generations [God] allowed the nations to walk in their own ways," declared Paul, "Nevertheless He did not leave Himself without witness, in that He did good, gave us rain from heaven and fruitful seasons, filling our hearts with food and gladness" (Acts 14:16–17). Of these same nations Paul later says: "He has made from one blood every nation of men to dwell on all the face of the earth," whom during "these times of ignorance God overlooked, but now commands all men everywhere to repent" (Acts 17:26, 30).

The Missionary Mandate

Our Lord gave the Great Commission to His eleven disciples on a mountain in Galilee just before His ascension. Even if it wasn't until after Pentecost and the coming of the Holy Spirit that the nascent Church could fully understand her vocation, still, Christ's command, the Great Commission, was simple and succinct:

A DECLARATION:
"*All* authority has been given to Me in heaven and on earth."

A COMMANDMENT:

> "Go therefore and make disciples of *all* the nations, baptizing them in the name of the Father and of the Son and of the Holy Spirit, teaching them to observe *all things* that I have commanded you;"

A PROMISE:

> "and lo, I am with you *always* (lit. *all* the days), even to the end of the age." (Matthew 28:18–20)

The "Son-of-God-Son-of-Man," Jesus Christ, soon to take His seat at the right hand of the Father and receive all authority in heaven and on earth from the Trinitarian God, gives to His Church, represented here by the eleven, a great mandate. As we shall see, this missionary mandate both encompasses and expands upon the cultural mandate given to mankind at the very dawn of history. The scale of this mandate is emphasized by the fourfold use of the word "all" — twice in relation to the commandment — marking its three parts.

The commandment hinges upon the declaration, hence the "therefore" (*oûn* in Greek) — omitted in some translations. It is because Christ has received — and possesses — all authority that He commissions His Church to go to all nations. It is because Christ's authority is with, behind, and above His mission that the Church, the ambassador of her powerful Lord, can go.

While living on the earth, Jesus went only "to the lost sheep of the house of Israel" (Matthew 15:24). Only on occasion did the others receive "the crumbs which fall from the table," to use the humble and admirable expression of the Canaanite woman whose petition Jesus granted and whose faith He commended as *great*. In this same vein, He sent His disciples only to Israel (Matthew 10:5–6; 15:24).

But from this point forward, without forgetting the sons and daughters of Israel, Christ turns himself and His Church toward the nations (*ethnê* in Greek).

In giving the Church a mission to the nations, Jesus does not diminish the importance of the individual. The offer of the Gospel must be sincerely extended to individual persons in all times and places. After all, at stake is the salvation of human beings, called to repent and believe. But also at stake is the salvation, well-being, and peace of the nations, that is, societies as God would have them. The Son of God must "rule all nations" (Revelation 12:5). The nations must bow down before the Lord and come to walk in His light (Revelation 15:4; 21:24). These nations,[1] with their cultures, traditions, and religions turned away from the God of Holy Scripture, are called to be converted to a sure salvation. This conversion of a nation does not happen apart from the individual lives of faithful Christians, but precisely through the influence of such lives. Moreover, each nation's conversion is to reflect the uniqueness of that nation.

Our view of the scope of Christ's salvation should be not only individual and national, but also cosmic. The Lamb of God, John the Baptist tells us, has come to "take away the sin of the *world (kosmos)*" (John 1:29). God "so loved the *world* that He gave His Son." God "sent His Son into the world that the *world* through Him might be saved" (John 3:16–17). Jesus said: "I came to save the *world*" (John 12:47). And "He Himself is the propitiation for our sins, and not for ours only but also for the whole *world*" (1 John 2:2). Paul tells us that "God was in Christ reconciling the *world* to Himself" (2 Corinthians 5:19).

The world, the *kosmos*, is the universe of men and all sub-human realities. It is all that God created, all that was subjected to futility, all that groans and labors, eagerly waiting for the revealing of the sons of God (Romans 8:18ff.). All aspects of existence, both human and sub-human, make up the world. Christ desires to rule over all since He is now "above every name that is named" and "all things" have been put under His feet (Ephesians 1:21–22). Also, being sent by her Lord, the Church can — and must — take up the fight with arms which are not of the flesh, but are mighty before God for "pulling down strongholds, casting down arguments and every high thing that exalts itself against the knowledge of God, and bringing every thought into captivity to the obedience of Christ" (2 Corinthians 10:3–5). And that is to become, and will become, reality.

Make Disciples of the Nations

When we read the mandate to "make disciples of all nations," we should be careful to recognize all that is meant here. It is not "make disciples *from* the nations," as if the conversion of individuals from within every nation is all that is intended, but "make disciples *of* the

---

1. The word *ethnê* "people; nation," is far too often translated "gentiles; pagans."

nations" themselves. The Greek verb *mathéteuô* corresponds to the noun *mathétês*, "disciple," and can be equated with the English verb "to disciple." Just as individuals can be "discipled," so all nations must be "discipled." The personal, individual sense can and certainly must be upheld, as we have previously said, but the social scope of the commandment must not be downplayed.

Whether individual-disciples or nation-disciples (a disciple being one who hears and follows the Master), each must be baptized and taught to obey all that Christ has commanded. Concerning the baptism of the nations, Isaiah's prophecy speaks of the Servant of the Lord (the Messiah) who, after His ascension, "shall sprinkle many nations. Kings shall shut their mouths at Him; for what had not been told them they shall see, and what they had not heard they shall consider" (Isaiah 52:15).

Paul, the apostle to the uncircumcised (that is, non-Jews), cited this text from Isaiah when he wrote: "And so I have made it my aim to preach the gospel where Christ had not been named" (Romans 15:20).

"To make disciples of all nations" is to lead both individuals and nations to faith in, and obedience to, Christ, God made man. Without question, everything depends on the sovereignty of the efficacious grace of the Lord-Savior. But, under this sovereignty, the call goes forth to individual people and, where there is a great number of people, to entire nations, to be baptized and taught to observe all that Christ has commanded. To such persons and nations it may be necessary to ask: "What has become of your baptism?"

When it comes to observing all that Christ has commanded, there is a real and profound unity between *baptism* and *teaching*. First, both baptism in the triune Name and the apostolic teaching (the apostles' teaching and/or the teaching faithful to the apostles' teaching) are under the authority of the Trinitarian God. Additionally, baptism in the triune Name and the apostolic teaching are both part of the revelation of the Triune God — the name of the Father, Son, and Holy Spirit are none other than the revelation of the Holy Scriptures from beginning to end of the One who is the Lord, Creator, and Savior.[2]

---

2. Biblically, the "name" reveals the person (his character traits, his works). Cf. in the Old Testament — and this is only a sample! — Psalm 5:11; 9:10; 22:22; 23:3; 25:11; 75:1; 76:1; 89:16, 24; 119:55; Jeremiah 10:6; Ezekiel 20:44; Micah 4:5; Malachi 3:16; in the New Testament: John 17:6; Acts 9:15. Also, blasphemy is neither the only nor even the principal aim of the third word of the Decalogue, but rather what is forbidden above all is the spurning or refusal of God's revela-

The baptized person (or nation) is sent to the school of the Bible to learn from the Holy Spirit and through the faithful Church to unlock the mystery of God's Word and observe its commandments.

*

The Church, that is, this Jerusalem above, the mother of us all (Galatians 4:26), this heavenly Jerusalem where all the baptized are citizens (Hebrews 12:22; Philippians 3:20), this new Jerusalem descending from heaven (Revelation 21:2), this holy Jerusalem which has the twelve apostles of the Lamb for its foundation (Revelation 21:10–14), has a mission — a mission that it has received from Christ and from His power "on earth and in heaven." It is "to make disciples" of individuals and families from all nations, and to make disciples of all nations themselves (Acts 2:38–39), baptizing them and teaching them to observe *all that Christ has commanded*. By this we understand Him to mean:

- *the Bible* (the Torah of Moses, the Prophets, and the Writings) which Christ received, acknowledged, and guaranteed and sealed as the authoritative Word of God even in its smallest details (Luke 24:44; Matthew 5:17–20);
- and *the Tradition* (the Truth to be passed down) that Christ, even before it was *written*, entrusted to His apostles, which He declared, communicated, guaranteed, and sealed as having divine authority, first, when He was on earth, until His ascension, by His teaching, His promises and prayer, then, after Pentecost, by the Holy Spirit whom He had especially promised them (Luke 10:16; 24:44–48; John 14:25–26; 16:13–15; 17:6–19).

THE APOSTLES

True to the promise accompanying the missionary commandment: "*I am* with you always, even to the end of the age," and the prophecy of the Resurrected One: "You shall be witnesses to Me in Jerusalem,

---

tion of Himself (Exodus 20:7; Isaiah 52:5; Jeremiah 34:16; Proverbs 30:9).

and in all Judea and Samaria, and to the end of the earth," the apostles will live to see the immediate fulfillment of these words between the years A.D. 30 and 70.

There were *twelve plus one* apostles (twelve to signify the faithful remnant of Israel and the continuity of the Covenant of Grace; one to signify the grafting of the nations into Israel). Three of these — Peter, Paul, and John — will illustrate this unique period.

Peter

The apostle Peter (Simon, *Képhas*) was one of the very first disciples, the spokesman for the Twelve, and appointed their leader by Jesus himself (Luke 22:32; John 21:15–19). His figure dominates the first part of Acts (1–12), from Pentecost in A.D. 30 until his arrest in 44 during the persecution ordered by Herod Agrippa I, grandson of Herod the Great, in the course of which the apostle James, John's brother, was beheaded (Acts 12:2). After leading the mother church in Jerusalem — which he did at least until the stoning of the first martyr, the deacon-preacher Stephen, in 37 — Peter was one of the evangelists, along with the deacon-preacher Philip, who spread the Gospel throughout Judea, Galilee, and Samaria. Although officially "the apostle to the circumcised," he was the first to baptize the uncircumcised, the non-Jews, of whom the first was Cornelius. Cornelius was a centurion of what was called the Italian Cohort. He was also a "God-fearer," a term used for those who, though Gentiles, had some spiritual kinship to the Jews. Before visiting him, Peter had the strange vision of a large sheet descending from heaven containing all sorts of animals, *both clean and unclean.* By the Holy Spirit, Peter understood that the Lord, through these symbols, was showing him there was no further distinction between Israelites and Gentiles in the Church, the New Israel descending from heaven.

Peter took part in the Jerusalem Council in the year 49 with the other apostles, including Paul and the elders, presided over by James, one of Jesus' brothers, who had succeeded Peter as the leader of the Church. This council gathered to address the question of the relationship between the Church and the Gentiles. After hearing the reports of Peter and James, they addressed a letter to "the brethren who are of the Gentiles in Antioch, Syria and Cilicia" along the southern coast of Asia Minor. According to the letter, these Gentile brethren would not have to be circumcised, and the uncircumcised would have their place in the Church (Acts 15).

At a date not precisely known — around 60? — Peter went to Rome. At least one of the two letters we possess by Peter in the New Testament was written from Rome (cf. 1 Peter 5:13). Reliable traditions also tell us that it was in Rome in A.D. 67, during the persecution ordered by Nero after the burning of Rome in 64, that Peter died a martyr (being crucified like Jesus, but upside-down).

Paul

The apostle Paul (Acts 13–28) is sometimes called "the supernumerary apostle," meaning "the apostle in addition to the Twelve." He is more commonly known as "Apostle to the Uncircumcised," the "Apostle to the Nations," and he is the dominant figure of the second part of the Book of Acts (Acts 13–28).

Born a Roman citizen in the city of Tarsus in Cilicia, Paul was a Jew of the tribe of Benjamin, a Pharisee, trained under the renowned Rabbi Gamaliel (Acts 22:3). In the immediate aftermath of Pentecost, Saul, as he was then known, was one of the fiercest persecutors of the Church. He had approved the stoning of Stephen. He "made havoc of the church, entering every house, and dragging off men and women, committing them to prison." In A.D. 37, while "still breathing threats and murder against the disciples of the Lord," Saul journeyed to Damascus, intent on discovering Christians there to "bring them bound to Jerusalem." Instead, on the way, he was confronted by Jesus, who called to him in a vision.

Abruptly converted, then baptized, Paul immediately proclaimed the Gospel of the Son of God in the very city of Damascus (Acts 7:55–8:4; 9:1–22; Galatians 1:15–17)! The apostles initially received this news with skepticism. However, thanks to Barnabas, a Christian of Jewish and Cyprian background, Paul was able to convince them of the genuineness of his faith and conversion.

He subsequently stayed in Jerusalem for some time, accompanying the apostles in their preaching of the Gospel. But when they learned of planned attempts on Paul's life, the disciples urged him to take refuge in his hometown, Tarsus. He remained there ten years, from 37 to 47, in complete anonymity. We know nothing about this time other than that it served to prepare him for the ten years that followed, from 47 to 57, when, over the course of three "missionary journeys," he planted churches in Asia minor, Macedonia, and Greece.

After his arrest in Jerusalem in 57, he spent two years as a prisoner in Caesarea (Acts 24:27). Being a Roman citizen, he "appealed to Caesar," thus invoking his right to be judged in Rome, and thus he was sent to Rome in 59.

Paul died a martyr in Rome in 67, as did Peter. He was beheaded, rather than crucified, since Roman citizens could not be executed by crucifixion. In all he spent ten years as a prisoner, though the conditions of his detainment were at times less restrictive (cf. Acts 28:23, 30).

John

The figure of John, in large part thanks to his Book of Revelation, dominates the last *seven* of the old covenant, being the seven years from 64 (the beginning of Nero's great persecution) to 70, when the Temple was destroyed. More specifically, his ministry deals with the "time, times and half a time," the three and a half years spanning from the martyrdom of Peter and Paul in 67 to the destruction of Jerusalem in 70 (Daniel 7:25; 12:7; Revelation 12:14). John experienced the tribulation of a great many of his brothers in the faith, spending at least part of this span of time in exile, banished "for the word of God and for the testimony of Jesus Christ" to the isle of Patmos, between Greece and Asia Minor (Revelation 1:9).

Both John and his brother James[3] were cousins of Jesus, and both were apostles as well.

---

3. This James is not to be confused with another among "the twelve," James the son of Alphaeus (Matthew 10:3; Acts 1:13), nor with James the brother of Jesus, as were also Joseph, Simon, and Jude (Matthew 13:55). While all we know of his father is his name, Zebedee, we know that his mother, Salome, was the sister of the Blessed Mary (all that is needed to prove this is to align Mark 15:47 and 16:1 with Matthew 27:55–56 and John 19:25). When recounting Jesus' crucifixion and entombment, the Gospels mention four women in particular: three Marys (the mother of Jesus, the mother of James and Joseph, and Mary Magdalene) and a fourth whom Mark names Salome, while Matthew calls her "the mother of the sons of Zebedee" and John calls her "His mother's sister," that is, the sister of Jesus' mother. Just as John does not give his own name in his Gospel, referring to himself simply as "the disciple whom Jesus loved" (13:23; 19:26; 20:2; 21:20), in the same way does he veil his mother's name (cf. Matthew 27:55; Mark 15:40; John 19:25–27). As one very close to the Lord, it was he to whom Jesus, while hanging on the cross, entrusted the care of the Blessed Mary: "Behold your mother!"

On three occasions we find the apostles Peter and the brothers James and John taken aside from the other disciples: at the raising of Jairus' daughter, at our Lord's transfiguration, and at the hour of His testing and temptation in the Garden of Gethsemane (Mark 5:37; 9:2; 14:33).

Immediately after Pentecost we find John working alongside Peter (Acts 3:1ff.; 4:7, 13; 8:14). He remained in the mother church in Jerusalem for quite some time (Galatians 2:9), but solid patristic tradition has him eventually residing in Ephesus with the Blessed Mary, and then from Ephesus he was exiled to Patmos. It was from Patmos, around 67 or 68, that he wrote his *Apocalypse* and *1 John*. Intended to encourage the persecuted Church as it passed through the tribulation, he revealed to them ("apocalypse" means "revelation") a series of visions, things he had seen and heard on the Lord's Day. He describes in detail the next Epiphany (that is, appearance) of the Lord Jesus Christ, the sovereign Rector over all history, the Judge of His own people, the One to whom the seven churches of Asia, and through them all churches, are to pray, worship, hear, and follow: *the One who is and who was and who is to come* (Revelation 1:4).[4]

The Apocalypse of John, like the *apocalypses* of the three synoptic Gospels (Matthew 24; Mark 13; Luke 21), is in no way comparable to the Jewish writings of the second and first centuries B.C., nor with those of the first century A.D. These writings are often called "apocalyptic" (that is, revelational), but wrongly so — it is worth noting that they never refer to themselves as "apocalyptic." In fact, these "apocalyptic" Jewish writings are riddled with gratuitous and incomprehensible *symbols* in stark contrast to the symbols of *The Apocalypse* of John which are grounded in the *Jewish Bible*: the Torah, Prophets, and Psalms. Furthermore, the "Jewish apocalyptic" writings are typically pessimistic and show little regard for history, flying off into arbitrary speculations; John's *Apocolypse*, by contrast, is not only fundamentally optimistic, but also holds fast to history, for it is over history that John sees the Lord reigning. Finally, these writings are not concerned with the moral life and behavior of their readers; in *The Apocalypse*, however, the emphasis on ethical living is plain and clear.

---

4. It has been said that this expression makes for atrocious Greek, but excellent theology!

Jews against Jews

The apostolic times experienced a spiritual war waged within Israel, a spiritual war between the Jews who rejected the Messiahship of Jesus and the Jews who converted to receive Jesus Christ. Far from being localized in Palestine, this spiritual war affected those in the Diaspora abroad as well.

But whereas the Jewish converts to Christ and, with them, the entire Apostolic Church, limited themselves to *spiritual weapons*, the same cannot be said of their adversaries (Ephesians 6:10–18; 1 Thessalonians 5:8; 1 Peter 5:8–9). Jewish opposition to the Gospel — usually sporadic, though at times more epidemic, such as the years 37 and 44 — did not hesitate to employ violence and hatred. Persecuting, beating, imprisoning, and sometimes even putting to death those who followed Christ, they shamelessly sought the support of the secular arm of Rome. Both the book of Acts, from beginning to end, and the apostolic letters, witness to this. Though not spared from these persecutions, the churches and Christians in great number not only survived, but indeed thrived, as the Church grew prodigiously throughout the whole Empire.

God's covenantal indictment against unfaithful Israel was clearly spelled out in the sum of Jesus' preaching during His ministry, and it was repeatedly set forth by the apostles, elders, and deacons when they addressed the Jews in the synagogues, in the Temple, or elsewhere. This indictment announced that "the wrath of God is revealed from heaven against all ungodliness and unrighteousness of men," including those among both the Jews and the nations (Romans 1:18; 2:12–24; 3:27–30). Because the people of the covenant have manifested their apostasy in rejecting God's Messiah-King and calling for His crucifixion (John 19:14–16), there are now coming upon them the "days of vengeance, that all things which are written may be fulfilled" (Luke 21:22). These are the days that Jesus had earlier foretold would take place in "this generation" (Luke 21:32). Revelation says they are going to come "quickly" and "soon." And indeed they did, for it was in 67 or 68 — within a generation of Christ's crucifixion in A.D. 30, quite quickly! — that judgment came.

But in the preaching of Jesus and the apostolic circle, the indictment is never the whole message. It is always accompanied with a sincere and insistent appeal, addressed first to the Jews, to be reconciled to God through Christ. At the very end of Revelation comes the last beatitude, which is also an exhortation:

> Blessed are those who wash their robes,
> that they may have the right to the tree of life,
> and may enter through the gates into the city. (Revelation 22:14)

The Seven Signs

The Seven Warning Signs Fulfilled

Just as Jesus had foretold, "this generation" — being the time of the apostles — would see the fulfillment of the seven signs that warned of His coming as the Son and Judge of His people.

Sign #1 — "False Christs" (Luke 21:8)

Not wanting the Apostolic Church to be deceived concerning the things to come, Jesus put her on guard. The first sign would consist in the arrival of false Christs, those claiming to be Christ himself: "For many will come in My name, saying, 'I am He,' and 'The time has drawn near.' Therefore do not go after them" (Luke 21:8).

Still, many Christian converts from Judaism failed to heed this warning and were deceived. The longing for a conquering Messiah-King to liberate the land from the oppressive yoke of Rome and win back the kingdom for Israel was strong. Many false Messiahs preyed on that longing, and with no small measure of success. A precursor to these false Christs is doubtless found in Simon, of whom many said, "This man is the great power of God!" (Acts 8:9–11). The apostle John draws attention to this growing number of false Christs in two of his letters, written around A.D. 60–65, in which John refers to them as "antichrists" to be revealed in "the last hour" — "even now many antichrists *have come*, by which we know that it is the last hour" (1 John 2:18–19, 22–23, 26; 4:6; 2 John 7–11).

As Jesus had forewarned, the generation of the apostles indeed witnessed the arrival of many false Christs.

Sign #2 – "Wars and Rumors of Wars"

The Mediterranean world enjoyed the famous *Pax Romana* (Roman Peace), beginning with the long reign of Augustus from 27 B.C. to A.D. 14. This peace, which would continue through the reigns of Tiberius Caesar (14–37), Caligula (37–41), Claudius (41–54), and Nero (54–68), facilitated the swift expansion of the faith and of the Christian Church; the triumphant advance of Christ. As the French poet Péguy sang in his *Eve*, "The steps of legions marched for Him."

But the peace would not last; things fell apart at the end of Nero's reign:

- Even during Nero's own lifetime, there was the conspiracy of Piso, which was quelled by a severe repression (64–65).
- After Nero's death came civil wars which nearly destroyed the empire. At this time, three emperors — Vitellius, Otho, and Vespasian — vied for power with Emperor Galba (68). Over the course of the next year, each of these would proclaim themselves emperor. Thus 69 is remembered as the "year of the Four Emperors." From this confusion Vespasian would emerge and remain the lone emperor from A.D. 69–79
- In addition to recording the end of the Julio-Claudian dynasty with Nero and its aftermath up to the death of Domitian in A.D. 96, the historian Tacitus (A.D. 55–120) also chronicles significant troubles outside of Rome. He reports that several provinces, in dividing Gaul, attempted to take advantage of the civil wars to regain their own independence.
- Finally, there was the Jewish War (A.D. 66–70), which we will examine later.

The *Pax Romana* was no more. "Wars and rumors" — the second warning sign! — had come indeed. "Nation against nation, kingdom against kingdom," just as Jesus had foretold.

Sign #3 — "Famines and Earthquakes"

The third warning sign was "famines and earthquakes in various places." The Book of Acts tells us of a prophet in the Jerusalem Church named Agabus. This man, who came down to Antioch with the other apostles, "declared by the Spirit that there would be a great famine throughout all the world" (Acts 11:27–30). This phrase "all the world" (*olen ten oikoumenen* in Greek) refers in this case, as it does elsewhere in the apostles' writings, to the Mediterranean world, the world of the Roman Empire. We learn in Acts that "[this great famine] happened in the days of Claudius Caesar," who ruled the Empire from A.D. 41–54. In another book, *The Annals*, Tacitus alludes to this famine — "Scanty crops too, and consequent famine were regarded as a token of calamity." The food supply in the capital dwindled to the point that "Rome had provisions for no more than fifteen days." Furthermore, in that same year, "houses were thrown down by frequent shocks of earthquake."[5]

From A.D. 55–57, Paul had to call upon the churches of Macedonia, including the churches of Philippi, Greece, and Corinth, to take up large collections for the believers and the poor in the church of Jerusalem, who were lacking even basic necessities (Romans 15:26; 1 Corinthians 16:1; 2 Corinthians 8:20).

We also learn from the reports of Flavius Josephus (A.D. 37–101) that Jerusalem, in the year 67 (a year in which the city was already threatened by attacks from Roman and Edomite assailants), was struck by an earthquake.

In his *Annals*, Tacitus also tells of earthquakes during that time from Crete to Phrygia and from Rome to Asia Minor.

"Famines and earthquakes in various places" were notable during the apostolic generation, in the years before the destruction of Jerusalem, just as Jesus had foretold.

Josephus' The Jewish Wars

Since we have just mentioned him, and will be referring to his work often, let us point out here the importance of Josephus' *The Jewish Wars*, a book which sheds light on the last seventy years of the old administration of the covenant.

Of priestly origin, Joseph ben Mallathias ha-Cohen became a military officer and historian, though not one remembered for his courage! Having become a general in the Jewish army, and having quickly understood that their defeat at the hands of the Romans under

---

5. Tacitus, *The Annals*, Bk. XII, 43.

Vespasian's command was all but assured, he abandoned his post and defected to the enemy. Once on the Roman side, he assisted in the storming of Jerusalem and the destruction of the Temple. He was subsequently showered with the favors of the new emperor Vespasian and his successor Titus, and eventually settled in Rome. There he wrote his three principal works, all in Greek: *Contra Apion*, a defense of Judaism; *Jewish Antiquities*, a history of Israel from the Creation to the Jewish War of 66; and *The Jewish Wars*. Josephus' works reveal that The Jewish War lasted from the month of Artemesios (May–June), A.D. 66, until the storming of Jerusalem by Titus on the 8th of Gorpialos (September 26), A.D. 70. The war comprehended three significant phases:

1st phase: A period of troubles and insurrection under the procurator Genius Florus, from May to October of A.D. 66.

2nd phase: A military expedition by Cestius, procurator of Syria, from October to November of A.D. 66.

3rd phase: The Jewish War "proper," comprising four campaigns (the first three under Vespasian):
- The first, from April to November of A.D. 67.
- The second, from March to June of A.D. 68.
- The third, from April to June of A.D. 69.
- The fourth, from May to September of A.D. 70, under the command of Titus (Vespasian had become the Emperor). On May 1, Titus sets up camp outside of Jerusalem. On August 5, the perpetual sacrifice is interrupted. On August 29, the Temple is burned down. On September 26, there were massacres and fire in the Holy City.

Josephus' works record for us the extent and intensity of the suffering and death experienced by the Jews in A.D. 70, but we will examine the events of that crucial year only after we conclude our brief look at the rest of the warning signs Jesus gave to "this generation."

Sign #4 — The Martyrdom of Those Who Endure to the End

The false Christs, the wars and rumors of wars, the famines and earthquakes, were only "the beginning of sorrows" (a Greek expression referring to the pains of childbirth; Matthew 24:8). The Kingdom of God, ushering in the new era of the Covenant of Grace, would not be established without such pains. The sufferings of the Head, Christ, would be filled out with those it lacked: the sufferings of the Body, the Church (cf. 2 Corinthians 4:10, Colossians 1:24, Acts 9:4). It is this time of persecution that the twelfth chapter of Revelation, using symbols drawn from the prophets, describes: "And the dragon was enraged with the woman, and he went to make war with the rest of her offspring, who keep the commandments of God and have the testimony of Jesus Christ" (12:17).

The martyrdom of those who endured, foretold by Jesus (Matthew 24:9, 13), is the continuation of the birth pangs. The Book of Acts, the letters of the Apostles, and Revelation witness to their martyrdom.

Hupomonè

The kind of endurance of the faithful that Jesus foretells and encourages is better understood when we grasp the meaning of the Greek word *hupomonè*, translated in our English Bibles as "patience" in some places, "perseverance" in others. The etymology is instructive. The noun, *hupomonè*, and also the verb, *hupoménô* (from the verb *menô* meaning "to rest" or "to exist," and the preposition *hupo* meaning "under"), evokes the sense of "to bear" or "to hold up." By "patience" we do not buckle under the weight of trials and suffering; we "endure." By "perseverance" we bear the duration of the ordeal with patience; we "wait" to the end. The virtue and power of *hupomonè* are manifested spectacularly in martyrdom, in which one who is faithful both holds up and holds out under the weight and duration of trials.

The verb *hupoménô* appears fifteen times, and the noun *hupomenè* thirty times, in the apostolic writings, for good reason. It aptly characterizes the faithful Christians of "the last times," that is, the apostolic times that were also the "first times," the times that gave birth to the Kingdom of God.

In the face of persecution, it was necessary that God supply, stir up, sustain, and renew "the *hupomonè* [the persevering patience] and the faith of the saints" (Revelation 13:10). After all, when the Son of Man would soon come to bring judgment on Israel, would He find faith on the earth (i.e., the land of Israel) and would God speedily avenge His elect who cry out day and night to Him (Luke 18:7–8; Revelation 6:9–11)?

Following the first wave of tribulations faced by the Apostolic Church at the hands of their Jewish persecutors, there came a second wave of tribulations, this time under the fierce direction of Rome. The execution of two of the three great apostles, Peter and Paul, in A.D. 67, was only the beginning of this second wave — a great number of believers would "persevere" in their wake. Still, the martyrdom of both Peter and Paul was significant in that it confirmed the newfound truth held dear by the Church. The Jewish converts to Christianity who had received Christ through the ministry of the apostle to the circumcised were indeed *one, in Christ*, with the Gentile converts to Christianity who had received Christ through the ministry of the apostle to the uncircumcised.

The third of these great apostles of the Apostolic Church, John, was banished and secluded on the island of Patmos. From there he would write the Book of Revelation, whose message was intended to strengthen the faith and patience of the contemporary cross-bearing Apostolic Church. The Roman Empire, "the beast rising out of the sea," and apostate Judaism, the "beast coming up out of the earth," will be powerless to stop the New Jerusalem from descending from heaven, the Church and Bride who celebrates its eternal wedding to the Lamb in the Lord's Supper. Though that serpent of old, the dragon, rears up against the woman, he is definitively conquered by the incarnation, death, resurrection, and ascension to heaven of the God-man, who now judges the former house of God. Satan is progressively beaten back as the Church knocks down his gates one by one throughout the course of history — these gates cannot prevail against her. He will be crushed once for all when Christ returns in glory to raise the dead, judge the world, and make all things new. This powerful vision fortified the faith of the saints in John's day, enabling them to endure, with courage and hope, the various tribulations that came upon them. All the powers of the visible world arrayed against them, coming from the earthly Jerusalem and Rome, were doomed to fall before the power of the new Jerusalem above.

The Beginning of the Roman Persecution of Christians under Nero

Until the year A.D. 64, the Christians had been afforded protection under Rome's laws and by several of its high-ranking officials, such as Gallio the Roman proconsul in Corinth (Acts 18:12–16), the tribune Lysias in Jerusalem (Acts 23:12–35), and procurator Festus in Caesarea (Acts 25).

It was the burning of Rome, which began in the middle of the night on July 18th, in the year 64, that triggered the first persecution of Christians at the hands of the nations (the Roman Empire being composed of many nations). It compounded the persecution already wrought by the Jews, and certainly surpassed it in intensity. Numerous waves of persecution would follow until the Edict of Milan, enacted by Constantine the Great in 313.

Nero became emperor in A.D. 54 at the young age of 17. While under the restraining influence of Seneca, the leader of the Senate, and Burrus, the head of the legions, he posed no threat to the Christians. But that changed when, in 62, Burrus died and an anxious Seneca resigned.

That year an unleashed Nero, and Rome with him, became the beast of Revelation 13 (by contrast, Romans 13:1–7 was written in A.D. 57, in the first part of Nero's reign). An actor, both a comedian and a tragedian who enjoyed organizing and putting on various spectacles, and a true megalo*maniac* in every sense of the word, Nero resorted to murders of a most infamous sort, thinking they would secure his mad and bloody reign. Those meeting a tragic fate included his brother, Brittanicus, his own mother, Agrippina, his successive wives, Octavia and Pompei, and his master, Seneca. After the Senate finally deposed him in A.D. 68, he committed suicide. He was 31 years old.

The burning of Rome in 64 was grandiose, a real spectacle in Nero's eyes. It broke out in the wooden booths on the southeastern side of the Circus Maximus, near Mount Palatin, and burned seven nights and six days. Fanned by relentless winds, the fire broke out again and consumed the Field of Mars, burning for another three days. Only four of the city's fourteen districts were spared. Temples, monuments, and centuries-old collections of Greek art were reduced to dust and ashes. Thousands of human lives fell victim to the flames.

According to Tacitus and his contemporary Suetone, Nero himself had the city burned, desiring to rebuild a more modern and glorious city in its place, which he planned to name Neopolis.

The Christians were immediately accused by Nero and the populace of having started the fire. By this time, and owing largely to Paul's trial and proclamation of the Word of God, they were no longer considered a sect within Judaism, but had come to be thought of as a *genus tertium*, a third race. That Nero and others blamed them is no great surprise. After all, Tacitus and Suetone referred to the Christian faith as an *exitiabilis superstitio*, a baneful superstition. Tacitus even went so far as to accuse Christians of hating the human race (*odium generis humani*). They were rumored to have committed secret crimes, including the eating of child sacrifices. They were proclaimed atheists because of their refusal to sacrifice to the gods, and anti-Romans because they appealed to a King greater than Caesar.

Writing from Rome to the Church in Corinth in A.D. 70, Clement reports that "a vast multitude of the elect" have "suffered many torments and tortures."[6] The Epistle to the Hebrews, written around 67, speaks of those who "were made a spectacle by reproaches and tribulations" (Hebrews 10:32–34). Peter's first epistle, composed in the spring of 65, contains this exhortation: "Beloved, do not think it strange concerning the fiery trial which is to try you.... [B]ut rejoice to the extent that you partake of Christ's sufferings." This is followed by a prophecy pertaining to events that are soon to take place: "For the time has come for the judgment to begin at the house of God; and if it begins with us first, what will be the end of those who do not obey the gospel?" (1 Peter 4:12–13, 17).

History records that a large number of enduring faithful — those who displayed *hupomonè* — were massacred. Some were crucified. Some were thrown to the beasts in the arena. Others were smeared with pitch and used as torches to light the imperial gardens through which Nero would triumphantly parade his chariot, whipping his horses all the way to the applause of the crowds.

It is abundantly clear that Jesus' fourth warning sign was fulfilled in the *oïkoumené*, the inhabited land, that is, the Roman Empire. Rome, queen of the nations, and Jerusalem, the apostate Holy City, are joined together in Revelation as one symbolic city, "Babylon the Great, the

---

6. Clement of Rome, *First Clement*, 6.1.

mother of harlots and of the abominations of the earth... drunk with the blood of the saints and with the blood of the martyrs of Jesus" (Revelation 17:5–6).

Sign #5 — The Apostasy of a Great Number

Jesus had announced the external danger that would menace the Apostolic Church. They would face persecution, but would overcome it by *hupomonè*, persevering patience. But He also forewarned of a second and equally formidable threat, this time arising from within. "Many false prophets will rise up and deceive many" (Matthew 24:11).

The apostles followed Jesus in this admonition, warning Christians and the Church throughout their ministries. Paul used the occasion of a stopover in Miletus in 47 to warn the leaders of the Church in Ephesus:

> Therefore take heed to yourselves and to all the flock, among which the Holy Spirit has made you overseers, to shepherd the church of God which He purchased with His own blood. For I know this, that after my departure savage wolves will come in among you, not sparing the flock. Also from among yourselves men will rise up, speaking perverse things, to draw away the disciples after themselves. (Acts 20:28–30)

In his letters Paul constantly warns the faithful against heresies. (Every heresy, according to the meaning of the Greek noun *haïresis*, "to choose," consists in preferring one aspect of Revelation to the whole. For this reason, *Sola Scriptura* is not enough; we must also hold to *Tota Scriptura*.) He calls on them not to be "tossed to and fro with every wind of doctrine, with the trickery of men, in the cunning craftiness of deceitful plotting" (Ephesians 4:14). He reminds Timothy that there is one holy and good "doctrine which accords with godliness," and warns him, with an eye toward the future, against other doctrines, "doctrines of demons."[7] Paul is emphatic on this point:

> Now the Spirit expressly says that in the latter times some will depart from the faith, giving heed to deceiving spirits and doctrines of demons, speaking lies in hypocrisy, having their own conscience seared with a hot iron. (1 Timothy 4:1–2)

---

7. 1 Timothy 1:3, 10; 4:1, 6; 6:3.

> But know this, that in the last days perilous times will come.... [There will be men] having a form of godliness but denying its power. And from such people turn away! (2 Timothy 3:1–5)

At the time of his writing Timothy, Paul had already encountered apostates such as Demas and Alexander the coppersmith.[8]

The concerns and warnings expressed by Paul are prevalent in other epistles. John, writing around A.D. 65, expressly says:

> It is the last hour; and as you have heard that the Antichrist is coming, even now many antichrists have come, by which we know that it is the last hour. They went out from us, but they were not of us; for if they had been of us, they would have continued with us; but they went out that they might be made manifest, that none of them were of us. (1 John 2:18–19)

And once more:

> For many deceivers have gone out into the world who do not confess Jesus Christ as coming in the flesh. This is a deceiver and an antichrist. Look to yourselves,... Whoever... does not abide in the doctrine of Christ does not have God. He who abides in the doctrine of Christ has both the Father and the Son. If anyone comes to you and does not bring this doctrine, do not receive him into your house nor greet him. (2 John 7–10)

As early as A.D. 62 we find Jude, the brother of the Lord and of James, urging his audience to:

> Contend earnestly for the faith which was once for all delivered to the saints. For certain men have crept in unnoticed,... ungodly men,... who deny the only Lord and our Lord Jesus Christ.... [B]eloved, remember the words which were spoken before by the apostles of our Lord Jesus Christ: how they told you that there would be mockers in the last time who would walk according to their own ungodly lusts. These are sensual persons, who cause divisions, not having the Spirit. (Jude 3–5, 17–19)

---

8. 2 Timothy 4:10, 14.

And the Epistle to the Hebrews, written around A.D. 67, issues this warning: "Do not be carried away with various and strange doctrines" (Hebrews 13:9).

Not only will the persecution intensify, but the heresies will worsen as well, culminating in the apostasy of many. Jesus had announced this fifth warning sign: "Then many false prophets will rise up and deceive many. And because lawlessness will abound, the love of many will grow cold" (Matthew 24:11–12).

Sign #6 — The Gospel Preached to All the Nations

The sixth and penultimate warning sign in Jesus' Olivet Discourse is His declaration that the good news of the Kingdom "will be preached in all the world as a witness to the nations" (Matthew 24:14; Mark 13:10; Luke 21:13ff.).

One of the extraordinary evidences of the power of the Holy Spirit advancing and accompanying the preaching of the Word of God in apostolic times was the rapidity with which the Gospel made its way to all the nations of the *oïkoumené*. In the New Testament, this Greek word, translated as "world" or "land," most often refers to the Roman Empire, such as when Luke tells us that "a decree went out from Caesar Augustus that all the world (*oïkoumené*) should be registered" (Luke 2:1).[9] In the same way, "all the nations" was understood to mean the *oïkoumené*, the Roman Empire. The Jews were likewise considered part of the *oïkoumené*, though the Gospel was preached first to them to the end that many of them might escape the impending judgment on Jerusalem.[10]

Furthermore, we have Paul's own testimony that the Gospel was indeed preached to all the nations during his own lifetime. He writes to the Romans: "I thank my God through Jesus Christ for you all, that your faith is spoken of throughout the whole world" (1:8). He addresses the Colossians concerning the Gospel "which has come to you, as it has also in all the world," later referring to it as "the gospel which you heard, which was preached to every creature under heaven" (1:6, 23).

---

9. Cf. also Luke 4:5; 21:26; Acts 11:28; 17:6, 31; 19:27; 24:5; Romans 10:18; Revelation 3:10; 12:9; 16:14.

10. Cf. Romans 1:15; 2:9–10; Acts 2:29–41; 21:21; 24:5, etc.

Sign # 7 — The Abomination of Desolation

Jesus comes to the last of the seven warning signs — "the abomination of desolation of which the prophet Daniel spoke, set up in the holy place" (Matthew 24:15).

The Book of Daniel speaks of the "seventy weeks" — literally, the "seventy sevens" — leading up to the last *seven* of the ancient era of the Covenant of Grace. Its "desolations" and "abominations" mark this last *seven* (9:26–27). Later, it indicates that "forces shall be mustered, ... they will profane the sanctuary, ... they will take away the daily sacrifices, and place there the abomination of desolation" (11:31). Later still, it speaks again concerning the "time that the daily sacrifice is taken away and the abomination of desolation is set up" (12:11).

In the Hebraic Bible, "abomination," *shiqûs*, or "abominations," *shiqûsîm*, designate blasphemous acts of idolatry intended to insult the Name of God, whether they be committed by the Israelites or by the nations. Molech is called "the abomination of the Ammonites" (1 Kings 11:5); while it is said of those Israelites who offer sacrifices irreverently that "their soul delights in their abominations" (Isaiah 66:3).[11]

In his parallel passage to Matthew 24:15, Luke records, "When you see Jerusalem surrounded by armies, then know that its desolation is near."[12]

The surrounding of Jerusalem, the Holy City, happened one night in the year A.D. 68, when 20,000 Idumean soldiers (formerly "Edomites"), allied to the Romans, encircled the City of David and its holy mountains. Both Idumeans, sons of Esau, and the Jews, sons of Jacob-Israel, committed their atrocities, even within the Temple. Flavius Josephus recounts:

> [T]here broke out a prodigious storm in the night, with the utmost violence, and very strong winds, with the largest showers of rain, with continued lightnings, terrible thunderings, and amazing concussions and bellowings of the earth, that was in an earthquake. These things

---
11. Cf. Also Deuteronomy 29:17; Jeremiah 7:30; Ezekiel 5:11; 11:18, 21; 20:7–8, 30.

12. *Translator's Note:* Courthial is convinced that much of the Greek employed by the apostolic writers is a "Hebraized" Greek, meaning that they were consciously trying to convey Hebrew words and thoughts with the Greek language. This is an excellent example of his employment of this hermeneutical principle. For more on this, see Pierre Courthial, *De bible en bible* (Lausanne: L'Age d'Homme, 2001).

were a manifest indication that some destruction was coming upon men, when the system of the world was put into this disorder; and any one would guess that these wonders foreshowed some grand calamities that were coming. (*The War of the Jews*, IV, 4:5)

He adds:

[T]he Idumeans passed through the City and up the slope to the Temple.... No one was spared by the Idumeans, by nature most barbarous and bloodthirsty.... There was no room for flight, no hope of safety; they were crushed together and cut down until most of them, driven back, with no way of retreat left, relentlessly assailed by their murderous foes and, in a hopeless position, flung themselves headlong into the City, choosing for themselves a fate more pitiable, it seems to me, than the one they were fleeing from. The entire outer court of the Temple was deluged with blood, and 8,500 corpses greeted the rising sun.[13] (IV, 5:1)

Josephus reports that the Jewish insurgents "used the Temple of God as their fortress." There were "three treacherous factions in the city" — those who followed Eleazar, those who followed John, and those who followed Simon — who "made the Temple a mass grave of civil war" (IV, 3:7; V, 1:4). The high priests of the apostolic times, who held to a more or less Sadducean Judaism, had done everything in their power to undermine the Christian faith. Their efforts contributed to the apostasy of a great number of Jews who, having once become Christians, then returned to Judaism. Only the continued proclamation of the Gospel and the presence of the Church in Jerusalem "restrained," for a time, the working of "the mystery of iniquity" and the revelation of "the lawless one" (Nero?), as Paul had foretold (2 Thessalonians 2:9).[14]

In the warning which follows (Matthew 24:16–22), Jesus goes into the most concrete details:

[T]hen let those who are in Judea flee to the mountains. Let him who is on the housetop not go down to take anything out of his house. And

---

13. Flavius Josephus, *The Jewish Wars*, trans. G. A. Williamson (New York: Penguin, 1981), 259.

14. Cf. also Genesis 18:20–23; Revelation 11:3–13; 14:12–20.

let him who is in the field not go back to get his clothes. But woe to those who are pregnant and to those who are nursing babies in those days! And pray that your flight may not be in winter or on the Sabbath. For there will be great tribulation, such as has not been since the beginning of the world until this time, no, nor ever shall be. And unless those days were shortened, no flesh would be saved; but for the elect's sake they will be shortened.

Once again, Jesus was referring to the Book of Daniel: "And there shall be a time of trouble, such as never was since there was a nation" (12:1ff.).

Let us note, in passing, that when the Gospel of Matthew underwent a final redaction in the late 40s, a *prophet*, that is, an inspired scribe, inserted these few words: "let the reader understand" (24:15). Thus warned, the Christians who read this Gospel in the 50s and 60s could plan accordingly, as they should have. The seven warning signs, and this last one in particular, called them — indeed urged them — to flee Jerusalem and Judea when they had the chance and, in any case, when they saw the army encircling the Holy City and the abomination of desolation.

What is more, the saints, divinely and duly warned, observed the gradual fulfillment of these warnings and determined their course accordingly.

Heeding these signs, it was doubtless in 67 that most of the Christians in Jerusalem fled the Holy City and the region. One ancient historical tradition, which can be substantiated in spite of the opposition of certain historians, places a large number of refugees in Pella, beyond the Jordan, in the Decapolis, having come safe and sound through the tribulation. This was the same tribulation John mentions several times in his Revelation, in which he himself took part, considering himself a "companion in the tribulation" (Revelation 1:9; 2:20–25; 7:13–17).

This tribulation lasted three and a half years, which lines up with the prophecies of Daniel — "the middle of the seven" (9:27); "a time and [two] times and half a time" (7:25; 12:7); and "one thousand three hundred and thirty-five days" (12:12).[15]

---

15. Cf. also Revelation 12:14 — "But the woman was given two wings of a great eagle, that she might fly into the wilderness to her place, where she is nourished for a time and times and half a time, from the presence of the serpent."

The Coming of the Lord

The Sign of the Son of Man in Heaven

On the heels of the seven warning signs appear the sign of the Son of Man in heaven, the decisive sign announced by Jesus on the Mount of Olives:

> For as lightning comes from the east and flashes to the west,
> so will the coming of the Son of man be.
> For wherever the carcass is, there the eagles will be gathered together.
> Immediately after the tribulation of those days
> The sun will be darkened, and the moon will not give its light;
> The stars will fall from heaven and the power of the heavens will be shaken.
> *Then will appear the sign of the Son of Man in heaven,*
> And then all the tribes of the earth will mourn,
> And they will see the Son of Man coming on the clouds of heaven
> with power and great glory.
> And He will send His angels with a great sound of a trumpet,
> And they will gather together His elect from the four winds,
> From one end of heaven to the other. (Matthew 24:27–31)

Cosmic Images in Biblical Prophecy

If we wish to understand these words of Jesus and see their fulfillment in the events of A.D. 70, we must hold them up to the light of the Jewish Bible and, in particular, the *Nevi'im*, the Prophets. Otherwise, we are bound to misinterpret them.

First, let us note that certain translations give: "Then the sign of the Son of Man will appear in heaven," turning around the Greek word order when it requires no modification.

Jesus' prophecy concerning "the advent (that is, the coming) of the Son of Man on the clouds of heaven" (vv. 27 and 30) and the whole host of cosmic images that come with it, reveals and conveys the utmost gravity of the Judgment of the Lord and the drastic upheaval brought on by the day of His coming.

The cosmic images of the sun, moon, stars, and powers of the heavens hearken back to the prophecies of the Hebraic Bible, in light of which their real — almost literal — meaning becomes clear.[16] In Isaiah, cosmic upheaval attends the coming of the Day of the Lord against Babylon (13:9–10). It is prophesied later when it concerns the sword of the LORD against Edom (34:4). Cosmic disturbances concerning the judgment of the LORD upon Israel are found in Amos 8:9 and Ezekiel 32:7–8, concerning his lamentation over Egypt. Zechariah prophesied about "the inhabitants of Jerusalem" who "will look on Me whom they pierced" (12:10; cf. John 19:37; Revelation 1:7).

"The coming of the Lord on the clouds of heaven" is a symbolic and poetic expression quite customary to the Bible and the prophets, as we see, for example, in the following passages:

> The earth shook and trembled;
> The foundations of the hills also quaked and were shaken,
> Because He was angry.
> Smoke went up from His nostrils,
> And devouring fire from His mouth;
> Coals were kindled by it.
> *He bowed the heavens also, and came down*
> *With darkness under His feet.*
> And He rode upon a *cherub* and flew;
> He flew upon the wings of the wind. (Psalm 18:7–10)

---

16. *Translator's Note:* New Testament scholar R.T. France addresses the use of cosmic images in the Olivet Discourse as recorded in the Gospel of Matthew: "... vv. 29–31 are to be understood as Jesus' way of speaking, in the colorful language of OT prophecy, of the climactic event of the destruction of the temple and of his own authority the vindicated Son of Man, which provides the necessary counterpart to the loss of what has been hitherto the earthly focus of God's rule among his people.... [I]f these texts are understood against the background of their meaning in OT contexts, they provide a striking and (for those who are at home in OT imagery) a theologically rich account of the far-reaching developments in the divine economy which are to be focused in the historical event of the destruction of the temple. The problem is that modern Christian readers are generally not very comfortable with OT prophetic imagery, and are instead heirs to a long tradition of Christian exegesis which takes it for granted that such cosmic language, and in particular the imagery of Daniel 7:13–14, can only be understood of the parousia and the end of the world. But Jesus was speaking before that tradition developed, and his words must be understood within their own context, where it was the OT that provided the natural template for interpreting such imagery.... Language about cosmic collapse, then, is used by the OT prophets to symbolize God's acts of judgment within history, with the emphasis on catastrophic political reversals. When Jesus borrowed Isaiah's imagery, it is reasonable to understand it in a similar sense. If such language was appropriate to describe the end of Babylon or Edom under the judgment of God, why should it not equally describe God's judgment on Jerusalem's temple and the power structure it symbolized?" (R.T. France, *The Gospel of Matthew* [2007], 920, 922).

At that time it will be said
To this people and to Jerusalem
"A dry wind of the desolate heights blows in the wilderness
Toward the daughter of My people..."
I beheld the earth,
And indeed it was without form, and void (cf. the *tohu-bohu* of Genesis 1:2)
And the heavens, they had no light.
I beheld the mountains,
And indeed they trembled,
And all the hills moved back and forth....
For this shall the earth mourn,
And the heavens above be black. (Jeremiah 4:11, 23–24, 28)

Behold the LORD *rides on a swift cloud,*
And will come into Egypt;
The idols of Egypt will totter at His presence,
And the heart of Egypt will melt in its midst. (Isaiah 19:1)

Let all the inhabitants of the land tremble;
For *the day of the* LORD *is coming,*
For it is at hand.
A day of darkness and gloominess,
A day of clouds and thick darkness. (Joel 2:1–2)

God is jealous, and the LORD avenges;
The LORD avenges and is furious....
And the clouds are the dust of His feet. (Nahum 1:2–3)

The great day of the LORD *draws nigh.*

Dies Irae, Dies Illa

"The great day of the LORD is near,...
That day is a day of wrath,
A day of trouble and distress,
A day of devastation and desolation,
A day of darkness and gloominess,
A day of clouds and thick darkness." (Zephaniah 1:14–15)

We should not simply assume that whenever the Bible speaks of judgment, it is always speaking of the Last Judgment; nor that when it speaks of the Day of the Lord, it only has in mind the final day of His return in glory at the end of time; nor when it tells of the coming — the advent of the Lord — that it refers exclusively to His last coming to resurrect the dead and transfigure the universe.

Indeed, Scripture teaches two, and only two, bodily comings of Christ in the world:

- the first, *when God the Son became man*, becoming incarnate when Blessed Virgin Mary conceived (this first bodily coming, in humiliation, occurred at the center of history);
- the second, *when God the Son will return*, in His humanity, a humanity glorified since the Ascension, to resurrect all who have died, to judge them with the living, to take His own to be with him and to transfigure the universe (this second bodily coming, in glory, will occur at the end of history, at the day and the hour known only to the Father).

But in actual fact, the whole Bible, from Genesis to Revelation and, consequently, the whole life of the people of God and its members, is "advental," "parousiac" — that is, looking forward to the appearance of the Son of God. In many ways, *the Lord is always the Coming One*; and the Church and the faithful are always those expecting, looking and praying as they carry out their assignments, missions, tasks, and ministries to which they have been ordained by the Law-Word of God. The Lord God who came in the Garden of Eden after the fall to announce the first judgment and the first Gospel (Genesis 3:8, 14–24), who came to walk with Enoch, then with Noah (Genesis 5:24; 6:9), who came to judge Babel and its inhabitants (Genesis 11:5–9), who then came to Moses (Exodus 20:24) and Samuel (1 Samuel 3:10), etc., is the One who is always coming.

Nunc

He is the *Ever-Coming One*, provoking or following the prayer of His people. He is the one always coming now, "as long as it is called today" (Psalm 95:7–8; Hebrews 3:7–8; 4:7; 2 Corinthians 6:2).

Et in Hora Mortis Nostrae Sursum Corda!

He comes at the departure of His people, to meet them at the hour of their death. He receives unto Himself their souls, their persons, whilst their bodies return to the ground until the resurrection (Philippians 1:23–24; 2 Timothy 4:6, 8). At their death He ushers the faithful, through their deepened sense of awareness, into a new revelation of the spiritual world, into a new intercession with Christ in this heavenly, unimaginable praise in which, in its liturgy, the Church still on earth is included: "Lift up your hearts! We lift them up to the Lord!" (Revelation 5:8; 8:3–4; Hebrews 12:22–24).

Throughout the centuries the people of God come to live ever more fully, ever more faithfully, under the reality of the "coming," the "parousia" of the Lord pressing in upon them. "And the Spirit and the bride say, 'Come!' And let him who hears say, 'Come!' And let him who thirsts come.... He who testifies of these things says, 'Sure I am coming quickly.' Amen. Even so, come, Lord Jesus!" (Revelation 22:17, 20).

Amen! Come Lord Jesus!

He comes to His people assembled on the Sabbath day, and later, on the Lord's Day (Revelation 1:10), the first day of the week (Acts 20:7; 1 Corinthians 16:2) — He comes to them with the Word, bread, and wine.

So He came at His incarnation!

So He came, present in another (in the Holy Spirit), on the day of Pentecost (John 14:18, 20; 16:16, 22).

And so He came in A.D. 70, just as He foretold while He still walked the earth:

- to judge the ancient Church, Israel, to establish thenceforth in its place, for the Jews no less than for the nations, the New Israel, the Church;
- to turn over the page of the ancient era of the Covenant of Grace and begin the new era of the same;
- to seal the completion of the Holy Scriptures;
- and to bring His Church from the apostolic times into the post-apostolic times in which we still live.

And so He will come at the end, at a given day and hour, for the *apokatastasis pantas*, the restoration of all things (Acts 3:21).

"This Generation"

In His prophecy in Matthew 24:1–34, Jesus made it clear that His imminent coming — in *this generation* — would not be a physical and corporeal coming, since He compared His coming to "the lightning coming from the east and flashing in the west" (v. 27). Moreover, in the immediately preceding context He said, "If anyone says to you, 'Look, here is the Christ!' or 'There!' do not believe it" (vv. 23, 25).

The coming of Christ in A.D. 70, a real and spiritual coming, would be accompanied by the sign of the Son-of-Man-in-heaven, a sign that was altogether physical and visible. This sign was the destruction of the Temple and the ruin of Jerusalem. With that sign the Son of Man, sitting and reigning at the right hand of the Father, made it abundantly clear that He had indeed received all power. On the day of His death, when Jesus came before the Sanhedrin (the Jewish tribunal), the high priest asked Him: "Are you the Christ, the Son of the Blessed?" Jesus answered: "I am. And *you will see* the Son of Man sitting at the right hand of the Power, and coming with the clouds of heaven" (Mark 14:61–62). And so it came to pass, when members of the Sanhedrin still alive in A.D. 70 beheld with their own eyes exactly what Jesus had foretold they would see: the execution of judgment which the Trinitarian Tribunal pronounced on Israel.

The hour had now come, as Jesus had announced to the Samaritan woman at Jacob's well, when it would no longer be in the earthly Jerusalem that the Father would be worshipped (John 4:21–24). Worship in Spirit and truth would take place in the heavenly Jerusalem (Hebrews 12:22–24), where men, women, and children from all nations — both Jews and Gentiles — would be gathered together. The Temple, from that time on, would be Christ in His totality — Head and Body (John 2:21; 1 Corinthians 3:16–17; 6:19; Ephesians 2:20–22).

Lamentations for the End

All the tribes of the *earth* (*gê*, in Greek, sometimes refers to the land of Israel, the meaning confirmed here by "the tribes") will mourn: the Holy City is gone!, the Sanctuary is gone!, the perpetual Sacrifice is no more!, and, for many of Jerusalem's inhabitants: our houses are gone!, and even for some: our parents are gone!, our friends are gone!

The events of A.D. 70, the sign and all that came with it, sent shockwaves throughout Judea and all the Diaspora. Israel, wrote Josephus, was "plunged into the greatest misfortune imaginable." The terrifying advent-event signaled "the end of the era," the end of the world under the old covenant administration, the end of the perpetual sacrifice and the Temple. Israel never recovered from this catastrophe. Jesus foretold that it would be a disaster "such as has not been since the beginning of the world until this time, no, nor ever shall be" (Matthew 24:21; Daniel 12:1). These lamentations have persisted throughout the twenty centuries Israel has since known.

In *The Syriac Apocalpyse of Baruch*, or *The Second Book of Baruch*, written between A.D. 75 and 100 (not to be confused with the Book of Baruch in the apocrypha of the old covenant), we read:

> Blessed is he who was not born,
> Or he, who having been born, has died.
> But as for us who live, woe unto us,
> Because we see the afflictions of Zion,
> And what has befallen Jerusalem . . . (1.6–7)
>
> And do ye, O heavens, withhold your dew,
> And open not the treasuries of rain:
> And do thou, O sun, withhold the light of your rays.
> And do thou, O moon, extinguish the multitude of your light;
> For why should light rise again
> Where the light of Zion is darkened? . . . (1.11–12)
>
> Would that you had ears, O earth,
> And that you had a heart, O dust:
> That you might go and announce in Sheol,
> And say to the dead:
> "Blessed are you more than we who live." (2.6–7)

All those among the Jews who refused to hear the Gospel of the Kingdom proclaimed by Jesus, by the Twelve, and by the Seventy, and who rejected the ultimatum (and time of patience) issued by the Lord and by the apostolic circle (Matthew 23:37), all the sons and daughters of the covenant who did not receive their Messiah (John 1:11), now saw the sign of power and glory of the Son of Man coming on the clouds of heaven. However, the Lord, having gathered His elect from the four winds (many called, but few chosen; Matthew 22:14) by His angels (His messengers, His sent ones, His apostles, His ambassadors) at the sound of a trumpet, snatches them away from judgment and saves them. The sounding trumpet is a clear allusion to the trumpet of Jubilee. The year of Jubilee (Leviticus 25) celebrates symbolically the liberation and redemption of men — not Jews only, but the nations as well (Ephesians 2:12, 21) — by the One who would release them from all their debt by paying it for them. The theme of the Jubilee is taken up again and again throughout the entire Bible (cf. Isaiah 61:1–2 and Luke 4:17–21).

The Carcass and the Eagles

One further prophecy remains to be considered. Jesus foretold: "Wherever the carcass is, there the eagles will be gathered together" (Matthew 24:28).

We cannot help but see within this prophecy an allusion to the capture and destruction of Jerusalem. The comparison of the holy people to a corpse, and even to dry bones, had been made by Ezekiel (37:1–14). We also read in that chapter of the Spirit coming "from the four winds" to "breathe on these slain, that they may live" (v. 9). In the last week — the last seven — of the old covenant, Israel is spiritually dead, like a desert (Matthew 23:38). Deuteronomy 28, beginning with verse 15, announces the cursings that would come upon God's people if they should disobey the word of their Lord. It is said there that "the LORD will cause you to be routed before your enemies;... Your carcasses shall be food for all the birds of the air and the beasts of the earth, and no one shall frighten them away" (vv. 25–26).

This happened at the end of the last *seven*. The Romans were the enemies routing Israel. All that remained of Israel was a carcass around which the eagles gathered. The light of the flames engulfing the sanctuary even flickered on eagles set up within by the Roman army, for whom the eagle was the symbol of the Empire, a sign under which the legions marched. Josephus reports: "Now the Romans, upon the flight of the seditious into the city, and upon the burning of the holy house itself, ... brought their ensigns ['sacred objects'] to the temple, and set them over against its eastern gate; and there did they offer sacrifices to them, and there did they make Titus imperator, with the greatest acclamations of joy" (*The Jewish War*, VI, 6, 1). Josephus had previously noted concerning these "ensigns" (or "sacred objects") that they were "encompassing the eagle, which is at the head of every Roman legion, the king, and the strongest of all birds" (III, 6, 2).

The Scriptural Canon

The Closing of the Biblical Canon

The apostolic times of A.D. 30 to 70 (and, more particularly, from 40 to 70) were those during which the holy Book was sealed — that is, finished, completed, closed — according to Daniel's prophecy (9:24). Though Daniel had received the order to "seal up the vision, for it refers to many days in the future" (Daniel 8:26), John, writing the last book of Holy Scripture, was commanded: "Do not seal the words of this book, for the time is at hand" (Revelation 22:10). This raises for us the question of the biblical canon, to which we now turn.

The word "canon" comes from the Greek word *kanôn*, meaning a reed, measure, or rule. It can be understood in two different ways, each equally acceptable.

The Canonical List

The first sense of *biblical canon* is *the ecclesiastical list of books contained in Holy Scripture*. Understood in this way, we may say that the Roman Church and the Churches of the Reformation have the same canon, the same list, of twenty-seven books of the New Testament. On the other hand, they have different lists of books, and thus different canons, for the Old Testament.

It does not seem that the Roman Church had a rigorously defined list of books before the Council of Trent, 1545–1563. The early Fathers and medieval Doctors held varying opinions on the matter. But with the Council of Trent, the Roman Church officially approved a supposed Alexandrian canon, the same used by the Greek translation of the Old Testament called "the Septuagint,"[17] which adds several apocryphal books to the traditional Hebrew canon (Tobias, Judith, 1 and 2 Maccabees, Wisdom, Ecclesiasticus, Baruch, and a letter of Jeremiah) and also includes additions to the books of Esther and Daniel.

I say "supposed" Alexandrian canon, because the evidence favors the traditional Hebrew canon. This was the canon endorsed by such Fathers as Melitus of Sardis (second century), St. Athanasius (295–378), St. Cyril of Jerusalem (315–386), and St. Jerome (347–420), the consummate master of Greek, Hebrew, and Latin, whose admirable translation of the Bible from the Hebrew and Greek into Latin is known as the *Vulgata latina* (the Vulgate). This Hebrew canon was also the one strictly held to by the Reformers as was right and proper for several reasons.

First, there is the witness of the first-century historian, Josephus, that only the Hebrew canon had authority in the time of Jesus and the apostles.[18] Another external evidence is found in the prologue to the *Book of Ben Sira* or *Ecclesiasticus*, an apocryphal book dating to the early second century B.C. The prologue twice refers to the Old Testament as the Law, Prophets, and Writings (*Torah, Nevi'im,* and *Ketuvim*), which is the three-fold division of the Hebrew canon.[19]

---

17. Regarding the *seventy,* or the *Septuagint,* let us note:
a. The expression "septuagint" (seventy) in no way refers to the legend disseminated by the *Letter of Aristea* (second century B.C.) according to which 72 aged Jewish men (six from each tribe) came from Jerusalem under the authority of the High Priest and at the request of the Egyptian sovereign Ptolemy (third century B.C.), and, being placed in Alexandria in 72 separate and self-enclosed cells, were said to have miraculously composed 72 absolutely identical Greek translations of the Hebrew manuscript of the Bible. St. Augustine, getting a bit carried away in this instance, gave credence to this legend, causing it to spread with its pretense of justly authenticating the *divine* authority of the Septuagint! (cf. *The City of God,* Book *XVIII,* 42–43)

    The truth of the matter is that the Septuagint draws its name from the fact that it was destined by the Alexandrian Jewish translators for the non-Jews, the Gentiles, the nations, symbolically numbered 70 because, at their origin (Genesis 10), they constituted such a number.
2. The New Testament frequently uses *The Septuagint* when quoting from the Old Testament because this facilitated the inclusion of these quotations into a text already written in Greek.
3. If, as it appears, there are allusions (but not quotations) in the New Testament to the apocryphal books added by the Septuagint to the Jewish Bible, these no more attest to the divine origin of these texts than the quotations (not allusions here!) of pagan authors in the New Testament "sacralize" the author quoted and the text from which they are drawn (Aratus in Acts 17:28, Menander in 1 Corinthians 15:33, and Epimenides in Titus 1:12).
18. *Contra Apion,* 1, 8.
19. *Ecclesiasticus* 1.10 and 1.20.

Second, there are several passages (the Word of God!) in the New Testament which clearly allude to the three parts of the Jewish Bible: "The Law, the Prophets, and the Psalms" (the Psalms were the first book of the Writings). This was often shortened to "the Law and the Prophets," or even "the Law" (cf. for example Matthew 5:17–18; 22:36–40; Luke 16:16; 24:44; John 1:45; Acts 13:15; 28:23; Romans 3:21; James 2:10).

Third, Matthew 23:35 and Luke 11:51 use the expression "from the blood of Abel to the blood of Zechariah" (cf. 2 Chronicles 24:20–22). These verses show quite clearly that the Jewish Bible used by Jesus and the apostles began with Genesis and concluded with 2 Chronicles.

Fourth, and most importantly, Romans 3:1–2 (the Word of God!) speaks precisely to the matter of canon. It reveals that the Jews do have a *privilege* (*perissos* in Greek), a superiority, an advantage: namely, that to them were entrusted the oracles, the words of God (*ta logia tou theou*).[20] The old Church, Israel, had in their possession the tradition, the transmission (*paradosis*) of the written Word of God which began with Moses. It was this tradition, this *paradosis*, that the faithful remnant of the old Church, Israel, passed down to the Church, the New Israel; and it was this tradition that would go on to be completed with the Tradition of the Apostles of the New Testament.

Whereas the Roman Church, at least since the Council of Trent, has received a canon that includes several books and additions to the traditional Hebrew canon, the Churches of the Reformation have held fast, with good reason, to the latter.

In all of this, we have dealt with the *historical question* concerning the canon — that is, which *list* of Holy Books are recognized and declared by the Church, the guardian of the Scriptures, to be canonical (the ancient Church, Israel, having recognized and declared which are the holy books of the old administration of the covenant; the New Israel having recognized and declared which are the holy books of the new administration of the covenant).

The Dogmatic Canon

The second sense of *biblical canon* differs from the first in that it confesses that *these books have divine authority that imposes itself* on

---

20. Cf. also Romans 9:4.

the Church and on the faithful as being the very Word of God and thus the sovereign norm.

Here we are dealing with a *dogmatic question*. Though the Church recognizes and declares the list of canonical books, it is *the Holy Spirit* who is the sure and certain Witness, who was operating in the hearts of the Fathers, Doctors, and Reformers of the Church in times past, and operates in the hearts of the simplest believers in all times, that they may grasp, with the certainty of divine faith, that this Holy Scripture is truly the Word of God.[21] He is the Guarantor of the truth and authority of the infallible Holy Scriptures (John 3:31–34; 1 Corinthians 1:4–6; 1 John 5:6, 9–13; Revelation 19:10).

For this reason, whenever the churches and faithful read or hear the Scriptures, they must humbly receive this word as if, gazing on the Lord, they were hearing it from His own lips.

The Tradition of the Apostles

The Church of Christ, the Church of the new administration of the covenant, has never been without Holy Books, the written Word of God. Let us never forget that the Church was, at the beginning, almost exclusively made up of the faithful remnant of Israel. Consequently, they "received" from Israel (or rather "held to") the *Torah, Nevi'im,* and *Ketuvim* (the *TaNaKh*) from the very start. Furthermore, the apostolic circle, carrying out the command given them by Christ, gave the Church quite early, book by book, the writings composing the New Testament. These writings, one by one, and then as a whole, gradually established themselves in the churches as having the same divine authority as the Bible of Israel.

The divine authority of the writings of the apostles is clearly attested to within the writings themselves. This Apostolic "Tradition," this apostolic "transmission" of these new Holy Writings, is spoken of as the Gospel which is proclaimed by the Holy Spirit sent from heaven (1 Peter 1:12); as the words taught by the Spirit (1 Corinthians 2:13); as prescriptions to be received as though proceeding from the Lord himself (1 Thessalonians 4:2), so much so that if anyone should choose

---

21. *Translator's Note:* Courthial distinguishes between the Church, which *fait connaître le canon* as it concerns the historical question, and the Holy Spirit, who *fait savior... que cette Écriture Sainte est vraiment la Parole de Dieu* as it concerns the dogmatic question.

not to obey them, one must "note that person and not keep company with him" (2 Thessalonians 3:14), since the things written by an apostle were "the commandments of the Lord" (1 Corinthians 14:37).

When one or several churches received a Gospel, letter, or writing bearing the authority or seal of an apostle, it was received as the Word of the Lord. It was consequently classed with the Scriptures of the Hebraic Bible, thus becoming, in turn, Scripture. It was to be read publicly to the brethren (1 Thessalonians 5:27). Moreover, it was to be passed on to the sister churches, to all in the spiritual fellowship of the Father and the Son. "Now when this epistle is read among you," commanded Paul, "see to it that it is read also in the church of the Laodiceans, and that you likewise read the epistle from Laodicea" (Colossians 4:16; cf. Revelation 1:3). In this way all the Churches in the *oîkouméné* gradually came to recognize a new collection of books as the Law-Word of God.

Moreover, this new collection of Holy Writings came to be recognized over time as a fourth part of Holy Scripture, alongside the three main parts of the Hebraic Bible. It was first known as "the Gospel and the Apostles" — or, in shortened form, "the Gospel." The subsequent works of the Church Fathers spoke of a single great collection in four parts: "the Law and the Prophets with the Gospels and the Apostles" or, more simply, "the Bible and the Tradition," or "the Law and the Gospel."

Regarding the first sense of "canon," the sense of a list defined by the Church, the first known attempt in the Church to define a list of the new Holy Writings comes toward the end of the second century (the "Muratorian" canon, named in 1740 for its Milanese compiler, which did not include Hebrews, James, 2 Peter, 2 and 3 John, Jude, and Revelation) and it would not be until Athanasius in 367 that we find the exact canon of twenty-seven New Testament books.

But regarding the second sense of "canon," the dogmatic sense under the control of the Holy Spirit, we may say that the New Testament canon was sealed in apostolic times, before A.D. 70. The apostles and their assistants exercised their authority immediately, an authority received from the Lord, to care for the Church and protect her faithfulness. Accordingly, each of the twenty-seven New Testament books was not only written, but was also immediately recognized and confessed, at least in certain churches, as the Scripture-Word of God.

Peter, writing around 65, declares that his "well beloved brother Paul, according to the wisdom given to him, has written to you, as also in all his epistles, speaking of these things, in which are some things hard to understand, which untaught and unstable people twist to their own destruction, *as they do also the rest of the Scriptures*" (2 Peter 3:15–16). Paul explicitly refers to both Deuteronomy and Luke as Scripture, a truth he considers self-evident (1 Timothy 5:18; cf. Deuteronomy 25:4 and Luke 10:7).

When John wrote Revelation, which stands not only as the last book of the New Testament, but of the whole Bible as well (Nero, who died in June of 68, is still living when the Revelation is written), he also "canonized," in his own way, the whole collection of writings in the New Testament. Concluding and sealing "the vision and the prophecy," he ends his book with these words:

> For I testify to everyone who hears the words of the prophecy of this book: If anyone adds to these things, God will add to him the plagues that are written in this book; and if anyone takes away from the words of the book of this prophecy, God shall take away his part from the Book of Life, from the holy city, and from the things which are written in this book. He who testifies to these things says, "Surely I come quickly." Amen. Even so, come Lord Jesus! The grace of our Lord Jesus Christ be with you all. Amen. (Revelation 22:18–21)

PART THREE

The New Order of the World

*From the End of the Apostolic Epoch
to Christ's Return in Glory*

6
The Genuinely *Catholic* Ecclesial Tradition

7
The Church Sick with Humanism

8
Humanism Defeated by the Law of God

6

THE GENUINELY *CATHOLIC* ECCLESIAL TRADITION

*Tradition is the living faith of the dead;
traditionalism is the dead faith of the living.*

JAROSLAV PELIKAN[1]

Preliminary Remarks

The Ecclesial Time

Taking into account the order that Jesus reveals and follows in His high priestly prayer in John 17, we see that the life of Christ (A.D. 1–30) is followed by the apostolic times (A.D. 30–70) after which comes *the ecclesial time* (post-A.D. 70).[2] The ecclesial time is the time from the destruction of Jerusalem to the present, in which we find ourselves, continuing up until the time of our Lord's glorious return.

With the destruction of the Temple in Jerusalem, the turning of the ages was completed. From that time on, the old order, having disappeared, has been giving way to the new order. "All things have become new" (2 Corinthians 5:17), Paul announces. Christ, sitting at the right

---

1. Jaroslav Pelikan, *The Emergence of the Catholic Tradition* (University of Chicago Press, 1971), 9.

2. Cf. John 17:1–5; 6–19; 20–26.

hand of the Father, declares and promises: "Behold, I am making all things new" (Revelation 21:5). This newness is not only a present reality, but the end toward which all of history is pressing, leading up to the day of the universal *apokatastasis* — that is, the day of the universal renewal, restoration, and transfiguration (Acts 3:21).

During the apostolic time (A.D. 30–70), on account of God's patience and slowness to anger, the Church continued to observe many Hebraic ceremonies and rites. The Church was considered to be for the most part a mere sect within Judaism. But after the destruction of the Temple, the Church cut loose from these moorings of the old order and set sail into the new.

In the apostolic books, we already find the Church set forth as the new Jerusalem, the heavenly Jerusalem, the Jerusalem above, the free woman, "which is the mother of us all" (Galatians 4:26), as opposed to the old Jerusalem, the earthly Jerusalem, the bondwoman with her children. She is now the mystical Mount Zion, the holy mountain of the Kingdom of God, which, according to Daniel's prophecy, "became a great mountain and filled the whole earth" (2:35). In relation to the holy mountain of the Church, the physical Mount Zion in Jerusalem was only a *type*.[3]

We have already seen and spoken of the mountains of God — Eden, Ararat, Moriah, Sinaï, and Zion. All of these were but *typological* signposts intended to direct the gaze of our eyes (and the longings of our hearts — *sursum corda!*) to the mountain of God. We are now given to draw near, ever and always, to the mountain of God. And we may do so only by grace, only by means of faith, for this mountain is ever and always descending and drawing near to us. "Now it shall come to pass in the latter days that the mountain of the Lord's house shall be established on the top of the mountains... and all nations shall flow to it" (Isaiah 2:2; cf. also Micah 4:1).[4]

> But you have come to Mount Zion and the city of the living God, the heavenly Jerusalem, to an innumerable company of angels, to the

---

3. Accordingly, although Psalm 2:6 ("Yet I have set My King on My holy hill of Zion") was first realized with king David, it finds its much better and fuller realization with the "Son of David," our Lord Jesus Christ, enthroned as King of kings and Lord of lords at His ascension to the mystical, and no less real, heavenly Zion.

4. Isaiah must be read with this mountain as its major theme.

general assembly and church of the firstborn who are registered in heaven, to God the Judge of all, to the spirits of just men made perfect, to Jesus the Mediator of the new covenant, and to the blood of sprinkling that speaks better things than that of Abel. (Hebrews 12:22–24)

Then I looked, and behold, a Lamb standing on Mount Zion. (Revelation 14:1; cf. ch. 21)

Removing the Veil from the Hebraic Bible

With the addition of the twenty-seven apostolic writings comprising its fourth and final part, the Book of the Covenant — Holy Scripture — was now completed and sealed and, as such, was taken up by the Church, the New Israel, not to be hidden away, but rather to be understood in its depths, from beginning to end, under the gentle and brilliant light of Christ, and also to be put into practice.

The apostolic writings, testifying to the Christ prefigured and foretold in the Hebraic writings, restored the true meaning of the Hebraic Bible, which had been distorted almost beyond recognition by the man-made tradition taught by the Jewish *rabbis* (the *rabbis* claimed to base their teachings on an *oral tradition* going back to Moses himself; cf. Mark 7:5–13). By removing the veil from the old covenant (the Old Testament), Jesus and His apostles led people back to the true meaning, and sole standard, of the Law, the Prophets, and the Writings (2 Corinthians 3:14–17). In the same way they showed that the literal meaning, intended and expressed by the Holy Spirit, was different from the *literalist* meaning, which many were imposing upon, or substituting for, the former. With the apostolic writings, the literal sense came to be received as it had been given, in images and symbols, in parables, which were properly understood by those to whom "it [was] given to know the mysteries of the kingdom of heaven" (Matthew 13:10–17).

As an example, let us consider the Gospel of John. When Jesus speaks about the wine at the wedding in Cana (2:1–11), the Temple (2:13–22), the new birth (3:3–6), blindness (ch. 9), shepherds (ch. 10), the resurrection and the life (ch. 11), etc., He is simply taking up in depth, and unveiling, symbols, images, and parables from the Hebraic Bible — things that Israel had, amazingly, forgotten! This explains why Jesus says to Nicodemus, after teaching him about the need for the new birth, "Are you the teacher of Israel, and you do not know these things?" (John 3:10). It is significant that when Christ died on the cross, "the veil of the Temple was torn in two from top to bottom" (Matthew 27:51; Mark 15:38). St. Paul tells us that when recalcitrant Jews read the Torah, "a veil remains," "a veil lies on their hearts," which can only be "taken away in Christ" (2 Corinthians 3:14–16).

The Holy Spirit reveals — that is, He pulls back the veil that conceals — the covenantal Lordship of the one-and-many God through the completed book of the one-and-many Holy Scriptures. In and through Scripture, God names Himself by speaking His personal Word, which is both transcendent, sovereign, mysterious, and exalted, as well as, and inseparably, immanent, near, concrete, and applicable to every area of existence (1 Corinthians 2:7; Deuteronomy 30:11–14; Romans 11:33–34).

Consequently, the living Church of God is "the pillar and ground of the Truth" only insofar as she is faithful to "the mystery of godliness," and only insofar as she applies herself to the reading, meditating, and searching of Scripture. This she must do in a spirit of humility, submission, and obedience, so that she will be able to exhort and teach with all faithfulness (1 Timothy 3:15–4:16; 2 Timothy 3:14–4:5).

A Warning to All Unfaithful Churches

When a church that is unfaithful to Scripture refuses to repent, convert, and reform, it will inevitably, sooner or later, bring upon itself the judgment of the Lord of the Church, the Lord of Scripture.

What happened *in* Israel just before A.D. 70 was followed by what came *upon* Israel in A.D. 70. Their rejection of Christ and His apostles led to a great judgment within one generation. In this we find an example and warning to all apostate churches until the end of time. It has already happened many times that God has brought historical judgments on this or that church or churches. Therefore the judgment on Israel in 70 — which has, since that time, given witness to Israel's need to repent and recognize her Messiah — should in no way justify and/or fuel even the slightest form of anti-Semitism whatever. To the contrary!

It is not as though Christians are less immune to self-righteousness than were the Jews, or that Christians are somehow exempted from the judgment God brings down on such self-righteousness. Listen to Paul as he addresses the non-Jewish faithful from the nations:

> And if some of the branches were broken off, and you, being a wild olive tree, were grafted in among them, and with them became a partaker of the root and fatness of the olive tree, do not boast against the branches. But if you do boast, remember that you do not support the root, but the root supports you. You will say then, "Branches were broken off that I might be grafted in." Well said. Because of unbelief they were broken off, and you stand by faith. Do not be haughty, but fear. For if God did not spare the natural branches, He may not spare you either. Therefore consider the goodness and severity of God: on those who fell, severity; but toward you, goodness, if you continue in His goodness. Otherwise you also will be cut off. And they also, if they do not continue in unbelief, will be grafted in, for God is able to graft them in again. For if you were cut out of the olive tree which is wild by nature, and were grafted contrary to nature into a cultivated olive tree, how much will these, who are natural, be grafted into their own olive tree? (Romans 11:17–24)

God's Sovereignty and Man's Responsibility

With Paul's warning above, we see the personal responsibility expected of Christians and the corporate responsibility expected of churches. The Covenant of Grace, placed under the lordship of God, includes inalienable instructions that require our responsibility.

History, and principally the history of the Church and churches, is both the temporal realization of God's eternal plan *and* the result of free and responsible human actions. We recall that human beings cannot be *autonomous*, for God alone is autonomous (a law unto Himself). Human beings are *theonomous* (under God's law). But man's theonomous condition in no way minimizes, alters, depreciates, or removes human liberty and responsibility — far from it! Rather, it serves to give reality to our liberty and responsibility, to grant possibility and meaning to these aspects of our nature.

It seems that each of these truths were so thoroughly imbued in the minds of the apostles Peter and John that they could refer at once to God's sovereignty and man's responsibility without getting hung up on the enormity of this paradox — a paradox, we might add, which runs from one end of the Bible to the other. When praying with the first community in Jerusalem several days after Pentecost, the believers say to God: "For truly against Your holy Servant Jesus, whom You anointed, both Herod and Pontius Pilate, with the Gentiles and the people of Israel, were gathered together [the liberty, responsibility and indisputable culpability of men!] to do whatever Your hand and Your purpose determined before to be done [the undeniable sovereignty of God!]" (Acts 4:27–28).

Likewise, at the Last Supper, on the eve of His death, our Lord Jesus Christ says to His apostles concerning Judas: "And truly the Son of Man goes as it has been determined, but woe to that man by whom He is betrayed!" (Luke 22:22). The Lord has sovereignly determined it and therein is established the liberty, responsibility, and culpability of Judas.

Thus the threat of the righteous covenantal judgment of God is as present in the new administration of the covenant as in the old. Accordingly, John receives the order to write the churches on the Lord's behalf. To the church in Ephesus, he writes: "Nevertheless I have this against you, that you have left your first love. Remember therefore from where you have fallen; *repent* and do the first works, or else I will come to you quickly" (Revelation 2:4–5). To the church in Sardis: "Remember therefore how you have received and heard; hold fast *and repent*. Therefore if you will not watch, I will come upon you as a thief, and you will not know what hour I will come upon you" (3:3). And to the church in Laodicea: "As many as I love, I rebuke and chasten. Therefore be zealous *and repent*" (3:19).

The Covenant of Grace and Law

We now return to an important and oft-neglected point: namely, the fact that the covenant is a Covenant of Grace with commands, a covenant of promises with warnings, a covenant of Gospel and of Law.

The Biblical prophets were all sent by God to call the people and the members of the covenant to stand firm, endure, persevere, and wait patiently if they were faithful, or to repent and turn back without delay if they were unfaithful.

Jeremiah declares: "'I will yet bring charges against you,' says the LORD, 'And against your children's children I will bring charges'" (Jeremiah 2:9).

The charges are always the same. They are those that the faithful Lord of the covenant brings against His unfaithful, covenant-breaking vassal. On account of breaking the commandments, the stipulations, the vassal incurs — and justly so — the execution of the covenant threats, the "vengeance" of the Lord of the covenant (Deuteronomy 32:35, repeated in Romans 12:19, Hebrews 10:30 and Luke 21:22).

The history of the Church, like the Biblical history of Israel before it, is significant in this regard. It reveals blessings and progress when the people of God are faithful, cursing and regress when they are unfaithful. Throughout the centuries, the true Fathers, Doctors, and Reformers of the Church are those who, whenever the times call for it, have been sent and rise up as "God's prosecutors." In the name of the Law, according to the covenant, they announce the charges that have been brought against the criminals — i.e., the heretics or notoriously ungodly men (Jude).

Though many are shocked by this *juridical perspective* of Scripture and refuse to acknowledge it, it is undeniably there. Scripture contains a formidable set of covenantal terms and conditions (cf. only a few of many such examples: Job; Isaiah 45:9; Jeremiah 2:35; 25:31; Hosea 4 and 5; Micah 6; Matthew 3:10–12; 5:13 and 17ff.; Romans 3:4–6; 9:20).

Rather than stop our ears, let us hear:

> Woe to him who strives with his Maker! Let the potsherd strive with the potsherds of the earth! Shall the clay say to him who forms it, "What are you making?" Or shall your handiwork say, "He has no hands?" (Isaiah 45:9)

> Behold, I will plead My case against you, because you say, "I have not sinned." (Jeremiah 2:35)

> Hear, O you mountains, the Lord's complaint against His people, and He will contend [bring charges against] Israel. (Micah 6:2)

> If the salt loses its flavor, how shall it be seasoned? It is then good for nothing but to be thrown out and trampled underfoot by men. (Matthew 5:13)

> But if our unrighteousness demonstrates the righteousness of God, what shall we say? Is God unjust who inflicts wrath? (I speak as a man.) (Romans 3:5)

Viewing the Catholic Ecclesial Tradition in Light of the Covenant

The above remarks are by no means a digression. We have not strayed from our present subject: the *catholic* ecclesial tradition.

The Church should be the first to admit, and truly to believe, that she is not inherently infallible, that her faithfulness is not to be taken for granted and that she is never exempt from the Lord bringing suit against her should He determine to do so according to the terms of the covenant. There are several necessary questions the Church must ask of herself:

1. Do I fear (= adoring respect) the one Trinitarian Lord, transcendent and immanent, Creator and Savior, as is His due?
2. How well am I carrying out my responsibility to Him and my responsibility to the mission committed to me by Him? Does the *salt of the earth* still have its flavor? Am I shining *the light of the world* before men? Is there anything hiding or darkening it? Am I the *pillar and ground of the truth*?[5]
3. Are my life, teaching, and worship in Spirit and truth that I owe God presently in accordance with what He commands and forbids?
4. Am I prepared for the righteous sanctions — the covenantal blessings or cursings — that my faithfulness or unfaithfulness will bring about?
5. Have I made a better future for those entrusted to my love and motherly care?

The "double-edged sword" is not brandished over the Church with delight, for the Lord takes no pleasure in the death of the wicked, but rather with the hope that she might turn from her evil ways, repent and live (Hebrews 4:12–13; Revelation 1:16; 2:12; Ezekiel 18:21–32; 33:11; Luke 15:7).

What to Make of Traditions?

Introduction

The word "tradition" (*paradosis* in Greek) does not always carry the best connotations in the New Testament, especially in Jesus' own

---

5. Matthew 5:13–16; 1 Timothy 3:15.

teaching. Our Lord vigorously opposed "the tradition of the elders," which refers not to the divine tradition of the Hebraic Bible, the Word of God, but rather to the man-made tradition claimed by the Pharisees and scribes of His day:

> Why do you also transgress the commandment of God because of your tradition?... You have made the commandment of God of no effect by your tradition. (Matthew 15:1–6)

> For laying aside the commandment of God, you hold the tradition of men.... All too well you reject the commandment of God, that you may keep your tradition... making the word of God of no effect through your tradition which you have handed down. (Mark 7:1–12)

Pleading guilty for his past, St. Paul the Apostle writes to the Christians in Galatia:

> For you have heard of my former times, how I persecuted the church of God.... And I advanced in Judaism beyond many of my contemporaries in my own nation, being more exceedingly zealous for the traditions of my fathers. (Galatians 1:13–14)

And so did he warn the Christians in Colossae: "Beware lest anyone cheat you through philosophy and empty deceit, according to the tradition of men" (Colossians 2:8).

But at the same time we find St. Paul commending the tradition of Christ and the apostles. He commands the Christians in Corinth to "keep the traditions just as I delivered them to you" (1 Corinthians 11:2). Those in Thessalonica he exhorts to "stand fast and hold the traditions which you were taught, whether by word or our epistle" (2 Thessalonians 2:15), reminding them later of the "tradition" they received from him (3:6). (Let us recall that when the most ancient Fathers spoke of *the Bible and the Tradition*, they meant "the Jewish Bible *and* the Tradition of the Apostles," or "the Old Testament *and* the New Testament.")

The tradition of Jesus and His chosen apostles who kept His Word consisted of the words that Jesus delivered to them, which they received, and which they were to hand down faithfully as the truth. So could Jesus pray to His Father: "For I have given to them the words which You have given Me; and they have received them," and send them out with the confidence that "he who hears you hears Me, he who rejects you rejects Me" (John 17:6, 8, 17, 19, 20; Luke 10:16). Having been permanently set down in the New Testament collection of writings (displaying both unity and diversity), which was completed with the closing of the canon of apostolic writings in the year 70, this tradition is to be found surely and securely there, and there only. This tradition of Jesus and His apostles should be regarded as authoritative, and therefore not doubted, distorted, altered, or set aside according to any other (pretended) tradition — even, and especially, ecclesial tradition — or any other (pretended) authority of any kind.

The Church, the New Israel, did not receive the neo-testamentary tradition as something independent from the divine tradition handed down in writing by ancient Israel. Rather, the holy writings of ancient Israel, as already contained in the three parts of the Hebraic Bible: the *Torah*, the *Nevi'im*, and the *Ketuvim*, were understood as finding their ultimate completion in the neo-testamentary tradition, in which they were affirmed, deepened, and transfigured. Indeed, the New Israel, the Church, received from the old Israel "the adoption, the glory, the covenants, the giving of the law (the *Torah*), the service of God, the promises and the fathers" which they now shared, for "salvation is of the Jews," and from them, "according to the flesh, Christ came, who is over all, the eternally blessed God" (Romans 9:4–5; John 4:22; cf. also Luke 24:27 and 44).

Man-made traditions, and especially ecclesial ones, have always pretended to locate their authority not in holy writings, but in oral transmissions which are alleged to go back to the beginnings: for the Jews, back to the truths supposedly revealed by God to Moses; for the Catholics, both Roman and Eastern Orthodox, to the truths supposedly revealed by Christ to the apostles. Such oral tradition amounts to darkness and fog, a plain and simple esoterism, harnessed by those in power to promote their own power, as well as the errors in their doctrines. For the Jews, the appeal to oral transmission served the pretensions of their teachers, elders, and *rabbis*, those in authority; for the Catholics, both Roman and Eastern Orthodox, it served to enshrine the infallibility of popes and/or councils.

With the *Kabbala* (= tradition!) and the *Talmud* (an immense compilation of seven to eight centuries'-worth of rabbinical teachings dating back to before our era), the Jewish tradition was elevated above the Hebraic Bible and was thus adhered to even where it contradicted the very meaning of the Hebraic Bible. Much of the opposition to Jesus and His apostles sprang from adherence to this tradition. To this day the Talmudists appeal to Exodus 24:3 to justify their stance: "So Moses came and told all the people all the words (*devârîm*) of the Lord and all the judgments (*mishepâtîm*)." They draw a distinction between that which would be written: *devârîm*, and that which would inaugurate the oral tradition taught from *rabbi* to *rabbi* through the ages.

A similar appeal to non-biblical traditions was used by the Catholics, both Roman and Eastern Orthodox, in Nicea II. Whereas the first six ecumenical Councils were faithful to the Word of God, the Holy Scripture (Nicea, 325; Constantinople, 381; Ephesus, 431; Chalcedon, 451; Constantinople II, 553; Constantinople III, 680–681), a seventh ecumenical Council (Nicea II, 787), approved, authorized, and promoted the veneration and worship of images and relics in blatant opposition to Scripture. Baptized as a "living tradition," a "vivifying presence," this tradition can be discerned and defined only *a posteriori*, that is, only after the people have pressed their adamant claims, after the theologians have proffered their speculations (which further undercuts the supposed identification of *theology* with the one Holy Scripture!), and after various *mystical* phenomena, such as apparitions and alleged miracles, have made their mark. This has left room for the rising tide of dogmas of human invention,[6] such as, in the West, the transubstantiation of the Eucharist, indulgences, the immaculate conception of Mary, the infallibility of the pope speaking *ex cathedra*, etc.

The Ecclesial Tradition

The Church, from the first beginnings of her existence on earth as a *covenantal people* under Moses, has had and received the Holy Scriptures as a *covenantal Book* (even if it was just the first part of the book, the Torah), which is the Word of God. This Word has contained for the Church in all ages the norms of her faith (the *credenda*, realities to be believed) and of her life (the *agenda*, those things to be done).

---

6. *Translator's Note:* One thinks of the apt phrase coined by Jacques Le Goff when he speaks of "the riot of imagination" that characterized much doctrinal formulation in the early Middle Ages (*The Birth of Purgatory*, trans. Arthur Goldhammer, 1986).

Indeed, as we have already seen, the covenant began with the creation of the world and man. By the grace of God there have always been *sons of God* among the human race to respond faithfully to the *words of God*. But it is only in the time of Moses, from the Exodus and precisely on Mt. Sinaï, that there began to exist, under the unction of the *blood of the covenant* (foretelling, prefiguring, and "typifying" the blood of Christ to come), a *people of the covenant* with a *Book of the Covenant*, the written Word of God (Exodus 24).

Since then the Church with the Holy Scripture, and the Holy Scripture with the Church, have always remained, and will always remain until the end of history. Both exist only by coexisting: the Holy Scripture as the truth; the Church as the pillar and ground of the truth — with it being well understood that the truth has "precellence," that is, pre-excellence, over the Church.

Beginning with the stone tablets "written with the finger of God" (Exodus 31:18), the Holy Scripture would expand. There will first be the Torah; then the Torah and the Prophets; then the Torah, the Prophets, and the Writings. Finally, in the fullness of time, when the Son of God has come, when He has been raised up into glory, has sent the Spirit and has begun to build *His* Church on the foundation of the apostles with the faithful Jewish remnant (whereas the old Israel with the Temple and its sacrifices is passing away), then the fourth and final part is added to the other three, giving us the Torah + the Prophets + the Writings + the twenty-seven Books of the Tradition of the Apostles.

From that time forth, the holy catholic Church — the people of the covenant now in the new and definitive era of the *ecclesial time* — approaches the Holy Scripture — now complete and inexhaustible — determined to listen to it, to apply our minds to understanding it, to meditate on and follow it, to translate and transmit it, and to explain and faithfully apply it. Without adding to or taking anything away from it. By respecting its unique and diverse meaning.

"Tota Scriptura" and the "Catholic" Tradition

The fourth-century ecumenical Creed of Nicea-Constantinople, together with the western Apostles' Creed (so named because it summarizes the Faith of the apostles), speaks of the *catholic* Church.

Similarly, the fifth-century Athanasian Creed speaks of the *catholic* Faith. In no way do the traditionally named Catholics, Roman or Eastern Orthodox, have exclusive rights to this word. The sixteenth-century Reformers also took this word for themselves. The common explanation of the meaning of *catholic* that is satisfied to equate the *Catholic* Church and the *Catholic* Faith with the *universal* Church and the *universal* Faith is not only an error, it is to deny the word its full meaning.

The Greek word *katholicos* comes from two words juxtaposed: *kath*, meaning "according to," and *holon*, meaning "the whole." When the word "catholic" is reduced to its merely *quantitative* sense, it is taken to have either a spatial or temporal meaning: "according to the whole of space" (that is, universal); or "according to the whole of time" (that is, continual, perpetual, permanent). When someone confesses, "I believe in the *catholic* Church," he is merely saying, "I believe in the universality of the Church," or "I believe in the continuity, perpetuity and permanence of the Church." There is, however, something more important, something more essential to this word: its *qualitative* sense. In fact, the quantitative sense (both spatial and temporal) follows from the qualitative sense, the latter being principal and primary. According to the *qualitative* sense, "catholic" means "according to the whole of normative revelation which is, for the Church, the Holy Scripture."

We must certainly believe in the *universality* of the Church in space and in the *perpetuity* of the Church in time. But first and foremost, we must believe in the *catholicity* of the Church of God (*tota ecclesia*), whose obedience consists primarily in being, and remaining faithful, to the *whole* Word of God (*tota scriptura*).

Consider St. Athanasius (296–373). When he found himself *solus contra mundum*, alone against the world—and even against the whole Church universal, its bishops and pastors—it was he alone who remained catholic. For it was Athanasius who stood firmly, "according to the whole of Holy Scripture," for the divinity of the person of Christ, consubstantial with the Person of the Father, truly God and truly man, whereas the *universe* (that is, the world) which surrounded him and relentlessly persecuted him had succumbed to the Arian heresy (the Arians, disciples of Arius, rejected the doctrine of the Trinity and the divinity of Jesus).

To be *catholic* is to respect the text of Scripture as an inseparable whole, worshipping Him who is its primary and sovereign Author. It is to refuse to choose one part of Scripture over another — that is to say, it is to refuse heresy.

The opposite of *catholic* is *heretical*, and vice versa.

Moreover, the principle of *sola scriptura* (professing that the Church's standard is Scripture alone) must be accompanied by the principle of *tota scriptura* (professing that the Church's standard is Scripture in its entirety). When we say "according to Holy Scripture," we must mean according to the *whole* of Scripture — nothing more (*sola*), nothing less (*tota*).

Our separated Catholic brethren, Roman or Eastern Orthodox, cannot — nor should they — object to our calling ourselves *catholic*. In fact, we must be, and in principle are indeed, more *catholic* than they. By adding a pretended "oral revealed tradition" to the Holy Scripture, they have allowed their own traditions — which are not only without foundation in Holy Scripture, but are blatantly opposed to it — to interfere with, and in the end smother and distort, the tradition following from Scripture (*Traditio e Scriptura fluens*, as our ancient Doctors put it). To choose one part of Scripture over another is heretical. But to choose something outside of Scripture is no less heretical. Nothing is to be taken away; nothing is to be added. The Lord made that as clear to the old Church, Israel (Deuteronomy 4:1–2; 13:1–3; Ecclesiastes 3:14; Proverbs 30:5–6), as to the New Israel, the Church (Revelation 22:18–19). The Church coexists with Scripture, but being the very Word of God, Scripture rules the Church until the end of history (Matthew 5:17ff.). The Church cannot claim power over Scripture. The ecclesial tradition, throughout the ages, must always remain humbly submitted to Scripture. The voice of the Mother (Galatians 4:26), of the Bride (Revelation 21:2), who is the *catholic* Church, must be faithfully in agreement with the voice of the Father, the Husband who is the Lord, expressed in Holy Scripture, of which He is the primary and sovereign Author.

The Progress of the Ecclesial Tradition

Completed since the end of the apostolic times in A.D. 70, centered entirely on Christ and illumined by Him and by the Holy Spirit whom

He has sent, and given to the Church as *regula fidei et vitae* (the rule-standard-law of faith and life), Holy Scripture is the inexhaustible source of the genuinely ecclesial tradition (*Traditio e Scriptura fluens*).

This unique source is truly inexhaustible. The Church, *mater et magistra*, like (only better than) "every scribe instructed in the kingdom concerning the kingdom of heaven, is like a householder who brings out of his treasure things new and old" (Matthew 13:52). The job is never done. Tasked "to fully carry out the preaching of the word of God, that is, the mystery which has been hidden from the past ages and generations; but has now been manifested to His saints, to whom God willed to make known what is the riches of the glory of this mystery among the Gentiles, which is Christ in you, the hope of glory" (Colossians 1:25–28, NASB), the Church, following the apostles, and faithful to their normative tradition, can and must always promote the knowledge that she progressively receives, with greater and greater precision, "that their hearts [those of the saints] may be encouraged, having been knit together in love, and attaining to all the wealth that comes from the full assurance of understanding, resulting in a true knowledge of God's mystery, that is, Christ Himself, in whom are hidden all the treasures of wisdom and knowledge" (Colossians 2:2–3, NASB).

The genuinely ecclesial tradition neither shrinks nor stretches the fixed revelation of Holy Scripture, but rather, under the leading of the Holy Spirit, serves to draw out and apply, translate and transmit, the fullness of its meaning. Gradually over time, and not without conflicts and difficulties, a more and more distinct tradition emerges, with more and more precise clarifications (even though, on account of Scripture's inexhaustibility, absolute precision remains beyond reach).

During His earthly life (to say nothing of His heavenly intercession!), the Lord Jesus prayed "for those who will believe in Me through their word," referring to the word of the apostles (John 17:20). If we can and must believe that there is a quantitative catholicity of the Church in time (continuity, perpetuity) and space (universality), then we can and must also believe that there is also, and more importantly, a growing qualitative catholicity of the Church in her understanding of the meaning of the Trinitarian and Christological Revelation of Holy Scripture. This qualitative catholicity of the Church grows as she plumbs the depths of the now-completed canon and passes down what becomes increasingly refined throughout the span of *ecclesial time* (from A.D. 70 onwards) until the days come in history when "the earth shall be full of the knowledge of the LORD as the waters cover the sea" (Isaiah 11:9; cf. 65:17–25; Matthew 28:18–20; and Romans 15:11–13).

The risk, the temptation, the error, is for the Church, or a church, to violate tradition by straying from fidelity to Scripture on this or that point, and by choosing ("*heretizing*") pretended truths found beyond, and contrary to, Scripture. Since this is always possible, *the ecclesial tradition will always have to be critiqued and be ready to critique itself.* Further, every true Reformation of the Church — or of a church — is nothing more than the putting into practice, the application regardless of the cost, of this self-criticism which does not work *against* the tradition and legitimate church authority, but, to the contrary, works to recover, purify, liberate, and strengthen the same. Not only does the Church profit from the truths that her tradition assumes, she likewise can and must profit from the errors into which her tradition has fallen, for only in correcting them can a true progress in the ecclesial tradition be made or regained.

The Two Great Epochs in the Progress of Ecclesial Tradition

If we define an *epoch* as "*a moment*, an historical movement of characteristic and decisive importance,"[7] then there are two epochs of the first order in the progress of the ecclesial tradition: the epoch of the first four ecumenical Councils (325–451), and that of the Reformation (1530–1647). The remarkable fact — and one that is rarely mentioned — is that these two epochs, however different they may be, have one and the same *raison d'être*. With fearless fidelity to Holy Scripture, both answered the call to confess the Faith: *God, and God alone, the Father, the Son, and the Holy Spirit, is the Lord and Savior and there is none besides Him.*

That is not to say that such a faithful confession was totally absent during the times preceding or following these two epochs. There were certainly those who prepared the way, followed by those who stayed the course — humble men, unknown today, whose names are written in heaven, who, like the Fathers and Doctors so justly named,

---

7. In Latin, *momentum* is a contraction of *movimentum*.

continued to read and meditate assiduously on Scripture and offer up incessant prayers which have not failed to bear fruit.

The Epoch of the Early Ecumenical Councils

The Early Heresies and the First Four Ecumenical Councils

From the earliest days of ecclesial time, the theological meditation of the Church and of faithful Christians has centered on the fact that God has revealed Himself in His Word as the God who is always both One and Many. From the earliest formulations of the Apostles' Creed and the *Baptismal Formula* going back to Jesus Himself — "I baptize you in the name (singular) of the Father, of the Son, and of the Holy Spirit (plural)" — the *Regula Fidei* (the Rule of the Church's Faith) drew attention to the *Trinitarian* mystery, which was itself bound up in the *Christological* mystery. Even before these mysteries were formally recognized and taught, they were part of the Church's confession.

During the century which followed the apostles (from the end of the first century to the second half of the second century), the "Apostolic Fathers" such as Clement of Rome, Barnabus, Ignatius of Antioch, and Hermas, together with the "Apologists" such as Justin Martyr, Melito of Sardis, and the anonymous author of the *Letter to Diogenese*, gave attention to the Scriptural foundations of these mysteries. This must be acknowledged. However, it is a quasi-contemporary of Irenaeus (130–202) who stands out for his insistence on the consubstantial unity of the Father, the Son, and the Holy Spirit. We owe this development in the doctrine of the Trinity, which came more than a century before the first ecumenical Council of Nicea (325), to Tertullian (155–230). While Irenaeus had also spoken of the *consubstantial unity*, it was Tertullian who completed Irenaeus by speaking also of the *distinction, without separation*, of the three divine persons. Moreover, it was Tertullian who coined the word *Trinitas* (Trinity), which had the advantage of combining "One" and "Three" and thereby pointing to the mystery, One and Many, of the one God, the Father, the Son, and the Holy Spirit, who has revealed Himself in Jesus Christ and throughout Holy Scripture.

The *Christological mystery*, that the divine Person of the Son has assumed human nature in addition to divine nature without ceasing to be God — put another way: the mystery of Jesus Christ being both *vere Deus* (truly God) and *vere homo* (truly man) — is intimately linked to the *Trinitarian mystery*. Thus the Church has always given attention to these two mysteries together, both well before the first ecumenical Council of Nicea (325) and long after the fourth ecumenical Council of Chalcedon (451). The goal has not been to explain these mysteries comprehensively (such comprehension is impossible!) but rather to apprehend them faithfully, which is both needful and sufficient.

The rationalistic impulse that favored comprehensive explanation over faithful apprehension led to the rise of many heresies that departed from the ecclesial Faith (the *fides quae creditur*, the Faith which is believed, and confessed, by the Church, as opposed to the *fides qua creditur*, the faith by which one believes). These heresies added elements to the Faith here, subtracted elements from it there — in each case departing from the Scripture! — with the result that such heresies did not further illumine the revealed mysteries of the ecclesial Faith, but rather suppressed them. And yet the introduction of these heresies also provoked the catholic Church — catholic "according to the *whole* of Scripture and according to Scripture *alone*" — to clarify the Faith of which she is "the pillar and ground." Thus it has often been on account of heresies — though thanks must be to God! — that the ecclesial tradition has made progress. Whatever the devil may do, God always turns it to good. Heresies tend to deviate from the catholic Faith and deform it in spite of the partial truths they contain. In responding to them, the Church benefits from this rigorous exercise in doctrinal clarification, from which she emerges better able to redirect and restore the true form of the Faith.[8]

---

8. *Translator's Note:* Cf. Harold O. J. Brown, *Heresies: The Image of Christ in the Mirror of Heresy and Orthodoxy from the Apostles to the Present* (1984). Brown writes: "Heresy... presupposes orthodoxy. And, curiously enough, it is heresy that offers us some of the best evidence for orthodoxy, for while heresy is often very explicit in the first centuries of Christianity, orthodoxy is often only implicit. If we hope, today, that the orthodoxy we believe is the 'faith once delivered to the saints' (Jude 3), then it is necessary to assume that it is older than heresy. But heresy appears on the historical record earlier, and is better documented, than what most of the church came to call orthodoxy. How then can heresy be younger, orthodoxy more original? The answer is that orthodoxy was there from the beginning and heresy reflected it. Sometimes one catches a glimpse of another person or object in a mirror on a lake

In the early centuries several heresies challenged the *vere Deus* and/or the *vere homo,* or the relation of the *vere Deus* and *vere homo* to the Faith.

The Heresy of Arius (256–336)

Arius and Arianism denied that Christ was truly God. At its highpoint, the Arian heresy was found throughout the whole of the Empire and even, for a time, held sway over the majority of the churches (the fact remains, however, that it has always had followers and to this day includes many within churches across all denominations). The maintaining of the faithful confession of the Faith called for a fight against Arianism. St. Athanasius (296–373) in the East and St. Hilary (315–367) in the West, together with the first two ecumenical Councils (Nicea, 325, and Constantinople, 381), answered the call. In accordance with Scripture, they declared the Faith in "one Lord Jesus Christ, the only-begotten Son of God, begotten of the Father before all worlds, God of God; Light of Light, very God of very God; begotten, not made, being of one substance with the Father, by whom all things were made. Who, for us men and for our salvation, came down from heaven, and was incarnate by the Holy Spirit of the Virgin Mary, and was made man..." (the Nicene Creed).

The Heresy of Apollinarius (died 390)

Apollinarius, of Laodicea, taught that the divine *Logos* (the Word) in Christ replaced His mind, which amounted to an attack on the *vere homo* — Christ was not fundamentally human in the same way that we are human; he did not have a *human* mind. St. Athanasius took great pains to oppose his former ally who had now lapsed into an error, a heresy that was the opposite of the Arian heresy. Arius was guilty of denying Christ's full divinity; Apollinarius denied Christ's full humanity. Athanasius was joined by St. Ambrose of Milan (340–397), who had also battled against Arianism, and now brought his abilities into the fight against Apollinarianism. In the year 381, the Council of Constantinople, in accordance with Scripture and against

---

before seeing the original. But the original preceded the reflection, and our perception of it. The same, we would argue, is true of orthodoxy — the original — and heresy — the reflection. The heresy we frequently see first, but orthodoxy preceded it" (4).

Apollinarius, confessed that Christ had assumed a fully human nature — that is to say, *vere homo*, truly man. Thus every imaginable *division* of His human nature was rejected.

The Heresy of Nestorius (380–451)

Nestorius contended that Christ was not one person with two natures, but rather two different persons — the one divine, the other human — and in so doing he effectively reduced the Incarnation to a moral union between God and the man Jesus, which is no Incarnation at all. Thus it could not be said that Jesus was *vere Deus,* truly God. The third ecumenical Council, the Council of Ephesus in the year 431, took it upon itself to condemn Nestorianism. In so doing, the real union of the divine and human natures in the one person of Christ was vigorously attested in a manner following Scripture, and the heresy of the *separation* of the two natures into two different persons was rejected.

The Heresy of Eutychius (378–453)

A contemporary of Nestorius and holding to the opposite error, Eutychius was a monophysite (a partisan of "one nature only"). He mixed the divine and human natures, arguing for a *confusion* of the two, a mixed divino-human nature (= theanthropic) of the Person of Christ. His proposed explanation thus amounted to a denial of the *vere homo*, Christ's truly human nature. The fourth ecumenical Council, the Council of Chalcedon in the year 451 (concerning which we will have more to say), condemned the doctrine of Eutychius by affirming — again, in conformity to Scripture — that the one Person of Christ had two natures, divine and human, *without confusion, without change, without division, without separation.* And so it was formulated yet more precisely still, after the Councils of Nicea, Constantinople, and Ephesus, that our Lord is indeed *vere Deus et vere homo* (truly God and truly man).

The Fifth and Sixth Ecumenical Councils

The period we are considering had two more councils which followed the epoch of the first four ecumenical Councils (325–451).

The fifth and sixth ecumenical Councils, the last of the ecumenical Councils to be faithful to Holy Scripture, are known as Constantinople II (553) and Constantinople III (680–681). In passing, we note two things.

First, in keeping with the Council of Ephesus (431), Constantinople II condemned the worship of Jesus' human nature; worship and adoration can only be directed to God, to the divine Person of Jesus Christ who took on human nature while remaining fully divine. With that, *the Council forbade, according to Scripture, any introduction whatsoever of the worship of man — and,* a fortiori, *the worship of any creation — into the Faith and Christian worship.*

Second, the Council of Constantinople III condemned the heresy of the *monothelytes* (partisans of the "one will" of Christ). Taking a much more subtle approach than the monophysites, the monothelytes mixed and confounded the divine will and human will of Christ into one will. With this move, the will of man was made to enter into the will of God, and the way opened for man to become one with God.

By condemning the worship of human nature (even that of Jesus Himself) and the confusion of the divine and human wills (even within Christ), Constantinople II and III laid the groundwork for the condemnation of modern heretics who would equate "belief in God" with "belief in man," and "human rights" with "the truth of God."[9] Consequent to the great councils of the period 325–451, Constantinople III affirmed once for all, according to Scripture and according to the catholic Faith proceeding from it: "We will not exalt into the divine essence what is created, nor will we bring down the glory of the divine nature to the place suited to the creature."

Returning to Chalcedon

With beauty and truth, and out of faithfulness and submission to the Word of God, Holy Scripture, the Council of Chalcedon concluded this defining epoch for the catholic Faith by clarifying the mystery of the Trinity and, above all, the mystery of the Person of Jesus Christ. By working out and stating in clear and precise terms — as far as is humanly possible — the confession of the catholic Faith, the

---

9. Cf. Jean-Marc Berthoud, *Une religion sans Dieu. Les Droits de l'Homme contre l'Évangile* (L'Age d'Homme, 1993).

Christological mystery, the "truly God, truly man" of the one and only Mediator, our Lord Jesus Christ, this council definitively and faithfully rejected every human pretension, whether personal or social, to self-divinization (the Church, the state, a philosophical or scientific school of thought, etc.). None but the Lord Jesus Christ can ever say: "All authority has been given to Me in heaven and on earth" (Matthew 28:18). In Him alone — the Sovereign Word Incarnate, seated at the right hand of the Father in heaven both now and until His coming in glory, and teaching through the Holy Scriptures, now complete for all time, that which His Church must guard and transmit (Matthew 28:20) — in Him alone is found the source of man's true liberty and all legitimate authority, which are instituted by Him, placed under His sovereignty, responsible to Him, and limited to the domain assigned by Him.[10]

Yes! God alone is the Lord-Savior and there is no other besides Him.

East and West after Chalcedon

The Orthodox Churches of the East after Chalcedon

For the Eastern Orthodox Churches, the period following the six ecumenical councils has continued rather smoothly up to the present day.[11] Unlike the Western Churches, whose understanding of Scripture has deepened, the Eastern Orthodox Churches have not seen any need (or even possibility) of moving beyond the dogmatic (*dogma* being Greek for "indisputable truth") statements concerning the Trinitarian and Christological mysteries: the one exception being the dogmatic vindication of the worship of icons and relics, as positively defined — though unfaithful to Scripture — by the seventh ecumenical

---

10. Cf. Pierre Courthial, "Actualité de Chalcédoine," *Foi et Vie*, No. 10, 1976, 59–66.

11. The Reformation, for example, made contact with the Orthodox Churches, but failed to influence them. Cyril Lucaris, patriarch of Constantinople, did write a *Confession of Faith* (1629) that favored the development of Reformed thought in Eastern Orthodoxy. However, not only did his confession go unheeded, it also served to provoke a reaction within Eastern Orthodoxy that further reinforced its uniqueness. The Ottoman authorities succeeded in drowning Lucaris, thus putting an end to whatever influence the Reformation might have had in the East. See George Hadjantoniou, *Protestant Patriarch, The Life of Cyril Lucaris (1572–1638), Patriarch of Constantinople* (Richmond: John Knox Press, 1961).

Council (Nicea II, 787). Holding both Scripture *and* the seven ecumenical Councils (seven being a symbolic number) as its unchanging foundation, Orthodoxy — "a green tree founded on a rock," we are told — would nevertheless become rife with mystico-gnostic speculations such as the "deification" of man,[12] the "divine energies" by which God manifests His immanence,[13] and "sophiology" (the doctrine of Wisdom).[14] That is not to say that Orthodoxy has nothing to teach us. We have much to learn from its vivid perception of the Resurrection and from its radiant liturgy, to name but two of the several things that display great faithfulness to the Word of God.

Since 1917, in the aftermath of the October Revolution and the two World Wars, Orthodoxy has been slowly but steadily advancing throughout the world: from Japan to the United States, Europe, Africa, and Latin America. In making many new contacts with both Protestantism and Roman Catholicism, and through suffering persecution in many countries throughout the decades, its understanding of Holy Scripture, its prayer, and its Christian vision of the world have been deepened, as is seen, for instance, in Alexander Schmemann's *For the Life of the World* (St. Vladimir's Press, 1973). Moreover, the Orthodox Tradition has become aware of the dangers posed by Humanism, even those harbored within the Church. This concern is evident in the works of Solzhenitsyn, as well as the works of the Serbian theologian, Father Justin Popovitch (1894–1979), particularly in his study *Man and the God-Man* (1969 in Serbian, 2009 in English).[15] Orthodoxy seems to be emerging from centuries of theological stagnation, and such development — which can only happen if it is the true extension of the reign of Christ through faith and obedience to His Word — holds out many promises for Christianity.

We have spoken above of "dogmas" (the same word in Greek as

---

12. Deification (*theosis*): "God was made man so that man might become God"; cf., for example, Maximus the Confessor (died 662).

13. Cf., for example, Gregory Palamas (1296–1359).

14. Cf., for example, Serge Boulgakov (1871–1944) and Paul Florensky (1882–1943). It needs to be added, however, that in spite of the attention given to risky and biblically unsound speculations on the subject of *Sophia*, there remains much in the works of these theologians that is faithful to Scripture.

15. *Translator's Note:* The English translation of *Man and the God-Man*, published in 2009 by Sebastian Press, was not available when Courthial wrote this book, in which he commended the French translation of Popovitch published by L'Age d'Homme in 1989 (*L'homme et le Dieu-homme*).

in English), an expression which must be intimately associated with "mysteries." The word "dogma" designates *a major and incontestable point of doctrine* which compels the faith of the Church and the conscience (the heart) of Christians because it is revealed not only in the several specific passages of Scripture which stand together, but in the whole fabric of the written Word of God. Gradually, and accompanied by great spiritual struggle, the Church and Christians individually have come to accept these dogmas as fundamental points of revelation. Their truth is grasped progressively.

The Catholic Church of the West after Chalcedon

If we date the Middle Ages in the West from Chalcedon (451) to the Reformation (1530, the date of the Augsburg Confession), then we may say that this period lasted a little more than a millennium. It was an epic period in history far more luminous than is portrayed by many a humanist scholar. During this long period, the *catholic* Tradition was maintained, though it was often obscured and disfigured by unbiblical teachings and practices. Throughout these centuries the faithful, and above all the "pastors and teachers," did not watch over the Faith as they should have. But Christ the King did — the King will never be without subjects. Also, there has never been a total break in the lifespan of the *catholic* Church, according to the indestructible promise: "I am with you always, even to the end of the age" (Matthew 28:20). It was from this Church, even when she seemed most shrouded, though ever present and tangible, that the Reformation gratefully received (1) the Holy Scripture that the ancient Fathers as well as the medieval Doctors of the Church had always, unanimously, confessed to be the very Word of God, (2) the Creed of the Fathers (Nicene-Constantinople Creed) and the Athanasian Creed, and (3) the fundamental and biblical teachings of the first six ecumenical Councils. Thus the Reformed Catholics had no need to trace their authority back to pretended spiritual *ancestors* or *fathers* who founded, or led, obscure and dubious sects. Rather, as we shall see, the Reformation sought to locate itself within the *continuum* of the Church and of the catholic Tradition maintained since the apostles, while recognizing that these were stifled and compromised by lapsed institutions and/or doctrines. Two citations from Calvin require our attention here:

> For the Lord's covenant remains, and shall forever remain inviolable, which he solemnly ratified with Christ, the true Solomon, and his members in these words: "If his children forsake my law and walk not in my judgments, if they profane my righteousnesses...and keep not my commandments,...I will visit their transgressions with the rod, their iniquities with stripes. But my mercy I will not utterly take from him.[16]

And:

> But because it is now our intention to discuss the visible church, let us learn even from the simple title "mother" how useful, indeed how necessary, it is that we should know her. For there is no other way to enter into life unless this mother conceive us in her womb, give us birth, nourish us at her breast, and lastly, unless she keep us under her care and guidance until, putting off mortal flesh, we become like the angels (Matthew 22:30).[17]

Let us further ask, has the Church ever been pure and clean? Is it not enough to consider the churches in the time of the apostles — Corinth, Galatia, Ephesus, Pergamum, Sardis, Laodicea, for example? These were all called by the Lord to repent and reform themselves. How can we then fail to find positive elements in the medieval Church which, even in its decline, included so many men and women passionately devoted — more so than we are on several points — to the Trinitarian God, to Christ the God-man, and to the Holy Scriptures received and heard as the very Word of the Lord, our Creator and Savior?

*

The figure who unquestionably marches at the head of this great procession of the western medieval Church is St. Augustine (354–430), whose vast literary production has exercised its influence and borne abundant fruit in every century since to this day. From his conversion to his death — that is, from his *Confessions* to his *Retractions*,

---

16. John Calvin, *Institutes of the Christian Religion*, IV.1.27.
17. *Ibid.*, IV, 1, 4.

passing through his mature works, such as *On Christian Doctrine* (396–426), *On the Trinity* (400–428), and *The City of God* (413–426), among others — we see St. Augustine's thinking moving further and further away from classical pagan thought, especially Platonism, on which he first heavily relied, and more and more toward a thoroughly Christian — that is, biblical — theology. This theology carried him decisively in at least three directions.

First, he battled against Pelagianism by affirming the sovereignty of divine grace.[18]

Second, he denied the pretended primacy and autonomy of human reason, one of several distinct features of Greek philosophy, by affirming the primacy of the Faith, of the Truth of God's Word. This was encapsulated in his famous phrase *credo ut intelligam* — "I believe so that I may understand."

Third, he rejected any amalgam, any false synthesis, by affirming the spiritual antithesis between the City of God (*civitas Dei*) and the earthly city (*civitas terrena*), the city of covenant-breaking men, between Jerusalem and Babylon, an antithesis that lies even within us as individuals. These two cities are "formed by two loves: the earthly by the love of self, even to the contempt of God; the heavenly by the love of God, even to the contempt of self. One seeks glory from men, but the greatest glory of the other is God, the witness of conscience. One lifts up its head in its own glory; the other says to God, 'Thou art my glory, and the lifter up of mine head' (Psalm 3:3)."[19]

Augustine's influence was carried into the Middle Ages by three principal figures who received, and continued to build upon, the main of his thought: a *philosopher*, St. Anselm (1033–1109), a *mystic*, St. Bernard (1091–1153), and a *theologian*, St. Bonaventure (1221–1274). St. Anselm's *Proslogion* — which first bore the more Augustinian title of

---

18. Pelagius (c. 360–c. 422) and his disciple Caelestius, condemned by an African Council held in Carthage in 418, gave primacy to the value and autonomy of man. They rejected original sin: sin was limited to present, isolated acts without ontological consequences. According to Pelagianism, God and man relate reciprocally in total freedom; man always acts freely of his own accord: if he so desired, he could be sinless. Whether in their more or less attenuated forms, or in their extreme form, Pelagianism or semi-Pelagianism have always been present in the history of the Church. A latent Pelagianism has manifested itself as much throughout Eastern Orthodoxy as in the Western Church ("Molinism," named after the Spanish Jesuit Luis Molina, 1535–1601, who was attacked by the Thomists [disciples of Thomas Aquinas, 1225–1274] in the sixteenth century in the Roman Church; and "Armianism," named after Jacob Arminius, 1560–1609, attacked by the Calvinists in the Reformed Churches).

19. *The City of God*, trans. Marcus Dodds (Random House), Book XIV, ch. 28.

Fides quaerens intellectum (Faith seeking understanding) — concluded its first chapter with these words taken straight from Augustine: *neque enim quaero intelligere ut credam, sed credo ut intelligam* (I do not seek to understand that I may believe, but I believe that I may understand). In his *Cur Deus Homo?* (Why the God-man?), St. Anselm advanced the Church's understanding of the atonement by brilliantly laying out, for the first time, the doctrine of expiation.

When studying a specific point of Christian doctrine, it is not unusual to uncover a progressive thread of truly catholic thought running through several key figures over time. To take one significant example, the *satisfaction* of Christ, we can trace this theme as it runs from St. Anselm to the Doctors of the Reformation, passing through St. Bernard of Clairvaux and Thomas Aquinas (1227–1274):

1. In his *Cur Deus Homo*, Anselm shows that God, in Jesus Christ, has *made satisfaction for* the justice of the thrice-holy God by His expiation of sin, and has *merited* our salvation.
2. St. Bernard — *the Bible was held in honor among his disciples!* — resolutely opposed the baneful Abelard (1079–1142), a *modernist* before his time whose thought combined the heresies of Arius, Pelagius, and Nestorius. In this struggle St. Bernard extended Anselm's thought by presenting and developing the biblical doctrine of the relation of Christ, the Head, to His own, the members of His body, by showing how the merit of One brought *satisfaction* for many.
3. Further extending the line established by Anselm and Bernard, Thomas Aquinas brought to light Christ's *satisfaction*, which includes His taking upon Himself the penalty of our sin, including death, and His *expiation*, which was the demonstration of God's unmerited love toward the sinful human race.
4. The Doctors of the Reformation did not depart from this line, nor from this specific point concerning *satisfaction*. In fact, they would establish that Christ's satisfaction consisted not only of His *passive obedience* in His passion, but also of His *active obedience* throughout the entire course of His incarnate life.

The Epoch of the Reformation

Introduction

The Reformation in the Church of the West in the sixteenth and seventeenth centuries stood right in line with the catholic Faith of the first six ecumenical Councils, the ecclesial tradition flowing from Scripture. It claimed as its own the Creeds and decisions of the aforementioned Councils.

This was explicitly acknowledged in several Reformed Confessions. For example, *The Gallicana* (The French Confession of Faith drafted in Paris in 1559, confirmed at La Rochelle in 1571) declares in articles VI, XIV and XV:

> These Holy Scriptures teach us that in this one sole and simple divine essence, whom we have confessed, there are three persons: the Father, the Son and the Holy Spirit. The Father, first cause, principle, and origin of all things. The Son, his Word and eternal wisdom. The Holy Spirit, his virtue, power and efficacy. The Son begotten from eternity by the Father, The Holy Spirit proceeding eternally from them both; the three persons not confused, but distinct, and yet not separate, but of the same essence, equal in eternity and power. *And in this we confess that which hath been established by the ancient councils, and we detest all sects and heresies which were rejected by the holy doctors, such as St. Hilary, St. Athanasius, St. Ambrose, and St. Cyril.*

> We believe that Jesus Christ, being the wisdom of God and his eternal Son, has put on our flesh, so as to be God and man in one person; man, like unto us, capable of suffering in body and soul, yet free from all stain of sin. And as to his humanity, he was the true seed of Abraham and of David, although he was conceived by the secret power of the Holy Spirit. *In this we detest all the heresies that have of old troubled the Church.*

> We believe that in one person, that is, Jesus Christ, the two natures are actually and inseparably joined and united, and yet each remains in its proper character: so that in this union the divine nature, retaining its attributes, remained uncreated, infinite, and all-pervading; and the

human nature finite, having its form, measures, and attributes; and although Jesus Christ, in rising from the dead, bestowed immortality upon his body, yet he did not take from it the truth of its nature, and we so consider him in his divinity that we do not despoil him of his continuity.

At the end of its article on the authority of Scripture, *The Gallicana*, demonstrating its willful and unreserved loyalty to the ecclesial tradition faithful to Scripture, declares: "And therefore we confess the three creeds, to wit: the Apostles', the Nicene, and the Athanasian, because they are in accordance with the Word of God" (Article V).

Such statements can be found throughout the teachings of the Reformers and confessing reformed Doctors. A simple look through Calvin's *Institutes of the Christian Religion*, which is full of quotations from the Councils and Fathers, will suffice to show this. Faithful to the Word of God, the Reformed Churches stated:

> In this way we willingly embrace and reverence as holy the early councils, such as those of Nicaea, Constantinople, Ephesus, Chalcedon, and the like, which were convened to refute the errors and evil opinions of heretics. We honor and reverence them in so far as they relate to the teachings of faith. For they contain nothing but the pure and genuine exposition of Scripture, which the holy Fathers applied with spiritual prudence to crush the enemies of religion who had then arisen.[20]

Where the ancient Fathers and/or Councils differed with Scripture, the Reformers clearly did not go along with them. Luther, as early as 1525, had said: "We must take the sayings of the Fathers with a spirit of liberty, and declare worthless those which are not based on Scripture." Accordingly, out of faithfulness to the Scripture-Word of God, the Reformers and confessing Reformed rejected, and always shall reject, the decisions of the second Council of Nicea (787) which imposed the worship of holy images, icons. So did Calvin rightly add:

> [T]he restoration of images...has subsequently prevailed among the people. But Augustine says that this practice involves an ever-present

---

20. Calvin, *Institutes*, IV.9.8.

danger of idolatry. Epiphanius, of a previous period, speaks much more harshly, for he states that it is unlawful and abominable for images to be seen in the churches of Christians.[21]

Otherwise said, the decisions of the Councils and the teachings of the Fathers of the ancient Church and the Doctors of the Middle Ages are such that

> [w]e modestly dissent from them when they are found to set down things differing from, or altogether contrary to, the Scriptures. Neither do we think that we do them any wrong in this matter; seeing that they all, with one consent, will not have their writings equated with the canonical Scriptures, but command us to prove how far they agree or disagree with them, and to accept what is in agreement and to reject what is in disagreement.

So summarizes the second chapter of *The Second Helvetic Confession* (1566), which the Synod held at La Rochelle in 1571, the Synod of *The Gallicana*, solemnly recognized and adopted.

The Necessity of the Reformation

Nothing is more important in the life and mission of the truly *catholic* Church than her call, her service, her responsibility, and her duty to be faithful to the Scripture-Word of God. It is upon this sole fact that the Reformation, from its earliest conception in 1520, was justified and necessary, and it was from this fact that it drew its authority. The papacy and its ministers, in order to maintain their extravagant traditions, had no more right in the sixteenth century to wield their power of the institutional Church against the biblically faithful teaching of the Reformers, than the leaders of Israel, the officials of the Jews, had in the first century to wield their power (instituted clearly by God in Deuteronomy 17:8–13) against the biblically faithful teaching (at that time, the Old Testament) of Jesus and the apostles.

The apostles report approvingly of the faithful in Berea who "received the word with all readiness, and searched the Scriptures daily to find out whether these things were so" (Acts 17:11). And that was

---

21. *Ibid.*, IV, 9, 9.

precisely what the Reformers desired to see of Rome — that Rome would examine its tradition under the light of the Scriptures.[22]

At certain decisive moments in church history, whether in the old administration of the covenant or the new, the Lord of the Church has exceptionally called men to extraordinary offices, parallel yet distinct from that of the ordinary "ordained ministry," an office requiring of them, often in great loneliness, to call the people of God back to renewed obedience to His Word. We need only think of such men as an Elijah in the old administration (1 Kings 17ff.), or a St. Athanasius in the new — both condemned and rejected as much by those who wielded the ecclesial authority as by the people of God in general. In a letter addressed to his fellow bishops, St. Athanasius dared to speak of "the whole dismembered Church," for at that time the Arians and their bishops ruled nearly three quarters of the churches and, being exceedingly skilled in the art of ecclesiastical politics, succeeded in convening more than ten great Councils favoring their heresy, including: Tyre, 335; Arles, 353; Milan, 355; Sirmium, 357 (with this gem: "Everyone doubtless knows that the catholic Faith teaches that there are two persons: the greater one being the Father, and the lesser one under Him, the Son"); and Rimini, 359–360 ("the Son like unto the Father!"). St. Athanasius was excommunicated on several occasions, and in 357 he was condemned by Pope Tiberius. And to think that all this transpired between the ecumenical Council of Nicea (325) and that of Constantinople (381)! This merely demonstrates that heresy, like a pesky weed, never stops spreading.

Even in 1859, Cardinal John Henry Newman (1801–1890), whose convictions led him to become Roman Catholic, wrote — and I believe he observed and spoke rightly — "I see, then, in the Arian history a palmary example of a state of the Church, during which, in order to know the Tradition of the Apostles, we must have recourse to the faithful."[23]

When Pope Leo X excommunicated Martin Luther, he not only challenged a Doctor and Reformer of the Church, but what is more,

---

22. What the Reformers desired of Rome was, in this respect, similar to what Jesus desired of the Jews in his day.

23. John Henry Newman, "On Consulting the Faithful in Matters of Doctrine," *Rambler*, July, 1859. *Translator's Note:* Newman drew tremendous criticism for the position he advocated in this article. See John R. Connolly, *John Henry Newman: A View of Catholic Faith for the New Millenium* (Lanham, MD: Rowman and Littlefield Publishers, 2005), 8.

without knowing or intending it, he disrupted the deepening of the whole western Church's interpretation of the Word of God. His action not only put a stop to the Reformation of the still united Catholic Church, but also halted her advance along the trajectory set by the first ecumenical Councils. The pope's hasty decision, rendered before a Council could be called — which Luther, along with many others, had insistently sought — produced another split among Christians in the West (the first being the split between the Eastern and Western Churches dating at least to the beginning of the thirteenth century, the sacking of Constantinople under Innocent III by the 4th Crusade). Ignoring the precedent established in Scripture (cf. Acts 15) that enjoins church leaders to seek the resolution of a controversy in a spirit of *conciliation* according to the Tradition proceeding from normative Scripture, Pope Leo X chose instead to single-handedly put an end to the matter with his Curia.[24] With a grave sense of the rising threat, and with no intention of heeding the widespread call for Reformation, the Roman ecclesiastical system, the Roman Establishment, moved to protect its power positions.

> The more one loves the Church, the more one should strive for her deliverance from the evils which distress her, especially when these evils push her to the verge of visible ruin.... A corrupted Church is composed of two societal elements — the one good, the other evil; the one which makes her the Church, and the other which corrupts her. The first of these ought to be respected and preserved in its entirety, insofar as it depends on us. But the second is a disastrous element which no one has the right to establish and which those who love the Church are called and obliged to destroy. We may even add that the first of these elements gives us the right and duty to take action against the second.[25]

The Abiding Significance of the Pre-Reformation Ecclesial Tradition

Let us say again: up until the Reformation, our Mother of all, our Church common to all, with her shades of light and darkness, to all who are today Roman Catholics, or Anglicans, or Lutherans, or

---

24. It is true that at this time even Cardinal Cajetan (1468–1533), master general of the Dominicans and the German legate, dared affirm that the pope was "above the Council, above Scripture, and above all that which is the Church!"

25. This quote is taken from *Défense de la Reformation*, II, IV, by Jean Claude (1619–1687).

Reformed, was *the Catholic Church of the West.*[26]

We thus *recognize* and *receive together* the ancient Fathers of the Church and the Doctors of the Middle Ages who were unanimous in their confession of the great dogmas of the Trinity and of Christ, and in their conviction that Holy Scripture is truly the Word of God. This does not, however, make them infallible. Some of the teachings of these writers we are compelled to accept with gratitude, while others we are compelled to challenge and refute. While examining various doctrinal points under the authorative light of Scripture, the Reformers gave considerable attention to what the Fathers and Doctors had said concerning them (afterall, the true ecclesial Tradition welcomes scrutiny). They found that the convictions among the Fathers and Doctors on a majority of these doctrinal points were not consistent, but varied widely and were often conflicting. This was the case with such doctrines as Scripture and tradition[s], salvation by grace, justification and sanctification, Mariology, mediation[s] and intermediaries, the worship of angels, saints, images and relics, sacraments, faith, works and merit, purgatory, etc. Such was to be expected, since every theologian of every age is influenced to some degree by personal idiosyncrasies, by his cultural milieu, by the intellectual spirit of his age, by social pressures, etc. But what matters above all is the degree of his attention and obedience to Scripture coupled with humble prayer. We must add that, despite their present division between distinct churches, all Christians today who aim to be *catholic* and *orthodox* give attention, as to brothers, to the Fathers and Doctors before the Reformation. Proof is found in the fact that many Doctors of the Reformation in addition to Calvin were considered experts in patrology (the study of the Fathers of the early Church). Such was the Reformer Pierre Martyr Vermigli (1500–1562), a friend of Calvin and Bucer, whose *Treatise and Disputation on the Doctrine of the Eucharist* (1559) is a commentary on the works of the Fathers. Such also were the Lutherans Martin Chemnitz (1522–1586), who demonstrated his grasp of the Fathers in his *Examination of the Council of Trent* (published from 1565–1573) and his treatise *On the Two Natures of Christ* (1574),

---

26. *Translator's Note:* Courthial is keen on making this point because there are many splinter groups who try to trace the history of the "true Church" back to the apostles through small and relatively unknown Christian communities standing outside the Catholic Church. As he has said previously, this creates great problems for such historians since these groups were usually caught up in one heresy or another.

and Johann Gerhard (1582–1677), author of the first *Patrology* ever written (we owe the very term *patrology* to him) and a *Catholic Confession* which is a treatise on the catholic Tradition of the Fathers. But within these we must, as Chemnitz noted, "separate the straw from the gold." More recent proof is found in the several denominational or ecumenical editions of the works of the Fathers and particular works of the medieval Doctors published on both sides of the Atlantic.

Two more things should be known about the long period of the Middle Ages.

First, the role of the pope during this period was far from being defined as it would finally be at the Council of Trent (1545–1563), a uniquely *Roman* council — and the doctrine of papal infallibility, contested by many within the Roman Church, would not be proclaimed until Vatican I (1870–1871), also a uniquely *Roman* council.

Second, the Church in the West during the Middle Ages was far from centralized. The *Roman* Church would become even more centralized over the four centuries from Trent to the Second World War. An apparent weakening of this centralization could be observed as it moved to Vatican II (1962–1965). But during the Middle Ages a *tolerated liberty* reigned, even in doctrine and worship, that is difficult for us to imagine today. This allowed a great many Christians, both clerics and laymen, to bear with the unbearable on many issues of doctrine because they were unhindered from confessing and pursuing their Christian life according to the Tradition flowing from Scripture.

Examples:

1. The Carolingian Church successfully and freely resisted the unfaithful decisions of the seventh ecumenical Council (Nicea II, 787) for more than a century, even stating its opposition to the worship of icons (or worship through the mediation of icons) in several of its particular councils. Thus it was not until the tenth century, 900 years after the apostolic times, that this form of worship was finally established. And it would not be until the Reformation that the Church would at least in part repent of this.
2. In the ninth century, the great defender of the ecclesial tradition faithful to Scripture, Ratramnus of Corbie (died after 868), freely published his *De corpore et sanguine Domine* on the Eucharist and his *De praedestinatione* on the sovereign election of God, which

would influence the Reformers seven centuries later.

3. Much later, at the turn of the fourteenth and fifteenth centuries, Pierre d'Ailly (1350–1420), Chancellor of the University of Paris and Archdeacon of the Church of Cambri, could write without fear of reprisal: "It is necessary to distinguish the Church universal from particular churches, that of Rome not necessarily being the 'head' of the others," or again: "The foundation of the Church is not Peter, that is, the pope, but Sacred Scripture, the Truth of the Word of Christ."[27] At the same time the French theologian Nicolas de Clamanges (died 1437) openly attacked the late scholastics for abandoning themselves to word games, "as do all who ignore Scripture and hold it in derision."[28] One sees how Auguste Lecerf (1871–1943), my professor in the Faculty of Protestant Theology in Paris, could write: "The real faith of believing [Roman] Catholics is formally so similar to our own, and so different from their present definition of theology, that they may eventually feel that there is something to reform and move closer to the ideas concerning Scripture once held by Pierre d'Ailly, Nicolas de Clamanges and so many other of the ancient doctors with whom M. Gilson was so familiar and quoted so favorably on many an occasion."[29]

Jaroslav Pelikan, in the fourth volume of his masterly *The Christian Tradition*, entitled "Reformation of the Church and Dogma: 1300–1700" (in chapter 1: "Doctrinal Pluralism at the end of the Middle Ages"), quite clearly shows the doctrinal pluralism that existed in the thirteenth and fourteenth centuries on a number of *Loci*, or doctrinal points — from the redemptive work of Jesus Christ to Mariology, the sacraments and their number, the Eucharist and transubstantiation, etc.[30] It was a pluralism that, after the Reformation, the more

---

27. *Encyclopedia Universalis*, first edition, vol. 18, 32.
28. Étienne Gilson, *La philosophie au Moyen Age* (Payot 3rd ed.), 747–753.
29. This quote comes from the fourth and final Appendix which concludes the second volume of Lecerf's *Introduction à la dogmatique réformée* (Paris: "Je Sers," 1938), p. 260. The appendix deals with the definition of faith given by the post-Tridentine catechisms, a definition which the great medievalist and Thomist Etienne Gilson (1884–1978) dealt with in his book which had then just come out, *Christianisme et philosophie*. In passing, it is interesting to note that Gilson, in his *La philosophie au Moyen Age* (cf. earlier citation) writes: "The influence of the theology of the Fathers and Doctors goes well beyond the bounds of the [Roman] Catholic Church," referring then to the "Anglican Church" and ... "Calvinism." [*Translator's Note:* The translation from the appendix is mine, although the reader can find an English translation published in Lecerf, *op. cit.*, 403.]
30. Jaroslav Pelikan, *The Christian Tradition: A History of the Development of Doctrine*,

centralized and monolithic Roman Church would no longer tolerate.

It is remarkable that the English Augustinian theologian John Wycliffe (1328–1384), who was a precursor to the Reformers on certain points (cf. his *De veritate Scripturae*, 1378) and enjoyed the faithful support of the University of Oxford and of the Christian people, was never excommunicated. Rather, his punishment was posthumous! It was not until 1428, well after his death, and after the martyrdom of John Huss and the Council of Constance (1414–1418), that his bones were exhumed, burned, and their ashes cast into the Swift. As for John Huss (1370–1415), he was the dean of the Faculty of Theology in Prague and was also a precursor to the Reformers on certain points whose life, though cut short, bore much fruit. Although he was in the end imprisoned (in 1414, and despite the Emperor Sigismund's promise of safe passage), then condemned as a heretic and burned at the stake by order of the Council of Constance on July 6, 1415, still he had been, even as late as 1411, an officially recognized preacher of the Bohemian church, faithfully supported by the Christian people and the University of Prague, of which he became the rector in 1401. He was also protected by the archbishop of Prague and King Wenceslas IV.

The Soteriological Dogma

Justification by Faith before the Reformation

We have seen that during the period of the first four ecumenical Councils (325–451) two grand dogmas, the Trinitarian and Christological dogmas, were developed (in the light of Holy Scripture and the ecclesial tradition) proclaiming the basic Truth that *God alone is the Lord-Savior and there is no other besides Him*.

With the epoch of the Reformation — and always to shed light on the same basic Truth — two more grand dogmas will be drawn from Scripture: the *Soteriological* dogma and the *Scriptural* dogma.[31] And, again, these emerge from within that continuum of ecclesial tradition faithful to Revelation.

---

vol. 4, "Reformation of Church and Dogma (1300–1700)" (University of Chicago Press, 1984).

31. In the absence of a better adjective, I say "soteriological" since in Greek *sôtêr* = Savior and *sôtêria* = salvation. As for "Scriptural," it is defined as "of or pertaining to Holy Scripture."

The Soteriological and Scriptural dogmas are closely correlated, as are the Trinitarian and Christological. What is more, each pair of dogmas is closely related to the other. The close relation of these dogmas follows the fact that the four fundamental dogmas taken together — Trinitarian, Christological, Soteriological, and Scriptural — help us to understand who God is, according to His self-revelation (His revelation of His Name) in Scripture.[32]

Throughout Church history (as much the history of Old Israel as the New), the Soteriological truth that "the God of Abraham, Isaac, and Jacob, the Trinitarian God, is THE SAVIOR: salvation is the work of God's sovereign and unmerited grace" — was written on every heart of the faithful. The reality did not have to wait for the Church to define it dogmatically: before it was defined, it was. Since the Incarnation, the prayer of every faithful Christian has been, and will be until the hour of his death, "Lord Jesus Christ, Son of God, have mercy on me a sinner!"[33] This is his first, constant, and last appeal (even if the doctrine of his particular church be tainted, penetrated by Pelagianism or semi-Pelagianism),[34] because *no man* in this world, whether Christian, Muslim, Buddhist, atheist, agnostic, etc., *no man can save himself,* but

- "with God all things are possible" (Matthew 19:26);
- "for the Son of Man has come to seek and to save that which was lost" (Luke 19:10);
- "for by grace you have been saved through faith" (Ephesians 2:8);
- "Christ Jesus came into the world to save sinners" (1 Timothy 1:15);
- "God our Savior... not by works of righteousness which we have done, but according to His mercy He saved us,... that having been justified by His grace we should become heirs according to the hope of eternal life" (Titus 3:5–7).

The Trinitarian God is, in Jesus Christ, the one and only Savior — one hundred percent, without the least autonomy on our part, not even 0.00001 thousandth!

---

32. The Revelation of Scripture is simply a long and mysterious "Naming" of God.
33. This simple evocation is the "Jesus Prayer" at the heart of the Eastern Orthodox spiritual tradition.
34. See earlier footnote on Pelagianism.

- "I, even I, am the Lord, and besides Me there is no Savior" (Isaiah 43:11).
- "Help us, O God of our salvation, for the glory of Your name; and deliver us, and provide atonement for our sins" (Psalm 79:9).
- "Nor is there salvation in any other, for there is no other name under heaven given among men by which we must be saved" (Acts 4:12).

We do not have in God *a lifeguard*, someone *rescuing us*, helping us toward salvation, but a Savior who definitively saves — who, in His love, alone has the power to save.

The same holds true even where the Soteriological dogma is unrecognized or rejected by the Church, as is the case within the more-or-less-Pelagian Eastern Orthodox Church. The piety of her faithful — and her theologians — often falls in line with the Soteriological dogma clarified by the Reformation. Thus could the Serbian theologian Justin Popovitch (1894–1979) write:

> How does the orthodox believer feel before the person of Christ the God-man? — Wholly sinful. That is his feeling, his attitude, his posture, his confession, his very self whole and entire. This sense of being nothing but sinful, personally sinful, before the most gentle Lord Jesus is the soul of his soul, the heart of his heart.... This attitude is a sacred duty and a sincere prayer for every orthodox Christian without exception. It is toward this that our immortal teachers, the holy Fathers, walked and guide us. We need only mention two: St. John of Damascus and St. Symeon the New Theologian. Their holiness is certainly worthy of the Cherubim, their prayers surely seraphic; yet even they had a complete awareness and recognition of their sinful state coupled with an attitude of profound conversion. This same antinomy pervades our orthodox faith, evangelical and apostolic, and our life lived in this same faith.[35]

In his response to Erasmus, Luther makes a similar observation about the very theologians whose "words about the power of free choice" Erasmus has cited.

---

35. *L'homme et le Dieu-homme* (Lausanne: L'Age d'Homme, 1989), 156.

In fact, I can easily prove to you the exact opposite of your position: namely, that whenever such holy men as you boast of approach God to pray or deal with Him, they approach Him in utter forgetfulness of their "free-will"; in self-despair they cry to Him for pure grace alone, as something far other than they deserve. Augustine was often thus; so was Bernard when, at the point of death, he said: "I have wasted my time, for I have lived a waster's life." I see no mention here of a power that could apply itself to grace; all power is here condemned, because it was entirely turned away from grace.[36]

Again, throughout church history, the faithful have known that "the Trinitarian God, is THE SAVIOR: salvation is the work of God's sovereign and unmerited grace."

Justification by Faith Expounded by the Reformers

Prior to the Reformation, the specific doctrine of justification by faith had not been expounded. Even when the topic was broached by the Fathers and medieval Doctors,[37] the biblically essential distinctions between justification and regeneration, justification and sanctification, justification of sinners and justification of righteous persons (the justified) were not to be found. Even St. Augustine, who had expounded with such excellence upon the liberty, sovereignty, and efficacy of the grace of God who saves covenant-breaking men, did not teach justification by faith.

In the absence of a precise definition of this ecclesial dogma — which maintains, preserves, and brings to the fore this revealed mystery — there arose the doctrines of merits, supererogatory works of the saints, and indulgences. Such heretical and semi-Pelagian ideas accompanied the impious idea that justification is partially obtained and *earned* by human works.

The leading contribution of the Reformation to the ecclesial tradition was that it defined the grand soteriological dogma of *justification by faith*, and it did so in the name of the catholic Church and of the ecclesial tradition following from Scripture. At the forefront of this

---

36. Martin Luther, *Bondage of the Will*, trans. J. I. Packer and O. R. Johnston (Grand Rapids: James Clarke & Co. Ltd, 1957), 114–115.

37. So could Calvin refer to the excellent statements on this subject made by St. Ambrose. Cf. Calvin, *Institutes*, III.11.3 and 11.23.

great effort was Martin Luther. And what Luther first discovered and brought to light, the ecclesial Confessions of faith would go on, with him (such as Augsburg, 1530) and after him (up to Westminster, 1647), to proclaim concerning this doctrine:

> Those whom God effectually calleth, He also freely justifieth:
> - not by infusing righteousness into them, but by pardoning their sins, and by accounting and accepting their persons as righteous;
> - not for anything wrought in them, or done by them, but for Christ's sake alone;
> - not by imputing faith itself, the act of believing, or any other evangelical obedience to them, as their righteousness;
> - but by imputing the obedience and satisfaction of Christ unto them, they receiving and resting on Him and His righteousness by faith; which faith they have not of themselves, it is the gift of God. (*Westminster Confession*, XI, 1)

And in Holy Scripture we find:

> For there is no difference; for all have sinned and fall short of the glory of God, being justified freely by His grace through the redemption that is in Christ Jesus, whom God set forth as a propitiation by His blood, through faith, to demonstrate His righteousness, because in His forbearance God had passed over the sins that were previously committed, to demonstrate at the present time His righteousness, that He might be just and the justifier of the one who has faith in Jesus. Where then is boasting? It is excluded. By what law? Of works? No, but by the law of faith. Therefore we conclude that a man is justified by faith apart from the deeds of the law. (Romans 3:22–28)

> Therefore let it be known to you, brethren, that through this Man is preached to you the forgiveness of sins; and by Him everyone who believes is justified from all things from which you could not be justified by the law of Moses. (Acts 13:38–39)

> For God did not send His Son into the world to condemn the world, but that the world through Him might be saved. He who believes in

Him is not condemned; but he who does not believe is condemned already, because he has not believed in the name of the only begotten Son of God. (John 3:17–18)

Most assuredly, I say to you, he who hears My word and believes in Him who sent Me has everlasting life, and shall not come into judgment, but has passed from death into life. (John 5:24)

The justification of the impious, of the sinner — "by pardoning their sins, and by accounting and accepting their persons as righteous" — is a judicial, legal act of the God of all power and love. In order to effect a change *in* man (but before the least change in him has taken place) God changes the condition, the standing, of man in relation to His law, which is holy, just, and good. This act of grace, unmerited by man, is solely and fully merited by the perfect and once-for-all sacrifice of Jesus Christ, the Son of the Father, "truly God" and made "truly man" "for us and for our salvation."

By His obedience and His perfect righteousness, all the requirements of the divine law having been satisfied, our Lord-Savior Christ bore the penalty of sin for many. As sinners, having been placed under the righteous wrath and judgment of God, they were restored to the honor and privileges befitting "children of God," of which they were otherwise unworthy of themselves. The Word, who was God, remained God, and is God, was made man. In and of themselves, none recognized or received Him: "But as many as received Him, to them He gave the right to become children of God, to those who believed in His name: who were born, not of blood, nor of the will of the flesh, nor of the will of man, but of God" (John 1:12–13).

To describe this justification of the impious, the sinner, the Reformation and its Doctors unanimously and rightly used the terms "forensic" and "imputed." "Forensic," derived from the Latin *forensis* meaning "from outside," conveyed the truth that no part of our justification comes from ourselves — it is from outside of ourselves, from the Trinitarian God, from Jesus Christ. "Imputed," from the Latin *imputata* meaning "accounted to," highlighted the fact that this same righteousness, the righteousness of Jesus Christ that is inherent within Him, is accounted to us by grace.

> For He made Him who knew no sin to be sin for us, that we might become the righteousness of God in Him. (2 Corinthians 5:21)

An Alien Righteousness

When the Reformation spoke of "justification by faith," what exactly did it mean?

It had already been said by a prophet that "the just shall live by faith" (Habakkuk 2:4), a statement taken up three times in the New Testament:

- "the righteousness of God is revealed (in the Gospel) from faith to faith, just as it is written, 'The just shall live by faith'" (Romans 1:17);
- "But that no one is justified by the law in the sight of God is evident, for 'the just shall live by faith'" (Galatians 3:11);
- "Now the just shall live by faith; but if any man draw back, My soul shall have no pleasure in him." (Hebrews 10:38)

What is it that makes one "just"? The verb "to justify" (*sâdaq* in Hebrew), means *to make righteous, to declare "not guilty," to acquit*. The just, the justified, is the one who *is accepted* by the Lord, reigning from His "throne of grace" (Hebrews 4:16), solely on account of the pardon, the mercy of God, in whom and by whom he believes, and places his trust. "He who believes in the Son has everlasting life: and he who does not believe the Son shall not see life, but the wrath of God abides on him." (John 3:36)

In his epistle to the Romans, Paul takes three chapters (2–4) to demonstrate that salvation is by grace, and that man, unless he disobeys by refusing this Gospel, lays hold of salvation by faith. Paul gives the example of Abraham, "the father of all those who believe":

> He did not waver at the promise of God through unbelief, but was strengthened in faith, giving glory to God, and being fully convinced that what He had promised He was also able to perform. And therefore "*it was accounted to him for righteousness*" (cf. Genesis 15:6). Now it was not written for his sake alone that it was imputed to him, but also for us. It shall be imputed to us who believe in Him who raised up Jesus our Lord from the dead, who was delivered up because of our offenses, and was raised because of our justification. (Romans 4:20–25)

The faith that Scripture speaks about is not some kind of meritorious work on man's part, as if he needed to contribute, or add "faith," to his justification.

As the Doctors of the Reformation made clear, following Scripture: faith does not contribute to our salvation; rather, it receives everything we lack for our justification from Christ. To be justified by faith — or *by means of faith* — means that faith is only the instrument through which we receive the righteousness of Jesus Christ, an *external* righteousness, offered in the Gospel. It is not our faith which justifies us, but the righteousness of Christ alone — on account of *His* righteousness alone are we sinners *declared* justified, made righteous. This is the righteousness of Another — *justicia aliena* ("an alien righteousness"). Our faith, which is God's gift to His elect (Ephesians 2:8; Titus 1:1), receives *His* righteousness with the awareness that such righteousness is wholly free and unmerited, with praise to Him who has given us this faith and has paid the price of the cross and hell to "redeem" us from God's curse, and with a joy which sings Alleluia!

Sanctification Accompanies Justification

Justification is by faith alone, but as the Reformers and the Reformed Confessions taught, justification is never alone.

Because justification is accompanied by regeneration, there proceeds from it — under, with, and through it — a life and a struggle for sanctification that can, should, and will develop in the faithful. Righteousness is thus infused *within* them, a *personal* righteousness.

Again, God justifies men by imputing to them, from without, by grace, the perfect righteousness of Jesus Christ to which they contribute nothing. Then, now and at the hour of death, this righteousness is the source, the cause and the ground of their glorification of God the Savior; it is their only assurance. And yet all those whom God has justified shall go on to know (not *in order* to be saved, but *because they are saved*) an inner life of union with Jesus Christ, a union giving them — infusing into them — the strengths and virtues needed to wage the fight in every area of life against the power of the Devil, sin, and death — a power over which Christ has already triumphed. These strengths and virtues are not for self-glory, as though they were the cause of our justification, but solely for God's glory.

... [T]he grace of justification is not separated from regeneration, although they are things distinct. But because it is very well known by experience that the traces of sin always remain in the righteous, their justification must be very different from reformation into newness of life [cf. Romans 6:4]. For God so begins this second point in His elect, and progresses in it gradually, and sometimes slowly, through life, that they are always liable to the judgment of death before His tribunal. But He does not justify in part but liberally, so that they may appear in heaven as if endowed with the purity of Christ. No portion of righteousness sets our consciences at peace until it has been determined that we are pleasing to God, because we are entirely righteous before Him. From this it follows that the doctrine of justification is perverted and utterly overthrown when doubt is thrust into men's minds, when the assurance of salvation is shaken and the free and fearless calling upon God suffers hindrance — nay, when peace and tranquility with spiritual joy are not established....

(St. Paul) mournfully exclaims: "Wretched man that I am! Who will deliver me from the body of this death?" [Romans 7:24]. But fleeing to that righteousness which is founded solely upon God's mercy he gloriously triumphs over both life and death, reproaches and hunger, the sword and all other adverse things. "Who will make accusation against God's elect," whom He justifies [Romans 8:33]? For I am surely convinced that nothing "will separate us from His love in Christ" [Romans 8:38–39]. He clearly proclaims that he has a righteousness which alone entirely suffices for salvation before God, so that he does not diminish his confidence in glorying, and no hindrance arises from the miserable bondage, consciousness of which had a moment before caused him to bemoan his lot....

[W]e say that those who were lost have their sins buried and are justified before God because, as he hates sin, he can love only those whom he has justified. This is a wonderful plan of justification that, covered by the righteousness of Christ, they should not tremble at the judgment they deserve, and that while they rightly condemn themselves, they should be accounted righteous outside themselves.[38]

Justification is accompanied by sanctification.

---

38. Calvin, *Institutes*, III.9.11.

Whereas justification completely removes the *guilt* of sin, sanctification progressively removes the *pollution* of sin and renews the *just*, the *justified*, that he may be conformed more and more to the image of his Lord.

Whereas justification is a *declarative act* of God imputing the righteousness of Jesus Christ to man, sanctification is an *inward work* of God in man resulting in man's cooperative obedience, that is, man's "willing" and "doing" according to His good pleasure (Philippians 2:13).

Whereas in *justification* the righteousness of Christ is *imputed* to us, in *sanctification* the righteousness of Christ is, little by little, and in part, *infused* into us.

Whereas justification knows no degree of being more or less justified (a man is either justified or he is not; *tertium non datur* — there is no third way), *sanctification* progresses little by little, never achieving perfection in this earthly life.

Whereas *justification* is a *total and perfect act*, the same for all the faithful, *sanctification varies* depending on the diversity of gifts of the Spirit, its radiance being sometimes more, sometimes less, among the faithful.

As with other doctrines where faithful Christian thinking requires that one unite them without dividing them, so with justification and sanctification: we must distinguish between them without separating them.

Faith and Works

Contra: But isn't it written: "You see then that a man is justified by works, and not by faith only" (James 2:14–26)? Is there not a conflict between the apostles Paul and James on this point?

Respondeo: When Paul and James speak of "justification," they are not talking about the same thing.

Paul is talking about the *justificatio peccatoris* — the justification of the impious, the sinner. James, however, is talking about the *justificatio justi* — the justification of the just, the justified. Both Paul and James appeal to Abraham, but in the case that Paul mentions,

Abraham is not yet just, he is not yet justified, and thus, says Paul, he is "justified by faith" (cf. Genesis 15, especially v. 6 — "Abraham believed the Lord, and He accounted it to him for righteousness"); the case that James mentions comes later, long after Abraham was justified by faith, and the matter of him obeying God's command to sacrifice Isaac concerns another justification: justification by works (cf. Genesis 22).

On this point Paul and James are not even addressing the same adversaries. Paul is opposing the *legalists*, those who pretend to find some kind of justification from sin in the works of the law. The false teaching of the legalists pushes aside justification by grace received through faith (*justificatio peccatoris*). James, on the other hand, is opposing the *antinomians*, those who pretend that their faith — a simple assent to the truth of God's existence (cf. James 2:19) — is sufficient in itself, even if unaccompanied by good works. The false teaching of the antinomians pushes aside another justification: justification (*justificatio justi*) by works. The *faith* of the *antinomians* is as dead as that of the demons — except that the demons at least tremble (James 2:14–19). True faith is never without works; works are the culmination of a life of faith.

Thus James shows, in concert with other statements of Paul (Romans 12; 13:8–10; Ephesians 4:17–31; 5:15–6:18; Philippians 2:12–18), that true faith leads to a life obedient to the Law of God, that works necessarily follow true faith — faith being not mere assent to a truth, but that which is "counted for righteousness" by the God of mercy. It is also worth noting that James, in the text in question (James 2:14–26), says that Abraham was justified by grace, by means of faith (James 2:23). There is no disagreement between James and Paul on this point.

Where there is justification from without by faith, there must also be an inner righteousness, a righteousness of life, a righteousness that is received and comes second — being grounded in this forensic justification — but nonetheless necessary and real, revealing and proving itself before men (including oneself!) by works. Imputed justification fully justifies us before God since it is the righteousness of Christ, and is always accompanied by our *infused* righteousness which confirms the righteousness of faith; it manifests itself through good works, which are signs both to others and to ourselves, of the beginning and growth of our inner infused justice.

When the apostle labels "faith" an empty opinion far removed from true faith.... He does not say "if anyone have faith without works" but "if he boast." He states it even more clearly a little later where in derision he makes it worse than devil's knowledge [James 2:19], and finally, where he calls it "dead" [James 2:20]. But from the definition you may understand sufficiently what he means. "You believe," he says, "that there is a God" [James 2:19]. Obviously, if this faith contains nothing but a belief that there is a God, it is not strange if it does not justify!... Surely it is clear that [James] is speaking of the declaration, not the imputation, of righteousness. It is as if he said: "Those who by true faith are righteous prove their righteousness by obedience and good works, not by a bare and imaginary mask of faith." To sum up, he is not discussing in what manner we are justified but demanding of believers a righteousness fruitful in good works.... [H]e is attempting only to shatter the evil confidence of those who vainly pretended faith as an excuse for their contempt of good works. Therefore, in whatever ways they may twist James' words, they will express but two ideas: an empty show of faith does not justify, and a believer, not content with such an image, declares his righteousness by good works.[39]

The Spiritual Battle

Every faithful believer, being fully justified by the perfect righteousness of Jesus Christ imputed to him by grace, is thus engaged in the advance of sanctification (with its highs and lows), in a spiritual battle. He is conscious of the fact that he will, and must, be unrelentingly engaged in this battle until his death (Romans 8:31–39). Defeatism is not an option, that is certain; but neither is pride or triumphalism. This bitter struggle (watch! pray!) includes sufferings to be borne with *hupomenè*, persevering patience, which enables one to hold up under tests and temptations (both are expressed by the same word in Greek: *peïrasmos*) for as long as is required for the realization of God's plan.

The more we advance in the light of the resurrected and victorious Christ throughout our earthly days, the more we measure our poverty against His riches, our weakness against His strength, our wretchedness against His holiness; and the more we grasp both how unmerited is that election which brings us into the service of such a

---

39. Ibid., III.17.11–12.

Lord-Savior and how unworthy are we who, if left to our own power, would be incapable of the least faithfulness in this service.

The standard of sanctification is the Word of God: the Word Incarnate, Jesus Christ, and the written Word, the Bible — both as *Law* and *Gospel*. The Law, which works its way deeper and deeper into our lives over time as the righteousness of Christ, always imputed, is infused into us, addresses our faithfulness, calling it into obedience. Always renewed, the Gospel provides the motive (gratitude) and the power (grace) to obey — to make the first steps of obedience, and to begin over and over again.

And thus we begin to see the *semper peccator, semper justus, semper penitens* of the Reformation:

- always a *sinner*, needing to beg for forgiveness;
- always *righteous*, in Him who has justified us by grace;
- always *repenting*, in a continual conversion and unending battle of faith, striving to put to death the sinner that we still are, and to vivify the righteous man that we are already in Christ.

The prayer goes on, without break: "Lord Jesus Christ, Son of God, have mercy on me, a sinner!"

> But we have this treasure (that is, the glorious Gospel of Christ, the glory of God in the face of Jesus Christ) in earthen vessels that the excellence of the power may be of God and not of us. (2 Corinthians 4:7; read together with 5:10)

> ...that I may know Him and the power of His resurrection, and the fellowship of His sufferings, being conformed to His death, if, by any means, I may attain to the resurrection of the dead. (Philippians 3:10; cf. the whole of ch. 3)

> ...we are children of God, and if children, then heirs — heirs of God and joint heirs with Christ, if indeed we suffer with Him, that we may also be glorified together. (Romans 8:17)

The Scriptural Dogma

Opening Remarks

Before setting forth the scriptural dogma proper, as defined by the Reformed Confessions, I will indulge in two opening remarks.

First Remark — Scripture's Own Testimony Concerning Itself

Holy Scripture itself declares, in several places and in several ways, that it is the Word of God. Thus when the Catholic Faith has confessed the divine origin and authorship of the sixty-six books that make up Scripture, it has simply followed Scripture on this point.

The Church has always claimed that Scripture is inspired, ever since the apostolic times. Unfortunately, the terms used today — such as *sacred* and *inspiration* — are far too vague and fall short of the plain meaning of *théopneustos*, the Greek word that Paul uses when he says that the Book, the Bible, Scripture (in his day, the Old Testament) is "inspired by God" (2 Timothy 3:16). To say that Scripture is *théopneustos* is to say that it proceeds from the Breath, the Spirit, of God, that it has been *breathed* (exhaled) *from God*. St. Peter expresses the same thing in another way. The human authors of Scripture, the Prophets, the Word-bearers of God, he says, were first "moved by the Holy Spirit," so much so that *their* speech, *their* prophecy, proceeded principally "not from the will of man," but from God (2 Peter 1:21).

The *mystery* of inspiration, or rather of the *divine spiration*, proceeds *above all* from the fact that what the human texts of Holy Scripture — which are, except for rare exceptions,[40] the work of veritable human authors bearing the marks of their personalities, situations, characters, and unique styles — have ultimately expressed is exactly that which God wanted to say not only to the people of that day, but also to men and women through the centuries to come, even down to the choice of the Hebrew and Greek (and sometimes Aramaic) words employed.

These "bearers of the Spirit" (or *pneumatophores*) were chosen by God, who governs all things with providential and covenantal sovereignty, whose creative knowledge — since He transcends time — is

---

40. For example, Exodus 34:27–28.

intimate and infinite, and whose holy, wise, good, and all-powerful will causes the future and all that is in it — things necessary as well as things contingent and free[41] — to exist. It was He who equipped these authors of Holy Scripture with all things necessary for their task, and by His Holy Spirit bore them in every aspect of their work — from their most personal and detailed studies (e.g. Luke 1:1–4) to the visions they received, interpreted, and passed down (e.g. Ezekiel, Revelation), and even to the expressions and exact words they employed (e.g. Matthew 5:18). In their unique styles, which were usually quite ordinary though at times quite brilliant, they were given to be the authors of Holy Scripture, though all the while the *transcendent-immanent* God was the ultimate Author.

Second Remark — The Apostolic Faith in the Inspiration of Scripture

Let us recall what we have previously stated concerning the development of Holy Scripture.

From the time Israel appeared on the scene of history in the days of Moses, inasmuch as they then became the people of God, God had given them the first installment of the covenantal Book, the beginning of Holy Scripture. Israel recognized and confessed that this embryonic Scripture was the Word of God to which they owed submission (Exodus 19 to 24; Deuteronomy 4:44–7:11).

Then, over the course of ten centuries, book by book, part by part, the *Torah*, *Nevi'im*, and *Ketuvim* (the Law, the Prophets, and the Writings) were sequentially revealed and given to Israel as the written Word of God. To this day the Orthodox Jews refer to these writings, in short, as the *TaNaKh*.

Finally, there arrived the time of the Church, the New Israel, which was at first comprised exclusively of the faithful remnant of ancient Israel that had received the Holy Scripture of the old manifestation of the covenant. Then, little by little before the destruction of the Temple in Jerusalem in A.D. 70, they received, from Christ reigning at the right hand of the Father and from the Spirit proceeding from the Father and the Son — the Spirit who had already "spoken by the prophets" and descended on the day of Pentecost — the twenty-seven Books

---

41. Here I adopt the terms used by Lecerf, *Études calvinists* (Delachaux et Niestlé, 1949), 22.

of the Tradition of the Apostles (*paradosis* in Greek, meaning "that which is handed down").

With that, the *dogmatic canon* of God-breathed holy books (*Torah + Nevi'im + Ketuvim* + Tradition of the Apostles; *TaNaKh* + Tradition) was completed and sealed. But it would require a long time before the *ecclesial historical canon* would catch up — and coincide — with the dogmatic canon. That is to say, while we affirm that the books of Holy Scripture we have today were indeed "canonical" (in the dogmatic sense) from the moment God, by His Spirit, finished *spirating* them, we acknowledge that time was needed for the Church of God to recognize these books as the very Word of God (which they already were), and to place them in her ecclesiastical canon. The true canonicity of a book, its authority as the Word of God, never depended on the Church; to the contrary, the book's dogmatic canonicity asserted itself in the Church, so that the ecclesial canonicity of Scripture thus followed from its divine canonicity.

Keeping the above in mind, we can now conclude this preliminary point. As the Apostolic Faith has been passed down through the ages, from the beginnings of the age of the Church throughout the centuries of the *Apostolic and Apologetic* Fathers, and up to our day, the Catholic Church, in the East as well as the West, has always held to the verbal inspiration of Holy Scripture, even the inspiration of its very words. Consequently, they have affirmed Holy Scripture as having the status of the Word of God.[42]

All of the Fathers, Doctors, and Reformers of the church, even to this day, would have agreed with St. Irenaeus of Lyon (130–202) when he said of the apostles: "This Gospel, first they preached, then, according to the will of God, they passed it down in the Scriptures, so that it might be the foundation and pillar of the truth."[43]

The Faith of the Church, the catholic and orthodox Faith, according to Scripture and concerning Scripture, has been expressed and

---

42. In his book *Inspiration and Canonicity of the Scriptures* (Greenville: A Press, 1993) in chapter 3 entitled "Verbal Inspiration in Church History," R. Laird Harris references several Church Fathers supporting this point: Clement of Rome (*First Epistle*), Ignatius of Antioch, died toward 117 (Letters to the Smyrnians, to the Magnesians, and to the Philadelphians); Polycarp, disciple of St. John, martyred in the same epoch (Letter to the Philippians); Justin Martyr (115–165) (*Discourse to the Greeks, First Apology, Dialogue with Trypho*); Irenaeus, (*Against Heresies*); Clement of Alexandria, etc., etc. The great Doctors of the Age of Faith would also need to be cited, from St. Augustine to Thomas Aquinas, etc., etc. The list is endless!

43. *Against Heresies*, III, I, 1.

is still expressed in these simple words: *Sacra Scriptura est Verbum Dei* — Holy Scripture is the Word of God.

Recognizing the Doctrine of Scripture as the Dogma of Scripture

In defining the *Scriptural dogma* of the Church, the Reformation — with its Doctors and Confessions — would raise the bar concerning what constitutes a *dogma* of the Church.

The bar most certainly needed to be raised, for although the ecclesial Faith maintained the doctrine of the *verbal* inspiration of Holy Scripture and its identification with the Word of God, there was to be found, even in several of the ancient Church Fathers, a drifting from a clearly defined Scriptural dogma. Whether influenced by pagan philosophies (especially neoplatonism) or by the approach of an original, genius, but often reckless Christian thinker, Origen (184–253), these Fathers embraced an *allegorical* interpretation of the Bible. As a result, their biblical commentary tended toward speculation that set aside the plain meaning of the text. If the ecclesial Faith of which I have spoken was, in theory, maintained, what the Holy Scripture of God said, revealed, and taught was, in practice, often distorted, and sometimes even completely obscured and eclipsed. As Henri Blocher has written: "*Spiritual* exegesis degenerated into allegoricalism. The devaluation of the literal meaning (which was not denied) loosened the grip of Scriptural authority."[44]

This drift away from the plain interpretation of Holy Scripture was further reinforced in the Middle Ages with the *rationalism* (simply *modernism* before its time) of Abelard,[45] the autonomous place accorded to reason by *Scholasticism*,[46] the *nominalism* of William of Occam (1285–1349),[47] as well as the lingering *pelagianism* or

---

44. *Prolégomènes* — Introduction to Theology — notes from a course taught at the Faculté de Vaux-sur-Seine in 1976, 53.

45. Abelard, a prophet of the exercise of methodological doubt, was an early precursor to Descartes and "modernity."

46. The "nature-grace" motif would long dominate Western thought, bifurcating not only nature-grace, but also, along the same lines, reason-revelation, creation-redemption and philosophy-theology. This left the door open to the accommodation of the Christian faith to non-Christian motifs, leading to the modern dualistic antithesis.

47. William of Occam "replaced words and ideas with mere signs, thereby transforming natural language into a simple algebra of thought. For Occam, words no longer convey truths or realities; they convey power." Arnaud-Aaron Upinsky, in his remarkable work *La tête coupée* (Paris: Guibert, 1991), 198.

semi-pelagianism (absent only from the works of those Doctors who chose to follow St. Augustine, such as St. Anselm or St. Bonaventure).

Eventually, and most significantly, a threat to the Scriptural dogma arose not only from individual theologians, but from the *representative authority of the Church* as well (popes and councils, both medieval and modern). Appealing to a pretended Tradition which, though strange and indefinable, had been steadily establishing itself as a new and second *source of Revelation*, the representative authority of the Church arrogantly accorded to itself the right to define doctrines and authorize practices which were not in accord with Scripture, and sometimes even opposed it. And thus scholars and devout Doctors who, on certain points, had carefully heeded Scripture began to encourage and teach that which, on other points, the ecclesial magisterium had dared to invent and define. The list of inventions includes the worship of Our Lady, to whom were attributed the titles of Our Lord ("Mediatrix," "Queen of Heaven," for example); the worship of saints who had essentially become small, specialized deities; merits, indulgences granted by the popes for staggering sums of money; transubstantiation and worship of the consecrated host; salvation by works; the sovereign authority (*spiritual* and *temporal*) of the bishop of Rome, etc. This corruption of doctrine by the representative authorities represented a far greater unfaithfulness than the public sins and the immorality of the clergy, which was often encouraged by the example of the Pope himself. Even the Church's exorbitant wealth and its commerce in ecclesial dignities were less damaging than these doctrinal deviations, for the latter would eventually leave their mark deep within the tradition, preaching, liturgy, catechesis, morals, and government of the Church — and, consequently, would penetrate the spiritual life and mores of Christians who came to accept them as being self-evident, incontestable, under pain of being accused of heresy or excommunicated. All of this shows the need for a dogma of Scripture, as Calvin puts it:

> Suppose we ponder how slippery is the fall of the human mind into forgetfulness of God, how great the tendency to every kind of error, how great the lust to fashion constantly new and artificial religions. Then we may perceive how necessary was such written proof of the

heavenly doctrine that it should neither perish through forgetfulness nor vanish through error nor be corrupted by the audacity of men.[48]

If Luther is remembered as the great Doctor of *justification by faith* — an ecclesial dogma espoused by all Reformed Confessions — then the whole host of Reformed Doctors, including Calvin, should be acknowledged as having contributed to the definition of the ecclesial dogma concerning *Holy Scripture and its authority* — which was also unanimously espoused by the Reformed Confessions.

I can do no better here than to cite the *French Confession of Faith* (1571) and the *Westminster Confession of Faith* (1647):

> We believe that the Word contained in these books has proceeded from God, and receives its authority from him alone, and not from men. And inasmuch as it is the rule of all truth, containing all that is necessary for the service of God and for our salvation, it is not lawful for men, nor even for angels, to add to it, to take away from it, or to change it. Whence it follows that no authority, whether of antiquity, or custom, or number, or human wisdom, or judgments, or proclamations, or edicts, or decrees, or councils, or visions, or miracles, should be opposed to these Holy Scriptures, but, on the contrary, all things should be examined, regulated and reformed according to them. (*The French Confession of Faith*, article 5.)

Extracts from *Westminster* (chapter I) on Holy Scripture:

1. ... for the more sure establishment and comfort of the Church against the corruption of the flesh, and the malice of Satan and of the world, (it pleased the Lord) to commit the same wholly unto writing: which maketh the Holy Scripture to be the most necessary....

4. The authority of Holy Scripture, for which it ought to be believed, and obeyed, dependeth not upon the testimony of any man, or Church; but wholly upon God (who is truth itself) and author thereof: and therefore it is to be received, because it is the Word of God.

---

48. Calvin, *Institutes*, I.6.3.

5. We may be moved and induced by the testimony of the Church to an high and reverend esteem of Holy Scripture. And the heavenliness of the matter, the efficacy of the doctrine, the majesty of the style, the consent of all the parts, the scope of the whole (which is, to give all glory to God), the full discovery it makes of the only way of man's salvation, the many other incomparable excellencies, and the entire perfection thereof, are arguments whereby it doth abundantly evidence itself to be the Word of God: yet notwithstanding, our full persuasion and assurance of the infallible truth and divine authority thereof, is from the inward work of the Holy Spirit bearing witness by and with the Word in our hearts.

6. The whole counsel of God concerning all things necessary for His own glory, man's salvation, faith and life, is either expressly set down in Scripture, or by good and necessary consequence may be deduced from Scripture: unto which nothing at any time is to be added, whether by new revelation of the Spirit or traditions of men. Nevertheless, we acknowledge the inward illumination of the Spirit of God to be necessary for the saving understanding of such things as are revealed in the Word: and that there are some circumstances concerning the worship of God, and government of the Church, common to human actions and societies, which are to be ordered by the light of nature, and Christian prudence, according to the general rules of the Word, which are always to be observed.

7. All things in Scripture are not alike plain in themselves, nor alike clear unto all: yet those things which are necessary to be known, believed, and observed for salvation, are so clearly propounded, and opened in some place of Scripture or other, that not only the learned, but the unlearned, in a due use of the ordinary means, may attain unto a sufficient understanding of them.

8. The Old Testament in Hebrew (which was the native language of the people of God of old [note that! — "of old" — P.C.]), and the New Testament in Greek (which, at the time of the writing of it, was most generally known to the nations), being immediately inspired by God, and, by His singular care and providence, kept pure in all ages, are therefore authentical; so as, in all controversies of religion, the Church is finally to appeal unto them. But, because

these original tongues are not known to all the people of God, who have right unto, and interest in the Scriptures, and are commanded, in the fear of God, to read and search them, therefore they are to be translated into the vulgar language of every nation unto which they come, that, the Word of God dwelling plentifully in all, they may worship Him in an acceptable manner; and, through patience and comfort of the Scriptures, may have hope.
9. The infallible rule of interpretation of Scripture is the Scripture itself: and therefore, when there is a question about the true and full sense of any Scripture (which is not manifold, but one), it must be searched and known by other places that speak more clearly.
10. The supreme judge by which all controversies of religion are to be determined, and all decrees of councils, opinions of ancient writers, doctrines of men, and private spirits, are to be examined, and in whose sentence we are to rest, can be no other but the Holy Spirit speaking in the Scripture.

The Essential Points of the Dogma of Scripture

Let us consider the essential points of the *Scriptural dogma* articulated by the Reformed Confessions.

Which Texts Are Ultimately Authoritative

The Confessions do more than simply enumerate, one by one, those books that are canonical in the dogmatic sense, that "have divine authority" (*The French Confession of Faith*, article 3; *The Belgic Confession*, article 4; *Westminster*, I.2).[49] They proceed to precisely define which texts have final authority for the Church, being "the Old Testament in Hebrew and the New Testament in Greek," "immediately inspired by God, and, by His singular care and providence, kept pure in all ages."

Until the Reformation, most of the Church Doctors, following Augustine's lead, put the Greek text of the Septuagint and the Latin Vulgate on practically the same level as inspired Scripture. This was true

---

49. Although the Old Testament of the Protestant Bibles have those books, and only those books, that are in the Hebraic Bible, they have not, however, ordered them according to the Hebraic Bible (that is, the Law, then the Prophets, then the Writings), but have followed the order of the *Septuagint* (Pentateuch, historical books, poetic books, and prophetic books)! It's a shame, and it will need to be corrected.

even of Augustine, who believed the legend of the *Lettre d'Aristée* to be the historical account of a miracle. Thus two translations of the holy texts came to be regarded as more authoritative than the texts themselves. In fact, after the Reformation had taken root, the Council of Trent — whose members were almost all ignorant of both Hebrew and Greek — would make St. Jerome's *Vulgata latina* (which Jerome himself had stated was not inspired!) a veritable "Verbal Icon."[50]

As it had done on several other matters, the Reformation would reclaim and uphold the ancient — that is, pre-Augustinian, pre-medieval — catholic Tradition.[51] The Reformers would return "to the sources," and that meant to the Masoretic text for the Old Testament and to the Byzantine Text for the New.

The Reformers would confess as canonical the Hebraic text handed down from Israel to the Church (Romans 3:1–2 and 9:4), the text of the synagogue, the text that the scribes (the *sopherîm*, or "men of the book," of the *sepher*) had passed down to the *Masoretes* (from *massora*, meaning "transmission," "tradition"). In their handling of the text, the Masoretes were more than careful: they were scrupulous, owing to the fact that they regarded the text as the inspired and sacred charter that indeed it was. From the fifth to the eleventh centuries they oversaw its transmission with renowned rigor — exact to the least stroke (to ensure precision, they would count the number of consonants both vertically and horizontally, and note the location of the middle letters and words of each book). They were "transmitters" of the Word of God in human words, in faith and prayer as well as in their detailed knowledge of its vocabulary and grammar. They were so eager to leave the inviolable consonantal text[52] as unaltered as possible that they chose not to mark down the implicit vowel points that would have gone above, below, or in the middle of the consonants, and

---

50. This expression is from T. P. Letis, a faithful disciple of the Reformation, from a conference in 1990: "The *Vulgata Latina* and the Council of Trent: The Latin Bible as Verbal Icon." In the pages that follow I am drawing from several articles published by this scholar in recent years in the excellent reformed reviews in *Christianity and Society* and *The Chalcedon Report*.

51. Jaroslav Pelikan, *Obedient Rebel* (New York, NY: Harper & Row, 1964) and *The Emergence of the Catholic Tradition, 100–600* (University of Chicago, 1971); and Robert Markus, *The End of Ancient Christianity* (Cambridge University Press: 1990).

52. The Hebrew script is consonantal, meaning that its words contain only consonants, generally three per word, and these three letters established the root meaning of the word; the reader supplied the vowels. For example, the three consonants Q-D-S carry the idea of holiness. The reader, according to the context, would know whether to read and say *QaDaS*, "He is holy," or *QaDoS*, "holy," or *QoDeS*, "holy place."

they put the accents and suggested corrections — "that which should be read" — only in the margins or to the side. From 1524 to 1525, the "Received Text," the Masoretic Text, was carefully edited in Venice by Jacob ben Chayyim (it is this edition that the Jewish scholar Cassuto used for his *Hebraic Bible*, published in Jerusalem in 1953).

For the New Testament, the Reformation would confess the Greek text as canonical (called the "Byzantine text," although it would be better called the "ecclesial text," since it was long regarded as the normative text by the Church, both in the East and the West). This is the "Received Text" (*textus receptus*) that Erasmus (1469–1536) would publish in 1516.

This is why the churches of the Reformation have so esteemed the *ordained ministry* of their "pastors and doctors" (Ephesians 4:11),[53] who were required to have the training necessary to be able to consult the Bible in the original languages.

Let me conclude this section with some quotations from the writings of Francis Turretin:[54]

> Although their utility is great for the instruction of believers, yet no version either can or ought to be put on an equality with the original, much less be preferred to it. (1) For no version has anything important which the Hebrew or Greek source does not have more fully, since in the sources not only the matter and sentences, but even the very words were directly dictated by the Holy Spirit. (2) It is one thing to be an interpreter, quite another to be a prophet, as Jerome says (*Praefatio in*

---

53. For example, see the *Second Helvetic Confession* (1566) which declares in chapter XVIII concerning the "ministers" of God that they should be "capable men distinguished by sufficient consecrated learning" so that they may "expound the word of God."

54. Francis Turretin (1623–1687), a Reformed theologian, and his contemporary Abraham Calov (1612–1686), a Lutheran theologian and author of a *Biblia Illustrata* (not illustrated but explained! — a masterly commentary on the whole Bible, 1672–1676) — should be considered as the last two great Doctors of the Reformation. Turretin's magnum opus was his *Institutes of Elenctic Theology* ("Teachings on much-debated theology"), published posthumously in 1688 in Geneva, where Calvin had long taught (*elenctica*, from the Greek verb *elenchein*, means the theology which Turretin wrote, as he said himself in his preface, "in order to refute — and, if possible, to convince — the opponents" on all sides). Those who, without having ever read them, speak of the orthodox Doctors of the seventeenth century as holding to a "dead orthodoxy," find, upon reading them, that they are dealing with a vibrant theology, woven of silence and prayer, as all theology should be. There has recently appeared a magnificent, three-volume edition in English (Presbyterian and Reformed Publishing, 1997). The work covers twenty-four themes (*Loci*, in Latin, or "topics") in all, ordered as "questions." Lecerf speaks of Turretin as "the Reformed Thomas Aquinas" (*Études calvinistes*, 128).

Pentateuchum [PL 28.182]). The prophet as God-inspired (*theopneustos*) cannot err, but the interpreter as a man lacks no human quality since he is always liable to err. (3) All versions are the streams; the original text is the fountain whence they flow. The latter is the rule, the former the thing, having only human authority.

Nevertheless all authority must not be denied to versions. Here we must carefully distinguish a twofold divine authority: one of things, the other of words. The former relates to the substance of doctrine which constitutes the internal form of the Scriptures. The latter relates to the accident of writing, the external and accidental form. The source has both, being God-inspired (*theopneustos*) both as to the words and things; but versions have only the first, being expressed in human and not in divine words....

Hence it follows that the versions... may be exposed to errors and admit of corrections, but nevertheless are authentic as to the doctrine they contain (which is divine and infallible).[55]

The Written Word Must Be Heard in the Church

One often hears that the Reformation is responsible for the rise of individualism. Roman Catholics and the Orthodox fault the Reformation for this, while modernist liberal Protestants praise the Reformation for the same. However, contrary to this pretended contention, the Reformation never extolled individualism. In fact, it always claimed that the written Word of God ought to be heard *in and with the Church*.

The Reformation did emphasize the sovereign authority of the Scriptures, but we should not miss the fact that it emphasized this dogma (along with the Soteriological dogma) *in its ecclesial Confessions of Faith*, which, furthermore, integrated the Christological and Trinitarian dogmas defined by the early ecumenical Councils. All of these dogmas took their place in the ecclesial *traditio e Scriptura fluens* (tradition following from Scripture).

Rather than supporting individualism, the Confessions of the Reformation clearly oppose individualism:

---

55. Turretin, *Institutes of Elenctic Theology*, 1, trans. George Musgrave Giger (Phillipsburg, NJ: Presbyterian and Reformed Publishing, 1997), 125–126 (I, Q. XIII, XIII–XV).

The French Confession of Faith
Now as we enjoy Christ only through the gospel, we believe that the order of the Church, established by his authority, ought to be sacred and inviolable.... We believe that no one ought to seclude himself and be contented to be alone; but that all jointly should keep and maintain the union of the Church ... wherever God shall have established a true order of the Church.... For if they do not take part in it or if they separate themselves from it, they do contrary to the Word of God (articles 25 and 26).

The Second Helvetic Confession
But we esteem fellowship with the true Church of Christ so highly that we deny that those can live before God who do not stand in fellowship with the true Church of God, but separate themselves from it. For as there was no salvation outside Noah's ark when the world perished in the flood; so we believe that there is no certain salvation outside Christ, who offers himself to be enjoyed by the elect in the Church; and hence we teach that those who wish to live ought not to be separated from the true Church of Christ ... so we teach that the true harmony of the Church consists in doctrines and in the true and harmonious preaching of the Gospel of Christ ... (chapter XVII).

The Westminster Confession of Faith
The catholic or universal Church, which is invisible, consists of the whole number of the elect that have been, are, or shall be gathered into one, under Christ the Head thereof; and is the spouse, the body, the fullness of Him that filleth all in all.

The visible Church, which is also catholic or universal under the Gospel (not confined to one nation, as before under the law), consists of all those throughout the world that profess the true religion; and of their children: and is the kingdom of the Lord Jesus Christ, the house and family of God, out of which there is no ordinary possibility of salvation.

Unto this catholic visible Church Christ hath given the ministry, oracles, and ordinances of God, for the gathering and perfecting of the saints, in this life, to the end of the world: and doth, by His own presence and Spirit, according to His promise, make them effectual thereunto. (chapter XXV)

Those who would charge (or praise) the Reformation for the rise of individualism would do well to examine the place given to the Church in the Reformation's Confessions.

Furthermore, the teachings of the Reformation, as found in its Confessions and the writings of its Doctors, emphasize that no preaching, teaching and faithful interpretation of Scripture can be separated from the catholic Tradition, and, consequently, that such preaching, teaching and interpretation should be carried out in cordial and professed submission to the ecclesial dogmas following from Scripture and clarified in the early centuries (the Trinitarian and Christological dogmas) as well as in the sixteenth and seventeenth centuries (the Soteriological and Scriptural dogmas).

Neither the early ecumenical Councils, with their Trinitarian and Christological definitions, nor the Confessions of the Reformation, with their Soteriological and Scriptural definitions, invented new doctrines in addition to what Scripture says. They simply preserved the *Fides catholica e Scriptura fluens* (the catholic Faith following from Scripture) by clarifying it against the many menacing heresies constantly sprouting up, and by confessing *Soli Deo Gloria* (to God alone the glory!), that:

GOD ALONE IS THE LORD-SAVIOR AND THERE IS NONE BESIDES HIM.

Let us state again: Holy Scripture, the Word of God, cannot be received, in accordance with its true meaning, outside the ecclesial context, outside the dogmatic consensus of the catholic Church. This consensus has weight and value by virtue of its faithfulness to Scripture. This consensus thus needs always to be defended and upheld for it is constantly threatened by those who, holding the catholic Faith in contempt and failing to understand the catholic Tradition, consequently deviate from the written Word given by the Lord Jesus Christ to the Church, His Bride. It is from this Word that the ecclesial dogmas in question necessarily follow.

One can then see why the Reformation, from its earliest days onward, produced so many catechisms expounding the Faith and catholic dogmas for all Christians, children, or baptized believers, and for anyone seeking the truth. These dogmas could only be neglected at great peril, for not only would Scripture then be misapprehended, but heresies would be assured a momentary triumph to the ruin of souls.[56]

The Scriptural Dogma Clarifies
that the Church Is the Servant of the Faith

We see that the Reformation's development of the Scriptural dogma was not intended to undermine the catholic tradition, a tradition that the Reformation beheld with (in the words of J. Pelikan) a critical reverence, as it did all of Church history.[57] The Reformation, whose leaders spoke of the Church as "the Mother that bears and begets every Christian"[58] and "the Mother of all for whom God is Father" (*la Mère de tous ceux dont Dieu est le Père*), was in many respects far more catholic than its adversaries.[59] With the Scriptural dogma, it clarified what should have been defined from the beginning of the Church and assumed during the early councils — what was already operative in the spirit of the ancient Fathers, as if it had already been codified, effectively witnessed by the Trinitarian and Christological dogmas defined by the first six ecumenical councils.

In all of its Confessions, the Reformation did what had been long needed (and this is the crux of the Scriptural dogma!): it dogmatically declared that Faith (the *Fides quae creditur*, the Faith which demands belief) comes before the Church, in the sense that the Church should be the servant of the Faith, and not the other way around. In the absence of this clear, faithful-to-Scripture, dogmatic declaration (you must "contend earnestly for the faith which was once for all delivered to the saints"; Jude 3), the teachings of the Church too often, in the end, put themselves above the Word of God. Luther firmly stated: "What can the Church settle that Scripture did not settle first?"[60]

The truth lies not in *what* the Church teaches. It lies in *the Word* (which teaches the Church).

---

56. Among such catechisms were counted: from the Lutherans: Luther's *Small Catechism* and *Large Catechism* (1529) and his *Smalcald Articles* (1537); from the Reformed: Calvin's *Instruction in Faith* (1537) and his *Geneva Catechism* (1545); and the Heidelberg Catechism by Olevianus and Ursinus (1563); from the Anglicans: the *Book of Common Prayer* and the *Thirty-Nine Articles* (1549). Lecerf stated again and again that the two masterpieces of the Reformation are Calvin's *Institutes of the Christian Religion* (1536–1560) for dogmatics, and *The Book of Common Prayer* for liturgy.
57. Pelikan, *Obedient Rebels*, 13.
58. Luther, *Larger Catechism*, II, III, 3rd paragraph.
59. Calvin, *Institutes*, IV.1.1.
60. Martin Luther, *The Bondage of the Will*, 69.

The Church has received a teaching mission (Matthew 28:19–20) which she can only effectively carry out by adhering firstly, continually, and strictly to the Truth: Jesus Christ, the Word made flesh, the Holy Scripture, the Word *breathed* of God.

According to Rome, the need for Holy Scripture to be clarified by the ecclesial traditions (which had been "baptized" then as "the Tradition") was greater than the need for such traditions to be clarified and authorized by the Scripture of the Lord.

In addition, as maintained by Calvin, "while the church receives and gives its seal of approval to the Scriptures, it does not thereby render authentic what is otherwise doubtful or controversial. But because the church recognizes Scripture to be the truth of its own God, as a pious duty it unhesitatingly venerates Scripture."[61]

The Reformation and the Council of Trent gave differing answers to the fundamental and inevitable question: who rules as the Sovereign endowed with full authority over the Church? The Council of Trent declared: "the sovereign Roman pontiff!" Thus Robert, Cardinal Bellarmine (1542–1621), one of the Doctors of the Roman Counter-Reformation, quite aptly summarized Trent when he wrote in his *De Verbo Dei* ("On the Word of God"), 19: "The supreme Judge cannot be Scripture but the ecclesiastical sovereign, whether alone or with the help and consent of his fellow bishops." In contrast, the Reformation declared: "No! The supreme Judge is the Holy Spirit speaking with and through Scripture!"

The crux of the Scriptural dogma, as confessed and defined by the Reformation, was that all ecclesiastical authority (Councils or Synods), in its necessary, though secondary, ministerial role, should always be able to show that its doctrinal decisions are clearly *according to Scripture*. The *leitmotiv*, the call issued by the Church *mater et magistra* (mother and teacher) should always be: "To the Law and the Testimony!" (cf. Isaiah 8:20).

For the Old Testament: "They have Moses and the prophets; let them hear them" (Luke 16:29).

For the New Testament, Jesus says to His apostles: "You who have followed Me will also sit on twelve thrones, judging [exercising authority over] the twelve tribes of Israel [the whole Church]" (Matthew 19:28b).

---

61. Calvin, *Institutes*, I.7.2.

Nor did Christ and His apostles themselves ever cease to appeal to the sovereign authority of Scripture (Matthew 4:1–11; 15:3; 22:32–33; John 5:39–47; 10:32–38; Acts 17:1–14; 18:1–11; 26:22–23, etc.).

By His Scripture, God Himself interprets His Scripture.

And if it is true in one sense that the Son of God incarnate never wrote anything, it is far truer in another sense that He is the Author, along with the Father and the Holy Spirit, of all Scripture.

Each time the New Testament introduces an Old Testament citation with "It is written," it is a synonym for "God has willed that it be written,..." or more profoundly still, "God, by His *spiration*, has written...."

> *Contra*: With the intention of relativizing the divine authority of Scripture, Roman theologians after the Reformation taught that the Word of God was written only *occasionaliter* — "because of circumstances."
>
> *Respondeo*: It is basically true that Scripture was written "in particular circumstances," remembering that (1) the composition of Scripture was always by God's order and "spiration" and (2) circumstances never happen other than according to the sovereign providence of God.

Moses was not the only one whom the Lord told to "write this for a memorial (*zikkâron* in Hebrew) in the book" or "write down this song" (the Song of Moses).[62] There was also Isaiah (8:1), Jeremiah (30:2), and Habakkuk (2:2), among others (cf. Exodus 24:12; Deuteronomy 31:9; Psalm 102:18; Revelation 1:10–11; etc.).

The principal cause of the Word of God being put into writing was the sovereign command of God. The circumstances themselves, which were in God's hand anyway, were only the secondary causes. The apostles certainly taught and wrote quite often on account of circumstances. But, in addressing these circumstances, they put their teachings down in writing only by the command of the Lord and according to their calling to "teach the nations."

According to the "divine economy," that is, the plan of salvation, the Holy Spirit has been — and remains until the end of the world — the sovereign Helper as much of Jesus Christ, the Word Incarnate, as of

---

62. Exodus 17:14; Deuteronomy 31:19; ch. 32 — "The Song of Moses."

Holy Scripture, the Word "breathed." (Philippians 1:9 says of the Holy Spirit that He is the *Épichorète* — the one who supplies, who acts in us; He is elsewhere called the *Paraclete* — the one who is called alongside, who carries, who supports.) But He is also the Helper (the *Épichorète*, the *Paraclete*) who unites us to Jesus Christ, who bears witness within us that Holy Scripture is indeed the Word of God, and who illumines Holy Scripture for the Church and all the faithful so that the Truth, which it is, shines forth in its tender and strong radiance.

Let us conclude this chapter with three brief quotations.[63]

We are brethren, why should we contend? Our father did not die intestate; he made a will. . . . Open it, let us read . . . (St. Augustine [354–430], on Psalm 21).

The inspired writing is the safe criterion of every doctrine (St. Gregory of Nyssa [335–394], *Contre Eunomius 1.22).*

Let the divinely inspired Writings be our Judge; and may the verdict of the Truth thus be received without qualification by those whose teachings must conform to the teachings of Scripture (St. Basil [c. 330–379], *Letter 189 to Eustathius the Doctor).*

---

63. Cf. Turretin, *Institutes of Elenctic Theology*, Second Topic, Q. 20, XIV.

7

THE CHURCH SICK WITH HUMANISM[1]

THE AGE OF FAITH

The "Age of Faith" Mispresented as the "Middle" or "Dark" Ages

We come now to the millennium spanning from the conversion of Constantine the Great (272–337) to the beginnings of the Renaissance. This period has been condescendingly deemed the "Middle Ages" (or even the "Dark Ages"!) by modern secular historians and intellectuals because it falls between the Classical period and the Renaissance, that is, between pagan antiquity and pagan renewal. It was a millennium during which civilization strove to be thoroughly Christian, and it is precisely for this reason that it is caricatured, maligned, misrepresented, and reviled by those approaching it from a more or less humanistic perspective.[2]

The Middle Ages should instead be called the *Age of Faith* in the West — and depicted accordingly.

---

1. *Humanism*, the subject of the following ages, can be defined as *the religion of Man* making himself divine, of Man as *the measure of all things*, of Man setting *Reason*, his reason, above everything.

2. For an excellent and introductory approach to the subject, see *Those Terrible Middle Ages: Debunking the Myths*, by Régine Pernoud (published originally in French in 1977 as *Pour en finir avec le Moyen Age*, and then in English in 2000 by Ignatius Press). Read also *Saint Louis*, by Jacques Le Goff (published originally in French under the same title in 1996, and then in English in 2009 by University of Notre Dame Press).

As a Christian of the Reformed faith, the American historian Otto Scott has shown the great spiritual revolution that was effected by the grace of God nearly everywhere the Christian faith went in history. The existing religions or ideologies ("idologies") that fostered and indeed required the abominable practices of slavery and human sacrifice were gradually supplanted by the true philanthropic religion (rooted in love for men, love for neighbor) uniting, submitting, and binding men ("religion" comes from the Latin *religare*, meaning "to bind") to the one true God who is love: the Father, the Son, and the Holy Spirit.[3]

The false gods, the idols, then as today, have always craved "the flesh and blood of men." (Anatole France's 1912 cautionary tale about the French Revolution was entitled, *Les Dieux ont soif*—"The Gods Are Thirsty.")[4] The last two centuries of modern, anti-Christian revolutions — tricolor, red, brown, or black — have only given further evidence of this fact. The worship of Moloch, mentioned several times in Holy Scripture, the worship rendered to the state as god, to the Welfare State, the totalitarian state, has always required complete and total control over men (that is, their servitude) and, when it so desires, their complete and total sacrifice. The reader would do well to turn again to 1 Samuel 8:11–18 which announces, in a rather moderate fashion, what will eventually happen to a people who reject the supreme reign of God in favor of that of a man or a state.

Modern historians and intellectuals, working from a humanistic bias, are not only inclined to disparage the Christian civilization of the Age of Faith, but their prejudiced adherence to Jean-Jacques Rousseau's myth of the noble savage (which touted the innate goodness of non-Christian man) leads them systematically to overlook the evils prevalent in pre-Christian societies (or post-Christian, insofar as it applies), such as slavery and human sacrifice. Such mischaracterizations of Christian civilization as oppressive on the one hand, and pre- or post-Christian societies as liberating on the other, are indefensible in light of history. It cannot be denied that the various forms of slavery were established by pre-Christian societies, while the challenge to slavery — gradual though it may have been (great change doesn't

---

3. Otto Scott, *The Great Christian Revolution* (Vallecito, CA: Ross House Books, 1991).

4. This famed work of French literature referenced by Courthial is available in English translation as *The Gods Will Have Blood* (trans. Frederick Davies, Penguin Classics, 1980).

come in an instant, or even in a generation) — came from the Christian faith. As soon as it appeared on the scene, the Christian Faith not only taught what true liberty was, it also lived it — often at the price of martyrdom.

Moreover, the very idea of civil liberty, of fixed limitations placed on the state's authority over individuals, ignored by many nations today (including those that have rejected the Faith of their baptism; Matthew 28:19), owes its demonstration and development to the Christian Faith: "Render unto Caesar that which is Caesar's and to God that which is God's." With this unchanging command, our Lord and Savior Jesus Christ designated at once the divine and limited calling of magistrates and the calling of God. To the magistrates must be rendered coins *with their image* when one pays taxes to support the safeguarding of justice and peace by means of the monopolized exercise of armed force at the magistrate's disposal over a given territory. And, correspondingly, what is owed to God? That which bears *His image*: man-in-the-image-of-God, returning, being converted, and rendering always his very self to his Creator and Savior.

In fact, under the sovereign working of God's grace, and by the faithful obedience of men working out their salvation with fear and trembling (Philippians 2:12–13), *the Age of Faith* was the most beautiful civilization that the world has yet known (though it was still far from perfect, having highs as well as lows, grandeur as well as misery). It is a wonder how the intelligentsia of the twentieth century, an abominable century of blood and slavery with its total wars on local and world-wide scales, with its gulags and concentration camps, with its torture and gas chambers, its massacres and its millions aborted each year, more numerous than the human sacrifices of the antiquity, and officially legalized as the legitimate practice of medicine, etc., would dare look disdainfully on the *Age of Faith*, an age when the incessant search for the truth coupled with respect for God were the lifeblood of a culture that made significant advances in every area of life.

The times in which we find ourselves today are just the opposite of those spoken of by the dear and great St. Athanasius at the threshold of the Age of Faith. In his *On the Incarnation of the Word*, he described the effects of the spread of Christianity:

> For as, when the sun is come, darkness no longer prevails, but if any be still left anywhere it is driven away, so, now that the divine Appearance of the Word of God is come, the darkness of the idols prevails no more, and all parts of the world in every direction are illumined by His teaching (55.3).
>
> For the race of men had gone to ruin, had not the Lord and Savior of all, the Son of God, come among us to meet the end of death (9.4).
>
> He it is that even before His appearing in the body won the victory over His demon adversaries and a triumph over idolatry (37.5).
>
> For formerly the whole world and every place was led astray by the worshipping of idols, and men regarded nothing else but the idols as gods. But now, all the world over, men are deserting the superstition of idols, and taking refuge with Christ; and, worshipping Him as God, are by His means coming to know that Father also Whom they knew not (46.4).
>
> For the Lord touched all parts of creation, and freed and undeceived all of them from every illusion; as Paul says: "Having put off from Himself the principalities and the powers, He triumphed on the Cross" that no one might by any possibility be any longer deceived, but everywhere might find the true Word of God (45.5).[5]

Athanasius saw the triumph of the Cross prevailing far and wide as masses of men and women were joined to Christ, united to Him by that mystical union proceeding from grace and received by faith. It is on account of the widespread reception of the one true faith, and of its significant permeation of all levels of society, that this time, even despite its regrettable errors, may truly be called the *Age of Faith*.

During this age, our *Fathers*, heeding the Scripture-Word of God guarded in the teaching of the Church, were able to walk in the light — a light which so many apostate churches today, sick with Humanism, have hidden under a basket. Throughout the *Age of Faith*, the three orders of society — those who worked, those who prayed,

---

5. *Nicene and Post-Nicene Fathers*, vol. 4, "St. Athanasius: Select Works and Letters" (Edinburgh: T&T Clark, reprinted 1991), 66, 41, 56, 62, 61.

and those who fought — pressed on under the radiant and gentle light of Christ the King. In his treatise *Politica* (1603), the Calvinist jurist Johannes Althusius (1557–1632) referred to the way in which medieval society, with its harmonious interplay of diverse institutions, associations, and organizations, exhibited a symbiotic character. This was possible because the presupposition underlying all of medieval society was that of a Christian theocracy (not to be confused with an ecclesiocracy or a cleritocracy!). Modern thinking, in stark contrast, argues that society and economic relations are ultimately forged from a base-level *conflict* of interests.

The Humanist Contagion

In order to grasp the perilous situation of the Church — without going back to that most ancient of temptations as reported in Genesis 3! — it is necessary to see how soon the temptation appeared in the Church to drift toward Humanism, to accommodate herself to it and to cede God's "thinking" and "speaking" as revealed in Holy Scripture to what man would rather hear. This was, of course, an echo of the temptation of old reported in Genesis: "Did God really say?"

So it happened that the Church soon found herself threatened by the prevailing Greek thought of the day, which was itself influenced by the fashionable Near-Eastern religions and, notably, Persian Zoroastrianism.[6]

The Christian dogma of creation, together with the Christian dogma of man, succumbed to the pressure of pagan thought which, on the one hand, asserted the continuity of Being (with disregard for the infinitely qualitative difference between God and His creation), and, on the other hand, claimed that all that exists resulted from *divine* activity giving *form* to preexisting *matter* (as human activity forms culture, or as an architect uses raw materials to bring his plan, his design, to fruition). This rational deity was not a creator, but an *artificer*, fashioning matter that was otherwise autonomous; thus whatever

---

[6]. Zoroaster or Zarathustra (seventh century B.C.), a more or less legendary character, was thought to have founded Mazdaism (from the name of the god Ahura Mazda and/or the word *mazda*, ancient Persian for "sage"). Zoroastrianism or Mazdaism is essentially dualism, teaching the irreducible opposition between Good and Evil, Light and Darkness, Matter and Spirit.

form was to be found in nature was evidence of the mind of the artificer imposing his design on matter, not the manifestation of any form intrinsic to matter itself. Likewise, just as this rational deity was set against matter that was, in principle, autonomous, so the *rational soul* of man was set against the material, earthly nature of the *body*. This Greek pagan thought had too easily accommodated the dualist theme of Zoroastrianism which set the divine principle of Light against the evil principle of Darkness. The Greek opposition of form vs. matter and the Zoroastrian opposition of light vs. darkness prove in the end to have a strong resemblance, presenting more or less identical challenges to the Christian dogmas of creation and man. The Gnostics soon posited a third opposition: the Savior God of the New Testament vs. the Creator God of the Old Testament. The influence of these three oppositions has clearly continued even to this day.[7]

The course laid out for the true Church is always one of faithful *reformation* according to Holy Scripture. In these first centuries, however, certain early Church Fathers chose instead to pursue a course of *accommodation*, seeking to harmonize the creation-fall-redemption theme of Biblical Christianity with the form-matter theme of Greek paganism. Thinking they had stripped these Greek concepts of their pagan elements, they failed to see just how deeply these concepts were rooted in the basic pagan schema. They also risked giving greater importance to a mystical, contemplative, theoretical knowledge of God than to the obedient faith of the faithful, thus relegating the Christian religion to nothing more than a superior ethic.[8]

In defense of the Fathers and of erudite Christians of the first four centuries, such as St. Justin (100–165), one must keep in mind that though the Church began in the Jewish milieu of Palestine, she spread out from there into the Greco-Roman world, where she found herself immersed in a pagan world. The education of those converted

---

7. The *Gnostics* have always added their own speculations to the revelation of Christ, speculations either modifying or opposing Scripture. They regarded their *gnosis* (that is, their "special knowledge") as superior to that of ordinary Christians, since it was esoteric, known only to initiates, whereas the common people knew only the ordinary and "exoteric" things. The Nicolaitans mentioned by St. John (Revelation 2:6, 15) may have been the very first gnostic "Christians."

8. For this paragraph and the one that follows, I have drawn upon the work of the Dutch Reformed philosopher Herman Dooyeweerd (1894–1977): *Roots of Western Culture* (Toronto, Canada, 1977), 114–117; as well as that of the American Rousas John Rushdoony, *The One and the Many* (1971), 185–229.

from paganism to Christianity had been, as one would expect, pagan. Once converted, it was simply not possible for such Christians, and the leading Fathers, to separate themselves from every trace of this pagan culture so thoroughly permeated by the gods, myths, and nature-grace scheme of Greek religion, *form-matter.*[9]

Moreover, although these early Christians were fully aware of the fact that God had revealed His Truth in His Word, they all too often gave undue weight to those elements of truth that Greek wisdom had seized upon by virtue of God's common grace (in distinction from His saving, soteriological grace). In their defenses of the Faith (such as Justin's *Apology*), the early Fathers had to use terminology of a thoroughly pagan origin, though they often lacked the mastery necessary to offer a thoroughgoing critique of its principles.

Scholasticism reached its full bloom in the thirteenth century, but its precursor and distant master lived and worked in the early stages of the Age of Faith. Boethius (480–524) was imprisoned after he was accused of having participated in a plot against Theodore the Great, the Ostrogoth prince become king of Italy. He died in prison, having suffered ghastly tortures.

As a theologian, Boethius wrote and compiled his *Treatises*, of which several set forth the catholic Faith and the dogmas of the Trinity and Incarnation (*De Trinitate* and *De Unitate et Uno*). But he is more renowned for his *Philosophical Treatises* on account of which he is considered, and rightly so, to have introduced Aristotle to the West — which was a mixed blessing — and for his *De consolatione philosophiae* ("The Consolation of Philosophy"). In this last work, composed in prison, knowing his sentence, death in sight, he claims to summarize everything that he knows and yet not a word is said about the revealed God, Christ, Scripture, or the Faith.

He faced death by confessing: "Now in tears to sad refrains am I compelled to turn. Thus my maimed Muses guide my pen, and gloomy songs make no feigned tears bedew my face."[10] This last testament, in prose and in verse, is animated from beginning to end by the old form-matter theme of Greek dialectic. The God of whom he speaks

---

9. For a differing view from that which I am presenting, one can consult the book of my Roman Catholic friend Daniel Bourgeois of La fraternité des moines apostoliques d'Aix-en-Provence, entitled *La sagesse des anciens dans le mystère du Verbe* ["The Wisdom of the Ancients in the Mystery of the Word"] (Paris: Téqui, 1981).

10. Boethius, *The Consolation of Philosophy*, Book One, trans. W. V. Cooper.

"is Form and truly One without plurality" (plurality, for Boethius, belongs to matter alone! What then is the Holy Trinity?).

The question can be asked (though it is not for us to answer): did Boethius consider the *Christian* faith to be nothing more than a means of expressing and representing the ancient Greek philosophy?

In his *Quomodo substantiae* ("The How of Substance"), he affirms:

VI. Anything that exists necessarily participates in absolute Being.

VII. Anything that exists possesses, as unity, a Being absolute and particular.

X. Opposites repulse; like things attract. It can be shown that whatever seeks something outside of itself is of the same nature as that which it seeks.

Here we have nothing more than the pagan belief in the continuity of Being, in which all realities participate. The particularity of a reality is its individual being; its absolute Being is God. How far we have strayed from the catholic Faith revealed in, and worked out under, the light of Holy Scripture!

Humanism and Scholasticism

In our endeavor to identify the extent to which Scholasticism succumbed to the seductive influence of Humanism, we must make clear from the outset that our problem is not with the scholastic method. Though often criticized, the scholastic method has great value, and a number of theologians of the Reformation employed it with success. It was a prominent feature in the work of Peter Martyr Vermigli (1500–1562), a professor at Oxford whose eucharistic theology, permeated with the Fathers, was hailed by Calvin as "leaving nothing more to be said."[11] It is also found in the work of Vermigli's contemporary and author of a superb *Treatise on Predestination*, Jerome Zanchi, and, much later, in the work of Francis Turretin, to whom I've

---

11. Cf. Joseph C. McLelland, *The Visible Words of God* (Grand Rapids, 1997), an exposition of Vermigli's sacramental theology.

already made abundant reference. It was not Scholasticism's method that proved harmful, but its intent to accommodate, to find a compromise between the base theme of the Bible (*Creation-Fall-Redemption*, with an absolute distinction between the Creator and creation) and the base theme inherited from Greek thought, and Aristotle in particular (*Form-Matter*, with a continuity of Being).

One can discern three stages in the history of this scholastic synthesis.

First, from the works of certain early Fathers on through St. Augustine, the scholastic synthesis was proposed as *a possible approach* to the apparent problem presented by the confrontation of Greek and Biblical thought systems (with many thinkers, such as Tertullian, objecting to the idea of synthesis altogether). Then, from St. Augustine to the twelfth century, the scholastic synthesis was refined as a *significant approach* as theologians and philosophers became increasingly confident that they had indeed succeeded in synthesizing the two thought systems. And finally, from the thirteenth century to "modern" times, the scholastic synthesis was championed as *an exclusive approach*.

St. Augustine, unlike Boethius who would follow, rejected the autonomy of theoretical thought. While recognizing that Greek thought contained certain true and useful ideas, he recognized that it must be illumined and governed by the Word of God or it would inevitably lead theology far off course and into serious error. It was useful so long as it remained the *ancilla theologiae*, the servant of theology. Augustine situated philosophical reflection within a theological framework so that human thinking was bridled by the Word of God, Truth itself.

In the thirteenth century, with Thomas Aquinas, the scholastic synthesis would become dominant as philosophy began to reassert its autonomy, not only as a discipline distinct from that of theology — which was a positive development — but also as an alternative authority to God and His Word. The real effect of this was to limit the lordship of Jesus Christ sitting at the right hand of the Father and to forget that Jesus Christ had said: "I am the truth" (John 14:6), that "in Him are hidden all the treasures of wisdom and knowledge" (Colossians 2:3) and that we should "take every thought captive to obey Christ" (2 Corinthians 10:5).

Thomas Aquinas (regrettably!) would masterfully proceed to construct a two-story system of thought:

THEOLOGY relying on the Revelation of Christ and the Bible (upper-level)

NATURAL PHILOSOPHY incorporating Aristotelian thought (lower-level)

Both the upper- and lower-stories then had their own dialectics: philosophy, with its Greek dialectic of FORM-MATTER; and theology, with its more complex and broad dialectic of NATURE-GRACE.

Since nature (and with it, the mind) had suffered the effects of the fall, it was the task of Revelation to take up again, to speak anew, those natural truths that had been more or less lost or forgotten (such truths as the divine creation of the world, the Decalogue, etc.).

Though Thomas Aquinas did accept the Augustinian vision of theology as the Queen of the sciences and of philosophy as the servant of theology, he nevertheless relied upon the kind of natural philosophy (and even natural theology) that pretended to draw its authority from the light of reason alone.

Thomist philosophy[12] is thus founded on an Aristotelian metaphysic of Being and pretends to answer in an autonomous manner (that is, without appeal to the Lord and His Word) the three fundamental problems of philosophy:

PROBLEM	SOLVED BY
1. How are diverse aspects of experience related and mutually connected?	A general metaphysic of Being as the foundation and connection of all diversity.
2. What accounts for the radical unity of the thinking self?	A metaphysical anthropology concerning the substantial unity of rational human nature.
3. What is the ultimate origin of the meaning of all creation?	A natural theology concerning the ultimate origin of the diversity of Being.

---

12. Cf. the masterful account by Etienne Gilson in *The Spirit of Mediaeval Philosophy* (University of Notre Dame Press, 1991), and Father Sertillanges, O.P., in *Le christianisme et les philosophes* ("Christianity and the Philosophers"), vol. 1 (Paris: Aubier éd., 1939), 244–354.

This is simply a recapitulation of Aristotelian Metaphysics of Being with its four transcendental attributes: the One, the True, the Good, and the Beautiful.

But what does this God of natural philosophy and natural theology have to do with the living and true God who reveals Himself in Holy Scripture and in Christ as the Creator and Redeemer?[13]

It all comes back to this double-presupposition:

- God is pure Form.
- Matter is the principle of imperfection.

Every natural movement is only a movement of *matter* being led towards the realization of a *form*. From this rule arises the pretended proofs for the existence of God: if every effect must be moved by a cause, then there must ultimately be a First Cause, "the Unmoved Mover."

It would be impossible to overstate the harm done to Christian thought and practice by this nature-grace scheme of Scholasticism.

Furthermore, as Dooyeweerd has rightly pointed out, the claim that this scheme has a biblical basis must be shown to be erroneous by holding it up to two passages in particular: Romans 1:19–20 and 2:14–15.

> What may be known of God (*to gnôston tou theou*, "the knowledge of God") is manifest in them [that is, in all men], for God has shown (*ephanerôsen*, "made it evident") it to them. For since the creation of the world His invisible attributes (*aorata*) are clearly seen (*katorataï*), being understood by the things that are made (*noumena*), even His eternal power and Godhead, so that they are without excuse. (Romans 1:19–20)

St. Paul is in no way stating that fallen man can now come to a knowledge of the true God *by the light of natural reason*. To the contrary, the immediate context (verse 18) emphasizes that rebellious men hold the truth captive by their ungodliness (*asebeïa*) and unrighteousness (*adikia*); this is why they are without excuse. In this

---

13. Consider the first words of Pascal's Memorial: "God of Abraham, God of Isaac, God of Jacob, not of the philosophers and savants!"

same immediate context it is clearly stated: "Professing to be wise, they became fools" (verse 22). What St. Thomas says concerning natural theology may follow Aristotle, but it certainly does not follow Holy Scripture.

> When the nations [*ethnoï*, non-Jews], who do not have the Law [*Nomos*, the Scriptures], by nature do the things in the Law, these, although not having the law, are a *law* unto themselves, who show the work of the law written in their hearts, their conscience also bearing witness, and between themselves their thoughts accusing or else excusing them. (Romans 2:14–15)

Here, St. Paul is in no way giving credence to the autonomy of natural thought apart from divine Revelation. Paul is not speaking of a natural law of reason that man can know by the natural light of reason, apart from the Faith. When Paul speaks of the "heart," we must not understand him to mean man's rational intelligence, or thought-life, as Thomas Aquinas interpreted it; rather, we must understand "heart" to mean the seat of all that man is and does, the mysterious center of his whole person. It is there, in the heart of man, that God, by the constant action of His common grace, ever inscribes some manner of His law, some sense of good and evil. Every man since the fall, whether Jew or non-Jew, is, in his rebellion, without excuse. Refusing to glorify God, losing himself to vain thoughts and plunging headlong into darkness (verse 21), he exchanges the truth of God for the lie, for he would rather worship and serve the creature than the Creator (verse 25).

Humanism and the Renaissance

Introduction

By identifying the Decalogue with a natural moral law rooted in the rational nature of man and in divine reason, and by teaching that the Decalogue could be known by the natural light of reason, apart from Revelation, there is no question that Thomas Aquinas cracked open the door through which modern Humanism would seep into the West. As the theme of *nature* became increasingly detached from the theme of *grace*, it would come to define itself more and more in reference to *man*, giving rise to a new base theme of *nature-freedom*.

Though the word "renaissance" has Christian and biblical origins (meaning "rebirth"), the period known as the *Renaissance* was that era during which Humanism would most forcefully penetrate Western Christendom causing immeasurable harm. Not even the resolute opposition of the Reformation would suffice to undo its damaging effects.

Considered superficially, the Renaissance and the Reformation were both returns *ad fontes*, "back to the sources," but the sources in question were not the same. The Renaissance sought a return to paganism, to the classical pagan authors of antiquity: theirs was a return to the period before *the Age of Faith*. The Reformation, on the other hand, sought a return "to the Law and to the Testimony"; that is, to the Holy Scripture of Christ and to the Christ of Holy Scripture: theirs was a continuation of *the Age of Faith*, albeit one corrected and reformed according to the Word of God.

Erasmus and the Spirit of Renaissance Humanism

Nothing better illustrates the opposing ideals of the Renaissance and the Reformation than Luther's debate with Erasmus over the question of free will.[14]

Known as the "father of Humanism," Erasmus (1469–1536) was more celebrated for his *In Praise of Folly* (1511) than for his *Diatribe on the Freedom of the Will* (1524). But it was in this latter and relatively brief work that Erasmus struck at the very heart of the Reformation. In 1525, Luther answered Erasmus with his *The Bondage of the Will* (*De Servo Arbitrio*).[15]

Unlike his contemporary Machiavelli (1469–1527), a staunch adversary of Christianity, Erasmus remained a loyal Roman Catholic. But

---

14. This does not mean that Luther and Erasmus were on the opposite ends of every issue, for Luther indeed drew from some of Erasmus' works, in particular his edition of the Greek New Testament (1516).

15. In the introduction to their translation of *The Bondage of the Will*, Johnston and Packer write: "*The Bondage of the Will* is the greatest piece of theological writing that ever came from Luther's pen. This was his own opinion. Writing to Capito on July 9th, 1537, with reference to a suggested complete edition of his works, he roundly affirmed that none of them deserved preservation save the little children's Catechism and *The Bondage of the Will*; for only they, in their different departments, were 'right' (*justum*)" (40).

the degree to which his "Christianity" was influenced by his "Humanism" provides a clear illustration of what we mean by "the Church sick with Humanism."

Although Erasmus never attacked the dogmas of his Church, he "saw the Christian religion more as a moral code than as the way of salvation for the human race lost in sin and spiritual death," wrote Dooyeweerd, adding, "Humanism began to reveal its true intentions even before its emancipation from the authority of Scripture was complete."[16]

Luther's Response to Erasmus concerning "Free Will"

In defending, in a somewhat unconvincing manner, his conception of free will, Erasmus was in fact defending *the autonomy of man*, and of science, from the "predestinating" lordship of God the Creator and Savior, and from the sovereign authority of His Word. For Erasmus, free will is nothing short of man's power to act *independently* of God.

The approach of Erasmus' *Diatribe* is Pelagian and anthropocentric, completely devoid of serious exegesis. He endeavors to defend at all costs his faith in what he calls "free will," this "power of the human will," he writes, "by which a man can apply himself to the things which lead to eternal salvation, or turn away from them."[17] He excuses himself from the constraints of Scriptural argument by claiming that "there are some secret places in the Holy Scriptures into which God has not wished us to penetrate more deeply and, if we try to do so, the deeper we go, the darker and darker it becomes, by which means we are led to acknowledge the unsearchable majesty of the divine wisdom, and the weakness of the human mind."[18] Under this language of seeming humility lies Erasmus' real thought: namely, that within God there is the contingent and the changing, the uncertain and the unstable. It therefore follows that one must not seek to affirm divine

---

16. Herman Dooyeweerd, *The Roots of Western Culture: Pagan, Secular, Christian Options* (Toronto: Wedge Publishing Foundation, 1979), 150. *Translator's Note*: In line with Dooyeweerd, Johnston and Packer write of Erasmus: "His reforming ideals were based on an undogmatic Christianity, an eviscerated Christianity precisely because it was a Christianity without Christ at the deepest level. The epigram is irresistible — Erasmus was shrewd but shallow, a man of cool calculation rather than of burning conviction. He could never stand *contra mundum*" (op. cit., 19).

17. *Luther and Erasmus: Free Will and Salvation*, trans. and ed. E. Gordon Rupp and Philip S. Watson, "Library of Christian Classics" (Philadelphia: Westminster Press, 1969), 47. All the following citations are taken from this edition; all emphases are mine.

18. *Luther and Erasmus*, 38.

predestination from Scripture with absolute certainty; such certainty is impossible, since it cannot be that the sovereign and certain Hand of an omnipotent God guides the universe and man.

What else could Luther do with these unacceptable assertions of Erasmus but demolish them? And that is what he did, not only with passion, but above all with precise exegesis. His *De Servo Arbitrio* ("The Bondage of the Will") "is clearly Luther's greatest work and one of the greatest documents in the history of thought."[19] Relying on Scripture from beginning to end, this lively and probing work is a solid witness to the Reformation's staunch opposition to every form of Humanism. It is a rigorous work, tackling each of Erasmus' appeals to the Bible one by one, showing them to be nothing more than arbitrary inventions (that is what they are!), sophisticated evasions and fanciful interpretations. Luther seeks to bring Erasmus, and all his readers, before the meaning of the text(s) of the Scripture-Word of God; the meaning which the Doctors of free will have, by inventing supposed contradictions in the text, shamelessly sought to confuse.

In his *Diatribe*, Erasmus time and again attempts to justify his reservations about the sovereignty of God's efficacious grace and divine predestination by appealing to the supposed obscurity of the text (as was commonly done by those Doctors defending the papacy).

In his response Luther writes:

> And what in the whole of the Old Testament, especially in Ps. 119, is more often said in praise of the Scripture than that it is a most certain and evident light? The psalmist celebrates its clarity thus: "A lamp to my feet and a light to my path" (Ps. 119:105).... In this way it is called both a "way" and a "path," no doubt because of its entire certainty....
>
> And what are the apostles doing when they prove their own preachings by the Scriptures? Are they trying to obscure for us their own darkness with greater darkness? Or to prove something well known by something known less well? What is Christ doing in John 5[:39], where he tells the Jews to search the Scriptures because they bear witness to him? Is he trying to put them in doubt about faith in him? What are those people in Acts 17[:11] doing, who, after hearing Paul, were reading the Scriptures day and night to see if these things were so? Do not

---

19. R. J. Rushdoony, *The One and the Many*, 248ff.

all these things prove that the apostles, like Christ himself, point us to the Scriptures as the very clearest witnesses to what they themselves say? What right have we, then, to make them obscure?[20]

Furthermore:

> For what sublimer thing can remain hidden in the Scriptures, now that the seals have been broken [Revelation 6:1, 3, 5, 7, 9, 12; 8:1], the stone rolled from the door of the sepulcher (Matthew 27:66; 28:2), and the supreme mystery brought to light, namely, that Christ the Son of God has been made man, that God is three and one, that Christ has suffered for us and is to reign eternally? Are not these things known and sung even in the highways and byways? Take Christ out of the Scriptures, and what will you find left in them?
>
> The subject matter of the Scriptures, therefore, is all quite accessible, even though some texts are still obscure owing to our ignorance of their terms. Truly it is stupid and impious, when we know that the subject matter of Scripture has all been placed in clearest light, to call it obscure on account of a few obscure words. If the words are obscure in one place, yet they are plain in another.... Now, when the thing signified is in the light, it does not matter if this or that sign of it is in the darkness, since many other signs of the same thing are meanwhile in the light.[21]

As it concerns free will:

> It is, you say, irreverent, inquisitive, and superfluous to want to know whether our will does anything in matters pertaining to eternal salvation or whether it is simply passive under the action of grace.[22]

> ...it is not irreverent, inquisitive, or superfluous, but essentially salutary and necessary for a Christian, to find out whether the will does anything or nothing in matters pertaining to eternal salvation. Indeed, as you should know, this is the cardinal issue between us, the point on which everything in this controversy turns.[23]

---

20. *Luther and Erasmus*, 161–162.
21. Ibid., 110–111.
22. Ibid., 114.
23. Ibid., 116.

But when the works and power of God are unknown, I do not know God himself, and when God is unknown, I cannot worship, praise, thank and serve God, since I do not know how much I ought to attribute to myself and how much to God.[24]

Here, then, is something fundamentally necessary and salutary for a Christian, to know that God foreknows nothing contingently, but that he foresees and purposes and does all things by his immutable, eternal, and infallible will. Here is a thunderbolt by which free choice is completely prostrated and shattered.... Do you, then, believe that he foreknows without willing or wills without foreknowing? If his foreknowledge is an attribute of his will, then his will is eternal and unchanging, because that is its nature.[25]

For if you doubt or disdain to know that God foreknows all things, not contingently, but necessarily and immutably, how can you believe his promises and place a sure trust and reliance on them? *For when he promises anything, you ought to be certain that he knows and is able and willing to perform what he promises;* otherwise, you will regard him as neither truthful nor faithful, and that is impiety and a denial of the Most High God.[26]

... you are of the opinion that *the truth and usefulness of Scripture is to be measured and judged by the reactions of men*, and the most ungodly men at that, so that only what has proved pleasing or seemed tolerable to them should be deemed true, divine, and salutary, while the opposite should forthwith be deemed useless, false, and pernicious. What are you aiming at with this advice, unless that the words of God should depend on, and stand or fall with, the choice and authority of men? Whereas Scripture says on the contrary that all things stand or fall by the choice and authority of God....[27]

---

24. Ibid., 117.
25. Ibid., 118–119. *Translator's Note:* Packer and Johnston's translation is also worth printing: "It is, then, fundamentally necessary and wholesome for a Christian to know that God foreknows nothing contingently, but that He foresees, purposes, and does all things according to His own immutable, eternal and infallible will. This bombshell knocks 'free-will' flat, and utterly shatters it.... Do you suppose that He does not will what He foreknows, or that He does not foreknow what He wills? If He wills what He foreknows, His will is eternal and changeless, because His nature is so" (Luther, *The Bondage of the Will*, trans. J. I. Packer and O. R. Johnston, 80).
26. *Luther and Erasmus*, 122.
27. Ibid., 135.

But no man can be thoroughly humbled until he knows that his salvation is utterly beyond his own powers, devices, endeavors, will and works, and depends entirely on the choice, will, and work of another, namely, of God alone. For as long as he is persuaded that he himself can do even the least thing toward his salvation, he retains some self-confidence and does not altogether despair of himself, and therefore he is not humbled before God, but presumes that there is — or at least hopes and desires that there may be — some place, time, and work for him, by which he may at length attain salvation. *But when a man has no doubt that everything depends on the will of God*, then he completely despairs of himself and chooses nothing for himself, but waits for God to work; then he has come close to grace, and can be saved.[28]

It is for the sake of the elect that these things are published, in order that being humbled and brought back to nothingness by this means they may be saved. The rest resist this humiliation, indeed they condemn this teaching of self-despair, *wishing for something, however little, to be left for them to do themselves; so they remain secretly proud and enemies of the grace of God*. This, I say, is one reason, namely, that the godly, being humbled, may recognize, call upon, and receive the grace of God.[29]

Thus when God makes alive he does it by killing, when he justifies he does it by making men guilty, when he exalts to heaven he does it by bringing down to hell, as Scripture says: "The Lord kills and brings to life; he brings down to Sheol and raises up" (1 Samuel 2:6).[30]

It follows, therefore, that "free-will" is obviously a term applicable only to the Divine Majesty; for only He can do, and does (as the Psalmist sings) "whatever he will in heaven and earth" (Ps. 135:6). If "free-will" is ascribed to men, it is ascribed with no more propriety than divinity itself would be — and no blasphemy could exceed that![31]

It is utterly iniquitous therefore, and the greatest pity in the world by

---

28. Ibid., 137.
29. Ibid., 137–138.
30. Ibid., 138.
31. *The Bondage of the Will*, trans. J. I. Packer and O. R. Johnston, 105.

far, that our consciences, which Christ redeemed by His blood, should be troubled by the ghost of this one little word, and a word of no certain meaning at that.[32]

We conclude this section with one last quotation. This passage was written by Luther after his thorough exegesis of all the texts he had quoted against the arguments that Erasmus (and other exegetes of the same cloth) had developed in contempt of these passages and of their direct and explicit meaning as understood in their immediate context.

> In a word, since Scripture everywhere *preaches Christ by contrast and antithesis,* as I have said, putting everything that is without the Spirit of Christ in subjection to Satan, ungodliness, error, darkness, sin, death, and the wrath of God, *all the texts that speak of Christ* must consequently stand opposed to free choice; and they are innumerable, indeed they are the entire Scripture. If, therefore, we submit the case to Scripture, . . . there will not be a jot or a tittle left that will not damn the dogma of free choice. Moreover, the fact that Scripture preaches Christ by contrast and antithesis, even if the great theologians and defenders of free choice are or pretend to be ignorant of it, is nevertheless known and commonly confessed by all Christians.
>
> For Christians know *there are two kingdoms in the world, which are bitterly opposed to each other. In one of them Satan reigns*, who is therefore called by Christ "the ruler of this world" (John 12:31) and by Paul "the god of this world" (2 Corinthians 4:4). He holds captive to his will all who are not snatched away from him by the Spirit of Christ, as the same Paul testifies, nor does he allow them to be snatched away by any powers other than the Spirit of God, as Christ testifies in the parable of the strong man guarding his palace in peace (Luke 11:21). *In the other Kingdom, Christ reigns*, and his Kingdom ceaselessly resists and makes war on the kingdom of Satan. Into this kingdom we are transferred, not by our own power but by the grace of God, by which we are set free from the present evil age and delivered from the dominion of darkness.[33]

---

32. Ibid., 117.
33. *Luther and Erasmus*, 327–328.

Humanism and the Enlightenment

Introduction

Humanism is the ever-present temptation of the Church; it is the constant *challenge*, the struggle against which the Church can never afford to let up, but must overcome by God's grace, "taking the sword of the Spirit, which is the word of God" (Ephesians 6:17). With Scholasticism and its effort to establish autonomous reason, Humanism gained a foothold in the Church. With the *spirit* of the Renaissance, Humanism swept through the life and thought of the Church. Consequently, in the centuries that followed — the eighteenth, nineteenth, and twentieth — the Church would find herself more and more corrupted by the presence and effects of Humanism. As a consequence, vast domains of culture and thought that had been for so long under the influence of — and indeed become expressions of — Christianity, were deformed by the scholastic scheme of nature-grace, which paved the way for the more modern scheme of nature-freedom. In the end, the Age of Faith, or what was left of it, capitulated to the spirit of modernity, with its belief that man, and not God and His Word, was the measure of all things.

The Influence of Immanuel Kant

Towards the end of the *Aufklärung*, the "Enlightenment" (once again a biblical word, like the word Renaissance, given the opposite meaning), one of the leading philosophers was Immanuel Kant (1724–1804), who was a *Protestant* philosopher no less. In the beginning of his *Critique of Pure Reason* (1781), he wrote: "Our age is the age of criticism, to which everything must submit. Religion through its holiness and legislation through its majesty commonly seek to exempt themselves from it. But in this way they excite a just suspicion against themselves, and canot lay claim to that unfeigned respect that reason grants only to that which has been able to withstand its free and public examination."[34]

But, one will say, didn't the Reformation extol this "free and public examination?" It most certainly encouraged men to subject everything

---

34. Immanuel Kant, *Critique of Pure Reason*, preface to first edition (1781), A, xi.

to questioning and examination, but according to the standard of the Holy Scripture-Word of God, not that of sovereign (human) Reason (Acts 17:11)!

According to Kant, when some aspect of reality is subjected to the examination of reason, reason is here understood to fall within the strict limits of a *closed* system of cause and effect, admitting only what can be accounted for by the laws of mechanistic Naturalism. It is precisely at this point that the nature-freedom scheme proves to be internally inconsistent. For within this mechanistic system, where does man, belonging to nature, derive his freedom and autonomy? Modern Humanism will have to make a choice (and an arbitrary one from its own standpoint): either nature is given priority and supremacy over freedom, or freedom is given priority and supremacy over nature. Having rejected divine predestination, which will *modern* man now choose — the predestination of Chance, of blind Necessity (that is, of nature); or the predestination of man himself, man making himself god (that is, of freedom)? Kant recognized this dilemma, and thought he had solved it by laying out his own version of a split, two-story world:

Upper Story: the noumenal world of thought and value/religion (or ideology)

Lower Story: the phenomenal world of the senses/science (or technology)

For the Reformation, God is the source, the principle, the sole interpreter of all things. For Kant, however, this source, this principle, is the autonomous mind of man. The objectivity of which he boasts is not that which God decreed, but the truth *invented* by the mind of man, by man's *reason*.[35]

Though daring to call themselves "heirs of the Reformation," the churches would prove to be truer heirs of the Renaissance and Enlightenment. From the Enlightenment and Kant up to the present day, the churches would gradually abandon the ancient dogmas of the Trinity and the Incarnation as well as the dogmas of salvation and Scripture — dogmas which, all flowing from Scripture, had once animated the Reformers and those churches which had followed them in order to follow the Word of God. They had been carried away by "the

---

35. Cf. Dooyeweerd, *op. cit.*, 152–153.

spirit of the age," "the spirit of the world" (1 Corinthians 2:12), which caused them to renounce their confession, their "testimony of Jesus Christ which is the spirit of prophecy" (Revelation 19:10). It is true that these churches were led astray by "false prophets," "ravenous wolves" (Matthew 7:15), "savage wolves not sparing the flock" (Acts 20:29); yet these were "ordained ministers," "pastor-teachers," who had been contaminated by the rationalism of the historico-critical method that shaped their university and seminary studies.

The Historical-Critical Method

The History and Presuppositions of the Historical-Critical Method

A powerful tool fashioned specifically to destroy Western orthodox Christianity, higher criticism arose from a confluence of various schools of Enlightenment thought: French *Skepticism* (à la Voltaire, 1694–1778, for example), British *Deism* (à la David Hume, 1711–1776, for example), and German *Rationalism* (à la Lessing, 1729–1781, for example). By the nineteenth and twentieth centuries, the *historical-critical method* had become a veritable dogma, and this predominantly *inside* the Church, her seminaries and theological faculties.

One of the most famous exponents of the historical-critical method was Julius Wellhausen (1844–1918), who built upon the work of Astruc (1684–1766), De Wette (1780–1849), Reuss (1804–1891), and Graf (1815–1869). The *a priori* governing his development of the historical-critical method are set forth by Wellhausen himself in his once-famous (though little-read today) *Prolegomena to the History of Israel.* The first of these *a priori* is his adherence to the *evolutionary schema,* leading him to reconstruct the history of Israel and biblical literature in such a way that Israel's religion begins as tribal polytheism that develops and matures into moral prophetism at a later stage. The second *a priori* is *the principle of analogy,* which declares that all historical facts are analogous to other historical facts, so that any historical claim that cannot be confirmed by present experience is rejected. The third is his presupposition of *the impossibility of miracles,* which entails his fourth *a priori: the impossibility of prophecy,* so that wherever he finds self-styled prophecy about an exact, specific historical fact in the text of Scripture, Wellhausen declares it must necessarily have been announced after the fact (*ex eventu*).

Are these not some of the very same *a priori* that we find set forth in Lessing's *Christianity and Reason* (1753)? And had not Darwin's (1809–1882) work in biology opened the way to evolutionary determinism, which sought to explain all things in terms of natural development? As Gary North has aptly concluded, "[h]igher criticism was the spiritual legacy of the Enlightenment."[36] As the historical-critical method made its way into the Church, the sovereign God (revealed in Jesus Christ, the Word incarnate; in Holy Scripture, the Word *breathed*; and in His works of creation, providence and salvation) was replaced with the sovereign Evolution decreed by Man.

With its plainly antitheistic[37] *a priori* and its contempt for the catholic ecclesial tradition ("catholic" in the sense of being faithful to all of Scripture), the historical-critical method was nothing more than a contagion, a contamination, introduced into the life and thought of the Church through Humanism. Having faced many threats from without, this method now presented a threat from within. The Church was, from that time forth, sick with Humanism.

And yet, the insane and intellectual response of a great many pastors and professors of theology to the threat was to adapt themselves to it, to concede the adversary's progress! They believed such a strategy would succeed in neutralizing the opposition, when in fact Humanism cannot be neutralized by accommodation, but only by meeting it

---

36. Gary North, *Tools of Dominion* (Tyler, TX: Institute for Christian Economics, 1990), 1064. North maintains vigorously that British Deism, even more than German Rationalism, is at the root of higher criticism and the historical-critical method. He quotes one of its spiritual heirs, Edgar Krentz, from his work *The Historical Critical Method* (Philadelphia: Fortress Press, 1975), "The rationalist Enlightenment radicalized the claim of reason and history; as a result it placed the claims of religion outside the realm of reason. In this division Orthodox theology lost its foundations in history. The cleft between reason and history triumphed among the learned — including theologians — and removed the basis of orthodoxy's epistemology.... [During this time the dogmatic church exhibited a] fear of change, fear of losing the basis for certainty of faith, and fear of posing questions in the area of authority.... The eighteenth-century deists treated the Bible with freedom when it did not, in their lights, accord with reason. For example, they argued that Isaiah was composite, the Gospels contradictory, and the apostles often unreliable" (North, *op. cit.*, 1064–1065). What these deists found truly untenable was that this Torah, this Law of Moses, this foundational Law of God, should stand in the way of the humanist civilization that they desired and sought to advance, a civilization founded not on God's Word, but on natural law.

37. By *anti-theistic* (or *anti-theist*) we mean anything or anyone opposing the God of biblical revelation, the true God and Savior of Abraham, Isaac, and Jacob ... and of Jesus Christ.

head on, by attacking it until it is defeated. This is the duty that the Church owes to her Lord. When she finds herself penetrated and infected by Humanism, she must fight it with the same resolution that Luther showed when, in the sixteenth century, he set himself against Renaissance Humanism which was exalting the pretended autonomy of man making himself god, the kind of Humanism personified by Erasmus. Taking aim against Man making himself the measure of all things (*anthropos metron ha pantôn*), the Reformer let fly the arrow of *De Servo Arbitrio*: O man, you boast of being free and autonomous, but you are still a slave of the Devil and of sin![38]

*

But one will say: isn't Holy Scripture a human book, subject to criticism like any other human book?

In answer to the first part of that question, we affirm that Scripture is indeed a truly human book — it is composed by men. But we acknowledge that it is not like any other human book, for this human book, unlike every other book, is also, and primarily, the Word of God!

In our nomenclature of the diverse human sciences as well as with regard to the specific science of theology itself, I would suggest that we coin two new terms, Mesitology and Hagiographology, so as better to describe the Mediation both of the Incarnate Christ and of the Inscriptured Word of God.

- Mesitology, the science of Christ the Mediator (from the Greek words mesitès = Mediator, and logos = Word), the admirable science of the mediation of the Divine Logos, Jesus-Christ, both God and Man, Mediator between God and men.

---

38. *Translator's Note:* For an example of this kind of all-out assault on Humanism, see the twentieth-century Serbian orthodox Father Justin Popovitch's *L'Homme et le Dieu-Homme* ("Man and the God-Man"), whom Courthial read with great appreciation. Popovitch grants nothing to reason operating apart from Christ. He declares: "In truth, the life of the mind is hell, unless, that is, it is transformed by the mind of Christ. Without the God-Word, human thought finds itself continually in dementia, in delirium, in a mad and satanic self-satisfaction, in this satanic activity that is thought for thought's sake, analogous to 'art for art's sake.' ... When it is not united with God the Word, the soul finds itself outside of itself, it finds itself in eternal dementia, eternally wandering from sin to sin, from passion to passion, from calamity to calamity" (*L'Homme et le Dieu-homme*, translated from Serbian by Jean-Louis Palierne (Lausanne: L'Age d'Homme, 1989) 53, 54; my translation from French into English).

- Hagiographology, the science of the mediation of the written Word of God, the Bible (from hagia = holy, and graphê = what is written), the science of the mediation of the Holy written Word, the Bible, both Old and New Testaments, both, at one and the same time, divine and human language, mediating thus between God's inscrutable Heavenly thoughts and man's created thinking.

With the aid of these terms, we can state that Mesitology has direct bearing on our understanding of Hagiographology.

Jesus cannot be critiqued or judged like any other man — not even Jesus in His humanity — because He is the Son of God incarnate, both in His divinity and in His humanity.

Likewise, Holy Scripture cannot be critiqued or judged like any other book — not even insofar as it is truly written by human authors — because it is the God-breathed, written Word of God, both in its divine and human authorship.

It should come as no surprise that a non-Christian would dare to use his academic training, with its anti-Christian presuppositions, to make critical judgments about the human Jesus. It follows from the fact that he denies the divinity of Him who, truly man, is also, and has always been, truly God.

Nor should it come as any surprise that a non-Christian would dare to use his academic training to make critical judgments about Holy Scripture. It likewise follows from the fact that he denies that it is the written Word of God.

What strikes us as abnormal is that a *Christian*, or a *Christian church*, would dare to make critical judgments about Jesus Christ, God the Son incarnate, *sine labe conceptus* (conceived without sin); or the Holy Scripture-Word of God, *sine labe concepta* (conceived without fault, without error).

Continuing along the lines of this analogy, *Mesitology*, the doctrine of the Mediator, does not teach of an intermediary who is neither God nor man (a third-party "go-between"), but of Him who is the true mediator because He is truly God and truly man, inseparably.

Likewise, *Hagiographology*, the doctrine of Holy Scripture, does not teach of a book that is neither human nor the Word of God, or that is partly human and partly the Word of God, but of a book that is entirely human because the whole of it was authored by men, and at the same time — and primarily — entirely the Word of God because the whole text as well as its meaning was sovereignly *breathed* by God (*théopneustos*).

As for the Church, she must seek to profit from the criticism directed toward *her* from those both within and without — God and His Word see to that better than anyone! But she cannot allow her own members, especially "theologians" and "pastor-teachers," to assume a critical posture toward the Trinitarian God and His Word incarnate (Jesus Christ) or written (Holy Scripture).

*

The Church has never lacked faithful theologians and pastor-teachers in her midst who have fearlessly upheld the catholic Faith and Tradition in strict obedience to the Word of God. The historical-critical method has always encountered opponents within the Church — not of the timid or trembling type, but combative, courageous, and scholarly. We turn to one now.

The Contribution of Louis Gaussen's Theopneustia

I have here before me the "second edition, reviewed and expanded by the author," of *Théopneustie, ou Inspiration plénière des Saintes Écritures* (1842), by Louis Gaussen (translated into English in 1867 by David D. Scott as *Theopneustia: The Bible: Its Divine Origin and Inspiration*). My copy bears the Latin inscription of a question posed by Francis Turretin:

> *Quaeritur — an, in scribendo, ita acti et inspirati fuerint a Spiritu Sancto, et quoad res ipsas, et quoad verba, ut ab omni errore immunes fuerint; adversarii negant; nos affirmamus.*[39]

---

39. *Institutio theologiae elenticae, locus* II, *questio* 4. The first edition of *Théopneustie* was published in 1830. Gaussen, a minister of the National Church of Geneva, was dismissed by *le Conseil d'État* on November 30, 1831. A leader of the Revival, he was accused of being too dogmatic, of being a literalist and of holding to "mechanical inspiration" (charges also leveled against César Malan and Henri Merle d'Aubigné, among others). It is true that the Venerable Company of Pastors had adopted, on May 3, 1817, a motion forbidding pastors from ever mentioning the divinity of Jesus Christ, original sin, grace and predestination in their sermons! Gaussen opened the Temple of Oratory in Geneva on February 9, 1834, and taught in the School of Theology, established in the same city in 1830 by the friends of the Awakening.

In response to the question whether the authors, as they wrote, were led and inspired by the Holy Spirit, not only concerning the subject matter but also the words, so as to be preserved from all error — our adversaries deny; we affirm.

In this lengthy work, Gaussen demonstrates his command of the works of the rationalist theologians of his day. He takes *critical science* to task, for "instead of being a scientific inquirer, it would be a judge; when, not content with collecting the oracles of God, it sets about composing them, decomposing them, canonizing them, decanonizing them; and, when it gives forth oracles itself! Then it tends to nothing less than to subvert the faith from its foundation."[40]

When the Fathers of the ancient Church, as well as the Doctors of *the Age of Faith* and of the Reformation, spoke of the action of the Holy Spirit on the authors of Scripture, they often said that the human authors wrote what the Holy Spirit had dictated to them (these authors were then referred to as secretaries, quills, scribes, flutes, used by the sovereign divine Author to transmit His Word, His song, His truth to us). But we *cannot* overlook the fact that when the Fathers or Doctors of the Church used such expressions to emphasize that God was truly the infallible and all-powerful author of Holy Scripture — Calvin spoke in the same manner of the apostles as "sure and genuine scribes of the Holy Spirit and their writings are therefore to be considered oracles of God"[41] — they also emphasized, often on the same page, that men were through and through real authors of the Holy Books.

Gaussen says repeatedly that God dictated the Scriptures in such a way that "the individuality of the sacred writers, so profoundly stamped on the books they have respectively written," was affirmed.[42] He explains:

Yes (we cordially unite with the objectors in saying), here is the phraseology, the tone, the accent of a Moses; there, of a John; here, of an Isaiah; there, of an Amos; here, of a Daniel or of a Peter; there, of a

---

40. Louis Gaussen, *Theopneustia: The Bible: Its Divine Origin and Inspiration*, trans. David W. Scott (Cincinnati: Hitchcock & Walden, 1867), 324.

41. Calvin, *Institutes*, IV.8.9.

42. Gaussen, *Theopneustia*, 38.

Nehemiah, there again of a Paul. We recognize them, listen to them, see them. Here, one may say, there is no room for mistake.[43]

Right in line with the Confessions of Faith and the Doctors of the Reformation, Gaussen goes on to say:

> It should not be forgotten, that the sovereign action of God, in the different fields in which it is displayed, never excludes the employment of second causes. On the contrary, it is in the concatenation of their mutual bearings that he loves to make his mighty wisdom shine forth.[44]

> The Father of mercies, while speaking in his prophets, behooved not only to employ their manner as well as their voice, and their style as well as their pen; but, further, often to put in operation their whole faculties of thought and feeling.[45]

He draws this section on "the individuality of the sacred authors" to a close with these words: "We conclude, therefore, that the abundance of humanity to be found in the Scriptures, far from compromising their divine inspiration, is only one further mark of their divinity."[46]

Despite these clear statements affirming the full involvement of the author's humanity, Gaussen was nonetheless accused of holding to a *mechanical* theory of inspiration that relegates the human authors to mere mouthpieces who had no real participation in the composition of the text! (Moreover, this accusation hangs over Gaussen's head to this day, even though few bother to read what he actually wrote!) Gaussen rejected any such theory outright, stating that "he found it utterly repugnant" and that "it had been loosely attributed to him" despite the fact that "never for a moment had he entertained the idea"; he was dismayed that men accredited it to him.

Soon after the middle of the nineteenth century, when higher criticism was *en vogue*, the German theologian Friedrich Adolf Philippi published his *Kirchliche Glaubenslehre* ("Doctrine of the Ecclesial Faith"), in which he also contended for verbal inspiration. Against the

---

43. Ibid., 41.
44. Ibid., 43.
45. Ibid., 54.
46. Ibid., 57.

critical theologians[47] who divided Scripture into contradictory parts, Philippi stated the necessary task of true theologians was the "task of harmonization" (*Aufgabe der Harmonistik*). Like Gaussen, he bemoaned that his opponents evaluated his work contemptuously, questioning his sincerity and honesty.

It would be improper to conclude this section on Louis Gaussen without mentioning the names of his fellow laborers in the Awakening, men such as the brothers Frederic and Adolphe Monod in France, and Ami Bost, César Malan, and Henri Merle d'Aubigné in Switzerland, who contended fearlessly for the preservation of the catholic Faith in the Churches of the Reformation.

Critiquing Biblical Criticism[48]

> We also have the more sure prophetic word, which you do well to heed ... Scripture. (2 Peter 1:19)

More than two centuries old now, Biblical criticism has established itself as a discipline in its own right. But we must not forget that its very appearance on the scene constituted a break from the catholic Faith and Tradition (again, "catholic" meaning "faithful to the whole of Scripture"). It departed from the consensus concerning the plenary (that is, "verbal") inspiration of Scripture, a consensus running from the literature of the Apologists and Church Fathers, on through the *Age of Faith* and the Reformation, and even up to our day.

As a result of this rupture, much of the Church has succumbed even further to the contagion of Humanism, and this to the detriment, rather than the advancement, of her reading, study, and meditation on Scripture. Especially saddening is the fact that a great many Christian scholars, many of them ordained ministers, have contributed to

---

47. Recalling the etymological meaning of "theologian," we see that it is oxymoronic to speak of "critical theologians" — like speaking of an "eloquent silence" or an "obscure clarity!"

48. For this section, I have made particular use of the following works: Gerhard Maier, *Das Ende der historish-kritischen Methode* ("The End of the Historico-Critical Method"), Wuppertal, 1974; Gerhard Maier, *Biblische Hermeneutik* ("Biblical Hermeneutics") (Wuppertal und Zürich, 1990); Moisés Silva, *Has the Church Misread the Bible?* (Grand Rapids: 1987); Gary North, *Tools of Dominion*, Appendix C (Tyler, TX: ICE, 1990); Theodore P. Letis, "The Language of Biblical Authority," *Christianity and Society* 5, no. 3 (July, 1995).

this backward step. Aside from the squandering of time and talent, their efforts have resulted in a large number of churches being led away from the *true* meaning of Scripture, some of which have now fallen into apostasy.

Some of these scholars were consciously breaking from the catholic Faith and Tradition. Ernest Troeltsch (1865–1923) was among them. A modernist theologian who taught at Bonn, Heidelberg, and finally Berlin, he famously stated of the historical method: "Once applied to the scientific study of the Bible and church history, it is the leaven, transforming everything and ultimately exploding the very form of earlier theological methods."[49]

Edgar Krentz, who has been called one of the spiritual heirs of higher criticism,[50] boldly declares: "The four-source theory of Pentateuchal origins[51] and the two-source theory of the Synoptic interrelationships[52] are its major results. Literary (source) criticism has achieved a more sharply contoured profile of the various sources and books, and the authors who stand behind them. It is indispensable for any responsible interpretation of the Bible."[53] His implication is clear: there was no "responsible interpretation of the Bible" in the Church until the arrival of "Modernity" in the nineteenth century, since only then did "criticism" come on the scene. What was needed was to approach the text with suspicion and skepticism toward the authority and inspiration of *Scripture just as it is*, an intellectual posture not advocated until the recent arrival and gradual acceptance of criticism, which was not satisfied to have its voice merely heard, but pressed on until it had established itself as the only academically acceptable approach to studying Scripture. Biblical experts (as well as more popular-level writers) were now free to interpret a *Scripture passage* by *desacralizing* it — that is, rejecting it as the written Word of God — then pulling

---

49. Cf. Moisés Silva, *op. cit.* 43.

50. North, *Tools of Dominion*, 1064.

51. These four sources are called Jawist (or Yahwist, from Yahweh), Elohist (from Elohim), Deuteronomic and Priestly, J-E-D-P, *defined* by the German school of Graf-Kuenen-Wellhausen and company, then carried on by their English epigones and imitators and others, since William Robertson Smith (*The Old Testament in the Jewish Church*, 1881). All of these sources are hypothetical and are increasingly rejected by eminent exegetes.

52. These two hypothetical sources — also increasingly rejected by eminent exegetes — are a primitive Gospel of Mark and the Q ("Q" meaning *Quelle*, or *source* in German, referring to a hypothetical document containing the sayings and parables of Jesus).

53. *The Historical-Critical Method* (Philadelphia: 1975); cited by North, *Tools of Dominion*, 1070 n. 22.

it apart into separate pieces. Certain pieces are discarded, and others kept, which are then reconstructed to promote a different meaning and rearranged according to a different chronology. And *voila!* you end up with an accommodating Scripture that is non-threatening to — and indeed in line with! — the spirit of Humanism!

This has given rise to the abundance of modern style Bibles, each devised and defended by the *new theologians,* experts in the *method,* working from their own particular dogmatic, philosophical, and political ideologies. These modern style Bibles draw from the old Bible, but *decontextualize* it according to the supplied ideology, and subsequently *recontextualize* it to better fit the humanist milieu of modernity that they have adapted for themselves.

What we are witnessing today is the *de facto identification of the* "Christian word" (sermons, publications, books, denominational declarations, etc.) *with the "humanist word"* that is disseminated by the various types of media into just about every part of the world. Is Romans 12:1 being reinterpreted? "Conform yourselves to this present world, let your minds be transformed by it until you no longer bother with the will of God of days gone by, which is neither good nor acceptable nor relevant to these changing times!"

The Works of Reformed Scholarship

Even within the critical camp we must distinguish between two groups. On the one hand are those who are rationalists through and through, holding to the critical method, fully committed to the aforementioned prejudices and thus radically opposed to the catholic Tradition and Faith. On the other hand are those who are more moderate practitioners of the critical method, but nonetheless (though it doesn't logically follow) strive to be faithful to this Tradition and Faith. Strange as it may be, these "pastors and teachers" profess the critical method to be, in theory, well founded and necessary, even though they seem to have no practical use for it in their sermons, catechizing and ministry (such inconsistency is perplexing, but we should thank the Lord for it!).

It is the task of the apologists to critique Biblical criticism, assuming as their audience the rationalists holding to the critical method. Theologians, on the other hand — and I am thinking particularly of those scholars seeking to examine, explore, and deepen our knowledge of the Bible in its original languages — need to be careful of responding to Biblical criticism in such a way that the themes and problems of Biblical criticism are allowed to set the agenda, for if that happens, the humanist ideology with its Kantian split between reason and faith will have been handed an easy victory. At the same time, theologians must guard against resorting to anti-scientific and obscurantist positions, ignoring or setting aside incontestable facts. After all, as Lecerf used to say: "The facts are among the words of God since no fact happens apart from Him."

Stated another way, theologians should be less concerned with the *critics* who, closed up with their anti-theistic *a priori*, are not listening to them anyway, and should instead forge ahead with their own theological scholarship which, when carried out in faithfulness to the written Word of God, not only prove indispensable to the wellbeing of God's people, but also, perhaps even unintentionally, answer the critics. They should do this, keeping in mind that the power of the Word and the Spirit of the Lord alone will prove able to break through to these critics and convert them (1 Corinthians 12:3). Isn't the better apologetic always to hold up and hold out the Truth, rather than to pick fights with the enemies of the faith by constantly harping on their errors and inconsistencies and speculations?

The theologians should focus on getting to the heart of these matters, of recovering the true base themes of thought and life revealed in the Word of God and putting them into practice.

For quite some time now — though most demonstrably since the 1970s — Reformation thought and the work of Christian Reconstruction have received a new and decisive impetus from the work of scholars, all of whom are *confessing Reformed* (Reformed or Anglican). Whether experts in ancient languages, exegetes, historians, or working from within other disciplines, their works draw on the *expressly Christian* philosophies and epistemologies of their predecessors, such as Herman Dooyeweerd (1894–1977) in the Netherlands, Hendrik Stoker (1899–1993) in South Africa, and Cornelius Van Til (1895–1987) in the United States. We must also mention the significant work of Kenneth Pike in the United States on philosophy and linguistics.

These men and their works (available in today's international theological language, English) are all deeply rooted in the catholic

Tradition of the four fundamental dogmas of the Trinity, the Incarnation, Soteriology, and Scripture. It is for this reason that I have labeled them as "confessing Reformed" and their thought as "expressly Christian."

I have also referred to them as scholars on account of the depth, breadth, and rigor displayed in their research and knowledge.

"We cannot fight today's Philistines with jawbones," Lecerf loved to quip in the 1930s, alluding to the book of Judges (15:15–17)! And he is right! It is with scholarship and rigor, getting to the very root of these matters, out of faithfulness to the written Word of God, that we must force the antithesis, that we must wage the fight between the two Cities spoken of by the likes of St. Augustine, Calvin, and Van Til:

- the Jerusalem above, the City of God-made-man for us and our salvation;
- and the city of Babel, the Babylon below, the City of Man making himself god, for the misery and death of all.

*

Several remarkable works have appeared in the vital area of *biblical studies and research,* an area too long dominated by humanist-inspired Criticism. These works have advanced several fronts of biblical scholarship, including:

- a renewed attention given to the diverse *manuscripts* which have made their way down to us (whether directly or indirectly), giving us a greater degree of confidence in the quality of our translations;
- the light that *archeological discoveries* of the past decades should shed on our understanding of the texts; cf. Deuteronomy 7 and 1 Samuel 15;
- renewed attention given to the *dating* of texts and books, which has yielded a return to recognizing the Mosaic authorship of the Torah, the unity of the Book of Isaiah, the chronological order of the synoptic Gospels (Matthew, Mark, Luke), the dating of the composition of all the neo-testamentary books before A.D. 70, etc.
- the more profound recognition of the *progressive* character of scriptural Revelation, so that differences from one stage to the

- next of God's dealings with His people are not mistaken for contradictions;
- an increased attention given to the diverse *manners of divine "spiration*," without in any way diminishing the quality of the inspiration of Scripture;
- showing the unity of diverse biblical texts through the practice of *interpretive harmonizing*, without forcing an artificial harmony on them; and while accepting that there are certain *phenomena* of Scripture that cannot be resolved at this time, and thus present difficulties which, nonetheless, must not be thought to contradict what Scripture says concerning itself, namely, that it is the written Word of God;
- the necessity of taking into account the *environment* and the *context* of the authors and the texts;
- the importance we must give to *diverse literary forms* of biblical Revelation, forms which are sometimes quite specific;
- the importance of the proper character of *biblical symbolism*; etc.

Hagiographology (the science of Holy Writings), which has too long treated biblical texts as the faulty witness of fallible men, is undergoing a renewal in which it is again affirming that these texts are *both* the Word of God and human texts authentically communicating this Word. Renewed in this way, hagiographology can and must play an important part in the Church's transmission (and that of the faithful) of the Truth, the Truth of which she is "the pillar and ground" (1 Timothy 3:15).

*

> Thus says the Lord God:
> "My sheep wandered... scattered over the whole face of the earth, and no one was seeking or searching for them. Therefore, you shepherds, hear the word of the Lord: 'As I live,' says the Lord God, 'surely because My flock became prey, and My flock became food for every beast of the field, because there was no shepherd, nor did My shepherds search for My flock, but the shepherds fed themselves and did not feed My flock...
> Behold, I am against the shepherds... for I will deliver My flock from their mouths, that they may no longer be food for them...

Indeed I Myself will search for My sheep and seek them out...

so I will seek out My sheep and deliver them from all the places where they were scattered on a cloudy and dark day...

I will bring them out...

I will feed them by the streams...in good pasture...

I will seek what was lost and bring back what was driven away, bind up the broken and strengthen the sick...

Thus they shall know that I, the Lord their God, am with them, and they...are my people." (Ezekiel 34)

Behold the royal declaration of Jesus Christ:

I am the good shepherd. The good shepherd gives His life for the sheep. But a hireling, he who is not the shepherd, one who does not own the sheep, sees the wolf coming and leaves the sheep and flees; and the wolf catches the sheep and scatters them...

I am the good shepherd; and I know My sheep, and am known by My own...

The shepherd of the sheep calls his own sheep by name...

He goes before them; and the sheep follow him, for they know his voice. (John 10:11–14 and 3–4)

8

HUMANISM DEFEATED BY THE LAW OF GOD

For law will proceed from Me,
And I will make My justice rest
As a light of the peoples.
(Isaiah 51:3)

...the darkness is passing away,
and the true light is already shining.
(1 John 2:8)

THE COVENANT: GOSPEL AND LAW

Introduction

Depending on which of several legitimate perspectives one uses to view the covenant (of which Holy Scripture is the Treaty), the covenant can be described as having five, six, or seven parts.[1] But viewed in the simplest possible terms, we may describe the covenant as consisting of two *main* component parts: *Gospel* and *Law.* At each of its

---

1. For example: for five points, Ray Sutton, *That You May Prosper: Dominion by Covenant* (Tyler, TX: Institute for Christian Economics, 1987); for six points, Meredith G. Kline, *The Structure of Biblical Authority*, rev. ed. (Grand Rapids: Eerdmans, 1972); for seven points, George E. Mendenhall, *Law and Covenant in Israel and the Near East* (Pittsburgh: The Biblical Colloquium, 1955).

historical stages (Adam, Noah, Abraham, Moses, David, and Christ Jesus), the covenant always includes both Gospel and Law, distinct yet inseparable.

In fact, the key to understanding and receiving the covenant is the recognition that it is composed of the Gospel and the Law conjoined. The Gospel can no more be separated from the Law than one side of a coin can be separated from the other. Moreover, the Gospel binds itself to the Law, as does the Law to the Gospel. This close relationship follows necessarily from the nature of each.

This is why the Reformation and its Doctors of yesterday and today, as well as Christian theologians of other creeds, have been able to develop a biblical doctrine of the covenant only insofar as they have grasped, with ever-greater precision, what the Gospel is: the good news of the unmerited grace of God; and what the Law is: the teaching of what God desires men to be and do across the various aspects and areas of life.

It is a mistake to think of the Law as that which was taught before Christ, and the Gospel as that which was taught with and after His coming. Though the word "Gospel" (*evangelion*) is found only in the Tradition of the Apostles, we nonetheless discern the essence of the Gospel already underlying the whole of the *TaNaKh*. Likewise, though the word "Law" (Hebrew, *Tôrâh*; Greek, *Nomos*) characterizes above all the *TaNaKh* (even when it is used in the Tradition of the Apostles), we nevertheless discern the essence of the Law underlying again the whole of the Tradition of the Apostles. That is simply to say that, from A to Z, the covenant treaty never ceases to explain, depict, and further uncover the inseparability of the Gospel and Law of God in their deep and intimate relationship.

The reader may already have sensed my reticence to use the terms "Old Testament" and "New Testament," as I prefer the terms *"TaNaKh"* (or Hebraic Bible) and "Tradition of the Apostles" — I would even prefer simply "Bible" and "Tradition"! I consider the word "testament" to be a regrettable translation of the Greek word *diathêkê*, which would be better translated as "covenant." We came to translate *diathêkê* as "testament" because of the influence of the Latin *Vulgate* (St. Jerome's Latin translation of the Bible), which rendered *diathêkê* as *testamentum*.

It is an error on the part of most of our English versions that translate *diathêkê* as *testament* in 2 Corinthians 3:14 and Galatians 3:17–29.

In 2 Corinthians 3:14 — "For until this day the same veil remains unlifted in the reading of the Old *diathêkê*" — it has to do with the reading (of the books) of the old covenant, and not the Old Testament; when translated as "Testament" here, the real meaning is lost, even if it has become common in our translations.[2]

In Galatians 3:17–29 (one must read the whole passage), the translation of *diathêkê* as *testament* proves even more harmful. In this text, St. Paul is essentially bringing the Abrahamic and Mosaic stages of the covenant together, demonstrating their remarkable unity and complementarity. The Abrahamic stage of the covenant emphasizes the two correlative gifts of God: His promise and one man's faith in this promise. The Mosaic stage of the covenant also emphasizes these two gifts, as St. Paul shows in his commentary according to which the focal point, the fulfillment, of the divine promise and of human faith is found only in Christ, who is both:

- the promised descendant, or more exactly, the seed (*sperma* in Greek) promised to Abraham;
- and the One in whom all the faithful of the old (arrangement of the) covenant believed in advance, and in whom the faithful of the new covenant do, and will, believe.

Paul clearly explains that the Law (*nomos*) given to Moses, which came 430 years after Abraham, was not intended to establish the possibility of obtaining life and justification by works, in which case it would annul the promise of the covenant made to Abraham and the example of justification by grace through faith according to which he obtained life. Rather, the point of Paul's argument is to show that the Law given to Moses is fully in accord with the promise of the covenant made to Abraham and with the teaching of justification by grace through faith; for the Law, rightly understood, exposes the inability of sinful men to keep it and thus leads them to seek and find Christ (in whom alone are found justification and life).

The only passage in which *diathêkê* can be translated as *testament* is Hebrews 9:15–17 — "For where there is a testament, there must also of necessity be the death of the testator...." Yet even in this single

---

2. *Translator's Note:* The ESV, NASB, NIV and RSV each render 2 Corinthians 3:14 as "old covenant," whereas the KJV and NKJV render it "old testament."

instance where it refers to "testament" it is being used to irrefutably emphasize that the new (arrangement of the) covenant, like the whole covenant of which Scripture speaks, is a sovereign and unilateral dispensation of God (Testament!), having nothing to do with a mutual contract.[3]

Another point regarding vocabulary: the biblical word "Law" (*Tôrâh, Nomos*) has a more vivid sense than in English. If it means ordinances, commandments, rules, prohibitions, injunctions, or directives, it also means, more generally, the basics of the body of laws. In its foremost and broadest sense, "Law" refers to the basics of doctrine, of teaching, akin to the Latin word *Institutio*, with which Calvin, for example, entitles his masterpiece *Institutes of the Christian Religion*.[4]

I have spoken above of how the two components of the covenant, the Gospel and the Law, are inextricably linked and intimately related.

> *Contra:* "But," it has been said, "doesn't Holy Scripture (and particularly St. Paul) oppose the Gospel to the Law?"

> *Respondeo:* Not at all! The only opposition set forth by Scripture (and particularly by St. Paul) is between those who, on the one hand, presume to use the Law as a means of justifying themselves (which is to abstract the Law from the covenant, as well as from the Gospel); and those who, on the other hand, know from the Word of God that it is impossible to depend on the Law and the works of the Law as a means of supposedly justifying themselves, and that justification is possible only in Christ, and by faith in Him.

The example and teaching of St. Paul — a *God-breathed* teaching — are plain and clear in this regard. In essence, St. Paul (formerly Saul of Tarsus) relates and declares concerning his relation to the Law:

- When I was Saul of Tarsus, I was boasting in what I thought to be my successful reliance on the Law, when in fact (as I now know)

---

3. Cf. Courthial's earlier essays on these subjects: "L'Ecriture comme traité d'Alliance," *Ichthus* 35 (1973), 8–12; and "La portée de Diathécé," *Etudes* évangeliques 1 (1976), 36–43; these and other of his essays are also collected in his *Fondements pour l'avenir* (Editions Kerygma: Aix-en Provence, 1981).

4. Cf. Gunnar Ostbahn, *Torah in the Old Testament: A Semantic Study* (Hahan Ohlssons, Lund, 1945).

I was transgressing the Law as all men do (Romans 2:17 and 23). I focused only on the letter of the Law and believed that I was keeping it (this "letter of the Law" which has only enough life in itself to condemn and kill those who claim to be following it faithfully; cf. Romans 2:27 and 2 Corinthians 3:6). I was "living" peacefully at that time *under* the Law (Romans 6:14–15) without yet seeing that this left me exposed only to "the law of sin and death" (Romans 8:2). I was seeking, and believed myself to have found, a righteousness proceeding from the Law, from the works of the Law, as did many of my compatriots, especially the Pharisees and scribes. I thought that the Law, the works of the Law, made it possible for men, and the Jews first of all, to establish and to be assured of their own righteousness (Romans 10:3).

- But when I became Paul after meeting Jesus Christ on the road to Damascus (in persecuting His Church I was persecuting Him), I was definitively delivered, freed from the so-called justificatory Law, and from the old regime of the letter that kills, in order to serve the new regime of the Spirit (Romans 7:6). And so was I transferred from being under the Law to being under grace (Romans 6:15), knowing from that time on that righteousness, justification, comes by grace (Romans 10:4), through faith (Romans 9:30; 10:6), in Christ, the Holy One. It is He who fulfilled the Law's demands, becoming a curse in my place, in our place (Galatians 3:13), though He Himself had perfectly obeyed the Law (Romans 5:19). I now saw that "I through the law died to the law" (Galatians 2:19) that I might live in Christ who "did not die in vain" (Galatians 2:21).

And so could this new man, Paul, exclaim — and let us exclaim with him!:

But what things were gain to me, these I have counted loss for Christ. Yet indeed I also count all things loss for the excellence of the knowledge of Christ Jesus my Lord, for whom I have suffered the loss of all things, and count them as rubbish, that I may gain Christ and be found in Him, not having my own righteousness, which is from the law, but that which is through faith in Christ, the righteousness which is from God by faith (Philippians 3:7–9).

The Rise of the Contemporary Theonomic Movement

The Law cannot be properly approached or understood when abstracted from the Gospel, for it is only by beginning with the Gospel, and in relationship to this Gospel proclaiming salvation by grace through faith (as the Church's Soteriological dogma clearly confesses against all adversaries), that the full meaning of the Law comes into view. In this context, holding Law and Gospel together, it becomes clear that the Law was not given as a means for man's justification, but as a guide for the man justified by grace to express his gratitude in a life given, and ever given again and again, to obedience to the Trinitarian God, the one and only Savior, who desires to be, and must be, the one and only Lord. Such obedience is God's rightful claim, due Him not only on account of creation and redemption, but also on account of the vivifying and sanctifying grace by which He has given to the man justified in Christ the efficacious power to render that obedience. "Work out your own salvation with fear and trembling; for it is God who works in you both to will and to do for His good pleasure" (Philippians 2:12–13).

The dogma of the Trinity, the dogma of the Incarnation, the dogma of Salvation, and the dogma of Scripture — these are the four fundamental dogmas of the ecclesial Faith, "catholic" in that they are faithful to the whole of Scripture. They came to mature expression during the course of the Church's history and in the midst of her struggles: the first two in the early centuries of the Church as she battled Arianism and a host of heresies concerning the Trinity and the two natures of Christ; the latter two in the sixteenth century as she battled the traditions of Rome obscuring the true nature of justification and biblical authority. As the Church moves into the future, it will be necessary to add a fifth dogma: the dogma of the Law (*nomos*) of God (*Theos*), the dogma of "theonomy," to battle the Humanism that reigns today.

Like the four dogmas preceding it, in fact, the coming dogma of theonomy will seek to expound upon the mystery that is, and must be, the permanent ecclesiastical confession: GOD ALONE, THE FATHER, THE SON, AND THE HOLY SPIRIT, IS THE LORD AND SAVIOR AND THERE IS NONE OTHER BESIDES HIM.

Indeed, the belief, thought, and life of the Church and faithful Christians have always been implicitly *theonomic*. But it remains for the Church's dogma of theonomy (theonomy meaning "faithfulness to the Law of God") to be explicitly set forth and raised up in every aspect of the lives (both individually and corporately) of God's people, of the covenant people — and this against all adversaries, against all competing allegiances.

It is true that we do not find an explicit theonomic doctrine in the works of the early Fathers and medieval Doctors, but this is owing to the fact that the soteriological dogma of justification would not be defined until the Reformation (as stated above, the Law cannot be rightly understood apart from the Gospel, apart from salvation by grace alone through faith, without which one falls into legalism and self-justification). However, the basic idea of theonomy, being intrinsic to the general thrust of Holy Scripture, was always present and active both in the Church and in the Christianized society.[5]

Among the Reformers, it was the Swiss pastor and theologian Pierre Viret (1511–1571) who, in the sixteenth century (better perhaps than Calvin, and certainly better than Luther), outlined a rigorous doctrine of theonomy, particularly in his 1564 masterpiece, *Instruction chrétienne en la doctrine de la Loi et de l'Évangile*.[6]

---

5. Three examples:
   1. The Code of Justinian, put together at the behest of the Roman Emperor Justinan I (482–565), introduced several elements of biblical law into the *Corpus juris civilis* (civil law code), especially regarding marriage. Those ancient Roman laws that were retained in the code were renewed with biblical meaning.
   2. A second example of theonomy is found during the reign of Alfred the Great (849–899), when several biblical laws were adapted to English Law. Concerning both examples, cf. Rousas J. Rushdoony, *The Institutes of Biblical Law* (Nutley, NJ: The Craig Press, 1973), 786–787. Rushdoony points out that "a very real defect of scholars has been their ignorance of Biblical law. As a result, much has been called pagan which was in reality Biblical" (ibid., 787).
   3. Furthermore, theonomy was evident in the feudal system, since "the feudal oath was strongly influenced by the biblical idea of the covenant. Even the term 'feudal' has its root in *foedas*, the Latin word for 'covenant.'" Cf. Jean-Marc Berthoud, "Social Contract Tradition and the Autonomy of Politics" (*Calvinism Today* 1, no. 1 1 (1991) 14. In this article, Jean-Marc Berthoud, referencing Régine Pernoud's work on Eleanor of Aquitaine, remarks that the feudal seed put social relations under the authority of a sovereign moral power, such that the relation between the sovereign and his subjects had the sacred quality of a conjugal covenant).

6. *Translator's Note:* Viret's *Instruction chrétienne en la doctrine de la Loi et de l'Évangile* was recently republished by L'Age d'Homme in 2009, and an English translation of the work is underway. See also two recent works on Viret published by Zurich Publishing: Jean-Marc Berthoud's *Pierre Viret: A Forgotten Giant of the Reformation* (2010) and R. A. Sheat's *Pierre*

An outline of the history of the doctrine of the covenant (with its Law and Gospel), even one confined to the confessing Reformed tradition, is beyond the parameters of this work. But we note that it was Calvin who began to emphasize the one covenant in two dispensations: the old and the new, with the Gospel and the Law throughout.[7] The same fundamental theme of the covenant: "I will be your God and you will be my people" runs through both the old and new dispensations.[8] As the first Adam was the covenantal Head and legal representative of the human race, so the second Adam, Christ, is the covenantal Head of His people who, though sinners deserving death, are, in Him, "legally," "judicially," declared to be alive and righteous (Romans 5:12–21; 1 Corinthians 15:22). Covenant theology, which has its ecumenical roots in the Age of Faith, has been progressively developed in confessing Reformed circles, with its five key concepts:

1. the *Transcendence of God*, even in His immanence;
2. the *Hierarchy* (that is, holy order) established by God, which represents His authority in each of the human societies that He has instituted: marriage, family, state, Church, ... ;
3. the *Ethic of the covenant* in Scripture, the gift of God as much for the personal as for the social life of human persons; not "works that save, but salvation that works";
4. the *divine Oaths*, including the legitimate sanctions, positive or negative;
5. *Succession*, the historical consequences of the promises and warnings of the covenant (note the mnemonic: THEOS, which is Greek for "God").[9]

Viret: *The Angel of the Reformation* (2013).

7. Hans Heinrich Wolf, *Die Einheit des Bundes: Das Verhaltnis von Alten und Neuem Testament bei Calvin* ("The Unity of the Covenant: the relation between the Old and New Testament in Calvin"), (Neukirchen, 1958). W. H. van der Vegt, *Het Verbond der Genade bij Calvÿn* ("The Covenant of Grace in Calvin") (Goes, 1938). *Translator's Note:* "The covenant made with all the patriarchs is so much like ours in substance and reality," writes Calvin, "that the two are actually one and the same. Yet they differ in mode of dispensation." Regarding the old covenant, he states clearly that "the covenant by which [the Israelites before Christ] were bound to the Lord was supported, not by their own merits, but solely by the mercy of the God who called them" (*Institutes*, II.10.2).

8. O. Palmer Robertson, *The Christ of the Covenants* (Phillipsburg, NJ: Presbyterian and Reformed Publishing, 1980).

9. Ray Sutton, *That You May Prosper* (Tyler, TX: Institute for Christian Economics 1987), 6–7.

Since the publication of Rousas John Rushdoony's *Institutes of Biblical Law*[10] in 1973, followed by Greg L. Bahnsen's *Theonomy in Christian Ethics*[11] in 1976, confessing Reformed scholars around the world have given steadfast attention to theonomy while others (or sometimes the same!) sought to put its applications into practice.[12]

The Knowledge of Good and Evil

Without God, there would be no true or false, no good or evil (as Dostoyevsky writes in *The Brothers Karamozov*, "If God does not exist, then everything is permissible"). The point of the forbidden tree in the garden was to make it clear that man could learn the knowledge of good and evil from God, and from Him alone. Otherwise stated: the Word of God is the sole source of morals and law.

It was at the fall that *another* source of morals and law was seductively suggested to man, a *pretended* source alongside of, and opposed to, the one true source. We know from the Word of God that the instigation of this other source, this *source-mirage*, was Satan, who was then — and always is — behind the alluring temptation that aims to draw man away from God as the source and standard of all truth. The fall happened because man, in Adam, rebelled, listening to the seducer and preferring an illusory source to the one true source.

The Church succeeds only in flattering Humanism — Humanism that has lost man! — whenever she, and her leadership in particular, *recoil* from pointing covenant-breaking man to the one true source of morals and law, and speak to him instead of a pretended alternative source, be it natural reason, natural law, or natural right (which today is not even presented as an alternative to the one true source, but is given priority over it!). In so doing, she succumbs to a spirit of compromise, and makes a pact with this disastrous religion of man-making-himself-god. Rather than call man to "repent," to turn back to God, the Church then leaves man to sink in death.

The Church, and her leadership in particular, has often given

---

10. Nutley, NJ: The Craig Press, 890 pages.
11. Nutley, NJ: The Craig Press, 619 pages.
12. For example: John Frame, Kenneth L. Gentry, Gary North, Vern S. Poythress, Moisés Silva, Ray R. Sutton, in the United States; Ruben C. Alvarado in the Netherlands; Thomas Schirrmacher in Germany; Owen Fourie in South Africa; Stephen C. Perks in Great Britain; Ian Hodge in Australia. Not all of these call themselves *theonomists*, but all have promoted reflection about theonomy.

priority to reason, nature, or some form of natural right or natural law, in an attempt to establish a no-man's-land, a neutral or common ground, or intermediary, between the true Faith and false faiths, where all men could hypothetically come together at ease, in "peace."[13] But in reality, this results in the Church deserting the battle of the Two Cities, and reinforcing the false sense of confidence of those in Babel, in Babylon here below, rather than leading them back, conquered, to the company of Christ, the Savior and Lord, in the Jerusalem above. In leaving man in the hands of man, in inviting man to continue in the faith in man, the Church, enfeebled by Humanism, turns away from her vocation of teaching all men that they must turn around and come back to the Father's House.

From Adam to Noah, to Abraham, to Moses, to Jesus Christ, and until the end of the world, the only true knowledge of good and evil, or what is just and unjust, has come, comes, and will come *only* from the faithful hearing of the Word of God, by apprehending and always re-apprehending the revealed Gospel-Law, by delving into it, examining it, and committing oneself ever anew to live it — by faith.

Good and evil are realities defined and described only by the God of the covenant in His Treaty of the covenant, Holy Scripture — and by no other source, and in no other place! The catholic Church, *Mater et magistra*, must tell and retell this truth, doing so gently, firmly, with perseverance and patience, under pain of no longer being "the salt of the earth," "the light of the world," "the pillar and ground of the Truth." She owes this to herself, she owes it to every man in every time and in every place, and first and foremost, she owes it to God. Striking a pact with Humanism, without and within, has only brought death to the Church — and not only from shame! In choosing synthesis rather than antithesis, in desiring to make only one City from the two Cities, the Church can only betray her mission, and, at the same time, betray both the men to whom she must communicate the Word of truth and salvation, and her Lord and Husband Jesus Christ.

Common Grace

Contra: But doesn't Paul say that the Gentiles (that is, the men of the non-Jewish nations), who do not have the Law (that is, Scripture), do

---

13. Matthew 10:34ff.; John 14:27.

by nature (Greek *physei*) the things of the Law, thus showing that the work of the Law is written on their hearts (Romans 2:14–15)?

Respondeo: That is exactly right, but we must keep the following in mind to understand this correctly:

1. As the context (Romans 1:18–3:20) makes clear, human reason since the fall has been led astray by sin, which leaves no faculty of man untouched. Thus, if it is always possible for men to have some practical knowledge of good and evil which moves the conscience, it is thanks to the work, the operation, of the Law in their heart. This is what our theologians call *common grace*, which God grants to the fallen human race in order to restrain the intensity of sin's effects (Romans 2:15).
2. As a result of common grace, even those human beings not motivated by a true faith manage to show some degree of obedience to God's law, and in so doing, allow men to know and enjoy certain benefits (blessings) throughout their history, such as a more or less viable political, civil or social order. That is to say, civilization is made possible by common grace.
3. This common grace, which is merited for the human race only by Jesus Christ, brings men to experience only temporary and temporal forms of "salvation and progress"; it does not bring regeneration of the inward man. Furthermore, instead of bringing them to a here-and-now experience of eternal salvation, common grace serves, should they persist in their rebellion against God, to render them yet more inexcusable.
4. And yet, in a great many of the issues and significant moments of life, touching on certain points or matters of significance, common grace allows for a real cooperation between believers and unbelievers (that is, between the faithful and the unfaithful). Believers freely accept, and even promote, this cooperation to advance the interests of Christ's reign, though our cooperation allows for no compromise or betrayal whatsoever of the Faith, since we are dealing here with the application of God's Law. But whereas the faithful cooperate with unbelievers because they are motivated to glorify God (the Law of God being written in their hearts; cf. Hebrews 8:10 and 10:16, citing Jeremiah 31:33ff.), the unfaithful

cooperate only for reasons that they consider pragmatic and in the interests of the common good. In fact we may say that they — the unfaithful! — cooperate to the glory of God *despite themselves*, and are unknowingly driven by "a work of God written in their hearts."[14]

The Theonomic Challenge to Humanistic Autonomy

It is worth noting that the Latin word *Lex* (law) has often been used as a more precise and encompassing term for religion.[15] This is what St. Augustine had in mind in his *De Vera Religione* (XXIII, 20) when he speaks of the *Christiana lex*.

John of Salisbury (1115–1180) was an Englishman of the Age of Faith who finished his life as bishop of Chartres and magnificently stated: "If the true God is the true Wisdom, then the love of God is the true philosophy."[16] In several places in his *Polycraticus*, he uses the word *Lex* to refer to religious worship or the profession of the Faith. Raymond Lulle (1235–1315),[17] who learned Arabic and made several trips

---

14. For those who believe, as I do, in the verbal inspiration of Scripture (a teaching belonging to the "catholic" ecclesiastical Tradition faithful to the Word of God), there is often great importance attached to the nuances of the terms used in Scripture. For example, in the whole of the New Testament, love of neighbor takes all men into consideration, whereas love of the brethren is that love which the Christian faithful owe to other Christians, all having become, by adoption, brothers of the one and only Son of God, by faith in Him and mystical union (as Calvin used to say) in Him.

In the same way, it is one thing to say that the Law of God is written in the hearts of the faithful, and another thing to say that the work of this Law is written in the hearts of all men. In the texts at hand (Romans 2 and Hebrews 8 and 10), in Greek, it is a question not only, as in English, of *o nomos* (the Law) and *to ergon tou nomou* (the work, the operation of the Law), but also the verbs, though each translated as "written," are, in Greek, different verbs: *epigraphô* and *graphô*. It would be better to translate the first as "inscribe" and the second as simply "write." Finally, we note that the inscription is "in their mind and on their hearts" of the faithful, whereas the writing is only "on the hearts" of the others.

15. Thomas Schirrmacher, "*Lex* (Law) as Another Word for Religion: A lesson from the Middle Ages," *Calvinism Today* 2, no. 2 (April, 1992), 5.

16. He wrote: *Philosophus amator Dei est* ("He is a philosopher who loves God"). Cf. Etienne Gilson, *La philosophie au Moyen Age* (Payot, 1947), 274–277, etc.

17. Ibid., 461–465, etc. *Translator's Note:* Historian Will Durant says of *Polycraticus*, "This is the first important essay in political philosophy in the literature of Christendom. It exposes the errors and vices of contemporary governments, delineates an ideal state, and describes the ideal man." Durant goes on to quote "the most famous passage in the Polycraticus" which concerns tyrannicide: "If princes have departed little by little from the true way, even so it is not well to overthrow them utterly at once, but rather to rebuke injustice with patient reproof until finally it becomes obvious that they are obstinate in their evil-doing.... But if the power of the ruler opposes the divine commandments, and wishes to make me share in its war against God, then with unrestrained voice I answer that God must be preferred before any man on earth.... To kill a tyrant is not merely lawful, but right and just" (*The Age of Faith* [1950], 951–952).

to evangelize the Saracens, compared the *Lex Mahumetana* (the Law of Mohammed) to the *Christiana Lex* when he sought to compare the Faith of Islam and the Faith of Christianity.[18] As for Roger Bacon (1220–1292)[19] — "The whole of wisdom was given by one God, to one world, for one purpose"; "There is only one perfect wisdom, and it is contained in the Holy Scriptures" — he also spoke of *Lex Christiana* to designate the Christian Faith and of *Lex Antichristi* to designate other religions.

Thus R. J. Rushdoony, one of the founders of contemporary Reformed theonomy, falls within an old and well-founded tradition when he said in his turn:

> Law is in every culture *religious in origin . . . the source of law is the god of that society*. If law has its source in man's reason, then reason is the god of that society. If the source is an oligarchy, or in a court, senate, or ruler, then that source is the god of that system. . . . Modern Humanism, the religion of the state, locates law in the state and thus makes the state, or the people as they find expression in the state, the god of the system. . . . In Western culture, law has steadily moved away from God to the people (or the state) as its source, although the historic power and vitality of the West has been in biblical faith and law.[20]

Every unbiblical system of faith, including those that pretend to be atheistic (godless!), and, consequently, every unbiblical system of law and morals, stand as rivals, if not self-professed adversaries, to the system of faith, law, and morals revealed in Holy Scripture (the *Lex*) of God. Man is always faced with the responsibility of choosing between theonomy and his desire for autonomy. In reality, God alone is autonomous (Law unto Himself and for His creatures). Calvin puts it succinctly: *Deus legibus solutus est quia ipse sibi et omnibus Lex est* (God is not submitted to laws, because He *is* the law for Himself and for all others.).[21]

The perennial question is: by what Standard? Who or what has authority here?

---

18. For example, *Lettera a Maometto II*, 115; cf. note 12 above.
19. Gilson, *op. cit.*, 476–482, etc.
20. Rushdoony, *The Institutes of Biblical Law*, 4–5.
21. *Commentaire du Deutéronome* (1563), *Corpus Reformatorum* 52, 49, 131.

And the perennial response is: the Standard, the *Lex*, is the covenantal Law, the Holy Scripture of Christ. Holy Scripture is at the heart of our religion (our relationship to God) and of our worship of God both within and beyond the church doors,[22] which worship Scripture identifies, defines, and ordains — for our salvation and our joy. Our authority is the Trinitarian God who has given His Word of the covenant once for all.

And there you have it — theonomy!

Humanism, by contrast, with its faith in *Man,* or in his *Reason,* or in whatever god he chooses (Evolution, Democracy, God revealed through the Welfare State, etc.), thinks that it can define any system of law and morals to its liking, with any conceivable variation, moving from one to the next or attempting to accommodate every variation at once (*pluralism*). And certain Christians, contaminated by Humanism, think that they can have a seat at the table by appealing to natural Revelation instead of to Holy Scripture. In each case, the effects of sin on our minds (the "noetic effects of the fall") are underestimated or ignored altogether. And so, to the humanist, it is necessary to say, with Lecerf:

> Sin has its seat in the very centre of the intellectual consciousness of man. If reason were normal [it no longer is on account of the Fall — P.C.], it would consent to remain *ratio ratiocinata* [reason that is "normed" by God — P.C.]. We should not see it aspire to become *ratio ratiocinens* [hair-splitting, abusive — P.C.]....[23]

The practical reason, which proclaims itself autonomous, sins: for there is only one lawgiver, namely God: and this lawgiver it ignores, in order to install itself in His place.

---

22. *Translator's Note:* Courthial speaks of *"notre service cultuel et culturel."*

23. *Translator's Note:* Analogous to Lecerf's distinction of *ratio ratiocinata* from *ratio ratiocinens*, Van Til speaks of non-Christian epistemology as *creatively constructive* in distinction from Christian epistemology which is *receptively reconstructive*: "This then is the most basic and fundamental difference between Christian and non-Christian epistemology, as far as it has a direct bearing upon questions of ethics, that in the case of non-Christian thought, man's moral activity is thought of as at once *creatively constructive*, while in Christian thought, man's moral activity is thought of as being *receptively reconstructive*. According to non-Christian thought there is no absolute moral personality to whom man is responsible and from whom he has received his conception of the good, while according to Christian thought God is the infinite moral personality wo reveals to man the true nature of morality" (Cornelius Van Til, "Christian Theistic Ethics," unpublished class syllabus [1964], 18).

The theoretical reason...sins also...when it ignores its subordinate role of organ or instrument conditioned by the true objective, in order to constitute itself the supreme norm and fallacious source of knowledge.

...in the order of knowledge as well as in the order of the moral law, God is everywhere displaced by man.... It follows from this that sin is...a conflict between the supreme reason, on which all depends, and the subordinate reason, which would rid itself of this dependence.[24]

To the Christians contaminated by the subjectivity of Humanism and who rightly claim that a natural Revelation of God is revealed before their very eyes, we must now repeat that

> what may be known of God is manifest in them, for God has shown it to them. For since the creation of the world His invisible attributes are clearly seen, being understood by the things that are made, even His eternal power and deity, so that they are without excuse (Romans 1:19–20),

while not forgetting, however, that these same men

> became futile in their thoughts, and their foolish hearts were darkened...who exchanged the truth of God for a lie...and even as they did not like to retain God in their knowledge, God gave them over to a debased mind, to do those things which are not fitting; being filled with all unrighteousness, malice...haters of God. (Romans 1:21, 25, 28–30)

In order for natural Revelation to come back into focus, to be perceived in all its color and meaning, the faithful must "put on the spectacles of Scripture" (Calvin), so that the gaze of their heart, now corrected, clarified, and restored, might apprehend the evidence that was under their eyes all along, but theretofore missed by their wayward minds. Then, and only then, does the natural Revelation that was always there finally come into view in its gentle, beautiful and radiant light.

---

24. Lecerf, *An Introduction to Reformed Dogmatics*, 80–81.

Rushdoony has quite ably discerned:

> The reason why men choose to look for a foundation [of morals or law] in man is because of their quest for a common ground with all men and all reality outside of God. They want to avoid what they call "a 'sectarian' system of thought." They declare that the need is for "the *philosophia perennis*," a philosophy common to all men as men, apart from theological considerations. By this means these thinkers claim that they can establish all the truths of Biblical religion in a rational manner satisfying to all men. Thus, instead of an exclusive or parochial revelation, a better, common ground can be established....[25]

Conversely, every faithful Christian is called to "set apart Christ as Lord in your hearts, and always be ready to give a defense to everyone who asks you a reason (*apologia* in Greek, from which we get the word "apologetics") for the hope that is in you, with gentleness and respect" (1 Peter 3:15–16); "For the weapons of our warfare are not of the flesh but mighty in God for pulling down strongholds, casting down arguments and every high thing that exalts itself against the knowledge of God, bringing every thought into captivity to the obedience of Christ" (2 Corinthians 10:4–5).

These Scriptures make a claim on our conscience to grow in our thinking according to the Faith, to grow in our knowledge of the Scripture of Christ and of the Christ of Scripture — and it makes this claim on all of us, not just the "pastors and teachers" (who are all too often lazy and unfaithful), but every member of the Church. Inasmuch as evangelization is everyone's calling and task, the first and foremost aspect of our witness must be the apologetic — giving an account for the difference in our thinking (because of our knowledge of the Scripture of Christ and of the Christ of the Scripture) in the course of our daily lives and constant contacts with our neighbors,

---

25. *Op. cit.*, 684–685. This serves to explain why one finds an intellectual drift in the work of Jacques Maritain (1882–1973) from his *Antimoderne*, in 1922 (driven by the scholastic "nature/grace" motif-de-base) to *Humanisme intégral*, in 1936, ending up finally with *Paysan de la Garonne*, in 1966. When I read *Antimoderne* in 1930 I greatly appreciated such thoughts as this one: "*les pentes de l'intelligence moderne sont contre nous; mais les pentes sont faites pour qu'on les remonte*" ["the inclinations of the modern mind are against us, but every slope of the mind, every decline, is made to be reconquered."]. But I have deplored the fact that the very author of *Antimoderne* eventually allowed himself to be overcome by Humanism...modernist Humanism [*l'Humanisme integral*]!

whoever they may be. The priority given to apologetics is, in any case, not only clearly commanded in the Word of God, but is also borne out in the history of the Church, beginning with the first three centuries under terrible persecutions, as well as many times since then. This is why the Church continues to give such great importance not only to preaching, but to "catholic" catechizing as well — that is, catechizing that is faithful to the Scripture-Word of God. It was understood to be essential not only by the Doctors of the ancient Church, but those of the Reformation as well, as evidenced by their larger and smaller catechisms.

It is also quite evident that a truly Christian way of life — one that is, whenever necessary, at odds with the world around us (Romans 12:1–2) — must accompany this apology and put it into practice each day. No area, no part, no square inch of our life should be exempted from the revealed Truth and the lordly reign of Christ our God. "Work out (*katergazomaï*) your salvation with fear and trembling; for it is God who works in you both to will and to do for His good pleasure" (Philippians 2:12–13).

We must defend the faith not only with sound arguments — giving reasons to all for the faith we profess — but also, inseparably, with the whole witness of our lives in word and deed. We must have in view every area of life here below, for the one Lord and Savior reigns over all, whether it be our individual, personal lives or our marriages, families, work, civic and ecclesiastical involvement, etc. . . .

And with that we come to consider the extension and deepening of the Law of God. We begin with its extension.

The Moral Law of God Extended

Israel and the Nations

We must begin by distinguishing between the Age of the old regime, the old administration of the old nature of the covenant, and the Age of the new regime, or the new administration of the new nature of the covenant. The first commenced with the beginning of history at Adam, and proceeded until the year A.D. 70; the second commenced with the beginning of our era, and will end at Christ's coming in glory, the resurrection of the dead, the Last Judgment, and the universal transfiguration — all arriving together. These seventy years (A.D. 1–70) in which the old and new administrations of the covenant overlap thus constitute the turning of the ages.

During the old administration of His covenant, God progressively established the separation between the members of the covenant and the nations.

Abraham, the first of the patriarchs marking the separation, was set apart from his Hebraic[26] family when he went out from Ur of the Chaldeans, together with his wife and nephew, to "go to a land that the Lord would show him" (Genesis 11:27–12:3; cf. Hebrews 11:8–10). His son Isaac was then set apart from his half-brother Ishmael, ancestor to the Arabs. Isaac's son, Jacob, was then set apart from his brother Esau, ancestor to the Edomites. And, finally, after the exodus from Egypt, under the leadership of Moses, was born the nation of Israel, a nation descended from the twelve sons of Jacob, who were ancestors to the twelve tribes of Israel. Israel, as a holy people (that is, a people "set apart"), was set apart from the other nations, the other peoples (*goyîm* in Hebrew; *ethnoï* in Greek).[27]

It is thus to Israel, to the holy people (the people set apart from the others), that God, through the ministry of Moses at Sinaï, gave the Book of the Covenant, the core of the Law that Moses received and wrote down over the course of his ministry — the *Law*, comprising the divine *Teaching* interwoven with the divine *Precepts*, forming a single piece called the *Torah* (our Pentateuch, the five books of Moses).

> *Contra:* Setting off from there, it is often claimed that the Mosaic Law — which the prophets and sages of Israel would thenceforth appeal to as the eternal standard of the (often unfaithful) people of God — was, since it was covenantal, exclusive to them.[28]

---

26. The lineage proceeded from the Hebrews to the Israelites, and thence to the Jews. The Hebrews took their name from Eber, Noah's great-great-grandson (Genesis 10:1, 21–24; 11:10–14). Abraham himself was the great-grandson of a great-grandson of Eber (Genesis 11:16–26). The Israelites obviously took their name from Israel (Jacob, Abraham's grandson). The Jews derived their name from the Hebrew word *yehuwd* which originally designated an inhabitant of Judea (2 Kings 16:6). The sons of Israel were eventually called Jews by the peoples surrounding Israel (cf. Jeremiah 34:9).

27. See Jean-Marc Berthoud, "The Bible and the Nations," accessed May 28, 2015, http://www.creationism.org/csshs/v15n2p22.htm.

28. Is it not surprising, paradoxical, and contradictory that these same people declare that

Respondeo: Not only is the reasoning behind this assertion specious (cf. note 28), but the assertion itself is contradicted by Holy Scripture, notably by the Torah. It is certainly true that the covenant that God established, then confirmed several times, with Israel, was particular and unique. He signified the uniqueness of this covenant by, among other things, the extraordinary commands that He gave them to take possession of the promised land, occupied at the time by the Canaanites (cf. Genesis 17:8; Exodus 3:8; 23:23; Deuteronomy 7:1–5), by the laws forbidding intermarriage with foreign nations, and by the sacrificial laws of worship specific to Israel. But the Law of God was never limited exclusively to the holy people:

a. Already, in the Adamic and Noahic stages of the covenant, before Israel existed, we find all men addressed by the Law (or laws) of God, before and after the fall, as it pertained to marriage (Genesis 2:24; 3:16), work (Genesis 2:15; 3:19), rest (Genesis 2:1–3), and above all, the cultural mandate and man's eminent place in creation (though under the authority of God, to be sure; Genesis 1:28; 2:15; 9:1).
b. As we saw above: the Law of God, by common grace, has never ceased to touch men, "who show the work of the law written in their hearts."
c. The Lord has always held foreign nations accountable to the Law. When coming to speak of Canaan (concerning incest, adultery, and homosexuality), the Lord says to Israel: "Do not defile yourselves with any of these things; for by all these things the nations are defiled, which I am casting out before you. For the land is defiled; therefore I visit the punishment of its iniquity upon it, and the land vomits out its inhabitants. . . . for all these abominations the men of the land have done, who were before you, and thus the land is defiled; . . . you shall not practice any of these abominable customs which were committed before you" (Leviticus 18:24–25, 27, 30).

  Already, long before, He had said by the mysterious visitors (angels, or men?) concerning Sodom: "For we will destroy this place, because the outcry against them has grown great before the

---

the Decalogue is for all nations even though it, like the rest of the law, is addressed by God to the people that he had "brought out of the land of Egypt, out of the house of bondage" (Exodus 20:2; Deuteronomy 5:6)?

face of the LORD, and the LORD has sent us to destroy it" (Genesis 19:13).

d. The Torah and Israel's faithfulness to this Torah were to instruct the other nations, and reinforce this Law of God that they already knew (not fully, but to a greater or lesser extent) through general revelation. The Torah and Israel's obedience were to serve as a model to foreign nations: "Therefore be careful to observe and practice the statutes and judgments of God; for this will be your wisdom and understanding in the sight of the peoples who will hear all these statutes, and say, 'Surely this great nation is a wise and understanding people!'... And what great nation is there that has such statutes and righteous judgments as are in all this law?" (Deuteronomy 4:6–8, ESV).

In the same vein, the book of Proverbs has more than just Israel in mind when it declares: "Righteousness exalts a nation, but sin is a reproach to any people" (14:34).[29]

e. If there is indeed *discontinuity* between Israel and the nations — on account of its particular vocation as a holy people, a people set apart, a *type* of the coming Kingdom of God in antithesis to the kingdoms of this world, with its blood sacrifices ordained by the Lord in order *to typify* the perfect, one-and-only sacrifice of the Incarnate Son of God offered to put away sin(s) — there is also *continuity* between Israel and the nations, for the moral standards (personal and social) of the Law of God are for all, and thus the same for Israel *and* the nations. God does not have two different moral laws: one for Israel, another for the nations.

The claim of theonomy, following Holy Scripture, is that the moral law revealed by God to Israel, the covenantal people, is normative for all men and all nations.

Greg L. Bahnsen, speaking of the Mosaic Law as the one moral law for Israel *and* the nations, finds evidence in support of this in:

> ...the examples of Sodom, Nineveh, the expulsion of the Canaanites, David's intentions, Ezra's praise of Artaxerxes, Daniel's experience in

---

29. The biblical meaning of the words "righteousness" and "sin," as well as "good" and "evil," is quite alien to the foreign meaning that modern discourse lends them; these are covenantal words, "of the Law of God."

Babylon, the prophetic rebukes of the nations, the wisdom literature, the "man of lawlessness," the testimony of Paul in court, Romans 13, etc.[30]

It is by the one and same moral Law of God that all men are justly condemned (Romans 1–3) and it is to this one and same moral Law of God that all nations must look for their model, their example (Deuteronomy 4:6–8). God alone, in His Scripture, has sovereignly defined and decreed, once for all, the foundations of ethics and law. We are all held accountable to the same law, the same objective and sovereign norm that God has revealed. We are held accountable to the same Lord. This norm is holy because God is holy, and it does not change because it reflects the immutable character of God.

From the Ancient Church to the New Israel

If the moral Law of God is not limited spatially to Israel, but, as we have seen, extends outward universally to encompass all nations, the Law of God is also not temporally restricted to the age before Christ — the old age of the covenant — but also extends forward covenantally.

The question before us is this: does the authority of the Law of God cease or continue as the covenant moves from the old administration in the ancient Church to the new administration in the New Israel? Is there continuity or discontinuity?

The Reformed confessions of faith generally identify three types of laws within the Law of God: the moral law, the ceremonial law, and the judicial (or political) laws.[31]

The Upholding of the Moral Law in its Entirety

When it comes to the matter of which of these three types of laws continue to abide from the old into the new administration of the covenant, it has been and remains the position of many *Reformed* thinkers

---

30. *No Other Standard* (Tyler, TX: Institute for Christian Economics, 1991), 120. *Translator's Note:* See also Bahnsen's exchange with Meredith Kline: Bahnsen, "M. G. Kline on Theonomic Politics: An Evaluation of His Reply," *Journal of Christian Reconstruction* 6, no. 2 (Winter, 1979–1980), http://www.cmfnow.com/articles/pe043.htm (accessed September 22, 2016)

31. For example, *The Second Helvetic Confession*, chapter XII; and *The Westminster Confession of Faith*, chapter XIV, 3 and 4.

that, at the very most, only the "moral" laws must be kept, and these are sometimes understood as the Decalogue alone. Accordingly, the "ceremonial" as well as "judicial" (or political) laws are denied to have abiding validity. The position of those who call themselves theonomists (who have illustrious predecessors — like Pierre Viret — at the beginning of the Reformation), together with many who do not refer to themselves as theonomists, teaches that the moral law revealed to Israel is a whole that includes also the case laws and the socio-political (or "judicial") laws, and that it is this whole body of law that must be fully kept. According to the theonomic position, those "ceremonial" laws — the ancient Church's sacrificial and sacramental laws and the laws concerning pure and impure things — though no longer having a direct and literal application, do nevertheless maintain an indirect and *typical* authority that can in no way be abolished.

In this, theonomy faithfully follows Christ and His Scripture.

I) Jesus plainly said:

> Do not think that I came to destroy the Law and the Prophets. I did not come to destroy but to fulfill. For assuredly, I say to you, till heaven and earth pass away, one jot or one tittle will by no means pass from the law till all is fulfilled. Whoever therefore breaks the least of these commandments and teaches men so, shall be called least in the kingdom of heaven; but whoever does and teaches them, he shall be called great in the kingdom of heaven. For I say to you, that unless your righteousness exceeds the righteousness of the scribes and Pharisees, you will by no means enter the kingdom of heaven. (Matthew 5:17–20)

II) The Tradition of the Apostles (the New Testament!) commands us to drop (and only allows us to drop) the direct and literal meaning of the "laws of separation" and the "sacrificial and sacramental laws" of the old service of worship (concerning the first, cf. Acts 10:10–15, 10:28, 11:4–10 and Ephesians 2:11–20; and concerning the second, cf. Hebrews 1–10). Writing shortly before A.D. 70 — the crucial year when the Temple in Jerusalem would be destroyed and the terrible judgment of Christ would arrive on a wicked, adulterous, sinful, and perverse *generation* — the author of Hebrews says that "what is becoming obsolete and growing old is ready to vanish away" (8:13). But the same author also recalls that in the Tabernacle, in the sanctuary, in the objects and sacrifices of the old service of worship, we have "copies" (*hypodeigmata* = images, replicas, representations) of "heavenly realities" (9:23–24). Likewise, in 2 Corinthians 6:14–7:1 and Romans 12:1, St. Paul teaches us — the Word of God! — that "the laws of separation," including here the laws forbidding the mixing of different kinds of seeds, animals and fibers (cf. Deuteronomy 22:9–11), still have much to say and reveal to us (consider the application for scientific research of the kind of genetic modification, for example, which dares to mix different species), to us who are under the new administration of the covenant, who "are the temple of the living God," who must "not be unequally yoked together with unbelievers" (2 Corinthians 6:14; cf. Deuteronomy 22:10), but must "offer our bodies as a living sacrifice" (Romans 12:1), which is our "logical worship" (= our worship according to the *Logos*, according to both the incarnate and written Word). But under the new administration of the covenant we must also understand and live out these laws of separation in an indirect and *typical* sense.[32]

If further confirmation of the necessary distinction between the moral and sacrificial laws is still needed, it is found in the divine declaration: "For I desire steadfast love (*hèsèd* in Hebrew) and not sacrifice" (Hosea 6:6, ESV).

Under the sacrificial and sacramental laws we must group the laws of purification dealing with matters specific to men and women (cf., for example, Leviticus 15; 18:19; 20:18; Numbers 19:11–22) or those of women after childbirth (cf. Leviticus 12). There is a great deal of confusion as to what these laws meant in the old administration of the covenant, and what relationship they have to the new administration of the covenant. We must begin by recognizing that this collection of laws relate, on the one hand, to the sin of the whole human race in Adam, which sin is ours from birth; and on the other hand, to the Covenant of Grace in Christ, the new Adam to come. There is nothing impure about the sexual relationship of marriage in and of itself, but original sin — as also the Covenant of Grace for the members of the people of God — flows from generation to generation. That is why such sacramental significance is attached to sexual relations and childbirth: it is at this point in human life, at the point of conceiving and bearing

---

32. On this point, cf. chapters 1–8 of Vern Poythress, *The Shadow of Christ in the Law of Moses* (Brentwood, 1991).

children, that the laws of purification serve to point back to the fall of the first Adam, and at the same time point forward to the coming salvation of many to be brought by the second Adam. To understand how this carries over to the new administration of the covenant, it would be necessary to begin with a detailed exegesis dealing with the purification of women after childbirth and the circumcision of male children of the covenant, and then go on to consider how these acts *typify* baptism for the Church of the new covenant. With that groundwork laid, attention could then be given to developing a biblical theology of blood, without which there is no expiation of sin (cf. Hebrews 9:22).

The Case Laws

In the numerous case laws of the Torah, we who live under the new administration of the covenant find normative examples of the Law of God applied to new historical and cultural situations and circumstances.[33] We must therefore heed, and seek to follow faithfully, in obedience, not only the general principles of God's moral law (which extend beyond just the Decalogue, though they are condensed in it, as the Decalogue itself is condensed in the summary of the law: Deuteronomy 6:5; Leviticus 19:18; Matthew 22:34–40), but also the examples of their application that are revealed.[34]

Casuistry — the practice of reasoning by case laws — needs to be revived, reformed, and constantly updated, out of our unending aspirations to be faithful to Holy Scripture.

If casuistry often carries negative, pejorative connotations, it is because it has been forgotten that there are two kinds of casuistry. There

---

33. To take an easy, elementary example, Moses tells us in Deuteronomy 22:8: "When you build a new house, then you shall make a parapet for your roof, that you may not bring guilt of bloodshed on your household if anyone falls from it." Here we have a normative case law applying the commandment: "You shall not murder." Though our houses today do not usually have flat roofs serving as terraces for our guests, this commandment teaches us that even in the way we arrange our homes we have the moral responsibility to protect our guests from any conceivable harm that could come as a result of our own negligence (simply "feeling" that your house is "safe enough," and having good insurance, would not suffice to absolve you of guilt). Concerning the case laws, cf. Greg Bahnsen, *By This Standard*, 137–138 and 317–318.

34. Cf. Gary North, *Tools of Dominion: The Case Laws of Exodus* (Tyler, TX: Institute for Christian Economics, 1990), 1280 pages (!). North (27–28) alludes to two Reformed treatises from the seventeenth century: Richard Baxter's *A Christian Directory* (1673), who desired, as he puts it, "the resolving of practical Cases of Conscience"; and Samuel Willard's posthumous work (d. 1717), *A Complete Body of Divinity* (1726). Cf. also volumes I, II, and III of Rousas J. Rushdoony's *The Institutes of Biblical Law* (1973, 1982, and 1999).

is the kind of casuistry that evades the clear teaching of the Law of God, with the result that the Law of God itself is called into question. This is the kind of abominable casuistry that was promoted by the Pharisees, the kind which Jesus vigorously contested (cf. for example Matthew 23:16–36) and which Pascal denounced in his *Provinciales*. But there is another kind of casuistry that seeks to follow the Law of God faithfully — and to have it faithfully followed — when dealing with specific and actual cases. It is then *we* who are called into question, according to God's law. This good kind of casuistry goes hand in hand with meditation on, and examination of, God's Law to the end that we may take delight in it (as is sung in Psalm 119).

The Humanism that plagues the Church and Christians today must be defeated, and the revival of the meaning of God's Law, even in its case laws, is going to play a powerful role in bringing about that defeat. Catechesis, preaching, and the Christian witness will be purged of that perverted thinking, à la Marcion, which teaches and proclaims a Word of God, a Gospel, amputated from the indispensable Law of God, with its commandments, examples, and warnings.

And as for those "pastors and teachers" who, under the pretext of being faithful to the Gospel, of sticking strictly to the message of "salvation by grace through faith," have become *a-nomians* (without the Law) or *anti-nomians* (against the Law), either they will convert (turn around), or, because their churches have come back to faithfulness and no longer tolerate their teaching, they will have to leave their ministry.

The days will come when we will not hear the laws contained in Scripture spoken of as *mythical* (inventions, for example, of primitive nomadism). The days are coming when we will not hear them spoken of as *passé*, as having had meaning only for bygone eras in the *progressive* history of humanity. The days are coming when Christians will not be persuaded to reject, or strike out, or annul the laws contained in Scripture because they are deemed prejudicial to modernity or to human rights.[35]

---

35. *Translator's Note:* R. C. Sproul displays the confidence Courthial calls for in his recent comments on chapter XIX.4 of the Westminster Confession of Faith: "Since the Old Testament came from God, who is holy and righteous, we should not be offended by any laws that we read there. If we are offended by them, it is because our thinking has been distorted by a secular perspective on law, righteousness, and ethics. God's standards, revealed to his people in the Old Testament, are as foreign to us today as they were to the ancient worshipers of Baal.

The Judicial and Political Laws

We now come to the important question for theonomy: how are we to understand the "judicial" (or "political") laws of the Torah, and what application do they have for us today? The "judicial" laws are those which we would largely call "civil law" today in both its private and public spheres: laws dealing with society, politics, economics, and penology,[36] which not only delineate the standards of socio-political life, but also the sanctions, the consequences — positive or negative — that follow.

On this point, theonomy not only collides with the humanists within and outside of the Church, but it also runs up against pietism. By surrendering entire areas of life to the humanists, pietism has unintentionally contributed to the spread of the humanist malady. Throughout the centuries, and especially since the eighteenth century, pietism has consistently limited the scope and authority of God's Word, of God's Law, to individuals, families, worship, and to the Church that isolates herself from the *world*. The Church influenced by pietism prefers to shelter herself from the world rather than engage it.

In minimizing the moral Law of God, in restraining it, in opposing its extension to those fields that constitute the greater part of the life of men here below, in claiming that only those areas of life likely to be "pious" are subject to the sovereignty of God's prescriptive will, pietists abandon *de facto* everything else — a massive betrayal! — to human design (or is it demonic design?). They leave humans to be masters of the world's battlefield. In this way pietism becomes an accomplice of Humanism: by deliberately keeping to themselves, by their willful abstention from the general affairs of men, it is ultimately the humanist agenda that benefits, and pietists who are swept along with it.

When faced with difficulties and times of crisis, as well as most other times, pietistic Christians can go so far as to look to prayer as an alibi for their disobedience to the moral Law of God — disobedience

---

We must go to the pages of Scripture and ask ourselves if it is really the law of God. If it is, it teaches us what is pleasing to God and what is odious to him" (Sproul, *Truths We Confess: A Layman's Guide to the Westminster Confession of Faith*, vol. 2 [2007], 267).

36. Penology concerns the field of sanctions (from the Latin *poena*, punishment). The expression "penal law" is derived from this word. Penal law defines the sanctions to be meted out to those who break the law.

not only to its general precepts but also to its particular "judicial" or "political" laws.

On the other end of the spectrum, Christians infected with Humanism exhaust themselves in their militantly aggressive engagement of the public sphere (politics, economics, social concerns, etc.), but their efforts are directed toward advancing humanist ideologies ("idologies") and their laws, not the Law of God as it applies to these areas.

Pietists and militant humanists agree on at least this point: God has neither said anything nor has anything to say to these areas of life. It then becomes obvious why the Church, siding with Humanism (if not infected with it), has nothing to say, or when she does feel the need to say something, falls in line with the prevailing and/or fashionable human opinions circulated by the media. When these areas of life are discussed, references to God or to Christ or to the Bible are only passing at best, and even then the words are carefully chosen and tailored to gain approval. These matters of the public sphere are not discussed with the aim of receiving and hearing the normative and objective Word of God, the sovereign Creator, Savior, and Lord (such authoritative appeals to the Word that has *spoken*, are they not silenced within the Church herself?).

Dismantling the various forms that Humanism takes, only Theonomy, in the strong sense of the Law of God, delineates what is good and evil, what is just and unjust, what are the various kinds of *governments* instituted by God (we will come to speak of these), what are the norms established by God for the various areas of the life of men; and this accompanied by the numerous examples of the application of the Law (the case laws) that must be faithfully adapted to present circumstances. To investigate what obedience to the law requires, what initial steps in obedience must be made, is not easy, but we must never let the difficulty deter us from this effort. The difficulty is not with the Law, but with us, on account of our lingering sin, our fondness for autonomy, our resistance to yield to Him who, with and by His Law — always inseparably accompanied by His Gospel — envelops and penetrates us with His mercy, and with the power and gentleness of His grace.

There are several places where the Tradition of the Apostles invokes and emphasizes the unfailing authority of the judicial laws (socio-political laws) of the Torah and the *TaNaKh*, for example:

- concerning the family (Matthew 15:4–6; cf. Exodus 20:12; 21:17);
- concerning incest (1 Corinthians 5:1; cf. Leviticus 18:8; Deuteronomy 27:20; Amos 2:7);
- concerning homosexuality (1 Corinthians 6:9–10; Romans 1:26–27, 32; cf. Genesis 1:27–28; 2:18, 23–24; 5:2; 19:1–29; Leviticus 18:22; 20:13);
- concerning relations with neighbors and even enemies (Matthew 5:44; Romans 12:19–20; cf. Exodus 23:4–5; Job 31:29; Proverbs 25:21–22; etc.).

A fortiori, even if a particular judicial law is not invoked by the Tradition of the Apostles — such as the laws concerning immigrants, foreigners in the community of Israel — it retains its normative authority (an authority equal to that of those listed above) into the age of the new administration of the covenant.

Moreover we have already seen that the Torah forbids taking anything whatsoever away from the moral Law that was given through the ministry of Moses, the moral Law that was given as example for all the nations (Deuteronomy 4:2, 5–8).

When it comes to civil government (or for simplicity's sake, "the state"), its form, whether it be a democracy, oligarchy, or monarchy, is entirely secondary to the main issue: whether or not the state is under the Law defined by the Word of God. It is a choice between theonomy on the one hand, or Humanism trying to establish some form of autonomy on the other. It is a choice between a legal state, which is to say a state of Law, seeking to govern a given territory in a manner consistent with the Law of God (applying both the principles and specific laws of the Bible): a state according to Romans 13:1–6; or a state according to Revelation 13, tending to arbitrary legislation and totalitarian Statism, putting its own Law on the same plane with, or above, the Law of God. It is a choice between a state that recognizes the limits of its own power and jurisdiction, whose hands bear the theonomic mark (Deuteronomy 6:8); or a state that, encroaching into every area of life, sets its own autonomous mark on the hands of every citizen (Revelation 13:16–17). It is a choice between a state exercising its legitimate authority in the specific domain entrusted to it by God, entrusted to it as a diaconate (a charge, a service, cf. Romans 13:4), to the end that those who do "what is good" may be approved and protected and that "evildoers" may be judged and condemned, for it is not in vain that the governing authorities bear the "sword" that manifests, when necessary, the righteous wrath of God (a "Romans 13" government in any time or place); or the tyrannical state of the Beast (a "Revelation 13" government in any time or place).

And this "totalitarianization" of the state — a true return to the humanistic paganism of Antiquity or of the pre-Christian times — tends to grow and intensify to the point that the question now pressing in on us from all sides as we face a wide range of ethical issues — from those occupying scholars and scientists, to those confronting the man on the street in his daily life — is, quite frighteningly, this question: "Which laws shall rule the land — those of God or those of the state?"

The history of the word "government" is, unfortunately, a clear illustration of our present social and political decline. It was not so long ago that this word referred to various kinds of governments — not only that of magistrates over the state, but also the authority of ordained ministers in the church; the authority of the husband in marriage, in the conjugal union; as well the authority exercised in self-control ("the government of oneself," Montaigne used to say). This diversity of governments, each having its own domain, and each submitted to the sovereign authority of God in accordance with Scripture, was as incompatible with Statism — in which authority over every sphere of life is monopolized by the state — as it was with clericalism — in which authority over every sphere of life is monopolized by the Church. But today, the word "government" is assumed to refer to the state (it is no longer necessary to qualify it as the "civil" government), because the state has encroached into all those areas of life which, according to Scripture, are not within its jurisdiction: the lives of individuals and families, the education of children, the operations of the economy, cultural life, etc. Moreover, having successfully established a separation between "public" and "private" spheres of life (thus denying the sovereignty of God and His Law-Word over every aspect of reality), the state has relegated the churches to the latter (which is by no means the full extent of their mission; cf. Matthew 28:18–20!), while at the same time, in complete contradiction to its policy, calling upon the churches to assist whenever it thinks their support would be strategically beneficial to its own aims.

The reason that it is so important for men to know and follow the judicial and political laws revealed in Holy Scripture is because God, in the short-run or long-run, blesses those nations whose people, having obedient hearts, institute and maintain laws that are outwardly conformed to the Law defined by His Word; and, on the other hand, punishes those nations that stray from it, and thus invite His Law to return upon them in the form of judgment (cf. Amos 1, 2:4–8; Jeremiah 50–51; Isaiah 19).

Penology and Penal Law

The socio-political laws, or "judicial" laws, would be incomplete if they did not also detail how those who have broken the law should be punished. And so it is that the stated obligations of the Law are followed by the stated consequences, punishments, and sanctions of the Law.[37]

When speaking of the judgments of the Law, we must begin by distinguishing between the direct and indirect judgments of God. The direct judgment of God is experienced throughout the course of our lives (e.g. Genesis 3:16–19a), at the hour of our death (Genesis 3:19b; Hebrews 9:27), and at the end of history. The indirect judgment of God, on the other hand, is that which is mediated through the various legitimate governments that He has instituted. In the realm of self-control, God's indirect judgment is mediated through the government of conscience, even though the conscience is fallen and in constant need of being reformed (Romans 2:14–16). In the life of the family and in the education of children, His judgment is mediated through the government of the parents. In the Church, it is mediated through the government of the ordained ministry. And in the realm of the state, God's judgment is mediated through the legitimate government of the magistrates.

When Holy Scripture speaks of the *direct* judgment of God, it means either temporal punishments, which serve the purposes of His common grace (promoting the general peace and welfare of a people by punishing those whose wickedness threatens it) or the purposes of His special and redemptive grace (which encourage, and result

---

37. In 1885, a now-forgotten French philosopher, Jean-Marie Guyau (1854–1888) published an *Esquisse d'une morale sans obligation ni sanction* ("A Sketch of Morality Independent of Obligation or Sanction")! Lecerf was fond of alluding to the irony of it. (*Translator's Note:* Guyau's work has been translated into English by Gertrude Kapteyn and republished by BiblioLife).

effectually in, the repentance and sanctification of the faithful); or eternal punishments, which uphold the Holiness of divine justice (Daniel 12:2; Matthew 13:24 and 37–40, 25:46; and 2 Thessalonians 1:6–10).

The judgments of legitimate governments, on the other hand, have a limited, temporal scope, with the general intention of bringing about positive effects in the lives of those under their authority. In view here are:

- Individual asceticism. The believer disciplines himself by abstaining from certain specific actions, by keeping himself from certain things, by "fasting," in the general sense of the word (cf. Isaiah 58:1–8 and Ezekiel 18:5–9), that he might provide no opportunity to inordinate desires, covetousness, lust, or habitual sin of any kind (cf. Exodus 20:17; and the metaphor of Matthew 5:29–30).
- The disciplining of children by parents. This discipline can — and often must — be corporal, provided such punishments are justified, tempered, and not carried out with the slightest hint of uncontrolled anger or undue violence (Psalm 37:8; Proverbs 13:24 and 29:15).
- The proper use of excommunication by the ministers of the church. This final and most serious step must be exercised, after warnings have been given, against blatantly obstinate and scandalous sinners or those teachers of grave heresies (keeping in mind that it is not given to the Church to judge their hearts — *de intimis Ecclesia non judicat*; Matthew 18:15–18; 1 Corinthians 5:9–13; Titus 3:10–11).

It is plainly clear that the Scriptures have set forth a divine penal law that is in no way contradicted by the Gospel, but is rather an integral part of it (1 Timothy 1:5–11). In His common grace as well as in His special redeeming grace, the Lord has deemed it necessary and good for the welfare of men in this fallen world that there be this penal Law to protect honest men (sinners who outwardly behave well) and to punish evildoers (sinners who outwardly behave wickedly).[38]

---

38. Proverbs 2:21–22; and, yet again, Romans 13:1–7!

"An eye for an eye..."

The basic rule of thumb of the penal law is *lex talionis*. Far from endorsing personal vengeance, as has often been thought and said, *lex talionis* comes to us as the imaged, metaphorical expression of the law of equity that magistrates must always follow when meting out judgment. This is made clear by the immediate context in which the principle is given (Exodus 21:20–23:9) and by the whole fabric of laws in the Torah, and is confirmed by Jesus Himself (Matthew 5:38ff.).

The principle of *lex talionis* — "a life for a life, an eye for an eye, tooth for tooth, hand for hand, foot for foot, burn for burn, wound for wound" (cf. also its repetition in Leviticus 24:17–21 and Deuteronomy 19:21) — formally declares that any legal punishment must, in the name of equity, fit the crime. The punishment must be proportional, or, to use the words of the *TaNaKh*, "according to his guilt" (Deuteronomy 25:2), "according to his wickedness" (2 Samuel 3:39), "according to the fruit of his doings" (Jeremiah 17:10), "according to his own ways" (Ezekiel 33:20). And considered at an even deeper level, the punishment must be in the image of the righteous and incontestable punishment that God inflicted on the one and only incarnate Son on the cross, on which the Son hung cursed and forsaken; and in the image of the final judgment that will be inflicted on some men (cf. Deuteronomy 21:23 and Galatians 3:13; Psalm 51:6; Obadiah 15; Romans 2:16; 1 Peter 1:17 and Revelation 20:12; among others). The criminal must receive his due (*cuique suum: to each what he deserves*).[39]

It is a curious thing that many Christians (and non-Christians), taking offense at the theonomic position allowing for the death penalty in whatever cases it is required by the Scriptural penal law for various crimes, are the same Christians (and non-Christians) who take equal offense at the theonomic position rejecting incarceration as punishment for other crimes, crimes which this same penal law would punish by restitution (that is, having the offender compensate the victim for what was suffered or lost rather than "do time," which

---

39. In his *Theonomy in Christian Ethics* (Nutley, NJ: The Craig Press, 1977), 437ff., Bahnsen makes some important observations about the great mystery of Christ on the cross (as the substitute for sinners) and about the light that this mystery sheds on the equity of divine judgment and of the revealed penal law. Concerning this mystery as it relates to the sacrifice of the Son, cf. John 1:29; Hebrews 9.11–15; 10:3 18; and 13:10–12; 1 Peter 1:18–20; and as it relates to substitution, cf.: Colossians 2:14; 2 Corinthians 5:21; and Galatians 3:10–13.

neither compensates the victim nor restores the offender).
Questions to consider:

1. Was God wrong to make the sword (*ê machaïra* in Greek; a clear picture of the death penalty) part of the justice system of the state, thereby making it the avenger (*ekdikos*) of His wrath (*orgê*), and to identify explicitly in His Law those crimes that deserve the death penalty?
2. Was God wrong to require offenders of certain other crimes to repay their victims for damages suffered (restitution) plus a certain additional portion as punishment (what the civil law today calls "punitive damages"), favoring this over imprisonment?
3. Should the principles and applications of the penal law be left to the discretion and changing tempers of man pretending to autonomy, even though what is at stake in these sanctions and punishments is justice itself?
4. Can the arbitrary opinions of any man, even the wisest of men, or those of any majority, even the most refined and elevated majority, be entrusted with the responsibility of framing penal sanctions?
5. Did God then act "in vain" (again, cf. Romans 13:1–6) when He entrusted His justice to be ministered through legitimate magistrates; that is, did He not have any real and sovereign intention that they would actually do so?
6. Do "humanist" Christians then take certain passages of the *Tradition of the Apostles* to be null and void, such as Matthew 5:18 with its "not one jot or one tittle," Matthew 28:20 with its "all power has been given to Me" and Hebrews 2:2 with "the word spoken through angels proved steadfast, and every transgression and disobedience received a just reward"?

When "the chief priests and the chief men of the Jews" brought Paul before the tribunal of the Roman governor Festus at Caesarea (since the Jews were not allowed by the Romans to sentence someone to death of their own accord), bringing "many and serious charges against him," Paul acknowledged quite plainly the enduring validity of the revealed penal law — valid for the nations as well as for Israel — when he declared: "If then I am a wrongdoer and have committed anything for which I deserve to die, I do not seek to escape death"

(Acts 25:1–12). In so doing he was acknowledging the continuity and inflexibility of the divine penal Law, willing that it should be applied to himself... if he had been guilty.[40]

The Moral Law of God Deepened

There are at least three places where a discernable deepening of the moral Law of God occurs: (1) in Holy Scripture itself, as the law moves from the completion of the *Torah* of Moses, through the *Nebîîm* and *Ketubîm*, and finally on to the *Tradition of the Apostles*; (2) in the individual conscience of the faithful, in which the law is deepened throughout the whole course of life; and (3) in the whole catholic communion, including its pastors and Doctors, where a deeper understanding of the law has been — and must continue to be — pursued, with the eventual goal of defining, as soon as possible, the dogma of theonomy, and in so doing defeat Humanism — first in the Church, then in the world. We will now examine each of these areas individually.

The Law of God Deepened in the TaNaKh

As we have already seen, in terms of the laws of reconciliation (sacrificial and sacramental) and the laws of separation (concerning pure and impure things), there is an evident discontinuity as the old administration of the covenant passes to the new, since the function of these specific laws under the old administration was to anticipate the once-for-all and perfect sacrifice of the incarnate Son of God and the breaking down of the wall of separation between Israel and the nations. But in terms of the moral law (personal and social), there is an evident continuity from the old administration to the new. The holy God has never given *a different set of morals* to the human race — there is one moral law found in the Revelation of both His common grace and His special grace. It remains necessary for us today to take seriously the moral Law of God as a whole, as found in the whole of Scripture, not

---

40. Concerning the revealed penal law, it is necessary to read chapters 21 and 22 of Bahnsen's *Theonomy*, as well as Bahnsen's response to the critics of theonomy — a response that further confirms the truthfulness of this teaching — in chapters 12 to 14 of his *No Other Standard*.

failing to observe how the holy books following the Torah of Moses reveal the progressive deepening of this law. If it is true that "the Torah, the Law, was given through Moses," it is also true that it has been continually deepened by the prophets and sages until "grace and truth came through Jesus Christ" (John 1:17).[41]

The *Nebîîm* and *Ketubîm*, books no less *breathed by God* than the *Torah*, clarify — and thus deepen — several points of the Mosaic Torah. Let us consider some examples.

In the episode of Naboth's vineyard alone (1 Kings 21), several points of the Mosaic law are clarified, including: the inviolability of inheritance, the lawfulness of the right to private property, the existence of certain limits on the legal power of the state, the fact that the various powers of the state (executive, legislative, and judicial) are all accountable to God (*coram Deo*), the gravity of giving false testimony and the penalties that follow, the need for the intervention of the prophetic ministry before the civil government, and, in 1 Kings 22, the dreadful nature of God's judgment that, with more or less long-term effects, falls on every state that oversteps and scoffs at its legal limits.

The Book of Proverbs commands one to seek, and then put into practice, the virtue of wisdom, that is, wisdom founded on the fear (worshipful respect) of the Lord (1:7; 9:10; 15:33; etc., cf. Job 28:28; Psalm 111:10). Such wisdom has never been taken to be an addition to the Law — it is nothing of the sort. Wisdom, according to Scripture, and especially according to the *Proverbs*, is a gift, a virtue, which serves specifically to enable one to receive and understand the commandments of the Law, to follow them (10:8), revere them (13:13), and keep them, that one may be wise (28:7) and blessed — "Happy is he who keeps the law" (29:18).

The Wisdom of God, which is God Himself, calls us to receive our

---

41. It should not be missed that the expression "grace and truth" (*ê charis kaï ê aletheia* in Greek; *hésèd we' èmèt* in Hebrew) is governed here by a verb in the singular (*egeneto*). The two words are joined to designate the steadfast and benevolent covenant-faithfulness of God as though it were a single word. Cf. Cornelius van der Waal, *The Covenant of God* (Alberta, Canada, 1990), 70–74. The fullness of the covenant comes through Jesus Christ. There is no antithesis between Moses and Jesus Christ, but complementarity, deepening and "fulfillment." This has been always affirmed, against Marcion and Marcionism, by the ancient Fathers (cf. Melito of Sardus) and the Reformation Confessions of Faith and Catechisms (cf. *Belgic Confession*, 1561, article 25; *Heidelberg Catechism*, 1563, question 19). The covenantal expression *hésèd we' èmèt* is also found, for example, in Exodus 34:6, Joshua 2:14, 2 Samuel 2:6 and 15:20, Psalm 85:11, Proverbs 3:3 and 20:28, and Zechariah 7:9.

wisdom from this divine Wisdom by keeping its commandments and writing them on the tablet of our heart (2:1–6; 3:3 — in this last verse, the commands of the law are referred to as *hèsèd we' èmèt*, the "steadfast and benevolent covenant-faithfulness of God"; cf. footnote 41 above).

So close is the relationship between wisdom and the commandments that we can say of the commandments that they constitute our wisdom, and of our wisdom that it applies these commandments without adding to them. Moreover, *to receive this wisdom* as a gift and virtue from above is, at the same time, *to keep the commandments* and wisely to put them into practice. Thus wisdom penetrates into our daily lives by our obedience to the Law of God.

The same Book of Proverbs specifically lays out the foundation, duty and principal elements of the civil government:

By Me kings reign,
And rulers decree justice.
By me princes rule, and nobles,
All the judges of the earth. (8:15–16)

A throne is established *by righteousness.* (16:12b)

[The authorities must not] forget *what has been decreed*
and pervert the rights of the afflicted. (31:5, ESV)

It is not good to show partiality in judgment.
He who says to the wicked, 'You are righteous,'
Him the people will curse;
Nations will abhor him. (24:23–24)

The king who judges the poor with truth,
His throne will be established forever. (29:14)

Judge righteously,
And plead the cause of the poor and needy. (31:9)

The Book of Proverbs also specifically addresses the tasks assigned to each member within a family:

> Hear, my children, the instruction of a father ... (chs. 4–7)

An excellent wife is the crown of her husband. (12:4; cf. 14:1; 15:20; 23:22; 30:17; 31:10–31; etc.)

A third example of the Mosaic Law being taken up and clarified in the later writings is found in the *Song of Songs*. A book that, as we have already mentioned, must be interpreted on two levels, the Song of Songs sheds light on the application of the moral Law of God to the conjugal life, with both the glory of God and the blessing of the human couple in view.[42]

A solid and careful exegesis based on a faithful translation of the Hebrew text reveals both the text's unity and the fact that the poem includes three characters: the couple made up of a shepherd and the Shulamite, his bride, with their faithful, passionate love, and King Solomon, who has not let this get in the way of taking her for himself to be one of the women in his harem, though he still has to win her over and is trying to do so, thus creating the plot tension of the story.[43]

This song, the song *par excellence*, also allows for a second level of interpretation, a sober typico-analogical exegesis (not allegorical, entirely subject to the reader's whim).

Whereas past interpreters have gravitated toward an allegorical interpretation, by which they force their own subjective interpretations onto the text, any second level of interpretation must instead look for the text's typological and analogical elements (typico-analogical interpretation) and be firmly founded on the first level of interpretation, the literal meaning. The soundness of such second-level interpretation will be judged by how well it fits and illumines the revealed mystery of the book, namely, that the union between the husband and his wife (Malachi 2:14) is related to the union between the Lord and His Church (Ephesians 5:25–32).

When the book is interpreted by typico-analogical exegesis, the central tension emerges between the tempter, seducer, and separator ("what God has united let no man separate") represented by the prince; and the Lord and His Church represented by the betrothed couple.

---

42. An excellent commentary by a Reformed theologian is *The Greatest Song* (Toronto: Tuppence Press, 1988), by Calvin Seerveld.
43. Seerveld, *The Greatest Song*, 19.

With its countless and mostly excessive variations, the traditional allegorical interpretation (known as the "spiritual" interpretation, though "spiritual" in the worst sense of the word), "originated as a defense against the complaint, 'how can such worldly love poetry be holy and a norm for the faith?'"[44] The complaint itself — and the "spiritual" response — arose from the *Greek* predilection for opposing soul and body: the soul being inherently good, the body more or less bad. This unbiblical opposition of body and soul continued as a dominant theme in the works of some ancient Church Fathers, while its contaminating effects were more subtly present in the works of others. The literal, obvious sense of the text was viewed with such suspicion that the Jewish *rabbi* Akiba declared in A.D. 110 that the Song *par excellence* must be taught in the synagogue according to its allegorico-spiritual sense.[45]

This kind of pseudo-exegesis can only be incorrect, getting in the way of biblical truth, so that the divine Word is eclipsed by such fantastical allegories, and the divine Word is left to be imprisoned within the subjectivity of man. The literal meaning alone (which must not be confused with unacceptable literalism — cf. the abusive interpretations of Matthew 5:29–30 or 7:1–2, for example) is the true and solid meaning, conformed to the "divine spiration," repelling all arbitrary gnosticism, be it of a rationalist or charismatic nature.

He who would interpret the Song must not come to it with the question posed by Pouget and Guitton: "What spiritual meaning[s] are acceptable for the catholic soul to find here?"[46] but rather must begin by asking: "What literal meaning[s] of the text must we honestly receive in this book of the written Word of God?"

> If the Bible does not actually mean what it says, how can one ever hope to find out what is revealed?[47]

The Song deepens our understanding of the divine institution of marriage, daring even to explore the sexual relationship and sexual desire, praising the singular beauty of the physical union within

---

44. Ibid., 12.
45. Ibid.
46. Quoted in Ibid., 17.
47. *Greatest Song*, 13.

marriage in contrast to all expressions of human desire outside of marriage (homosexuality, heterosexual adultery, bestiality, etc.).

The Song also deepens our understanding of love and faithfulness in marriage, bidding us to honor these things in our own lives and those of others. Despite the passionate, and sometimes grotesque, statements of Solomon the seducer, despite the exhortations of the women of the harem who invite her to join herself (what an honor!) to the royal line of David, the Shulamite remains faithful to the shepherd to whom she has betrothed herself: "I am my beloved's, and my beloved is mine" (6:3). As for the shepherd, he says to Solomon at the end of the book: "The thousands are yours, Solomon!... My vineyard here before me is for me alone (8:12; *trans.* Calvin Seerveld).

The author of the Book of Kings (1 Kings 11) recounts, with a mournful spirit, that Solomon eventually had a thousand women in his harem who "turned his heart after other gods," and in this he "did evil in the sight of the Lord ... so the Lord became angry with Solomon" (11:4, 6, 9). The "most beautiful of Songs" is a warning to any who would imitate Solomon ... that they might instead be converted to God and live.

The Law of God Deepened in Jesus' Teaching

But it is here, with Jesus and the Tradition of the Apostles, that the moral Law of God will be definitively deepened and clarified, renewed and transfigured, while remaining fundamentally what it has always been. That which was first revealed and instituted with the giving of the *Torah* through Moses and progressively deepened with the *Prophets* and *Writings*, will now be *fulfilled* in Jesus Christ, in the sense that it is "realized," filled to the brim. Three things require our attention: (1) Jesus identifies a hierarchical order within the law, (2) He shows that the Law aims for the heart, and (3) He identifies love with Law. Let us briefly consider each of these.

Hierarchical Order within the Law

> ... you pay tithe of mint and anise and cummin, and have neglected the weightier matters of the law: justice and mercy and faith. These you ought to have done, without leaving the others undone. (Matthew 23:23)

In rebuking the Pharisees, Jesus identifies a hierarchical order within the Law (an order which they had ignored or subverted). "Justice and mercy and faith" are the most important (*ta barutera* = the weightiest matters), yet these must not be performed in isolation from the less important laws, but must be done "without leaving the others undone."

It is significant that each of the three "weightier matters" are *communicable* attributes of God in relation to sin and the sins of human creatures: (1) justice (*ê crisis*) is the righteous judgment of sin and sinners; (2) mercy (*to eleos*) is the tenderness of the heart (*cor*) toward the miserable state (*miseria*) of sinners; and (3) faith (*ê pistis* = faithfulness) is the opposition to sin (Kierkegaard said: "The opposite of sin is not virtue but faith").

Mysteriously, it is only against the backdrop of the inexplicable entrance of sin into the world that these three things — justice, mercy, and faith — have, in God, in whom they are modeled, taken their meaning.[48]

Let us recall how the commandments exhibit an organic relation in which the first and most basic commandment forms the controlling center from which the others extend in their unique specificity. Every commandment serves to adorn and elucidate the central command to "love the Lord your God" together with its natural complement to "love your neighbor as yourself" (Matthew 22:36–40). On these two commandments hang all the others. Next comes the Decalogue, which summarizes the whole moral Law. And finally there are the other commandments, each related to one or more words of the Decalogue, which are ordered from those having the most weight to those having the least (though, as Jesus does not fail to add, these last must not go undone or unmentioned).

---

48. It was along the same lines of the theologian Robert Lewis Dabney (1820–1894), whom he greatly esteemed, that Lecerf wrote in his *Introduction à la Dogmatique réformée*, vol. 2 (Paris: Editions Je sers, 1938), 125: "As for sin itself, as for moral evil, if God, within the warp and woof of his decrees, gave room for the abuse of liberty, it is no doubt because He had determined that a world in which sin would open the possibility for repentance, for forgiveness, for heroism, for self-sacrifice, would be a world of greater worth and one in which His mercy and His justice would be more fully displayed (both with regard to angels and to men); that such a world would be morally and aesthetically superior to one composed merely of amoral innocent beings and just men impeccable because they could not be otherwise. Such a judgment of value pronounced by God Himself must satisfy us, if indeed we believe in Him. For those who do not believe in Him, the question itself disappears."

The Law Aims at the Heart

Jesus emphasized the fact that the primary aim of the moral Law is the heart, and not merely, nor even primarily, actions. In His constant struggle with Pharisaism, Jesus challenged its *externalizing* interpretation of the moral law, its exclusive focus on the external application of the moral law. This deviant interpretation not only distorted the law, but also led to the idea of justification by works. Any characterization of the Pharisees as careful and faithful practitioners of the Mosaic Law, any tendency to credit them with orthodoxy or orthopraxy, is patently false, as Jesus Himself reveals in His rebuke: "Even so you also outwardly appear righteous to men, but inside you are full of hypocrisy *and lawlessness*" (Matthew 23:28).

Jesus invites His disciples, and leads them, to judge rightly, to judge "justly," which must begin with an ever more honest and penetrating examination of oneself in the mirror of the moral Law of God (Matthew 5:19; 7:1–5). This exercise of judgment is right or "just" in a manner completely different from that of the Pharisees, and at the same time "exceeds" theirs — "Unless your righteousness exceeds the righteousness of the scribes and Pharisees, you will by no means enter the kingdom of heaven" (Matthew 5:20).

The Identification of Love with Law

> He who has My commandments and keeps them, it is he who loves Me. (John 14:21)

Jesus and the Tradition of the Apostles identify love of God, of neighbor, and of oneself, *with obedience to the commandments* of the moral Law.

The fact of the matter is that the moral law and its commandments serve to show forth just what is the concrete love of God, of neighbor, and of oneself. True love and law-keeping go together, hand in hand: without love, even the most heroic obedience is nothing (1 Corinthians 13:3), and without Law, apart from Law, love is nothing more than an empty sentiment. It is together that love and Law abide, it is together that they never fail (1 Corinthians 13:8; Luke 16:17). For, as a fruit of the Spirit, love fulfills the righteous requirement of the law in us, the righteousness that is our sanctification (Galatians 5:22; Romans 8:4;

2 Corinthians 7:1), the righteousness that from small beginnings becomes ours more and more though only in glorification are we made perfect: "If you love Me, you will keep My commandments," said Jesus (John 14:15). "He who has My commandments and keeps them, it is he who loves Me" (John 14:21). "If anyone loves Me, he will keep My word; and My Father will love him" (John 14:23). "If you keep My commandments, you will abide in My love" (John 15:10; cf. 1 John 2:3–11). "You are my friends if you do whatever I command you" (John 15:14).

> God's law... is *summarized* in love.... Certainly a summary does not nullify the *contents* of that which it summarizes![49]

Though clearly stated in the Tradition of the Apostles, the identification of love with law was already revealed, *in nuce*, in the Torah: "I command you today to love the LORD your God, to walk in His ways, and to keep His commandments, His statutes, and His judgments, that you may live and multiply; and the LORD your God will bless you..." (Deuteronomy 30:16; cf. Deuteronomy 6:4–6; 11:1, 13, 22; 13:2ff.; 19:9).

The Law of God Deepened in the Conscience and Life of the Faithful[50]

Richard Rogers, the Puritan pastor of Wethersfield, Essex, at the turn of the sixteenth century, was riding one day with the local lord of the manor, who, after twitting him for some time about his "precisian" ways, asked him what it was that made him so *precise*. "O sir," replied Rogers, *"I serve a precise God."*[51]

It's in its precision that Scripture makes us uneasy.

---

49. Bahnsen, *Theonomy in Christian Ethics*, 243. This quote is taken from the section entitled "Love and Law," 241–247.

50. Cf. among others: Calvin, *Institutes*, IV.10.3; J. I. Packer, *A Quest for Godliness* (Wheaton, IL: Crossway Books, 1990), 107–122; Robert L. Dabney, *The Practical Philosophy* (Harrisonburg, VA: Sprinkle Publications, 1984), 282–287.

51. From Packer, *op. cit.*, 114. Packer adds: "If there were such a thing as a Puritan crest, this would be its proper motto. A precise God — a God, that is, who has made a precise disclosure of his mind and will in Scripture, and who expects from his servants a corresponding preciseness of belief and behavior — it was this view of God that created and controlled the historic Puritan outlook. The Bible itself led them to it."

*

In the *TaNaKh*, the Hebrew word for "heart" (*lev, levâv*) can also, as in English, refer to one's conscience, such as when Elihu declares "my words come from my upright heart (*lev*)" (Job 33:3; cf. Joshua 14:7; Job 22:22; and 27:6, with *levâv*). Sometimes the Hebrew word *kileyâh*, or "kidney," is used to refer to the deep-seated conscience of a man, and likewise translated as "heart" — "My heart (or kidneys) also instructs me in the night seasons" (Psalm 16:7).

In the Tradition of the Apostles, the Greek word *syneïdêsis* (cf. *synoïda*, "to know with") is used to convey the same idea, though in this case it has exactly the same meaning as our English word "con-science." In this case the English word is actually traced back to the Greek.

According to the description given in Scripture, the conscience is the internal seat of judgment that accuses or excuses us, and in so doing declares us to be innocent or guilty (Romans 2:15). It is the "heart of hearts."

However, because of man's separation from God, his conscience is impaired to the point of being confused as to what is good and what is evil, what should be approved and what should be condemned. "Woe to those who call evil good, and good evil; who put darkness for light, and light for darkness" (Isaiah 5:20).

The Tradition of the Apostles speaks quite openly of the conscience as "weak," "defiled," "evil" (1 Corinthians 8:7, 10, 12; Titus 1:15; Hebrews 10:22; 1 Timothy 1:19). The operations of the conscience, its testimony (Romans 2:15; 9:1; 2 Corinthians 1:12), its leading (Acts 24:16; Romans 13:5), and its discernment or judgment (Romans 2:15; 1 John 3:20) can all give false testimony, can act as an evil judge. As Calvin put it (*op. cit.*), true con-science (knowledge with) is found only where there is a relationship *with* God, where the conscience is "a certain mean knowledge (a link) between God and man." Calvin adds:

> It is conceivable that man might have had a pure and simple awareness that remained smothered. It is for that reason that this feeling, which prods and draws men before the judgment seat of God, is like a watchdog assigned to him to observe and call out everything that the man would have otherwise kept hidden.[52]

---

52. *L'Institution chrétienne*, IV.10.3; — translation M. M.

The impaired conscience puts man in a difficult situation, as observed by Robert Lewis Dabney:

> Now, then, if conscience is supreme, and yet also fallible, this paradoxical consequence results: that in the case of a sincerely mistaken conscience, the man must sin if he disobeys it, and must also sin if he obeys it. He is placed in a desperate quandary.[53]

We are, in effect, accountable to our conscience insofar as it reflects God's Law, and we must follow our conscience. But we are also responsible for the condition of our conscience: finding ourselves at first with a *de*-formed conscience, we have to ask, and to seek, that it become progressively *re*-formed. We are bound to follow genuinely the promptings of our conscience; but we must also see to it that these stands be in strict accordance with the biblical moral law, for the conscience is only "a mirror to reflect the light of moral and spiritual truth so as to project its well-adjusted and concentrated beams on our actions, our desires, our aims, and our choices."[54]

Every faithful Christian in the catholic Church will thus apply himself to regaining a "good" conscience. To this end he will devote himself to God's moral law so that it might be written ever more and better both on, and within, his heart (cf. Jeremiah 31:33; Hebrews 8:10 and 10:16). He will do whatever he must to obtain "a clear conscience before God and men" (Acts 24:16), making regular use of the God-ordained and God-given means of grace: meditation and hearing Scripture, personal and communal prayer, communion of the Lord's Supper, Church, exhortation, spiritual counseling (counseling that relies upon the Spirit!), etc. He will be able to take up Paul's boast, having received "the testimony of our conscience that we conducted ourselves in the world in simplicity and godly sincerity, not with fleshly wisdom but by the grace of God" (2 Corinthians 1:12). He will desire that his conscience become pure (*kathara*), that is, capable of discerning every trace of lingering sin (1 Timothy 3:9). For the grace of the Lord so refines and sharpens the conscience that it comes to drive out the hidden and subtle sins that must be confessed as they are uncovered, sins which are far more dangerous than the more "gross and open"

---

53. Dabney, *op. cit.*, 283–284.
54. Packer, *op. cit.*, 113.

sins from which the work of God, with our corresponding effort, in our sanctification, has no doubt already freed us (cf. 1 John 1:8–2:3).

The question now presents itself to us: what remains today of the "examination of the conscience" that was once a personal and sometimes daily discipline for many of the faithful? Are we diligent to examine our own hearts, especially on the eve of the Eucharistic communion? Shall we reclaim the practice of self-examination, of humbly and prayerfully searching the heart before God and His Word? Such examination is not meant to discourage us, but to bring us back to Christ and His Gospel, and to an ever-closer communion with Him: "For if we would judge ourselves, we would not be judged. But when we are judged, we are chastened by the Lord, that we may not be condemned with the world" (1 Corinthians 11:31). In this self-examination, *coram Deo* (before God), we receive together the two inseparable realities of grace: the Law and the Gospel, the Gospel and the Law; and the peace and joy that accompany them.

The Law of God Deepened in the Church and the World

Since the Enlightenment, for two and a half centuries now, the Church and Christians have been influenced by the root by Humanism, with the result that little importance is given today to the Mosaic Law. Aside from Genesis and historical sections of Exodus and Deuteronomy, the greater part of the Torah dealing with the Law has for all practical purposes been excised from Holy Scripture. Furthermore, even though Scripture is still "consulted," and sometimes heeded and followed where it deals with piety, marriage, and the family, the Church, and theology (yet even here we must protest that these subjects cannot be properly treated apart from a thorough submission to the *whole* of Scripture!), it is nonetheless categorically dismissed where it deals with other areas of life (except for those rare points where it gives backing to what is being advanced by an otherwise humanistic agenda). And yet it is precisely to these portions of Scripture — portions that deal with the major part of our everyday lives — that we should devote the greater part of our attention! But "natural law" is touted here because it presents the advantage of being undefined, variable, and modifiable, at the mercy and whim of what is considered "practical."

Should the Church end up being carried away by Humanism — with which she is already infected and sickened across all confessions and denominations — surely one of the primary reasons for her demise will be that she loosed herself from the sovereign authority of the Word of God (incarnate and written) and subsequently capitulated to each new wave of the humanistic assault as her traditional positions became increasingly untenable. The Church's will to stand her ground has also been compromised by the spreading popularity of an eschatology (the study of the *eschaton*, the "end" or "last things") that, over the last century and a half, has made so much of a "near" return of Christ and a "looming," "any-moment" end of the world, that many Christians, waiting for this imminent end, no longer believe that history may — and no doubt shall — have a long way to go, which would mean that Churches and Christians are going to have a long-time horizon in which to work patiently, courageously, and perseveringly toward the conquest of the world in the name of Christ, and thus for His victory over every enemy (1 Corinthians 15:25; Hebrews 1:13).

Despite the prophetic promise that "the earth shall be full of the knowledge of the LORD as the waters cover the sea" (Isaiah 11:9; cf. 65:17–25) and the last word of Christ:

> *All* authority has been given to Me in heaven and on earth. Go therefore and make disciples of *all* the nations, baptizing them in the name of the Father and of the Son and of the Holy Spirit, teaching them to observe *all* things that I have commanded you; and lo, I am with you *all* the days (*pásas tàs hēméras*), even to the end of the age (Matthew 28:18–20),

these Christians lay down their arms with an easy conscience, welcoming the end of the world, convinced that no mid- or long-range ventures remain to be undertaken.

The biblical understanding of the Apocalypse is quite different from that which is more and more commonly taught today. The Book of Revelation is a revelation of victory, and the apocalypses of the synoptic Gospels (Matthew 24; Mark 13; Luke 21) and of numerous other passages in the Tradition of the Apostles are not revelations of *the end of the world*, but revelations of the near and imminent end *of the ancient world* before Jesus Christ (of the judgment of Israel, the destruction of the Temple, the end of the ancient sacrifices). The erroneous exegesis of these texts, twisting them to teach an any-moment end of the world, has powerfully contributed to the capitulation of the Church in the face of the present struggles, breeding a pessimistic and defeatist mentality among the majority of the Churches and Christians who misunderstand the biblical meaning of the words *Apocalypse* and *apocalyptic.* Whereas these words hailed the good news for the first-century Christians to whom St. John addressed the Revelation, and who drew encouragement from this teaching in the face of the temporary trial (temptation) through which they would have to pass victoriously — a trial which is now historically behind us — the mention of the *Apocalypse* in our day causes Christians and non-Christians alike to envision dreadful catastrophes at the end of the world (*Apocalypse Now!*).

Since our Lord will come "like a thief," we need not speculate about "a day" or "an hour," for only the Father knows these things (cf. Matthew 24:42–44). Our responsibility, on the other hand, is to be watchful (to not fall asleep), by making the best use of our time (Ephesians 5:16; Colossians 4:5), to the end that we may obey God's Law as it applies to our vocations, to our ministries (that is, our assigned tasks). And with what time we have (no matter how little!), we must work with our children and grandchildren in mind, preparing the generations to come (no matter how many!), paving the way for the *Christendom* that we hope for according to the unfailing promises of the Lord.

*

To speak truthfully, the looming judgment that we should expect as we now begin the twenty-first century is one that will begin with us, the churches and Christians: it is the judgment of Humanism, of the religion of Man that is a religion of death. For since sin first entered the world with Adam, men have — always unsuccessfully — sought to escape from the good and holy Law of God, set forth in the whole of Scripture and summarized in the Decalogue. But rather than escape from the Law, they have experienced the weight of its sanctions overtake and fall upon them. In the end they bore the brunt of the consequences that follow such disobedience, and of which the Law had warned them. We are no different. Whoever obstinately mocks the

Law of God, that in one sense he knows to be true, inevitably runs into the backlash of this same Law that in another sense he would rather ignore. Let us all hear anew:

> For the wrath of God is revealed from heaven against all ungodliness and unrighteousness of men, who suppress the truth in unrighteousness... so that they are without excuse, because, although they knew God, they did not glorify Him as God, nor were thankful... their foolish hearts were darkened.... And even as they did not like to retain God in their knowledge, God gave them over to a debased mind, to do those things which are not fitting... who, knowing the righteous judgment of God, that those who practice such things are deserving of death, not only do the same but also approve of those who practice them. (Romans 1:18, 20–21, 28, 32)

By their willful ignorance of God and His Law, men have lost the motivation and the power to live well. Having become *autonomous*, they have lost the *goal* of life on earth, in its most individual, as well as universal, sense. Created "in the image of God" (Genesis 1:26–27), they pervert, corrupt, and deny this foundational character of their being. Their refusal to be theonomous, to obey a Law of life designed for them, causes them to love death and leads them to their own, draining them of spiritual and ethical life (Proverbs 8:36), until they even give up their will to live and, bending their necks, become slaves. They prefer any ideology ("idology"), any abstract ideal, to the personal orders of their Creator and Savior.

Under the power of Humanism the present world is becoming ever more dark and lost, and only one thing is sufficient to illumine, lead and deliver it: the Word of God, the Gospel-Law, working first in each of us. It is by the Word-Gospel-Law that Humanism will be counterattacked and defeated — *first in the Church, then in the world*. There is no hope of deliverance and salvation in anyone other than Jesus Christ — it is found nowhere else. We must pass from submission and bondage to liberation and faith, remembering that our entrance into liberation and faith includes the summons to the fight of the faith (cf. 1 Timothy 1:18–19; 6:12), to the fight for theonomy (1 John 3 and 5:1–5), a spiritual fight that can and must be waged with every weapon of God (*ê panoplia tou theou*), a fight that attacks Humanism and does so for man's sake, a fight against "the prince of the power of the air" (the "air" of our own times as well, Ephesians 2:2), "against the cosmic rulers over this present darkness" and "the schemes of the devil" (Ephesians 6:11–12, ESV). We must hear and heed the call of Ephesians 6:14–18:

> Stand therefore!
> Having girded your waist with truth,
> having put on the breastplate of righteousness,
> and having shod your feet with the preparation of the gospel of peace!
> Above all, taking the shield of faith
> with which you will be able to quench all the fiery darts of the wicked one.
> And take the helmet of salvation,
> and the sword of the Spirit which is the word (*tô rêma*) of God;
> praying always with all prayer and supplication in the Spirit!

This leads us to a major point. At least since the Enlightenment (and Jean-Jacques Rousseau!) — though Thomas Hobbes (1588–1670) wrote *The Leviathan* as far back as 1651, and Niccolo Machiaveli (1469–1527) wrote *The Prince* in 1513 (though it was not published until 1532) — Humanism, so zealous for "liberty," has always moved toward the totalitarian state, the welfare state, the divine state, whether under the deceptively innocent and insidious form of the goddess Democracy or the harsh forms of communist Socialism (U.S.S.R., China, Cuba) or nationalistic Socialism (Fascism, Nazism). For the humanistic faith, the salvation of men — or at least their temporal salvation — can be assured by predominantly political means and by the sovereign authority of the state.

The spiritual fight and the spiritual conquest, on the other hand, is the mission of the catholic Faith (a mission from which it cannot turn away without betraying the Word of God and itself, as has grievously happened today, to its own judgment and sorrow). Therefore it cannot trust in "flesh and blood" (*aïma kaï sarka*) to fight "flesh and blood" (Ephesians 6:12) — the temptation of every power religion[55] — but must rely on the power proceeding from the omnipotent

---

55. Cf. Gary North, *Moses and Pharaoh: Dominion Religion Versus Power Religion* (Tyler, TX: Institute for Christian Economics, 1985).

Lord (6:10). This is the whole meaning and significance of the Book of Exodus, contrary to what the humanist, statist, self-styled "liberation" theologians make of it. The book's meaning is found in the opposition between[56] the servitude of the people of God under the arbitrary power of Pharaoh — the state — and their liberty under the prophetic leading of Moses and the Law promulgated at Sinaï by the unmerited grace of God alone.

Humanism, whether it be right, center, or left (I am using its own politically-correct language!), always and inevitably tends toward the deification of the state, to which it looks for salvation, unphased by persistent failure upon failure. Their illusions are opposed by Psalm 2, which speaks with such realism of "the raging of the nations," of "the peoples plotting in vain," and of states (of princes) "taking counsel together against the LORD and His Christ." The Lord, we are then reminded, "laughs" in the face of such deluded conceit. The states (the princes) must honor the One who was crowned "the Holy Son" with His Ascension (2:7; cf. Hebrews 1:5; 5:5) and who has received "the nations for Your inheritance and the ends of the earth for Your possession." "Kiss the Son," they are commanded, "lest He be angry, and you perish in the way." Men, images of God and their diverse societies, including the state, must all "render to God that which is God's"; and must only "render to the state" that which is returned to it: the taxes and respect that are necessary and owed so that it may exercise (under God's Law!) the limited service that has been entrusted to it from on High (Matthew 22:15–22).

*

This accounts for the essential difference between revolutions and reformations. Revolutions of human origin, *coups de force* aroused by "power religion," openly violate God's laws, scoff at liberties and end by installing dictators who are determined to achieve their goals at all costs, even if that means the bloody sacrifices of many human lives. The system they establish is a veritable form of slavery. Their hatred of men in God's image reveals their hatred for God Himself. Reformations of divine origin, on the other hand, peacefully and patiently

---

56. As does, for example, 1 Samuel 10:17–19.

pursue the extension of the Kingdom of God on earth and a deeper understanding of His Law, which they diligently keep and practice. In the end, such Reformations progressively liberate many men from slavery, work toward a renewal of culture, invest great efforts into all kinds of educational and relief efforts which serve not only to address short-term needs but also improve conditions in the long-term. There will then be a *Christianization* of society, a new *Christendom*, rising from the large number of those who are *converted* and *come back* to the Faith as a result of the faithful communication of the Word-Gospel-Law of God under the sovereign working of the Holy Spirit.

I will limit myself to two examples — the one considerable, the other quite modest — of such Reformations in Church history.

The first appeared during the first three centuries of our era, when the Gospel and the Law of Christ spread with astonishing speed throughout the Roman Empire, and this despite the hostility, and often persecutions, of the civil and military power in place.

The Truth, winning hearts, was shared from house to house, from city to city, from province to province, crossing land and sea. Not by taking up arms of "flesh and blood," but by the witness of the words and lives of the faithful across every segment of society — slave or free, rich or poor, descendants of Israel or of the nations, continuing in prayer and open to the needs of their neighbors — there occurred, at the price of a great many martyrs, one of the greatest mysteries in history.

As Athanasius of Alexandria wrote in the fourth century:

> For as, when the sun is come, darkness no longer prevails, but if any be still left anywhere it is driven away, so, now that the divine Appearance of the Word of God is come, the darkness of the idols prevails no more, and all parts of the world in every direction are illumined by His teaching (*On the Incarnation*, 55.3).

The second appeared in sixteenth-century France over the course of four decades (about 1520 to 1560). This time, the Gospel and the Law of Christ, being proclaimed by the Reformation which had in the steps of the ancient catholic tradition, recovered them in Holy Scripture, spread "like a fire that breaks out in several places at the same time so that the whole land is ablaze, here by the regular advance of the fire's front line, there by the sparks spread by the wind, and elsewhere by the spontaneous combustion of souls ready to catch flame."[57]

Even before over two thousand "Reformed Churches in France" had been established, each planted with its own pastor, the Word of God was spreading far and wide — again, at the price of countless martyrs. During these four decades, the persecuted Reformation did not cease to gain ground throughout the whole country. Then, once again, was the statement proved true: "The blood of the martyrs is the seed of the Church."

But then, in 1562, came the beginning of the disastrous and dreadful *Wars of Religion* (a terrible phrase if ever there were one), accompanied by the struggle for power between a Condé on the one side and a Guise on the other. As a result, the *Huguenots* took up arms, and this despite the protestations of Calvin, whose letters proliferated from Geneva to the churches and the faithful in his mother country. From the moment when the arms of "flesh and blood" were taken up, the Reformation in France began to recede.

The nature of the moral Law of God is such that it can never be imposed from without or by an act of force on those who reject it, who do not want it.

Contrary to the pan-Islamists armed with a pitiless "sword" who go so far as to use terrorism to impose their faith and to establish their totalitarian regimes, theonomists are anti-revolutionaries who use only spiritual arms (Ephesians 6:10ff.) with *hupomonê* (persevering patience, cf. Ephesians 4:1–6).

For theonomists, it has never been — nor will it ever be — a question of forcing the moral Law of God on a rebellious generation (or generations) who want nothing of it.

If the future should witness — and it will, according to the promises of God! — a widespread reign of "Christendom" (composed of a diversity of republics), it will be only on the heels of such a great number of true conversions that the Gospel, accompanied by the Law of God, will cover the earth (cf. Isaiah 11:9).

Until that day comes, it is in the heart of each faithful believer, in their families, in their churches, in the exercise of their professional vocation, in their legitimate political and cultural sphere of influence,

---

57. Emile G. Léonard, *Le Protestant français* (P.U.F., 1953), 9.

that the moral Law of God will find its field of action and, to the greatest extent, be put into practice. The witness that Christians, their families, and their churches owe to the Lord and to His Gospel-Law is to live according to that Gospel-Law in their spheres of influence, even if it be only a small beginning, and to do what they can to make it known in the same. Then, as happened in the first three centuries of the Roman Empire and during the four decades in France from 1520–1560, the *catholic* faithful must strive to share the Gospel-Law from house to house, from community to community, from country to country, doing so with patience, with persistence, "with gentleness and respect," until they gain future victory as fruit of God's promise, and that at a time God alone knows. The message must be passed on to everyone in every situation of life, without showing partiality to specific familial, professional, cultural, civic, or ecclesiastical groups on account of importance or heritage. Wherever the Christian may be, in whatever group or community he finds himself, he must bear witness to the Word-Gospel-Law of the Lord, giving as faithful an account as possible of his faith in the Gospel-Law of God, to whomever asks him (cf. the whole first letter of Peter, which is strikingly relevant on this point; in the very least read 1:1–9, 15–17; 1:22–2:10; 2:12–16; 3:8–17; 4:10–19 and 5:6–11).

It is significant that confessing-Reformed theologians who differ, and sometimes even clash, when it comes to certain points of theonomy, nonetheless agree that, with these points as well as others, more time and more rigorous interpretation (exegesis) are needed before the teachings of Scripture can be faithfully set forth.[58] The way to the formulation by the catholic Church of a clearly defined *theonomic dogma* must be paved, *a fortiori*, by such careful studies of the written Word of God.

After such a long and regrettable neglect of the in-depth study of the moral Law of God (taken both as a whole and in its details), it is not realistic to think that the Church could suddenly rise up and speak with clarity and comprehensiveness on this subject. It is precisely because of this disregard, and her consequently falling sick with

---

58. For example: Greg L. Bahnsen, *No Other Standard*, 45, 66–67, 94–95, 194, 273–275; James B. Jordan, *The Death Penalty in the Mosaic Law* (Tyler, TX: 1989); and *Theonomy: A Reformed Critique* (Grand Rapids: 1990), specifically the introduction by the editors, William S. Barker and W. Robert Godfrey (1–7) and the contributions by John Frame (89–99), Vern S. Poythress (103–123), Moisés Silva (153–167), and D. Clair Davis (389–402).

Humanism, that the Church has so often lost the thread of her own thought and ethical teaching. Consider four subjects which have recently come under discussion: whether they be abortion and sexuality, or the ordination of women and the marriage of ordained ministers, the different *confessions* have given to their consideration only a selective hearing to Scripture, carefully heeding some texts while ignoring others. When it comes to abortion, the pope has surely spoken better than most Protestants who recklessly continue to justify it. The same is true for the ordination of women, where the pope and the "Eastern" Orthodox hold the Biblical line while the Protestants yield to cultural demands. And yet the Protestants have spoken better regarding the marriage of ordained ministers than the pope or the "Eastern" Orthodox.[59] Concerning sexuality, each goes wrong in its own way: the *Eastern* Orthodox and, above all, the Roman Catholics, always influenced by *neo-platonic Hellenism*, have blindly held to the superiority of virginity and celibacy over marriage; on the other end, a number of Protestants have shown an outrageous and unbiblical laxity, going so far as to justify homosexuality.

But it's not just the formal position but also the reasoning by which one arrives at that position that is significant. For example, though the Roman Catholics, with the pope, condemn abortion, they do not take their stand in the name of the Law of God — as should be done — but in the name of the defense of life, the absolute sanctity of life, which puts them in an awkward and contradictory position when it comes to the death penalty (which the Law of God endorses for certain crimes). Once again — and this hurts the preaching of the Gospel — rather than standing on the written Word of God, these Roman Catholics rely on natural law, a wax nose that can be bent as one wishes.

The situation of the modern world is far from that of the Age of Faith and the time of the Reformation in Europe, when the Law of God was the foundation of society. In most countries today the Law is constantly changing, usually following (or rather being led astray by) humanistic public opinions. These opinions are themselves formed

---

59. Most of the apostles, including Peter, were married, and their wives (*gunaïkès*) accompanied them (1 Corinthians 9:5). Paul, though himself single, recommended the marriage of "bishops," for "if a man does not know how to rule his own house, how will he take care of the church of God?" (1 Timothy 3:2, 4–5).

and reinforced by the media and the enshrined doctrine of human rights (without God!) which are developed in every possible direction, and which ultimately serve to support a kind of "humanitarian" and "politically-correct" pseudo-justice that criminalizes pseudo-sins invented by men while excusing certain crimes clearly defined as such by the Law of God and its penology. Against this backdrop, the Psalmist's inspired cry to the Lord takes on its full meaning:

> Shall the throne of iniquity which devises evil by law,
> Have fellowship with You? (Psalm 94:20)

Christians in the twenty-first century face the strong possibility of finding themselves in a difficult situation, having to endure a time of crisis, of judgment, of unknown duration. Such a situation would be analogous, though not identical, to that experienced by the Christians of the first three centuries who found themselves, not through any fault of their own, at odds with the thought and life of the governing political authorities as well as that of their non-Christian fellow citizens. What is different is that the antinomian (opposed to the Law of God) "powers that be" avail themselves today of means of pressure, oppression, and disinformation on a scale far surpassing those available then to the second Beast (of propaganda) who served at the bidding of the first Beast (of power) in Revelation 13 (vv. 11–17).

It is incumbent upon us who are baptized, faithful Christians across all confessions — often closer to our brothers in other confessions than to the false-brothers in our own confessions — to carry out the urgent and necessary task of planting the seeds of the next Reformation in every area of life, beginning with the hearts of non-Christian men moved by the grace of God to receive it. As Humanism approaches, and perhaps fast approaches, the end of its road strewn with ruin and death, it is this next Reformation that will replace it. On this renewal depends the future of the life of the world.

Our Lord reigns, and from on High He acts on earth. But, paradoxically, He generally begins His works from below, beginning from the diversity of small communities — beginning with the family, the local church, professional or cultural undertakings that are faithful to Him, that hear and follow His moral law, revealed in Scripture (which is THE Scripture!). From small seeds sometimes spring forth great trees. We are not to be like Revolutionaries, who look to the day when they can take the reins of power in order to impose their top-down agenda. Rather, like the Reformers, we are to be humbly sowing, humbly planting, influencing from below, patient and steadfast in our hope. This is our time: this is the DAY OF SMALL BEGINNINGS.

In the Church it is time to hear anew the ancient SHEMA YISRAEL ("Hear, O Israel") which I now copy down as the sum and substance of God's call to us:

> Hear, O Israel: The LORD our God, the LORD is one!
> You shall love the LORD your God with all your heart, with all your soul, and with all your strength. And these words which I command you today shall be in your heart. You shall teach them diligently to your children, and shall talk of them when you sit in your house, when you walk by the way, when you lie down, and when you rise up. You shall bind them as a sign on your hand, and they shall be as frontlets between your eyes. You shall write them on the doorposts of your house and on your gates. (Deuteronomy 6:4–9)

> And it shall be that if you earnestly obey My commandments which I command you today, to love the LORD your God and serve Him with all your heart and with all your soul, then I will give you the rain for your land in its season, the early rain and the latter rain, that you may gather in your grain, your new wine, and your oil. And I will send grass in your fields for your livestock that you may eat and be filled. Take heed to yourselves, lest your heart be deceived, and you turn aside and serve other gods and worship them, lest the LORD's anger be aroused against you, and He shut up the heavens so that there be no rain, and the land yield no produce, and you perish quickly from the good land which the LORD is giving you. (Deuteronomy 11:13–17)

> And you shall...remember all the commandments of the LORD and do them...that you may not follow the harlotry to which your own heart and your own eyes are inclined, and that you may remember and do all My commandments, and be holy for your God. I am the LORD your God, who brought you out of the land of Egypt, to be your God: I am the LORD your God. (Numbers 15:39–41)

Let me close with these last words of our Lord and Savior Jesus Christ:

THE PROCLAMATION:
"All authority has been given to Me in heaven and on earth."

THE MARCHING ORDER:
"Go therefore and make disciples of all nations, baptizing them in the name of the Father and of the Son and of the Holy Spirit, teaching them to observe all things that I have commanded you."

THE PROMISE:
"And lo, I am with you always, even to the end of the age!" (Matthew 28:18–20)

Appendix

MY MEETING WITH PIERRE COURTHIAL

IN MAY OF 2006, ZURICH PUBLISHING FOUNDATION (THROUGH the generous gift of Ms. Elizabeth Conway) arranged for me to travel to Europe to meet the man whose works I'd been translating for the previous two years. Over that time, Dr. Courthial and I had carried on correspondence, but we had never spoken or met in person.

The meeting was arranged by our mutual friend in Switzerland, Jean-Marc Berthoud, and Dr. Courthial's wife, Hélène, who carefully looked after her husband in his last years. The date was set for Wednesday, May 17, a day that would prove unforgettable for me.

I awoke that morning in a hostel near the Gare de Lyon station in Paris, and found breakfast at a nearby café where I reviewed some of Courthial's essays and looked over the questions I intended to ask him. I also prayed that the Lord would give me special help that day with my spoken French (which He graciously did). From there I took the subway to the address.

After exiting in the fifteenth district of Paris and rounding the corner to the apartment block, I was greeted by the sight of a nine-story apartment building. Somewhere up there was this man who had poured out his life in service of Christ's Church during one of the most spiritually challenging centuries, in one of the most spiritually apostate countries in the history of Christianity.

Madame Courthial opened the door about the time I stepped out of the elevator at the eighth floor. She warmly greeted me as she invited me in, but was quick to inform me that her husband's health was not good that morning, so we should limit our visit to about twenty minutes. She then ushered me into the drawing room, a small but very nicely appointed room with several chairs and a coffee table. Taking my seat, to my left was a wall lined with books, to my right a dresser with various pictures and Courthial's morning reading (including the latest draft of Douglas Kelly's *Systematic Theology*). Across from me was a window looking out towards the rooftops of Paris. In the chair to my right sat the theologian, who welcomed me with a smile as I entered. He was quick to let me know that he was, indeed, not feeling so well on this day.

We sat, exchanged greetings, and began by speaking of our mutual friend, Jean-Marc Berthoud. M. Courthial had just finished reading with great appreciation Jean-Marc's recent essay on Theodore Beza.

After a few minutes, I began our more formal interview by opening his book, *De Bible en Bible* (2001), and reading a line that he had quoted from Hugues Kéraly:

> Amidst the evil of these difficult times, when all our eyes behold is blurred, mysterious bonds bring together those who travel different roads, whose paths would never have crossed apart from the often-strange workings of Providence.

"This meeting today is such a mysterious, providential crossing of paths," I said. Here I was, a twenty-seven-year-old American, sitting with a ninety-year-old French theologian whose books I'd translated, and it all hinged upon Jean-Marc Berthoud, our mutual friend, and Tom Ertl, the publisher whom neither Courthial nor I, nor even Jean-Marc, had heard of until three years ago. He and Hélène smiled with pleasure as we briefly reflected on how all of this came to be and the role Tom played in making it happen. Courthial's countenance lifted and he took a new posture, leaning forward in his chair.

My first question was one I'd prepared. Courthial's writings brimmed with hope for the future of Christianity, a strikingly different note from what one often hears from Western churchmen and theologians. I asked him how, given all of the spiritual and cultural defeats he'd witnessed in his lifetime, was he able to maintain and communicate such hope?

He hardly hesitated in answering: *"C'est la promesse de Dieu!"* ("It's the promise of God!"). He quoted Isaiah prophesying the spread of the knowledge of God over the whole face of the earth as the waters cover the sea. But he then added, "For now, all that remains for France is judgment. It is clear that God is judging us. Paul says in Romans 1 that homosexuality, for instance — it's a sign of the wrath of God being poured out! We see God's judgment in the prevalence of homosexuality, more and more, in France. But, on the other side of judgment is restoration. I believe that. I won't live to see it, but you might. You may live to see it!" And he added with vibrant eyes and a chuckle, "And if you do, then you can tell them I told you."

Reaffirming this hope obviously enlivened him. We discussed his decision not to pursue a Ph.D. at Free University, and the state of Reformed Christianity in the Netherlands, the U.K., and America. He shared his opinions on several recent pieces of theological writing, evidencing the degree to which he was still "on top of things."

Speaking of his books, I asked him if he would consider writing an additional section to be inserted in *Le jour des petits recommencements* (*A New Day of Small Beginnings*). In this book, tracing the history of the covenant from Adam to our present day, he devotes about thirty pages to the life of Christ, from his birth and baptism up to the Olivet Discourse. From there, he goes on to the birth of the Church, which opens with a transitional paragraph about Christ's move from his state of humiliation (incarnation to the cross) to his state of glorification (resurrection to ascension), from which He now sends His Spirit who gives birth to the Church. I told him I thought the book would be strengthened by a few pages specifically devoted to the Cross, expanding upon the Cross in light of this covenantal history. He had received my letter the day before in which I had raised this possibility. Referencing that letter, he quickly gave his assent, acknowledging that it could strengthen the work.

Apparently this was news to his wife, who gave him a tender but skeptical look. If I could have translated that look, it would have said: "Pierre, you're ninety; it's a little late to be adding pages to your masterpiece!" She did turn to me and say, with gentleness, "We'll see." She was obviously far more sensitive to her husband's age than was he.

What was to be a twenty-minute interview became an hour of animated, joy-filled conversation in the presence of a vigorous and engaging man. At the end of that hour, Hélène suggested that we draw things to a close, and Courthial agreed, saying that he was just beginning to feel tired. He stood with me for a photograph, which Hélène kindly took. Then he turned to me and, raising his hand, pronounced a benediction over me.

Having said my goodbyes and taken the elevator back down to the entrance, I sat down on the street curb and jotted down as much of our dialogue as I could recall. Twenty minutes later, I got up and made my way toward the subway. I had about six hours until my train left Paris for Lausanne. I first went straight to *L'Église Réformée de l'Annonciation* to see where Courthial had ministered for twenty-three years. Fortunately, there was a woman outside the church who saw me looking around and agreed to unlock the door and let me in for a bit. I took some pictures of the beautiful sanctuary, not knowing I would be back there in three years to attend Courthial's memorial service.

My train departed Paris for Lausanne at 4:30 that afternoon, and I had a wonderful window seat in which to reflect on the substance of Courthial's writings and on the hope he had sounded in them. Meeting the man in person had confirmed that he lived and breathed what he wrote. As the bright yellow fields of sunflowers in the French countryside whirled by outside my window, I was left to ponder: "In the face of this present darkness, is it really possible that we could witness, even in the West, a great restoration of Christianity? Could a vigorous, 'catholic' version of theonomy, as uniquely espoused by Courthial,[1] really emerge as the fifth grand dogma of the Church, guiding her into a third great epoch in her history? Could the saints really hold onto that kind of hope, or was it more realistic simply to acknowledge that 'things fall apart,' the 'center cannot hold,' and that there's no reason to expect anything more than steady decline?"

Apart from pondering this future possibility, I was deeply impressed by the present reality of a man, so late in age, having fought so many battles, who nonetheless sounded such a vibrant and uplifting

---

1. Courthial expounds more fully on this "theocosmonomic vision" in his final book, *De Bible en Bible,* currently in translation and forthcoming from Zurich Publishing,

note of hope. I began to realize that Courthial was among those rare men who judged everything, not only the present but also the future, according to the Word of God ("we walk by faith, not by sight," he was fond of quoting). The depth of his hope had exuded from him in his countenance and in the strength of his voice. He did not harp on how terrible things were, but seized the occasion to encourage a young man of the amazing things God has promised for His people who hold fast to His Word.

Courthial opens this book with a quotation from "The Old Man and the Three Younger Ones," a seventeenth-century French fable written by the famed Jean de La Fontaine. This particular fable tells of three young men, living for the pleasures of the present, who come across an eighty-year-old man planting saplings. In response to the sight, they mock him for spending his last days planting something, the fruit of which he will never live to see. But, as the fable goes on to show, the old man knew exactly what he was doing, and why.

Courthial was eighty-two years old when he wrote this book. It was his effort, at an age when most men have long retired, to invest himself in planting the seeds of the future — a future he doubted he would live to see, but was convinced others would. And so, confident that he knew exactly what he was doing, and why, Courthial took up his pen, dug down into the rich soil of decades of extraordinary study and experience, and produced what may well prove to be a seminal contribution to that which he saw from afar — a new day of small beginnings.

Rev. Matthew S. Miller
Erskine Theological Seminary
Greenville, South Carolina

History Index

THE PURPOSE OF THIS INDEX IS TO PROVIDE A TIMELINE OF THE material references so that the reader may see how the author traced certain themes in their historical contexts.

General entries are sorted in logical or loose chronological order. Dates used in the dated entries are based on the indexer's research, with deference given to any dates the author provided. The dates in the index are for the reader's convenience but are not to be relied upon as an infallible record. Italicized dates indicate the occupation of an office.

Ancient History (creation–a.d. 1)

Adam and Eve
    covenant responsibility of, 5–9, 14, 258
    and the mountain of God, 12
    fall of, 14–16, 259
    gospel and law, 40–41
    God's covenant and, 252
Cain and Seth, 16–17, 18, 21, 41
Noah, 9–10, 17–18, 252
Tower of Babel, 21–22
c. 2000 B.C.: Abraham, 23–26, 41, 252, 268
Moses

God's revealed covenant to, 4, 11, 14, 30, 34, 252
and Pharaoh, 27
God's promise to Abraham fulfilled during the time of, 24, 35, 268
at Sainaï, 27, 29, 31, 268
the Blood of the Covenant, 30
the Law, 31, 42, 77–78, 253, 278, 300
subsidiary, 32
c. 1400 B.C.: institution of the Passover, 28–29
Covenants at Sinaï
with Moses at the burning bush, 27
confirmation of the covenant with Israel, 27, 29–30, 48
Israel given the first installment of Scriptures, 200, 300
Joshua succeeds Moses, 34
The Judges and Samuel, 34–35
Saul, 35
David, 36–38, 252
Ministry of the Prophets, 49–54
Naboth's Vineyard, 285
Daniel's Visions, 56–58
c. 576–530 B.C.: Cyrus the Great ends the Babylonian captivity, 58–59
384–322 B.C.: Aristotle and his influence on Scholasticism, 224
74/73–4 B.C.: Herod's massacre of the children, 71
27 B.C.–A.D. 14: *Pax Romana* (Roman peace), 121

Early Church (1st–4th centuries)

Jesus Christ
   incarnation of Christ, 64, 67–68, 70, 74, 101
   childhood and pre-ministry years, 71–73
   baptism of, 78–79, 80–85
   ministry, 91–100
   the Last Supper, 156
   obedience and death, 73–75
   resurrection and rule, 101–104ß
   Great Commission and ascension, 110–113
   God's covenant and, 252, 258
1–70: The turning of the ages as the administrations of the covenant overlap, 267–268
14–37: Tiberius Caesar, 121
30: Pentecost, 104–106, 107, 118, 156
Apostolic Church
   early church in Jerusalem, 108, 118

Jewish opposition to the Gospel, 119–120
the Gospel spreads to all the Roman world, 130
continues many Hebraic ceremonies and rites, 152
Apostle Peter, 115–116, 147, 125
Apostle Paul
life and ministry of, 116–117
on faith and works, 195–196
did not teach autonomy of natural thought, 227
and the Law, 254–255
and famine in Jerusalem, 122
67: Martyrdom of, 125
Apostle John, 117–118
Apostolic fathers and the New Testament canon, 146
c. 35–108: Ignatius and the One and the Many, 167
37–41: Emperor Caligula and Pax Romana, 121
37–100: Josephus, 122–123
41–54: Claudius Caesar, 122
44, d.: Apostle James, 195–196
54–68: Emperor Nero, 121, 126–127, 147
55–120: Tacitus (historian), 121
c. 61, d.: Barnabus and the One and the Many, 167
64:
    Roman law protecting Christians, 126
    Pisonian Conspiracy, 121
    July 18: burning of Rome triggers first persecution of Christians, 126
66–70: Jewish-Roman war, 121, 123
67: earthquake in Jerusalem, 122
68: Roman civil wars, 121
68: Idumean soldiers surround and attack Jerusalem, 131–132
69: "Year of the Four Emperors," 121
70: destruction of the Temple, 139, 141–142, 152, 154
88–99: Clement of Rome and the One and the Many, 167
100–165: Justin Martyr, 221
    and the One and the Many, 167
    Apology and the use of pagan terminology, 222
130–202: Irenaeus
    and the One and the Many, 167
    This Gospel....the foundation and pillar of the truth, 201
c. 155–240: Tertullian and the One and the Many, 167
c. 170: "Muratorian" canon, 146
180, d. : Melito of Sardis and the One and the Many, 167
185–254: Origen's interpretation of Scripture, 202
256–336: Arius of Alexandria
    rejects doctrine of the Trinity, 163

rejects the divinity of Christ, 163, 169
    influence of, 169
c. 296–373: Athanasius of Alexandria
    alone against the world, 163, 181
    battles Arianism, 169, 178
    creed of, 174
    speaks of *the whole dismembered Church*, 181
    On the Incarnation of the Word, 218–219
        357: condemned by Pope Tiberius, 181
        367: we find the exact canon of 27 New Testament books for the first time, 146
313: Constantine's Edict of Milan ends major persecution of Christians, 126
315–367: St. Hilary battles Arianism, 169, 178
325–451: first four Ecumenical Councils, 166, 170, 186
325: First Council of Nicea, 167, 168, 170, 174, 179
    faithful to Scripture, 161
    battles Arianism, 169
335: Council of Tyre favors the Arian heresy, 181
c. 340–397: Ambrose battles Arianism and Apollinarianism, 169, 178
c. 350–425: Pelagius, 176
353: Council of Arles favors the Arian heresy, 181
354–430: Augustine
    writings of, 175–176, 262
    sanctified away from pagan thought, 176
    battles against Pelagianism, 176, 202–203
    rejects autonomy of human reason, 176, 224
    influence in the Middle Ages on Anselm, Bernard, and Bonaventure, 176
    did not teach justification by faith, 189
    puts Septuagint and Latin Vulgate on nearly same level as Scripture, 206–207
    and Scholastic synthesis, 224
355: Council of Milan favors the Arian heresy, 181
357: Council of Sirmium favors the Arian heresy, 181
359–360: Council of Rimini favors the Arian heresy, 181
376–444: Cyril of Alexandria battles heresies, 178
378–453: Eutychius argues for a confusion of natures in Christ, 170
380–451: Nestorius contends that Christ is two persons, 170
381: Council of Constantinople, 170, 174, 179
    faithful to Scripture, 161
    battles Arianism, 169
    denies Apollinarianism, 169–170
d. 390: Apollinarius of Laodicea, 169

Medieval Era (5th-15th Centuries)

Middle Ages, 246–220
    decentralization in the Church, 184
    should have been called "The Age of Faith," 216
431: Council of Ephesus, 170, 171, 179
    faithful to Scripture, 161
    condemns Nestorianism, 170
451: Council of Chalcedon, 65, 168, 179
    faithful to Scripture, 161
    condemns the doctrine of Eutychius, 170
    clarifies mystery of the Trinity and the Person of Christ, 171–172
480–524: Boethius, 222–223, 224
553: Second Council of Constantinople
    faithful to Scripture, 161
    condemns the worship of Jesus' human nature, 171
680–681: Third Council of Constantinople
    faithful to Scripture, 161
    condemns the heresy of Monothelitism, 171
    condemns the worship of Jesus' human nature, 171
    opposed by the Carolingian Church, 184
787: Second Council of Nicea, 184, 172–173
    approves, authorizes, and promotes the worship of images and relics, 161, 179
    rejected by the Reformers, 179
c. 870, d.: Ratramnus of Corbie
    faithful to Scripture, 184
    writes *Decorpore et sanguine Domine* and *De praedestinatione*, 184–185
1033–1109: Anselm
    influenced by Augustine, 176
    writes *Proslogion*, 176–177
    Cur Deus Homo and the doctrine of expiation, 177
    his followers avoid Pelagianism, 202–203
1079–1142: Abelard and modernism, 177
1090–1153: St. Bernard of Clairvaux,
    influenced by Augustine, 176
    opposes Abelard, extends thought of Anselm, 177
1115–1180: John of Salisbury
    If... God is the true Wisdom, then the love of God is the true philosophy, 262
    writes *Polycraticus*, 262
1198–1216: Pope Innocent III and the sacking of Constantinople, 182
13th century and bloom of Scholasticism, 222–225
1220–1292: Roger Bacon, 263

318 • A NEW DAY OF SMALL BEGINNINGS

1221–1274: St. Bonaventure
    influenced by Augustine, 176
    his followers avoid Pelagianism, 202–203
1227–1274: Thomas Aquinas, 177, 224–225, 227–228
1235–1315: Raymond Lulle, 262–263
1328–1384: John Wycliffe, 186, 187
1350–1420: Pierre d'Ailly, 185
1369–1415: John Huss, 186
1414–1418: Council of Constance condemns John Huss, 186
1428, Wycliffe's bones exhumed, burned, and ashes cast into the river, 187
d. 1437: Nicolas de Clamanges attacks Scholasticism, 185
1466–1536: Desiderius Erasmus
    wrote that France was the envy of the other kingdoms of Europe, xxxv
    remains a loyal Roman Catholic, 228
    debate with Luther regarding free will, 228–234
    1511: *In Praise of Folly*, 228
    1524: *Diatribe on the Freedom of the Will*, 228–229
    1516: Publishes the first New Testament in Greek, 208
1469–1527: Niccolò Machiavelli, 228, 299
1483–1546: Martin Luther
    response to Erasmus, 188–189, 228–234
    brings to light the doctrine of justification by faith, 189–190
    on Scripture and church authority, 179, 212
    1521: Excommunicated by Pope Leo X, 181–182
    1525: Writes *Bondage of the Will* in answer to Erasmus, 228

Reformation and Renaissance (16th–17th Centuries)

1500–1562: Peter Martyr Vermigli, 183, 223
1516–1590: Jerome Zanchi's *Treatise on Predestination*, 223
1509–1564: John Calvin
    life, theology, and ministry, xxxvi–xxxviii
    on the necessity of the church, 175
    on the veneration of images, 179–180
    and the authority of Scripture, 204, 213
    on God and Law, 263
    1559: completes final edition of *Institutes of the Christian Religion*, xxxvii
1511–1571: Pierre Viret outlines doctrine of theonomy, 257, 272
1521: Pope Leo X excommunicates Martin Luther, 181–182
1515–1547: Francis I calls himself "the most Christian King of France," xxxv
1520–1560: The Reformation spreads wildly through France, 300–301

1522–1586: Martin Chemnitz, 183–184
1530: Diet of Augsburg, 190
1530–1647: The Epoch of the Protestant Reformation, 178
   in France, xxxv
   as the second epoch of the first order in the progress of the ecclesial tradition, 166
   seeks to locate itself within the continuum of the church and catholic tradition, 174
   defines justification by faith, 189–193, 257
   teachings on sanctification, 193–195
   establishes the authority of Scripture alone over popes and pontiffs, 213
   return to Scripture, 228
   develops a biblical doctrine of the covenant, 252
Persecution of French Huguenots, xxxvi
1545–1583: Council of Trent,
   and canon of Scripture, 142–143, 144
   defines the role of the Pope, 184
   makes Jerome's *Vulgata latina* a "verbal icon," 207
   calls the Roman pontiff sovereign over the Church, 213
1550?–1618: Richard Rogers, 292
1559: The *Gallicana* (French Confession of Faith) drafted in Paris, 178, 179, 204
1571: The *Gallicana* confirmed by the Synod at La Rochelle, 178, 180
1582–1677: Johann Gerhard authors the first *Patrology* ever written, 184
1588–1670: Thomas Hobbes writes humanistic *Leviathan*, 299
1647: Westminster Confession of Faith, 190, 204–206
   1694–1778: Voltaire, 237

Modern Era (18th–20th Centuries)

Age of Enlightenment influences the church, 295
1711–1776: David Hume, 237, 815
1712–1778: Jean-Jacques Rousseau, 299
1724–1804: Immanuel Kant, 235, 236
1729–1781: Gotthold Lessing, 237
1787–1864: César Malan and the catholic Faith, 244
1789–1815: French Revolution's antinomian influence, xliii
1790–1874: Ami Bost and the catholic Faith, 244
1794–1863: Frédéric Monod and the catholic Faith, 244
1794–1872: Henri Merle d'Aubigné and the catholic Faith, 244
1801–1882: Friedrich Philippi, 243–244
1802–1856: Adolphe Monod and the catholic Faith, 244
1821–1881: Fyodor Dostoyevsky, 259

1844–1918: Julius Wellhausen and the historical-critical method, 237
1865–1923: Ernest Troeltsch breaks from catholic Faith and Tradition, 245
1870–1871: Vatican I proclaims the doctrine of papal infallibility, 184
1871–1943: Auguste Lecerf noetic effect of original sin, 264–265
1879–1890: John Henry Newman, 181
1894–1977: Herman Dooyeweerd, 247
1894–1979: Father Justin Popovich, 173, 188
1895–1987: Cornelius Van Til, 247
1899–1993: Hendrik Stoker, 247
1912–2000: Kenneth Lee Pike, 247
1914–2009: Pierre Courthial, xxxii–xxxiii
1916–2001: Rousas John Rushdoony, 263, 295
1917: October Revolution, the World Wars, and the advance of Orthodoxy, 173
1929: Westminster Theological Seminary, Philadelphia, founded, xxxi
1948–1995: Greg Bahnsen, 270–271
1962–1965: Vatican II, 184
1976: *Le Mal Francais* by Alain Peyrefitte, xxxvi

SCRIPTURE INDEX

Genesis

1	17, 41
1:2	22, 41
1:26	17, 22, 41, 50
1:26–27	298
1:26–28	14
1:27–28	278
1:28	6, 40, 41, 269
1:28–29	6
1:28–30	40
1:29	41
1:31	13
2:2–3	40
2:3	31
2:8	12
2:9	6
2:15	6, 269
2:15–16	40
2:17	16, 40
2:18	278
2:18–24	14
2:19–20	40
2:20	6
2:23–24	40, 278
2:24	269
3:6	21
3:7–10	15
3:8	137
3:11–13	15
3:14–19	40
3:14–24	137
3:15	9
3:16	269
3:16–19	16, 280
3:17–19	9
3:19	40, 280
3:22	50
3:24	7
4:4	17
4:15	18
4:23–24	21
5:2	278
5:24	137
6	9
6:1–7	21
6:2–4	9
6:3	50
6:5–7	17
6:8–9	9–10
6:9	137
6:13–8:19	17
6:16	41

6:17–18	9	17:1–14	41
6:18	9	17:8	269
8:8–12	41	17:9	25
8:20–9:27	17	17:9–14	24
8:21–22	17	17:12–13	25
9	9	17:14	26
9:1	17, 41, 269	17:15–22	25
9:2–7	18	17:23–27	24–25
9:3	41	18	23
9:5–7	18	18:1–16	51
9:6	41	18:2–3	23
9:7–17	20	18:4–5	23
9:9–17	19	18:17	51
9:11–17	18	18:17–19	42
9:12	18	18:19	25
9:17	19	18:20–23	132
10	22	19:1–19	51
10:1	268	19:1–29	278
10:21–24	268	19:13	269–270
10:32	20	20:7	51
11	20	21:12–14	23
11:1–9	22	22	23, 196
11:4	21	22:1–9	23
11:5–9	137	22:11	22
11:7	21–22, 22, 50	22:15	22
11:10–14	268	22:15–18	27
11–12	17	23	24
11:27–12:3	268	24:7	22
12:1–4	23	24:40	22
12:2–3	41	25:7–11	24
12:7–8	23	26:2–5	27
12–22	24	26:3	27
13:14–18	23	28:12–22	27
14	83	31:11	22
14:18–19	83	32:24ff	22
15	23, 196	35:6–15	27
15:5	24	35:9–10	27
15:6	24, 196	38	68
15:9–12	25	48:16	22
15:10ff	57	50:20	29
15:17ff	25		
16:7	22	Exodus	
17	9, 23	2:24–25	27
17:1	42	3	52

Reference	Page
3:6	27
3:7	29
3:8	269
3:16	27
3 and 4	27
4:5	27
4:15	50
5–11	27
6	9
6:7	29
7:1–2	50
7:10–13	31
9-40	27
12:1–25	28
12:7–8	28
12:13–14	28
12:24–27	28
12:49	109
17:14	50, 214
18:13	31
18:16	31
18:17–26	32
19:5	48
19:5–6	29
19:16–19	30
19:20	30
19-24	200
20	48
20:2	269
20:2–17	43
20:3	90
20:4	31
20:7	114
20:12	278
20:17	90, 92, 281
20:22	33
20:22–26	44
20:24	137
21:17	278
21:20–23:9	282
21–23	43, 45
22:20	31
23:4–5	278
23:16	109
23:23	269
24	162
24:1–8	30
24:3	30, 161
24:4	50
24:7	3, 48
24:12	214
25:8	34
25–31	44
26:23–40	33
27:1–8	33
28:1	81
28:41	80
29:4	81
29:7	80
29:43	34
29:45	29
30:1–10	33
30:17–21	33, 81
30:22–25	80
30:30	80
30–35	51
31:12–17	31
31:18	162
32:7–14	51
32:9	53
33:3–11	51
33:11	31
34:6	78, 285
34:22–24	109
34:27	31
34:27–28	199
34:29	31
35:1–3	31
35–40	45
40:12–15	80

Leviticus

Reference	Page
book of	27
1–25	45
4–5	33
8:6	81
8:12	80
12	273

15	273
16:1–14	33
16:32	80
18:8	278
18:19	273
18:22	278
18:24–25	269
18:27	269
18:30	269
19:12	92
19:16–18	92
19:18	43, 274
20:13	278
20:18	273
21:12	80
24:17–21	282
25	141
25:8–10	57
26:3–13	94
26:11–12	77
26:12	29
26:40–45	47

Numbers

book of	27
1:47–6:21	45
3:9–12	82
4:3	81
4:47	81
6	108
8:1–19	45
8:6–7	81
11:33	78
12:7–8	51
14:13–20	51
14:34	56
15:1–31	45
15:39–41	306
18-19	45
19:11–22	273
23:15–30:20	45
27:1–11	45
28:1–30:17	45
29:12–38	109

35:1–36:13	45

Deuteronomy

book of	27, 45
4:1–2	164
4:2	278
4:5–8	109, 278
4:6	73
4:6–8	270, 271
4:20	29
4:44–7:11	200
5:6	269
5:7–21	43
5:20	90
6:4–5	43, 55
6:4–6	292
6:4–9	306
6:5	274
6:8	278
6:25	81
7	248
7:1–5	269
7:8	33
8:2	90
9:6	53
9:13	53
10:12–21	46
10:16	26
11:1	292
11:13	292
11:13–17	306
11:17	78
11:22	292
11:26–28	45
13:1–3	164
13:2ff	292
14:2	29
14:27	32
14:29	32
17:14–20	35
19:9	292
19:21	282
21:23	74, 85, 282
22:5	13

22:8	274
22:9–11	273
22:10	273
23:5	33
24:1	92
25:2	282
25:4	147
27:20	278
28:1–14	94
28:15ff.	141
28:25–26	141
29:17	131
30:6	26
30:11–14	154
30:16	292
31:9	214
31:19	214
31:26	33
32	214
32:7–8	20
32:35	87, 157
33:1	50
33:4	42, 78
34	34
34:10	51

JOSHUA

book of	34
1	34
2:14	285
14:7	293
24:26	50

JUDGES

book of	34
Judges 15:15–17	248
Judges 21:25	35

RUTH

book of	55
2	68
2:3	l

1 SAMUEL

book of	34
2:6	233
2:10	80
2:27	50
2:35	80
3–6	37
3:10	137
8	35
8:11–18	217
9:6	50
10:1	80
10:6	80
10:17–19	300
12:12	36
13:14	36
15	36, 248
15:23	36
16	36
16:3	80
16:12	80
16:13	80
31	36

2 SAMUEL

book of	34, 36
1	36
2:4	80
2:6	285
3:39	80, 282
5:1–10	36
6	37
7:1–16	37
7:18–29	38
15:20	285
24:11	50

1 KINGS

book of	34
1–2	36
1:34–45	80
10:1–13	110
11	289
11:4	289

11:5	131
11:6	289
11:9	289
13:1	50
17ff.	181
18	50
19:16	80
21	285
22	285
22:19–23	51

2 Kings

book of	34
4:9	50
9:3–6	80
11:12	80
16:6	268
17:13	50
19:31	49
21:10	50
23:30	80

1 Chronicles

11–29	36

2 Chronicles

3:1	23
20:7	23
24:20	22
24:20–22	144
32:25	85
36:16	50
36:22ff.	58

Ezra

1:1–4	58
4:12	58
6:10	59
7:6	59
9:8	49
10:3	39

Nehemiah

8:9	59

Esther

book of, 55

Job

book of	54, 157
1:6–12	50
2:1–6	50
22:22	293
27:6	293
28:28	13, 39, 285
31:1	92
31:29	278
33:3	293
33:4	22

Psalms

2	83, 300
2:2	80
2:6	80, 152
2:7	300
3:3	176
5:11	113
7:10	39
9:10	113
16:7	293
18:7–10	135
21	215
22	67
22:3	39
22:22	113
22:28	20
23:3	113
25:11	113
27	xxxviii
27:5	77
37	54
37:8	281
40:7–9	75
41:9	100
45:8	80
49	54
51:6	282
75:1	113
76:1	113

Reference	Page
79:9	188
82:5	109
82:8	109
85:11	285
86:8–10	20
89:16	113
89:24	113
92:14	xlviii
94:20	305
95:7–8	137
102:18	214
110	82
111:10	13, 39, 73, 285
112	54
119	39, 230, 275
119:29	46
119:55	113
119:105	230
121	11
121:1	xlvii
121:2	xlvii
122	54
135:6	233
145:9	39

Proverbs

54, 285–287

Reference	Page
1:7	13, 39, 285
2:1–6	286
2:21–22	281
3:3	285, 286
4–7	287
4:23	90
6:16–18	90
6:25	90
8:15–16	286
8:36	7, 298
9:10	39, 285
10:8	285
12:4	287
13:13	285
13:24	281
14:1	287
14:34	270
15:20	287
15:33	285
16:12	286
19:22	92
20:28	285
22:9	92
23:22	287
24:23–24	286
25:21	92
25:21–22	278
28:7	285
29:14	286
29:15	281
29:18	285
30:5–6	164
30:9	114
30:17	287
31:5	286
31:9	286
31:10–31	287

Ecclesiastes

Reference	Page
book of	54, 55
3:14	164
12:13	39

The Song of Songs

Reference	Page
book of	55, 287–289
6:3	289
8:12	289

Isaiah

Reference	Page
book of	152, 248
1:9	49
1:17	92
2:2	11, 152
2:2–4	95
5:20	13, 293
6	52
6:1–7	51
6:3	39
7:14	70
8:1	214
11:2	22

11:9 . . . . . . 94, 166, 296, 302
11:11. 49
13:9–10 135
19. 280
19:1 136
28:5. 49
28:11. 108
28:12–14 108
30:10 50
34:4. 135
34:16 22
35:5 52
37:32 49
40:10–11. 84
40-55 84
41:14 84
42:1. 84
42:4. 84
42:6. 84
42:7. 52
43:11. 188
44:24–28 59
45:9. 157
49:8ff. 84
51:3 . . . . 12, 251
51:11–12 84
52:5 114
52:15. 113
53:4ff. 84
53:5–12 68
53:7 84
55:11. 103
58:1–8 281
60:3. 110
61:1 80
61:1–2 . . . . 80–81, 141
61:1–3 57
64:1. 64
65:17–25 . . . . 166, 296
66:1 32
66:3. 131
66:19ff. 49

JEREMIAH
1:6–7 50
1:11–12. 50
1:11–14. 52
2:9 156
2:35 157
4:11 136
4:23–24 136
4:28 136
5ff. 50
7:25 50
7:30 131
10:6 113
17:10. 282
23:3 49
23:16–18 51
23:18 14
24:7. 29
25:11–12 59
25:31. 157
30:1. 50
30:2. 214
31:7 49
31:33. . . . . .29, 294
31:33ff.. 261
31:34 xli
32:38 29
34:9 . . . . .58, 268
34:16 114
50:20 49
50–51 280

LAMENTATIONS
book of 55
3:41. 23

EZEKIEL
1 52
1:28 19
2:9–3:3 52
3:17 50
4:6 56
5:11 131
11:5 . . . . 22, 50

11:18	131
11:19–20	90
11:20	29
11:21	131
14:22	49
18:5–9	281
18:21–32	158
20:7–8	131
20:30	131
20:44	113
28:12–14	12
32:7–8	135
33:11	158
33:20	282
34	50, 249–250
36:25–27	90
36:33–36	12
37:1–14	141
37:9	141
37:9ff	22
37:23	29
37:26–27	77
37:27	29
39:25–29	59
44:23	13

DANIEL

56–58	
1–3	56
2	50
2:31–35	93
2:31–45	22, 56
2:35	152
2:44	93
4:34–37	56
6:1–2	56
6:28	56
7:13–14	56, 135
7:25	117, 133
8:26	142
9	51
9:24	142
9:24–26	80
9:24–27	56, 57
9:26-27	58
9:26–27	131
9:27	133
10:1	56
11:31	131
12:1	140
12:1ff.	133
12:2	281
12:7	117, 133
12:11	131
12:12	133

HOSEA

4-5	157
6:6	273
6:7	14
12:4	22

JOEL

2:1–2	136
2:28–32	106

AMOS

1	280
2:4–8	280
2:7	278
3:7	14, 51
7:1–3	51
8:9	135

OBADIAH

verse 15	282

MICAH

2:12	49
3:8	50
4:1	152
4:1–4	95
4:5	113
5:7	49
6	157
6:2	157
6:8	90

Nahum
1:2–3 136
2:13 50

Habakkuk
2:2 . . . . 50, 214
2:4 192
3:19 11

Zephaniah
1:14–15. 136

Haggai
2:6 64
2:7 109

Zechariah
4:6 . . . . vii, 50
7:9 . . . . 92, 285
7:9–10 90
7:10 92
8:8 29
8:17 92
12:10 135
14:16 109

Malachi
2:14 287
2:14–16 92
3:16 113

Matthew
book of 67, 248
1:1–17 67
1:18–24 72
1:18–25 69
2 69
2:11 71
2:16 71
2:19–23 71
3:1. 68
3:1–12 69
3:7 78
3:10–12 157
3:13–17 79
3:14–15 81
3:16 . . . . 81, 86
4:1–11 . . . . 67, 214
4:17 93
5 89
5:10 90
5:13 157
5:13–16 158
5:17–18 . . . . 78, 144
5:17–19 91
5:17–20 114
5:17–48 91
5:17ff. 157, 164
5:18 . . . . 42, 200, 283
5:19 291
5:20 291
5:21–48 91
5:23–26 92
5:29–30 . . . . 281, 288
5:33 92
5:38ff. 282
5:44 278
5:44–48 93
6 89
6:33 . . . . 83, 93
7 89
7:1–2 288
7:1–5 291
7:12–27 95
7:15 237
7:29 91
8:11–12 96
8:27 73
9:10–13 90
10 86
10:3 117
10:5–6 111
10:5–15 87
10:16–23 87
10:34ff. 260
11:7–15 68
11:9 79
11:9–14 51

11:21–24 96
13:10–17 153
13:24 281
13:31–32 94
13:33 94
13:37–40 281
13:52 165
13:55 . . . . 72, 117
15:1–6 159
15:3 214
15:4–6 278
15:24 111
16:21–23 67
18:15–18 . . . . 32, 281
19:17 39
19:26 187
19:28 213
21 82
21:34–41 97
21:42–44 108
21:43 97
22:2–10 96
22:14 . . . . 88, 141
22:15–22 300
22:30 175
22:32–33 214
22:34–40 274
22:36–40 . . . . 144, 290
23:1–12 97
23:13–36 97
23:16–36 275
23:23 . . . . 90, 289
23:28 291
23:32–36 87
23:33–36 90
23:35 144
23:37 . . . . 88, 141
23:37–39 97
23:38 141
24 . . . . 95, 118, 296
24:1–34 139
24:4–5 98
24:6–7 98
24:7 98
24:8 124
24:9 . . . . 98, 124
24:10–12 98
24:11 128
24:11–12 130
24:13 . . . . 98, 124
24:14 . . . . 98, 130
24:15 . . . . 131, 133
24:15–28 98
24:16–22 132
24:21 140
24:23 139
24:25 139
24:27 139
24:27–31 134
24:28 141
24:29–31 135
24:29–35 98
24:34 97
24:42–44 297
25:46 281
26:39 75
26:42 75
27:46 . . . . 67, 75
27:51 154
27:55 117
27:55–56 117
27:66 231
28:1–10 102
28:2 231
28:16ff. 102
28:18 . . . . 99, 172
28:18–20 . . . . . xli, 20, 111, 166,
                    279, 296, 307
28:19 . . . . xxvi, 65, 218
28:20 . . . . 172, 174, 283

MARK
book of 248
1:2 68
1:4 69
1:9 86
1:15 93
5:37 118

6:3	72	1:48	72
6:7–13	87	1:50	72
7:1–12	159	1:53	72
7:5–13	153	1:57–80	69
9:2	118	1:69	72
11	82	1:76	79
11:11–26	87	2:1	130
12:1–12	87	2:1–6	69
12:34	93	2:4	72
13	95, 118, 296	2:8–20	69
13:6	98	2:12	71
13:7	98	2:19	70
13:8	98	2:21–40	69
13:9	98	2:34	71
13:10	98, 130	2:40	72
13:11	98	2:41–52	69
13:12	98	2:51	72
13:13	98	3:1	68
13:14–23	98	3:1–9	69
13:24–31	98	3:1–20	69
13:30	97	3:21	85, 86
14:33	118	3:22	85
14:61–62	81, 139	3:23	81
15:38	154	3:23–38	67
15:40	117	4:5	130
15:47	117	4:14–21	81
16:1	117	4:16–21	57
		4:17–21	141
Luke		7:27–28	79
book of	67, 248	9:1–6	87
1:1–4	200	9:20	81
1:5	81	10	86
1:5–25	69	10:1–20	87
1:6	72	10:7	147
1:13	81	10:16	114, 160
1:17	79	11:9–13	93
1:26–38	69	11:21	234
1:27	72	11:51	144
1:28	79	15:7	158
1:38	72, 79	16:15	90
1:39–56	69	16:16	144
1:42	72, 79	16–17	69
1:45	72	16:17	291
1:47–49	79	16:29	213

17:21	93
18:7–8	125
18:9–14	90
19:10	187
21	95, 118, 296
21:8	98, 120
21:9–10	98
21:11	98
21:12–19	98
21:13ff.	130
21:16	98
21:20–26	98
21:22	97, 119, 157
21:22–23	78
21:24	110
21:25–33	98
21:26	130
21:32	97, 119
22:22	156
22:32	115
23:28–30	97
24:13–49	102
24:27	160
24:44	114, 144, 160
24:44–48	114
50–52	72

John

1	77
1:1–18	68, 76
1:6–7	68
1:11	141
1:12–13	191
1:17	42, 285
1:19	68
1:29	68, 83, 112, 282
1:30	68
1:32	86
1:34	68
1:45	144
2:1–11	153
2:12	72
2:13–22	153
2:19–22	77
2:21	139
3:3	93
3:3–6	153
3–4	250
3:5	93
3:5–8	88
3:10	154
3:16–17	112
3:17	65, 88
3:17–18	191
3:18–21	88
3:27	88
3:31–34	145
3:36	85, 88, 192
4:21–24	139
4:22	70, 160
4:24	39
4:25–26	81
5:21–30	88
5:24	191
5:39	230
5:39–47	214
6:37–39	88
6:39	106
6:44	88
6:65	88
8:16	88
8:31–40	41
9	153
9:39	88
10	153
10:11–14	250
10:32–38	214
11	153
11:24	106
12:24	94
12:31	88, 234
12:47	112
13:18	100
13:23	117
14:6	224
14:15	292
14:16	103, 104
14:17	104

14:18	138	21	102
14:19b	104	21:15–19	115
14:20	138	21:20	117
14:20–21	104	26:22–23	214
14:21	291, 292		
14:23	292	ACTS	
14:25–26	114	1:3–11	103
14:26	105	1-12	115
14:27	83, 260	1:12–14	103–104
15:10	292	1:13	117
15:14	292	2:4–11	105
15:16	105	2:16–17	107
15:26	105	2:17-21	106
16:7–15	103	2:29–41	130
16:12–14	105	2:36	81
16:13–15	114	2:38–39	114
16:16	138	2:42–46	108
16:22	138	2:43	105
16:33	83	3:1ff	118
17	99–100	3:12–26	108
17:1–3	99	3:14	39
17:1–5	151	3:21	69, 139, 152
17:4-5	99	4:7	118
17:6	113, 160	4:12	188
17:6-14	100	4:13	118
17:6–19	105, 114, 151	4:27–28	156
17:8	159–160	6:7	108
17:15-19	100	7:46	77
17:17	160	7:55–8:1	58
17:19	160	7:55–8:4	116
17:20	160, 165	8:9–11	120
17:20-26	100	8:14	118
17:20–26	151	9:1–22	116
17:24	88	9:4	124
18:1–11	214	9:15	58, 113
18:36	94	10:10–15	272
19:14–16	119	10:28	272
19:25	117	10:36	83
19:25–27	117	11:4–10	272
19:26	117	11:27–30	122
19:37	135	11:28	130
20:2	117	12:2	115
20:3–8	102	13:15	144
20:11-21:23	102	13–28	116

13:38–39 190	1:25 . . . . 227, 265
14:16–17 110	1:26–27 278
14:27 110	1:28 298
15 . . . . 116, 182	1:28–30 265
16:1ff. 108	1:32 . . . . 278, 298
17:1–14 214	2 262
17:6 130	2–4 192
17:11 . . . . 180, 230, 236	2:9–10 130
17:24–28 20	2:12–24 119
17:26 110	2:14–15 . . . . . 226, 227, 261
17:28 143	2:14–16 280
17:30 110	2:15 . . . . 261, 293
17:31 130	2:16 282
18:12–16 126	2:17 255
18:18 108	2:23 255
19:27 130	2:27 255
20:7 138	3:1–2 . . . . 144, 207
20:28 66	3:4–6 157
20:28–30 128	3:5 157
20:29 237	3:21 144
21:15–26 108	3:22–28 190
21:21 130	3:27–30 119
22:3 116	4:3 24
23:12–35 126	4:11 26
24:5 130	4:11–12 23
24:16 . . . . 293, 294	4:16 23
24:27 117	4:20–25 192
25 126	5:1 83
25:1–12 283–284	5:12–21 258
28:23 . . . . 117, 144	5:14 26
28:30 117	5:19 255
	6:4 194
Romans	6:14–15 255
1–3 271	6:15 255
1:4 81	6:23 14
1:8 130	7:6 255
1:15 130	7:12 39
1:17 192	7:14 39
1:18 . . . . 85, 119, 298	7:24 194
1:18–3:20 261	8:2 255
1:19–20 . . . . 226, 265	8:4 . . . . 43, 93, 291
1:20–21 298	8:11 101
1:21 . . . . 227, 265	8:17 198
1:22 227	8:18–22 41

8:18ff.	18, 112
8:26	104
8:31–39	197
8:33	194
8:38–39	194
9:1	293
9:4	10, 144, 207
9:4–5	160
9:7	41
9:20	157
9:30	255
10:3	255
10:4	255
10:6	255
10:18	130
11:17–24	155
11:33–34	154
12	196
12:1	14, 246, 273
12:1–2	267
12:19	157
12:19–20	278
13	271, 279
13:1–6	278, 283
13:1–7	126, 281
13:4	278
13:5	293
13:8–10	196
14:17	93
15:11–13	166
15:20	113
15:26	122

1 Corinthians

1:4–6	145
2:7	154
2:12	237
2:13	145
3:16–17	139
5:1	278
5:9–13	281
6:9–10	278
6:19	139
8:7	293

8:10	293
8:12	293
9:5	304
11:2	159
11:31	295
12:3	247
13:3	291
13:8	291
14:21	108
14:37	146
15:6	102
15:17	101
15:22	258
15:25	296
15:33	143
15:54	101
16:1	122
16:2	138

2 Corinthians

1:12	293, 294
3:6	255
3:14	252–253
3:14–16	154
3:14–17	153
4:4	234
4:7	198
4:10	124
5:10	198
5:17	xlvii, 76, 151
5:19	112
5:21	192, 282
6:2	137
6:14	273
6:14–7:1	273
6:16	29
7:1	292
8:20	122
10:3–5	112
10:4–5	266
10:5	224

Galatians

1:13–14	159

1:15–17	116
2:9	118
2:19	255
2:21	255
3:6	24
3:7	23
3:10–13	282
3:11	192
3:13	74, 85, 255, 282
3:17–29	252–253
3:27	16
3:29	41
4:4	81
4:26	114, 152, 164
5:22	291
6:9	xlvii

Ephesians

1:9–1	64
1:20–21	94
1:21–22	112
2:8	187, 193
2:11–20	272
2:12	10, 141
2:14	20, 83
2:20–22	105, 139
2:21	141
4:1–6	302
4:11	208
4:14	128
4:17–31	196
5:6	85
5:15-6:18	196
5:16	297
5:25–32	287
6:10	300
6:10–18	119
6:10ff.	302
6:11–12	299
6:12	299
6:12ff.	xxxviii
6:14–18	299
6:17	235

Philippians

1:9	215
1:23–24	138
2:7	101
2:7–8	66
2:12–13	218, 256, 267
2:12–18	196
2:13	195
3	198
3:7–9	255
3:8–14	93
3:10	198
3:20	114

Colossians

1:6	130
1:23	130
1:24	124
1:25–28	165
2:2–3	165
2:3	224
2:8	159
2:14	282
3:1–5	101
4:5	297
4:16	146

1 Thessalonians

4:2	145
5:8	119
5:27	146

2 Thessalonians

1:6–10	281
2:4	108
2:9	132
2:15	159
3:6	159
3:14	146

1 Timothy

1:3	128
1:5–11	281
1:10	128

1:15 187
1:18–19 298
1:19 293
3:2 304
3:4–5 304
3:9 294
3:15 . . . . 158, 249
3:15–4:16 154
4:1 128
4:1–2 128
4:1–3 106
4:6 128
5:18 147
6:3 128
6:12 298
6:14–16 103

2 Timothy
3:1–5 129
3:1–9 107
3:14–4:5 154
3:16 199
4:6 138
4:8 138

Titus
1:1 193
1:12 143
1:15 293
3:5–7 187
3:10–11 281

Hebrews
book of 146
1:2 107
1:5 300
1–10 272
1:13 296
2:2 283
2:4 105
3:7–8 137
4:7 137
4:12–13 158
4:15 67
4:16 192
5:4 81
5:4–10 81
5:5 300
5:5–6 83
5:6 84
5:7 67
5:8 67
5:9 95
5:10 83
6:20 83
7:3–4 83
7:11 84
7:17 83
7:24 84
7:26 84
8 262
8:5 26
8:6 xli
8:10 . . . . 29, 261, 294
8:11 xli
8:13 272
9:11 xli
9:11–15 282
9:15–17 253
9:22 . . . . 16, 274
9:23–24 273
9:27 280
10 262
10:3–18 282
10:5–7 75
10:5–10 16
10:16 . . . . 261, 294
10:22 293
10:30 157
10:30–31 87
10:32–34 127
10:38 192
11:4 xlviii
11:8–10 268
11:8–12 42
11:10 . . . . xlvii, 24
11:12 24
11:19 23

12:22	114
12:22–24	138, 139, 152–153
12:26	64
13:9	130
13:10–12	282

JAMES
book of	146
1:17	5
2:10	144
2:14–19	196
2:14–26	195, 196
2:19	196, 197
2:20	197
2:20–23	42
2:23	23, 24, 196
5:3	107

1 PETER
book of	303
1:1–9	303
1:3	101
1:12	145
1:15–17	303
1:17	282
1:18–20	282
1:21	101
1:22–2:10	303
2:6–8	108
2:12–16	303
3:8–17	303
3:15–16	266
3:20–21	18
4:10–19	303
4:12–13	127
4:17	127
5:6–11	303
5:8–9	119
5:13	116

2 PETER
book of	146
1:13–14	77
1:19	244
1:21	199
3:15–16	147

1 JOHN
1:8–2:3	295
2:2	112
2:3–11	292
2:8	251
2:18	107
2:18–19	120, 129
2:22–23	120
2:26	120
3	298
3:20	293
4:6	120
5:1–5	298
5:4	67
5:6	145
9–13	145

2 JOHN
book of	146
7–10	129
7–11	120

3 JOHN
book of	146

JUDE
book of	146, 157
3	168
3–5	129
17–19	106, 129

REVELATION
book of	146, 147
1:3	146
1:4	118
1:7	135
1:9	117, 133
1:10	138
1:10–11	214
1:16	158
2:4–5	156

2:6	221	12:14	117, 133
2:12	158	12:17	124
2:15	221	13	126, 278, 279
2:20–25	133	13:8	40, 47, 83
3:3	156	13:10	124–125
3:10	130	13:11-17	305
3:14	78	13:16–17	278
3:19	156	14:1	153
4:3	19	14:12–20	132
4:8	39	15:3–4	83
5:8	138	15:4	110, 112
6:1	231	16:14	130
6:3	231	17:5–6	127–128
6:5	231	19:10	145, 237
6:7	231	20:12	282
6:9	231	21	153
6:9–11	125	21:2	114, 164
6:12	231	21:3	77
7:11–12	78	21:5	76, 152
7:13–17	133	21:7	29
7:15	77	21:10–14	114
8:1	231	21:24	110, 112
8:3–4	138	22:10	142
10:1	19	22:14	120
11:3–13	132	22:17	138
11:15	94	22:18–19	164
12	9	22:18-21	147
12:5	112	22:20	138
12:9	130		

General Index

A

Aaron, 28, 32–33, 80, 82–83
Abel, 17, 144, 153
Abelard, 177, 202
abortion, 304
Abraham
    and Covenant of Grace
        God's promise to, 29, 34–36, 38, 41–42
        Gospel and Law under, 260
        historical marker of, 11, 14, 22–27, 52, 252–253, 260
        renewal of, 41–42
        revelation of, 4, 11, 46, 47
    faith of, 23–24, 83
    father of remnant, 68–69, 192, 268
    as prophet, 22–23, 46, 51
    relation to Christ
        Christ as seed of, 178
        genealogy of, 21–23, 41–42, 178, 268
        and Melchizedek, 83
Acts, Book of
    Apostles in, 115–119
    First Church described, 108
    martyrdom in, 124
    prophecy in, 104–107, 105, 107, 121–122
Adam
    covenantal head of human race, 258
    and Covenant of Grace
        administration of, 63, 104
        Gospel and Law under, 40–41, 46, 260
        historical marker of, 4–18, 29, 40–41, 46, 63, 69, 104, 252, 260, 267, 269, 310
        renewal of, 26
        revealed to, 4
    fall of man in, 14–15, 26, 67, 259, 273–274, 297 (*see also* Original Sin)
    father of man, 18, 21
    genealogy of, 16–18, 21
    relation to Christ
        Christ as new Adam, 19, 69, 73–74
        head of human race *vs.* Head of His people, 258
        Original Sin *vs.* Christ's perfection, 67, 74
Adamic time, 69
Advent, 134, 137, 140

Agabus, 121
Agag, 36
Age of Faith, 216–218, 242, 244. *see also* Middle Ages
Agrippina, 126
Alexander, 129
Alexandrian canon, 142–143
Althusius, Johannes, 220
Amalekites, 36
Ambrose of Milan, 169
Ammonites, 131
Amos, 51, 53, 135, 242
anarchy, 35
Angel of the Lord, 22, 27, 42, 50. *See also* God, names of
angels
    Christ described as, 19
    Gabriel, 56, 79
    Gathering of the elect, 141
    part of the Council of God, 50–51
    visits by, 71, 78, 134, 269
    worship of, 183
Anna, 70
Annals, The, 122
Annunciation, 79
Anoint, 35–36, 58, 78–86, 156
Anointed One, 79, 81, 84
Anselm, 176–177, 203
antichrists, 120, 129
antinomians, 196
Antioch, 115, 121
Apocalypse, 12, 118, 296–297
apokatastasis, 69, 139, 152
a posteriori, 161
apostles
    and Christ, 99–100, 103, 153–156, 213–214
    executions of, 125
    as foundation of the Church, 105–108, 114
    John, 117–118
    Paul, 116–117
    Peter, 115–116
    teaching of, 4, 113, 124, 128, 165, 180

The Tradition of the Apostles (*see* Tradition of the Apostles)
apostolic church, 100, 105, 108–109, 119–120, 125, 128
apostolic times
    Christ brings the Church from, 138
    Church's practices during, 151–152
    closing of Biblical canon, 142, 146
    definition of, 64
    as first times, 124
    as last times, 106–107
    spiritual war during, 119
    spread of the Gospel, 130
apostolic writings, 124, 153, 160
Aqiba, 55
Aquinas, Thomas, 177, 224–228
Ararat, 16–19, 64, 152
Arianism, 163, 169, 256
Aristotle, 222, 224, 226
Arius, 163, 169, 181
Ark of the Covenant, 32, 33, 36–37
Asia Minor, 115–117, 122
Athanasius, 143, 146, 163, 169, 181, 218–219, 301
Augustine
    On Christian Doctrine, 176
    the City of God, 175, 176
    Confessions, 175
    De Vera Religione, 262
    followers of, 203, 206–207
    and history of scholasticism, 224, 248
    on human thinking, 224
    influence of, 175–177
    progression from paganism, 175–176
    retractions, 175
    on theology, 176, 189, 224–225, 262
Augustus, Caesar, 117, 121, 130
autonomy, 5, 187–189. *see also* autonomy *vs.* theonomy
autonomy *vs.* theonomy
    autonomy of God, 155
    and God's sovereignty, 155
    human liberty, 155
    human *vs.* God, 5–6, 14–15

liberté-responsabilité, definition, 5, 6
man and God's Law, 14, 21–22, 29–30, 32, 39, 44–45, 66, 155–156
and Sadducees, 91
and society, 44
and the state, 44
theonomy, definition, 5
true liberty, 28–29
Awakening, The, 244

B

Babel, 20, 22, 137, 248, 260
Babel, Tower of. *see* Tower of Babel
Babylon, 56, 58–59, 63, 109, 135
Bacon, Roger, 263
Bahnsen, Greg L., 259, 270
baptism, 16
    baptismal formula, 65, 113, 167
    of Christ, 67, 78–86, 93, 104, 310
    of the nations, 113, 218
    part of revelation of god, 113
    symbols of, 274
bar-mitzvah, 71
Barnabus, 116, 167
Baruch, 140, 143
Benedictus, Domine Deus, 70
Benjamin, 116
Berea, 180
berîth, *berîthî*, 9, 19, 25
Bernard, Saint, 55, 176–177, 189
Bethlehem, 69, 71
Bethsaida, 96
Bible
    as Book of the Covenant, 33, 46–48, 63, 161–165, 251, 254
    books of traditions of the apostles, 162 (*see also* Tradition of the Apostles)
    Christ speaks about, 42, 91
    the Church's history and, 153, 161, 171, 173, 179–183, 228
    commandments of Christ, 89, 113–114, 159
    division of, 54–55
    dogma and, 174
    faithfulness to, 64
    Hebraic, 153, 160–161
    Holy Scripture, 162, 164–165
    humanism *vs.*, 224, 235–236, 275–278, 288, 296–299
    inspired by Holy Spirit, 63–64, 108, 114, 301
    as Law, 137, 144–146, 198, 259–260
    Logos, 14
    made flesh, 76–77, 86, 198
    modern, 246
    oneness of Scripture, 12
    and philosophy, 224, 230
    role in Reformation, 228
    sealing of, 138, 142, 153
    spread and teaching of, 54, 127–130, 219, 267, 273, 302–304
    Torah of Moses, 34, 35
    and The Tradition, 159, 162
    as treasure of treasures, 20
    as truth, 222
    without error, 240
    as Word of God, 199–215, 239–241, 245–249
    worship according to, 14, 32–34
Biblical canon, 142–144
Biblical criticism, 244, 246, 247
Biblical scholarship, 248–249
blessings, 54
Boethius, 222–223
Bonaventure, 176, 203
Book of the Covenant, 43, 45, 46, 48, 153. *see also* Bible; Covenant of Grace
Brittanicus, 126
burning bush, 27
Burrus, 126

C

Caesar, 117, 121–122, 127, 130, 218
Caesarea, 117, 126, 283
Cain, 17–18, 21
Cainites, 21
Caligula, 121
Calvin, John
    expert in patrology, 183
    Institutes of the Christian Religion, 179, 194
    on theology, 175, 242, 258, 263
Canaan, 23, 269
Canaanites, 68, 111, 269–270
Canaanite woman, 111
canonical list, 142
Capernaum, 96
Caroligian Church, 184
catechizing, 267
catholic (unified) church
    break from, 245
    call to faithfulness, 180
    call to repentance, 175
    continuation of, 174
    creeds speak of, 162–163
    importance of Fathers and Doctors pre-Reformation, 183
    meaning of, 163–164
    people of the covenant, 162
    refusal of heresy, 164, 168
    tasks of, 164–165, 168, 175, 182, 241, 260
    truth of unity in Christ, 125
Catholic Church, 164, 182–183, 201. *see also* Roman Church
central commandment, 43–44
Ceremonial Law, 30, 44–45, 108, 271–272. *see also* Law
Cestius, 123
Chaldeans, 23, 268
Chemnitz, Martin, 183–184
Christ. *see* Jesus Christ
Christian era, 69, 99
Christian liberty, 172. *see also* autonomy

Christological dogma, 186–187, 209, 211–212
Christological mystery, 167–168, 172
Chrysostom, John, 65–66
Church
    apostolic to post-apostolic, 138
    corruption of, 152, 154, 235, 259–260
    critique of paganism, 222
    defense of, 241
    faithful reformation of, 221
    growth of, 105, 119, 121, 221–222
    and humanism, 220, 244, 259, 260
    makeup of, 109
    as New Israel, 115, 160
    as New Jerusalem, 152
    role of, 110–111, 114, 125, 137, 154, 158, 161–162, 259
Cilicia, 115–116
circumcision, 24–26, 28, 41, 44, 69, 108, 274
Circus Maximus, 126
civil liberty, 218
Claudius Caesar, 121–122
Clement of Rome, 127, 167
clericalism, 44, 279
Colossae, 130, 159
common grace, 261
communion, 7, 13, 15, 23, 33
confessions
    Augsburg Confession, 174, 190
    of the Faith in ecclesial epochs, 166
    Gallican Confession, 178–179
    Peter's confession, 81
    Westminster Confession of Faith, xlv, 190, 204–206, 210, 271, 275
Constantine the Great, 126, 216
Corinth, 122, 126–127, 159, 175
Cornelius, 115
councils
    Council of Chalcedon, 65, 65, 170–171, 174, 179
    Council of Constance, 186
    Council of Constantinople, 169–170, 179

Council of Constantinople II, 171, 184
Council of Constantinople III, 171, 186
Council of Ephesus, 170, 179
Council of Ephesus II, 172–173
Council of Nicea, 167, 169, 179
Council of Nicea II, 179–180
Council of Trent, 142, 144
Council of Tyre, 181
development of trinitarian and christological dogmas, 186
epoch of, 166
heretical councils, 142, 144, 181
Roman councils, 184
councils of God, 50–51
Covenant of Grace
   administration of, 63, 104, 254
      new covenant, 73, 82
      new era, 124, 151–152
      old and new covenants, 267–268
      old covenant (see old covenant)
   banishment of, 117
   beginning of, 3, 4–8, 10, 104, 162
   and Christ, 66, 68, 87, 138, 191
   confirmation of, 17–18, 57, 58
   conflict between redeemed and rebellious, 9, 17, 21
   continuity of, 70, 115
   corporate responsibility, 14
   covenant of Gospel and Law, 156
   given in Old and New testaments, 160
   and God
      adoption by, 25
      His affirmation, 29
      His call to men, 181
      His commandment, 29
      His faithfulness in, 4
      His faithfulness to, 78
      His judgment, 15, 156
      His Lordship under, 155
      His plan in, 3
      His promise, 29
      His treaty, 260
   historical development of, 13–19, 29–31, 34, 37–38, 41, 46–48, 54–55, 58, 63, 66, 68–69, 110
   inviolability of, 175
   Jews as sons of the covenant, 29, 108
   Law under, 251–252, 254, 256, 264
   modified and deepened, 3, 10
   and the nations, 109
   progress directed by followers, 95
   prophecy about, 88, 131, 156
   questions of, 86
   renewed and confirmed
      with Abraham, 24, 27
      with Adam, 8–9
      with Christ, 73
      with Isaac, 27
      with Israel, 29–30, 31
      with Jacob, 27
      with Noah, 9–10, 17–19
   stages of
      Abrahamic, 252, 253, 260, 268
      Adamic, 252, 260, 269
      Davidic, 252
      Edenic, 14, 15
      Jesus Christ, 252, 260
      Moses, 252, 253, 260, 268
      Noah, 252, 260, 269
   terms and conditions of, 155–157
covenant theology, 258
creation, 41, 42, 76, 220
creeds
   Apostles', 162, 167
   Athanasian, 163
   Nicea-Constantinople, 162
   Nicene, 65, 169
Crete, 122
cross, 74, 75, 80, 219
crucifixion, 9, 58, 75, 81, 117–119
Cultural (Dominion) Mandate
   as command of God, 40, 111, 269
   continuity of, 17–18, 20, 41
   definition of, 6
   establishment of, 6, 13
   men addressed by, 269
   men as king, 13
   Noah, 17–18, 41

curse, 40, 54
Cyril of Jerusalem, 143, 178
Cyrus, 56–58, 57, 58

D

d'Ailly, Pierre, 185
Damascus, 116, 188, 255
Daniel, 56–58, 93, 110, 131–133, 142–143, 152
Darius, 110
daughters of men, 17, 21
David
    author of wisdom literature, 54
    consecration of, 36
    and Covenant of Grace, 4, 11, 24, 34, 35, 36–38
    genealogy of, 53, 67, 72, 178
Day of Atonement, 57, 80
Day of Pentecost, 87, 104–105, 107, 138, 200
deacons, 119
death, 7, 40, 66, 138
Decalogue. *see* Ten Commandments
decapolis, 133
de Clamanges, Nicolas, 185
deï, 74, 84, 176
deity of Christ, 9, 10, 16
Demas, 129
demons, 71, 91, 128, 196
Devil. *see* Satan
diaspora of Israel, 59, 108, 119, 140
disciples, 86–87, 95, 110, 111–113
Doctors of the Law, 59
dogma, 161, 174, 187–188, 247–248, 256–257
dogmatic canon, 144–145
Dominion Mandate. *see* Cultural Mandate
Domitian, 121
Dooyeweerd, Herman, xxvi, 226, 229
Dostoyevsky, Fyodor, 259

E

Easter, 101–102, 104
Eastern Orthodox Church, 172–173, 188
Eastern religions, 220, 221
Eber, 21
Ecclesiasticus, 143
Ecclesial time, 151, 162, 164, 165–167
Ecclesiasticism, 44, 47–48, 168
Ecumenical Councils, 161. *see also* Councils
Eden, 12, 18, 64, 67
Edenic covenant, 14, 20
Edict of Milan, 126
Edomites, 131, 268
education, 44, 73, 221, 279–280, 301
Egypt, 27–29, 31, 47, 71, 110, 136
elders, 31, 90–91, 115, 119, 159–160
Eleazar, 132
elect, 73, 85
Elijah, 50, 68, 181
Elizabeth, 69, 70, 72, 79
Elohîm, 22. *see also* God
éméth, 78
Enlightenment, 235–238, 295, 299
Enoch, 21, 137
ensigns, 142
Ephesus, 118, 128, 156, 175
Ephron, 24
epiphane, 103
Epiphanius, 180
epiphany, 86, 118
epistles, 83, 105, 129, 147
Erasmus, 188–189, 208, 228–230, 234, 239
Esau, 268
Esther, 55, 143
Euphrates, 59
Eve, 5–9, 7, 14–16, 18, 21, 40
Exile of the Jews, 53, 58–59, 63, 95, 109
Exodus, 29
Ezekiel, 19, 49, 52–53, 59, 135, 141
Ezra, 59, 270

F

faith
    and God's grace, 16, 26, 152, 193
    of God's people, 72, 102, 125, 138, 146
    in the Great Commission, 113
    of Israel, 109
    and justification, 193
    of King Saul, 36
    of man, 6, 8, 17–19, 21, 40, 42, 45–49, 52
    and obedience, 4
false gods. *see* idolatry
false prophets, 51, 128, 130, 237
family, 14, 40, 44. *see also* marriage
family-church, 22, 29, 32, 210
feasts, 96, 108–109
Festus, 126, 283
Field of Mars, 126
final judgment, 69, 106, 282
first Gospel, 137
flood, 9–10, 17–21, 41, 210

G

Gabriel, 56, 79
Galatia, 159, 175
Galilee, 71, 89, 115
Garden of Eden, 4, 11–12, 14–15, 137
Gentiles, 115–116, 139, 156, 165, 260
Gethsemane, 67, 75, 118
Gloria, 71
gnostics, 221
God
    Author of life, 7, 15, 43, 76, 112, 113, 158, 218
    Author of Scripture, 14–15, 33, 86, 164, 200
    commandments of, 3, 8, 36, 79
    continuity of His plan, 3, 4, 8–10
    Council of, 50
    counsel of, 14, 205
    establisher of Covenant of Grace, 5, 17, 87
    ever-coming One, 137, 138
    fear of, 72
    friendship with man, 23, 31
    glory of, 8, 12, 19–20, 30, 34, 193
    grace of, 4–8, 9, 15–16, 72
    grieved by rebellion, 17, 21
    immanence of, 4–5, 39, 52, 167, 173, 258
    inscribes grace on man's heart, 227
    interpreter of all things, 236
    as Judge, 134, 137, 153, 154
    judgment of, 9–10, 15–18, 21–22, 25, 27–28, 30, 34–35, 280–281, 283
    as King, 34, 68, 109
    as Law-Giver, 39, 42–43
    Living God, 64
    Lordship of, 5–6, 28–29, 35, 36
    love of, 9, 33, 64
    names of
        Adonaï, 27, 82
        Angel of the Lord, 22, 27, 42, 50
        El Chaddaï, 25
        Elohîm, 22
        Emanu-El, 70
        Father, 22–23, 22–23, 42, 50, 65–66
        Giver of the Law, 66
        God of Abraham, Isaac and Jacob, 27
        Holy God, 45
        Holy One, 74
        Husband, 164
        I Am, 27
        Iêsous, 70
        YHWH, 27
        King, 68
        Law unto Himself, 66
        Lord, 28, 30–31, 45, 46, 56, 59
        Master, 28
        as one-and-many, 21–22, 23
        the Trinity, 21–22, 23
        Word, 65, 76, 86, 191

Yehoshuah, 70
YHWH, 82
nature of, 49, 52, 119, 131
as One-and-Many
  Abraham meeting with, 51
  comparison to His Law, 42
  Father, 76, 79, 94, 99, 111, 139, 151, 163, 217
  Holy Spirit (*see* Holy Spirit)
  interpreter of all things, 236
  at Jesus' baptism, 85–86
  Jesus Christ, 79, 102–103, 111, 167, 187
  Lord
    accepts the just, 192
    announces judgment, 137, 141
    of the Church, 154, 166
    of the Covenant, 87, 109, 154, 157
    day of, 134–137
    of hosts, 109
    one and only, 256
    return in clouds, 135–136
    of Scripture, 145, 154, 164
  Mediator, 66
  Messiah-King, 119
  names Self, 21–22, 154
  Reconciler, 112
  revealed as Trinity, 64, 79
  revealed in His Word, 167
  Savior, 43, 113–115, 158, 166, 187–188, 189, 218, 256
  Son, 65–66, 79, 101, 108, 137, 187, 217
  Sovereign One, 79, 85, 113
  Spirit of God, 22, 39, 41–42, 44, 50–51, 65–66
  trinitarian mystery, 104, 165, 167, 169–170
  as Trinity, 79, 85–86, 101, 111, 139, 158, 165, 217, 241, 256
  truly God and truly man, 163
  Voice from heaven, 85
presence of, 32
promises of, 17–18, 19, 24–25, 27, 28, 30, 34, 35
sovereignty of
  Augustine on, 176, 189
  and authorship of Scripture, 3
  and Covenant of Grace, 5–8
  dependence of all on, 113
  Erasmus on, 230
  God's authority, 44, 48
  God's Law and, 5, 276, 279
  as Lord-Savior, 113
  man's responsibility and, 155–156, 172
  and prophets, 50
  in salvation, 3
  standard of sanctification, 198
  transcendence of, 4–5, 10, 39, 52, 200
  worship of, 14, 23, 28, 31–32, 35
Golden calf, 31
Gomorrah, 51
Gospel and Law. *see also* Gospel; Law
  and Covenant of Grace, 4, 15, 34, 46–47, 66
  as God's blessing, 40
  inseparable nature of, 6, 40, 46
  Law brought by Moses, 26, 42
  personal morals and, 42
  proclaimed in Jewish Wars, 132
  and the prophets, 49
  requirements of, 46
  in Roman Empire, 130
  sealed in Christ's blood, 66
  social morals and, 42
Gospels
  angels of the Gospel, 67
  attest to the one Gospel, 78
  Incarnation in, 67, 68
  and the individual, 111
  John, 67–68, 76, 78, 88–90
  Luke, 67, 69–70, 78, 85
  Mark, 68, 78, 82
  Matthew, 67, 69–70, 78, 82
  prophecy in, 105
  in relation to Jewish Bible, 108

government, 277, 279, 281
goyîm, 20
grace
    draws man to God, 152
    fulfillment of Law, 90
    Gospel of, 40
    of Jesus, 73, 76–77
    justifies sinner, 93
    Law as product of, 46
    necessity of, 93
    only means of justification, 40
    only source of salvation, 90
    and salvation of the nations, 113
    in the Torah, 78
    working on man, 218, 227
Great Commission, 4, 110–112, 114
Greece, 56, 117, 122, 126
Greek Empire
    arts, 126
    Bible, 21, 74, 205–206, 208
    philosophy, 176, 220–225, 288
    prophecy about, 56

H

Habakkuk, 53, 214
ha-Cohen, Joseph ben Mallathias, 123
Hades, 96
Hagar, 24
Haggai, 109
Halakhah, 91
Ham, 20
Hasmonean kings, 90
heavenly army, 50
Hebraic Bible, 131, 159. *see also* Bible
Hebrew canon, 143–144
Hebrews, 21, 26, 127, 130
Hebron, 23, 36
Henry, John, Cardinal Newman, 181
heresy
    Ambrose, 178
    ancient, 64
    Apollinarius, 169–170
    Arius, 169
    Athanasius, 178
    Cyril, 178
    denial of Christ as God, 169, 170
    denial of Christ as man, 169–170
    Eutychius, 170
    Hilary, 178
    and human works, 189
    modern, 64
    Nestorius, 170
Hermas, 167
Herod Agrippa I, 115, 156
Herod the Great, 71–72, 90, 95
heséd, 78, 273, 286
Hezekiah, 53
Hezron, 24
High Priest, 80
High Priestly Prayer, 99–100, 151
Hilary, 169, 178
Hillel the Elder, 89, 92
hiphil, 9
historical-critical method, 237, 238
Holy City, 123, 127–128, 131
Holy of Holies, 32–33, 58, 131
Holy Scripture. *see* Bible
Holy Spirit
    actions of, 104
    and the apostles, 103, 105
    authority of Scripture, 54, 86, 103, 114, 145, 199–200
    coming of, 87, 102, 110, 138
    coming upon Jesus, 79–81, 85
    and Council of God, 50–52
    in ecclesial tradition, 165
    gifts of, 104, 105
    literal meaning of old covenant, 153
    Lordship of God, 154
    miracles of, 105
    necessity of, 93
    and new Covenant of Grace, 104
    paraclete, 103
    person in the One God, 22
    predictions of, 106
    revelations to Peter, 115

salvation and, 104, 205, 234
spirit of Christ, 105
spirit of Truth, 103, 145
unity with Father and Son, 103–106, 166–167
and visions, 115
Horeb, 27
Hosea, 53
House of God, 13, 32, 125, 127
humanism
and autonomy, 236, 278
and the church, 219–220, 238–239, 259, 277
definition of, 264
desecration of Scripture, 245–246
faith in man, 264
and God's Law, 275
historical-critical method, 238
influence on scholasticism, 223
lost man, 259
media, 277
natural revelation, 264–265
neutralization of, 238–239
pietists, 276–277
return to paganism, 279
temptation of the church, 235
human sacrifice, 217
hupomone, hupomeno, 124, 127–128, 302
Huss, John, 186
Hyrcanus, John, 89

I

icons and relics, 172–173, 179, 184
idolatry, 31, 35, 131, 180, 217, 219
Idumeans, 131–132
Ignatius of Antioch, 167
incarnation, 74, 75
inspiration, 199–202, 241n39, 243–245, 249, 262n14
Irenaeus, 167, 201
Isaac
as climactic sacrifice, 23
and Covenant of Grace, 27, 47
genealogy of, 24, 268
justification and, 196
relation to Christ, 23, 96
set apart from Ishmael, 268
writings about, 22–24
Isaiah
announcement of Christ, 70
in Council of the Lord, 51
Jubilee of Christ's coming, 57, 68, 135
as prophet, 53, 58–59, 107, 113
on the remnant, 49
Ishmael, 24–25, 268
Islam, 64, 263, 302
Israel
apostasy of, 31, 34–35, 48, 96, 141
blessings of Jesus on, 89
called to repentance, 68, 86, 111, 119
and the church, 105, 109, 138, 144, 164
Covenant of Grace and, 58, 109, 268
days of vengeance, 97
descended from Jacob, 27, 268
destruction of, 53, 140
faithful remnant of, 70
and God's Law, 45
history of, 22, 123, 237, 268
Holy nation, 28–29, 268
house of, 111
as inheritance, 29
judgment of, 68, 87, 107, 125, 138, 139, 154
kingdom of priests, 29
leaders of, 97
missionary priority in, 87
as object of God's affection, 33–34, 46
poor of, 89
purposes of, 109
rebirth of, 58
rejection of Christ in, 154
relationship to the nations, 109, 115
restoration of, 58, 63
shepherds from, 71
shocked by end times, 140

spiritual war in, 119
Torah given to, 54–55, 145
worship of, 32
Israelites
    distinction from Gentiles, 115
    idolatry and, 131
    Law for, 109
    restoration of Israel and, 58
Italian Cohort, 115

J

Jacob, 22, 27, 32, 59, 96, 268
Jacob's well, 81, 139
Jairus, 118
James
    beheading of, 115
    brother of Jesus and Jude, 72, 115, 129
    brother of John, 117
    cousin of Jesus, 117
    Jerusalem Council, 115
    on justification of the just, 195–197
    as leader of Church, 115
    speaks about last days, 107
    witness to Lord's transfiguration, 118
Japhet, 20
Jebusites, 36
Jeremiah, 48, 49–50, 53, 59, 143, 156
Jerome, 143, 207–208, 252
Jerusalem
    built on Moriah, 23
    and Christ
        and the apostles, 114–115
        His entrance into, 82, 136
        His revelation to, 102
        prophecy about, 88
        taken to, 71
        weeps for, 88, 97
    Christians in, 70, 105, 108, 115–118, 122, 125–126, 152
    city of David, 36
    City of God, 248
    destruction of, 4, 58, 97, 123, 131–132, 139–140
    destruction of Temple in, 117, 151
    fighting Babylon, 248
    God with Israelites to, 33–34
    heavenly Jerusalem, 102, 114, 139, 260
    judgment of, 53, 107, 130
    location of Temple, 64, 69
    Matthew's warning to, 133
    opposition to, 109
    part of Babylon the Great, 127–128
    Paul arrested in, 117
    and Queen of Sheba, 110
    rebuilding of, 56, 58–59
    refers to book of Daniel, 133
    site of first church, 105
    Upper Room, 103
Jerusalem Council, 108, 108, 115
Jesus Christ
    arrest and crucifixion of, 57–58, 66–67, 73, 94, 119
    ascension of
        Christ receives authority, 99, 113, 300
        Daniel's prophecy of, 56
        omnipresence of Christ, 104
        as symbolism of heaven, 102–103
        as victory over evil, 94, 125
    authority of, 81, 83, 91, 93, 111, 139
    baptism of, 79–81, 84–87, 89
    blessing of, 38
    and the Church, 32
    circumcision of, 69
    coming of, 57, 134
    comprehensive lordship of, 4
    consecration of, 93
    conversion of Paul, 116
    and Covenant of Grace, 10–11, 16, 24–25, 58, 153
    cutting off of, 57–58, 73
    death of, 67, 74–75, 153–154
    denial of His divinity, 240

faith of, 78
fear of God, 73
followers martyred, 119
fulfillment of prophecy, 57, 84
genealogy of, 67–68, 253
glorification of, 102
Gospel of, 9, 15–16, 19, 24–25, 26, 108, 198
grace of, 73
and the Great Commission, 110–111
incarnation of
    birthdate, 71
    conception of, 69, 79, 240
    mystery of, 64–66
    virgin birth, 72, 79
judge of Israel, 99, 118, 125
as King, 71, 83, 94, 103
and the Law
    deepens the Law, 289
    embodiment of the Law, 44
    fulfillment of the Law, 73, 78, 91
    identifies order in, 290
    obedience of, 73, 83
    relationship with the Torah, 76
    satisfied divine Law, 191
    submission to the Law, 101
life of
    documentation of, 69
    early life, 71–72
    earthly life, 64, 151
    education of, 72–73
    humanity of, 68, 240
linked with Moses, 77
as Lord
    calling to God, 218
    coming of, 84
    in Council of Chalcedon confession, 65–66
    and Founder of the Covenant, 87
    of lords, 103
    reign in history, 118
    to wise men, scholars and sages, 71
Lord's Supper, 125
love for man as God, 67
man justified in, 256
and man's prayer for salvation, 187
moral pain of, 75
mysteries of, 102, 168, 191
names of (*see also* God, names of)
    Anointed One, 79, 84
    Anointed Priest, 85
    Anointed Sacrifice, 85
    Beloved of God, 85
    Bridegroom, 77
    Chosen One, 84
    Creator, 226
    Emanu-El, 70
    God-Made-Man, 24, 65–66, 70, 75, 77, 113, 125
    God the Son, 137
    Head of His body, 84–85, 124, 258
    High Priest, 82–83
    Holy One, 73
    Iesous, 70
    Innocent One, 85
    King, 38, 56, 68, 79, 93, 174
    the Lamb Who was slain, 40, 47, 83–84, 114, 125, 153
    Liberator, 84
    Life and Light, 76
    Master, 87
    Mediator, 79–80, 153, 239–240
    Messiah, 56, 79, 81, 88, 113, 119–120, 141, 154
    Messiah-Prince, 56, 79, 84
    New Adam, 18–19, 63, 69
    The One, 253
    as One-and-Many (*see* God, as One-and-Many)
    Only Begotten, 65, 83
    Potentate, 103
    Prince, 56
    Redeemer, 66, 84, 226
    Righteous One, 73
    Savior, 71, 218, 260
    Second Adam, 73–74, 258

Servant, 67, 73, 84, 113
Shepherd, 84
Son of David, 38
Son of God, 38, 64–65, 77, 103–104, 108, 111, 162, 240
Son of Man, 87–88, 98, 108, 111, 125, 141
Son of the Father, 191
Sovereign Rector, 118
Sovereign Word Incarnate, 172
Tabernacle of God, 77
Temple, 38, 69, 77, 139
True Solomon, 175
True Witness, 78
Word Incarnate, 86, 91, 198
Yehoshuah, 70
one with the Church, 85
prayers of
    for the apostles, 99, 151
    during baptism, 85
    at Gethsemane, 75
    on Mount of Olives, 85
    for those who believe in Him, 165
Priesthood of, 79, 81–84
pronounces cursings, 97
prophecy of, 86, 95, 140–141, 156
rejection of, 76, 88
resurrection of, 94, 102, 114
and salvation, 16, 57, 74–76, 79, 83–85, 88, 111–112, 191
second coming of, 63, 69, 125, 137, 139
sign of the Son of Man in Heaven, 99, 134, 139
teaching of
    about false christs, 120
    about new birth, 153–154
    call to obey Law, 85
    describes Kingdom of Heaven, 96
    disciples, 95
    ministry of, 79, 119
    of Nicodemus, 153–154
    Olivet Discourse, 95, 98 (see also Olivet Discourse)
    parables of, 94
    response to Scripture misuse, 91
    Sermon on the Mount, 42, 89, 91 (see also Sermon on the Mount)
    on tradition, 158–159
    warning signs, 120–133
at the Temple, 69, 71
temptation of, 67, 118
transfiguration of, 118
weeps for Jerusalem, 88, 97
Jethro, 31
Jewish antiquities, 56, 123
Jewish authorities, 82
Jewish Bible, 118, 134
Jewish Wars, 54–56, 121–123
Jews
    colony on Euphrates, 59
    diaspora of, 58, 59, 119 (see also diaspora)
    and the early church, 105, 108
    faithful to Torah, 81
    with Gentiles to worship, 139
    Judaism, 64
    Lord establishes New Israel for, 138
    making proselytes, 59
    opposition of the Gospel, 119
    part of oikoumene, 130
    persecution of Christians, 126
    privilege of, 144
    at Sermon on the Mount, 88
    Sons of Jacob-Isreal, 131
    Sons of the Covenant, 108
    spiritual maturation of, 59
    spiritual war within, 119
    traditions of, 71
    use of violence, 119
Job, 54
Joel, 49, 49, 105–108
Johannine prologue, 76
John the Baptist, 12, 19, 42, 51, 52
    on autonomy *vs.* theonomy, 155
    banishment of, 117, 125
    and baptism of Jesus, 79, 81, 85
    birth of, 69
    call Israel to repent, 68, 84

Christ comes after, 83
commandments to, 142
conception of, 69
on false Christs, 120
fiat of, 79
followers of, 132
genealogy of, 70, 72, 117
Gospel of, 76, 153
as illustration, 115
letters of, 120, 156
member of the remnant, 72
message to the remnant, 70
mission of, 68
and old Covenant of Grace, 104
opposition of Christ, 79
preaching of, 69
as prophet, 68, 79, 117, 129, 133
on sacrifice of Jesus, 83
witness to transfiguration, 118
Jonah, 110
Jordan, 85, 133
Joseph, 22, 70–73, 110
Josephus, Flavius
   Contra Apion, 123
   on Daniel, 56
   and destruction of Israel, 140–143
   the Jewish Wars, 122, 131–132
   military service, 122–123
   reported Israeli earthquake, 122
Joshua, 34, 34–35, 35
Josiah, 53
Jubilee, 57, 141
Judah, 36, 36, 53, 58–59
Judaism, 120, 123, 125, 127
Judas, 156
Jude, 72, 129
Judea, 114–115, 132–133, 140
Judges, 34, 286
Judgment of God, 53, 69
Judith, 143
Julio-Claudian dynasty, 121
justification, 191, 193–196. *see also* sanctification
Justin Martyr, 167, 221–222

K

Kabbala, 160–161
Kant, Immanuel, 235, 236
kârath, 25–26
kârath berîth, 25
Kerûbîm, 32, 36
Ketuvim, 54–56, 63, 143–145, 160, 200–201
Kingdom of God
   in Christ, 56, 68, 93
   coupled with righteousness, 93
   fifth kingdom announced by Daniel, 93
   growth of, 94
   Jesus talks of, 93, 103
   Noah's nations into, 110
   in the people's midst, 93
   progress of, 95
Kingdom of Heaven
   Christ as King of, 93
   entering, 272, 291
   instruction about, 165
   Jesus' descriptions of, 94, 96
   mysteries of, 153
King Herod, 71–72, 90, 95
King of Tyre, 12
King Solomon. *see* Solomon
Kline, Meredith, 13
kosmos, 112

L

Lamech, 21
Laodicea, 146, 156, 169, 175
Last Days, 69, 106–107
Last Hour, 69, 106–107, 120, 129
Last Judgment, 100, 137, 268
Last Supper, 156
Last Times, 69, 106–107, 124
Latter Times, 106, 128
Law. *see also* autonomy *vs.* theonomy; Covenant of Grace; Ten Commandments; theonomy

authority of, 271
Christ's obedience to, 74, 78, 91
condemnation of sinners, 74, 90
Covenant and, 25–27, 30, 34–35, 161
deepening of, 289, 292, 295
definition of, 273, 277–278
"eye for an eye," 282
on faithfulness, 198
and heart of men, 291
and Israelites, 109, 270
as Law of God, 34–35, 42–49, 54–55, 160
Mosaic law in Song of Songs, 287
and the nations, 109, 269
obedience to, 104, 137, 198, 277
as organic whole, 43
part of Old Testament, 63, 114, 118, 143, 145, 162
as part of the Gospel, 46, 54, 281
penal law, 280–282
three types of
    ceremonial, 43–44, 47, 108
    civil, 276
    moral, 44, 270–272, 276, 278, 284, 291
on work, 44
Lecerf, Auguste, 185, 247–248, 264
legalists, 196
leitmotif, 29
Letter to the Diogenese, 167
Levi, 32, 82
Levites, 31–32, 59
Levitical priesthood, 83
liberté-responsabilité, 5, 6
liberty, 218
literalist, 153
Logos, 13–14, 169, 239, 273
Lord. *see* God; Jesus Christ
Lord's Day, 118, 138
love
    celebrated in Song of Songs, 55
    and Covenant of Grace, 13, 55, 66
    God as, 64, 66–67
    in God's Law, 104
    Gospel as, 40, 55, 66, 74
    between the Lord and His bride, 55
    man's desire for, 74
    in marriage, 55
    of neighbor, 92
    obedience of God as, 45–46
    of the Trinity, 101
Luke, 67–70, 78, 85, 130–131
Luther, Martin
    on the apostles, 230–231
    Bondage of the Will, The, 189, 228
    debates Erasmus, 228–229
    De Servo Arbitrio, 230
    excommunication of, 181
    justification by faith, 188–190
    opposition to humanism, 230, 239
    sayings of the fathers, 179
Lutherans, 183
Lysias, 126

M

Maccabees, 143
Macedonia, 117, 122
Machiavelli, 228
Machpelah, 24
Magnificat, 70, 79
Malachi, 53
Mamre, 24, 51
man
    calling of, 13–14, 41–42
    fall of, 40, 137 (*see also* Original Sin)
    humanism (*see* humanism)
    as image of God, 4, 7, 13–14, 15, 18
marriage, 14, 40, 42, 44. *see also* family
Martyrdom, 87, 98, 124–125, 186, 218
martyrs, 70
Mary Magdalene, 102
Mary the Virgin, 65, 65, 69, 70, 71, 72, 73, 79, 103, 137, 169
massacres, 218
Matthew, 67–70, 78, 133, 248
mea culpa, 15

media, 277
mediation, 239–240
Medieval society, 220
Mediterranean world, 121–122
Medo-Persia, 56
Melchizedek, 82–84
Melito of Sardis, 167
Mesopotamia, 71
Micah, 49
Micaiah, 51
Michal, 37
Middle Ages, 174
Miletus, 128
Missionary Mandate. see Great Commission
modern church, 4, 44
Molech, 131, 217
Moral Law, 44, 45. see also Law
Moriah, 20, 23, 36, 64, 152
Mosaic Law, 89, 268–269. see also Law
Moses
    and Covenant of Grace, 4, 11, 14, 27, 29–31, 34–35, 42–43, 46, 268
    deliverer of Law, 44, 76–78, 144
    and Jesus, 77, 83, 137
    as judge, 31, 53
    Melchizedek over, 83
    oral tradition, 153, 161
    and people of the covenant, 24, 26, 32, 162
    as prophet, 31, 51, 52
    traditions of, 89
    Wisdom literature, 54
Mountains of God
    Ararat, 16–19, 64, 152
    the Church as, 152
    Eden, 12, 18, 64, 67, 152
    Galilee, 102–110
    in God's presence, 64
    Horeb, 27
    man's attempt to replicate, 22
    as markers of Covenant of Grace, 11
    Moriah, 20, 23, 36, 64, 152
    Mount of Olives, 85, 95, 134
    Sinai, 26–27, 29, 30, 31, 34, 64, 152, 268
    typological signs of, 152
    Zion, 34, 36, 37, 64, 152
Mount Nebo, 34
murder, 18, 21, 92, 96, 116, 126

N

Nahum, 53
Nathan, 37
Nations, The, 109–110, 112
nazar, 108
Nazareth, 69, 71–72, 80
Nazarites, 108
Nebuchadnezzar, 53, 56, 93, 110
Neopolis, 127
Nero, 116–117, 126–127, 132, 147
nestorianism. see heresy
Nestorius. see heresy
Nevi'im, 45, 49–50, 54, 56, 63, 143, 160, 200–201, 1134
New Israel, 115, 138, 144
New Jerusalem, 3, 114, 125, 152
New Testament
    authority of, 82, 85, 145, 160
    God as love and holiness, 87
    Greek text of, 74
    language of, 77
    letters of Peter in, 116
    and Old Testament, 144
    revelation of, 63
    tradition of Jesus and the apostles, 63, 158–160 (*see also* Tradition of the Apostles)
Nicodemus, 93, 153–154
Ninevites, 110
Nisan, 28
Noah
    and Covenant of Grace, 4, 9, 11, 17–20, 29, 31, 41, 46
    Lord walks with, 137
    seventy nations from, 110

Noah's Ark, 17–18, 31–32, 41, 210
Numbers, Book of, 26, 45, 108
Nunc Dimittis, 70, 137

O

Octavia, 126
October Revolution, 173
oïkouménê, 98, 122, 127, 130, 146
oil, 36, 80–81, 306
olam, 25
old covenant, 104, 117, 122
    apostasy under, 119
    Christ's offering, 82
    confirmed by God, 269
    and Israel, 109
    kings under, 80
    priests under, 80, 81, 83
    sacrifices under, 83
    sons and daughters of old, 140–141
Old Covenant
    symbols of
        altars, 23, 30
        Ark of the Covenant, 32, 33, 36–37
        blood of the Covenant, 30
        blood sacrifice, 30
        chronology, 57
        circumcision, 24–26, 41, 44
        Jubilee, 57
        Noah's Ark, 17–18, 31
        offerings, 37
        Passover, 27–28, 44
        pointing to Christ, 47
        rainbow, 19
        relation to New Covenant, 10
        sacrificial lamb, 28
        signs of redemption, 6–8, 12–14, 16
Old Testament
    on Christ, 134–137, 139
    on Jubilee, 141
    on Rome, 141
    symbolism in, 134–137, 139, 141
    anointing, 80
    blood of the covenant, 162
    circumcision, 108
    clean and unclean animals, 115
    Glory of God, 71
    Mount Zion as Church, 152
    ordination, 81, 82
    sacrifices, 83
    star, 71
    tree of Eden, 259
    wrath of God, 85
    on who God is, 87
olen ten oikoumenen, 122
Olivet Discourse, 95, 97–98, 130, 310.
    see also Sermon on the Mount
oral traditions, 153, 160, 160–161, 164
Original Sin, 8–9, 14–15, 26, 40, 73.
    see also Adam, fall of man in
orthodoxy, 168–169, 172–173
Otho, 121
Owen, John, 55

P

Palestine, 23, 119, 221
parable
    Abraham as, 23
    apostolic writings and, 153
    teachings of Jesus, 86–87, 93–97, 234, 245
paradosis, 144, 158, 201
paraklètos, 103
passion of Christ, 81–82, 85, 99, 177
Passover, 27–28, 32, 44, 71
Patmos, 19, 99, 117–118, 125
patrology, 183–184
Paul
    on Christ's sacrifice, 66, 101, 195
    on circumcision, 26, 108
    conversion of, 116
    execution of, 108, 117, 125, 127, 159
    explanation of the Law, 253–254
    faith of, 116

genealogy of, 116
on inspiration of Scripture, 199
on man's heart, 226–227
ministry of, 58, 108, 110, 113, 115–117, 122
opposed legalists, 196
persecutor of the church, 116
preaching of the Gospel, 113, 116–117, 199–130
prophecy of, 105, 127, 132–133
reported torture of Christians, 127
on salvation, 192
as Saul, 116
speaks of Temple, 108
speaks on foreign languages, 107
and the stages of the Covenant, 253
on traditions of Jesus and the apostles, 159
warns of heresies, 128

Pax Romana, 121
Péguy, 121
peïrasmos, 67, 74, 197
Pelikan, Jaroslav, 185–186, 212
Pella, 133
Pentateuch, 42, 42, 90, 245, 268
Pentecost, Day of
  baptism on, 105
  Church growth and, 104–105, 110
  coming of Holy Spirit, 87, 101–102, 107, 138, 200
  foreign languages during, 105, 107
  as marker of time, 114–116, 118, 156
people of God, 32, 33
Pergamum, 175
Persia, 71
Peter, 67, 81, 105–106, 115–118, 125, 199
Pharaoh, 27–28, 300
Pharisees. *see also* Scribes
  Christ's warnings about, 89–90, 159, 272
  Christ's words to, 77, 89, 97, 290–291
  disciples greater than, 93
  Sadducees and, 90–91
  schools of, 89
  twisting of Scripture, 89–90, 91–93, 275
phémi, 49
Philip, 115
Philippi, 122
Philippi, Friedrich Adolf, 243–244
Philistines, 36–37, 248
philosophy, 225
Phrygia, 122
Place of the Skull, 97
pneumatophores, 199
polytheism, 43, 237
Pompei, 126
pope, 184
Pope Leo X, 160–161, 181–182, 184–185, 203, 304
Pope Tiberius, 181
Popovitch, Justin, 173, 188
post-apostolic times, 100, 138
predestinarian, 87
prelapsarian, 4, 40
priests, 44, 81
procreation, 40, 49
prolapsarian, 40, 41
prologue to the Kingdom, 13
prophecy, 105
prophétes, 49
prophets
  biblical definition, 49–50
  commandments of Christ, 77, 86, 114
  communication with God, 50, 52
  false prophets, 51
  foundation of the church, 105
  origin of, 49
  teachers of the Torah, 49, 53
Proverbs, 285–287
Psalms, 11, 54–55, 70, 118, 144

Q

Queen of Sheba, 110
qûm, 9

R

Rabbis, 90–92, 153, 160
Rahab, 67–68
Ratramnus of Corbie, 184–185
Reformation
    comparison to Jews and Israel, 180
    in comparison to Renaissance, 228
    and convictions of the fathers and doctors, 183, 242
    developed scriptural dogmas, 186–187
    developed soteriological dogmas, 186–187
    dissented with the councils, 180
    gifts of the catholic Church, 174
    against humanism, 228
    justification and necessity of, 180
    in line with ecumenical councils, 178
    marker of Middle Ages, 174
    rejected Nicea II, 179–180
    rejected worship of icons, 179–180
    against Rome, 180–181
    semper peccator, semper justus, semper penitens, 198
    tenets of, 189–193, 228, 235–236, 244, 247, 252
reformers
    adopted use of "catholic," 163
    and critique of the church, 157, 166
    doctrine of theonomy, 257
    epoch of, 166
    example of, 306
    held to Hebrew canon, 143, 144
    justification by faith, 189, 193
    scrutiny of, 183
    use of "catholic," 163
    Word of God and, 143–145, 179–181, 185, 207, 236
Regula Fidei, 167
regula fidei et vitae, 165
Remnant
    apostles signify, 115
    gathered by Christ, 68–69, 162
    in history, 48–49
    of Israel, 72, 86, 88
    members of, 69–70
    Noah and family, 18
    passing down of the Word, 144–145
Renaissance, 227–228
resurrection, 101–102, 105
Revelation, Book of, 99, 105, 124–125, 133
Roman Church, 130, 142, 184. *see also* Catholic Church
Roman Empire
    "all the world" as, 122, 126, 130–131
    and "Babylon the Great," 127–128
    beast in Book of Revelation, 125–126
    death of Peter, 116
    destruction of, 116, 122, 126
    eagle as symbol of, 141
    enemy of Israel, 141
    ignores call for reformation, 182
    Jews in, 108
    New Jerusalem and, 125–128
    oppression of Christians, 119–120, 125
    and Paul's Judgment, 117
    Roman army, 141
    spread of the Gospel, 301, 303
    under threat, 122
    tribulations on the Church, 125
Rousseau, Jean-Jacques, 217
Rushdoony, Rousas John, 259, 263, 266
Ruth, 68

S

Sabbath, 31–32, 40, 57, 80, 138
sacrifice
    Christ as, 40, 66, 80, 84–85, 191, 284
    human, 127, 217–218, 300
    of Isaac, 196
    precursors of redemption, 16–19, 26, 30, 47, 273
    sacrificial law, 44–45, 123, 131, 139–140, 269, 273
    Saul's disobedience for, 36

Sadducean Judaism, 132
Sadducees, 90, 91, 132
Sages, 54, 59, 71, 268
Salem, 83
salvation
   Anselm on, 177
   and Christ
      author of, 95, 298
      His baptism, 79, 85
      His obedience to the Law, 73–74, 264
      incarnation of, 16, 24, 57, 101, 169, 248
   and Covenant of Grace, 9, 16, 24, 26
   dogma of, 236
   Erasmus on, 229–233
   faith and, 191–194
   Great Commission and, 111–112
   humanism and, 299–300
   Israel and, 28, 70, 160
   misconceptions about, 183, 188, 203
   new creation and, 76
   plan of, 214–215
   scope of, 111–112
   stages of, 7
   symbols of, 8, 274
   through grace, 16, 90, 187–189, 256–258, 261
Samaria, 53, 114–115
Samaritan woman, 81, 139
Samuel, 35–37, 52–53, 68, 137
sanctification. *see also* justification
   accompanies justification, 193–195, 197
   of the apostles, 100
   in conflicting doctrine, 183, 189
   by grace, 105
Sanctuary. *see* Temple
Sanhedrin, 90, 139
Sarah, 24, 25
Sardis, 156, 175
Satan
   and Christ's temptation, 91
   Christ's victory over, 94, 125
   conflict with, 9, 234
   as God's adversary, 15, 66
   malice of, 67, 204, 239, 259
   as ruler of the world, 234
   source-mirage of source of knowledge, 259
Saul, 34, 35–36, 37. *see also* Paul
Schmemann, Alexander, 173
scholasticism, 223, 224
Scott, David D., 241
Scott, Otto, 217
Scribes. *see also* Pharisees
   authors of Scripture, 242
   Christ's warnings about, 89–91, 159, 272, 291
   maintain the text, 59, 207
scriptural dogma, 187
Scripture. *see* Bible
Sea of Tiberias, 102
Second Adam, 73. *see also* Jesus Christ
Second Book of Baruch, The, 140
Semites, 22
Seneca, 126
Septuagint, 21, 77, 142–143, 206
Sermon on the Mount, 42, 89–93. *see also* Olivet Discourse
Seth, 9, 17, 19, 21
Sethites, 9, 17, 19, 21, 21
Seventy nations, 20, 110
Shamai, 89
Shechem, 23
Shem, 20–22
Sheol, 140, 233
Shepherds, 69–71
Sidon, 96
Sigismund, Emperor, 186
Simon, 70–72, 115, 120, 132
Sinai. *see also* mountains of God
   the Exodus and, 29–31, 34
   God's revelation to Moses, 26–27, 29–31, 51, 300
   the Incarnation and, 64
   and renewal of the Covenant, 29–31, 48, 152, 162, 268

skénôma, 77
skénoô, 77
slavery, 217–218
society, 219–220
sôd, 51
Sodom, 51, 51, 96, 96, 269–270
Sola Scriptura, 92, 128, 164
Solomon. *see also* Song of Songs
   in Book of Kings, 289
   death of, 53
   in genealogy of Jesus, 67
   harem of, 289
   as king, 110, 287, 289
   as sage, 54
   symbol of Christ, 175
   the Temple and, 37–38, 53
   wisdom literature and, 54
Solzhenitsyn, Aleksandr Isayevich, 173
Song of Mary, 70. *see also* Magnificat
Song of Songs, 54–55, 55, 287, 287–289. *see also* Solomon
Sons of God, 9, 16–17, 21, 41, 112
Sons of men, 16–17
sophiology, 173
soteriological dogma, 186–191, 209, 211, 256–257. *see also* dogma
soteriology, 187, 188, 190–191
Spirit of God. *see* Holy Spirit
State, the
   God's Law and, 44, 278–280
   Government of, 31–32
   humanism as religion of, 217–218, 263–264, 299–300
   legal power of, 283, 285
   self-divinization and, 172
Stephen, 70, 115–116
Sueton, 126–127
symbols
   Altars, 23, 30
   Ark of the Covenant, 32–33, 36–37
   circumcision, 24–26, 41, 44
   Jubilee, 57
   Noah's Ark, 17–18, 31
   offerings, 37
   Old and New Covenant and, 10
   Passover, 27–28, 44
   pointing to Christ, 47
   rainbow, 19
   redemption, 16
   sacrificial lamb, 28
   trees of Eden, 6–8, 12–14
synagogues, 119
Synod at La Rochelle, 180
Synod of The Gallicana, 180
Syria, 115, 123
Syriac Apocalypse of Barush, 140

T

Tabernacle
   Ark of the Covenant in, 37
   Christ as, 77, 272
   and Council of God, 51
   description of, 31–34, 37, 44
   Holy of Holies, 32
   Holy Place, 32–33
   institution of, 28, 31–34, 37
   the Law and, 44–45
   rise of, 28
Tacitus, 121–122, 126–127
Talmud, 160–161
ta logia tou theou, 144
Tamar, 67–68
TaNaKh. see Ketuvim
Tarsus, 116
taxes, 218
Te Deum, 95
Temple
   and Abraham, 23
   and Christ, 37–38, 69, 71, 77, 82, 139–140, 154
   destruction of
      in apostolic times, 64
      as end of old covenant, 99, 117, 151–152, 200, 272–273, 296–297

362 • A NEW DAY OF SMALL BEGINNINGS

and Joseph ben Mallathias ha-
    Cohen, 123–124
by Nebuchadnezzar, 53–54
prophecy about, 58–59
and the Sadducees, 90
as sign of Christ's coming, 88,
    139–140, 151
history of, 77, 95, 108–109, 131–132,
    162
judgments in, 53–54, 119
prophecy about, 57, 88, 95, 97
reconstruction of, 57–59, 95
Ten Commandments, 29, 31, 43–44,
    52, 92, 227
Tent of Meeting. *see* Tabernacle
Ten Words. *see* Ten Commandments
Tertullian, 167, 224
Theodore the Great, 222
theology, 225
theonomy. *see also* autonomy *vs.*
    theonomy
    and death penalty, 282
    explanation of, 262–264
    follows Christ, 272
    follows Scripture, 257, 272
    and humanism, 256, 276
    Law revealed to Israel, 270
    in lives of God's people, 256–257
Theophany, 86
théopneustos, 199
theotokos, 79
Thessalonians, 108, 159
Thessalonica, 159
The Tradition, 63, 114, 144–146, 159, 162
"this generation," 88, 97–98, 119–120,
    123, 139
Thomas, 227
Tiberius Caesar, 121
Timothy, 108, 128–129
Titus, 123, 142
Tobias, 143
Torah
    on anointment, 80, 81
    authority of, 91

and Christ, 69, 72–73, 76–83, 91,
    94, 114
circumcision in, 69
clarification of, 54
commandments of, 44, 49, 54, 73
and Feast of Tabernacles, 109–110
grace and truth in, 78
the Holy People, 29–30, 81, 154
and the Law (*see* Law)
and Moses, 78
obedience to, 53, 73, 89
and the Pharisees, 89–90
preaching of, 53
and the prophets, 53–54
symbols in, 54
and the Tabernacle, 33
and teaching of rabbis, 91
and the Ten Words, 44
twisting of, 89–92
unchangeable nature of, 54
writing of, 86
torture, 218
tota ecclesia, 163
tota scriptura, 92, 128, 162–164
Tower of Babel, 20, 22
Tradition of the Apostles
    authority of God's laws, 272,
        277–278, 284, 289
    New Testament as, 144, 145–146,
        252
    obedience and love, 291–293
    Paul's teaching of, 159–162
    received by the Church, 201
transfiguration, 118
Tribulation, 98–99, 117–118, 133–134
trinitarian council, 66
trinitarian dogma, 186
Troeltsch, Ernest, 245
Turretin, Frances, 223–224
typological, 26, 152, 287
typos, 26
Tyre, 96, 181

U

Upper Room, 103
Ur, 23
Uriah, wife of, 23, 67

V

Vermigli, Pierre, 183, 223
Vespasian, 121, 123
Viret, Pierre, 257, 272
Virgin Mary. *see* Mary the Virgin
Vitellius, 121
Vulgate, 143, 206, 252

W

wars, 173, 218
Wellhausen, Julius, 237
Westminster Confession of Faith, xlv, 190, 204–206, 210, 271, 275
wisdom
   divine wisdom, 224, 229, 243, 262–263, 270–271
   fear of the Lord as, 39
   Greek wisdom, 222
   human, 204, 294
   virtue of, 285–286
wisdom literature, 54–56, 143, 271
wise men, 69, 71
Word of God. *see* Bible
Wycliffe, John, 186

Y

Year of the Four Emperors, 121

Z

Zadok, 90
Zanchi, Jerome, 223
Zechariah, 70, 72, 81, 109, 135, 144
Zephaniah, 49, 53
Zion, 34–37, 64, 82, 140, 152–153, xlii, xlvii